BLUE GUIDE CATHEDRALS AND ABBEYS

THE BLUE GUIDES

ENGLAND
SCOTLAND
IRELAND
WALES AND THE MARCHES
LONDON
MUSEUMS AND GALLERIES OF LONDON
OXFORD AND CAMBRIDGE
CATHEDRALS AND ABBEYS OF ENGLAND & WALES
THE CHANNEL ISLANDS
MALTA
GREECE
ATHENS AND ENVIRONS
CRETE
CYPRUS
BOSTON AND CAMBRIDGE
NEW YORK
EGYPT
ISTANBUL
PORTUGAL
FRANCE
PARIS AND ENVIRONS
LOIRE VALLEY, NORMANDY, BRITTANY
NORTHERN ITALY
SOUTHERN ITALY
ROME AND ENVIRONS
SICILY
FLORENCE
VENICE
HOLLAND
SPAIN: THE MAINLAND
BELGIUM AND LUXEMBOURG
MOSCOW AND LENINGRAD

BLUE GUIDE

CATHEDRALS AND ABBEYS

OF ENGLAND AND WALES

Keith Spence

Ernest Benn Limited
London

W. W. Norton & Company Inc.
New York

FIRST EDITION 1984

Published by Ernest Benn Limited
Sovereign Way, Tonbridge, Kent TN9 1RW

© Ernest Benn Limited 1984

Published in the United States of America by
W. W. Norton & Company Inc.
500 Fifth Avenue, New York, N.Y. 10110

ISBN Paperback 0 510-00155-6   0 393-30071-4 (U.S.A.)
ISBN Cased 0 510-00154-8   0 393-01664-1 (U.S.A.)

Plans by Hilary Wright
Planning map by Thames Cartographic Services
Drawings by Jo Compton

PREFACE

Books on cathedrals, books on abbeys, and books that deal with both together are legion. Because of the vastness of the subject, they tend to fall into distinct and mutually exclusive categories: scholarly accounts of the evolution of medieval architecture as revealed in its masterpieces of construction; exhaustive treatment of one particular building; and, at the other extreme, short guides covering the major examples, often perceptive in their comments and ideal for listing the main features, but limited in their scope for reasons of space. It is hoped that this addition to the Blue Guides will go some way towards bridging the gap between these contrasted treatments of a vast subject. It includes every cathedral, both Church of England and Roman Catholic, in the country, plus London's Greek Orthodox cathedral; and some 200 abbeys and abbey churches, both standing and ruined. The amount of space given to each varies enormously, from several pages, together with a plan and illustrations, for the major buildings, to a few lines for a minor Roman Catholic cathedral, or a ruined abbey half-buried in a field.

The author of a new Blue Guide has an inestimable advantage over writers of other guide-books: he or she does not have to start completely from scratch, but can build the foundations at least on previous volumes in the series. Such is certainly the case with this volume, which, as far as the major cathedrals are concerned, draws to a large degree on the relevant sections in the Blue Guides to England and to Wales, amplified and brought up to date. The descriptions of the lesser cathedrals, and the abbeys both standing and ruined, are almost wholly new. The author's thanks are due to the many vergers and site curators who have pointed out details that would otherwise have gone unnoticed; and above all to the more than 50 deans, provosts and archivists of the great standing cathedrals and abbeys, who have meticulously corrected the text.

CONTENTS

MAPS AND PLANS

PLANNING MAP *at the end of the book*

INTRODUCTION

In spite of advances in structural techniques, which have made it possible to build skyscrapers three times as high as the spire of Salisbury Cathedral, or roof a stadium half a dozen times the area covered by the dome of St Paul's, our great churches are still unmatched for the variety and daring of their construction, and totally unapproached for their beauty and for the quality of their craftsmanship in stone, glass and wood. Any visitor wishing to get to know the heart of a city makes straight for its cathedral, whether it be Lincoln soaring above the plain on its ridge of rock, Winchester huddled low in its river valley, Durham looming majestically over the Wear, or Chester hemmed in by busy shopping streets. To the believer, the cathedral still provides a focus for faith and a goal of pilgrimage, as in medieval times; to the vast majority of visitors it is simply the finest building in any city, summing up centuries of history in its structure, and the essence of the city in which it stands. This remains true even of modern cathedrals, like Coventry which rose from wartime ashes and rubble as a symbol of hope for the future, and Liverpool's contrasting pair, the Protestant showing the survival into modern times of a medieval disregard for the passing years, and the Roman Catholic seizing the present with an enthusiasm and vigour just as typical of the great age of cathedral building.

Our ruined abbeys tell a different and more melancholy story. They are visited for a variety of reasons, the main one being that the best of them, like Tintern by the Wye, or Fountains and Rievaulx in the uplands of Yorkshire, stand in some of the most beautiful countryside to be found in England and Wales. The more fragmented and remote ones—Dunwich on the sea-eroded Suffolk coast, Cwmhir by a meandering stream in the heartlands of Wales, Monk Bretton among the Yorkshire coalfields—still offer the delights of finding an unexpected treasure in an unfamiliar place. Others again, like Glastonbury in the West Country and Lindisfarne in the extreme north-east, have names resonant with echoes from the first days of British Christianity. Fortunately not all our abbeys are in a state of ruin. Where the cloisters and monastic buildings opening off them were torn down at the Dissolution, often the churches were left, either in their totality (Sherborne and Tewkesbury Abbeys, and Great Malvern Priory) or in part (Waltham Abbey on the outskirts of London, and Lanercost Priory below the Roman Wall). There are the abbeys turned into houses (Mottisfont in the Test Valley, Lord Byron's Newstead, Sir Francis Drake's Buckland, Llanthony in the Welsh hills, now in part a hotel); and abbeys where the Tudor house has followed the abbot's lodging into oblivion (Titchfield in Hampshire, and Neath among the industry of South Wales). Finally there are the functioning abbeys where the monastic tradition of the Middle Ages has been revived or started from the beginning (Buckfast below Dartmoor, Ampleforth only a mile or two from Rievaulx, Prinknash on the edge of the Cotswolds).

The present decade is almost exactly as far distant from Henry VIII's Dissolution of the Monasteries at the end of the 1530s as the

Dissolution was from the spate of cathedral- and abbey-building with which the Normans opened the 12C. The same time span of four and a half centuries takes us back to the Synod of Whitby in 664—the meeting of churchmen that decided the youthful English Church in favour of Roman rather than Celtic dogma. Some 450 years before the Synod, at the beginning of the 3C, early Christians fleeing from persecution had sought safety in the deserts of the Near East, living at first as solitary hermits, and later coming together to form the earliest rudimentary monasteries. The buildings of our cathedrals and abbeys cover most of this huge span of time, nearly 1,400 years, if one takes St Augustine's foundation of a monastery at Canterbury in 598 as a convenient starting-point. During these 1,400 years the story has been intermittent rather than continuous. The early enthusiasm for monastic and church building in the 7 and 8C waned during the attacks by the Danes and Vikings; revived after the Norman Conquest, reaching a peak about 1300; declined with the start of the 100 Years War in 1337 and virtually stopped with the coming of the Black Death a decade later; and saw a brief revival in the 15C before the axe of the Dissolution severed the long tradition.

At this distance in time it is hard for us to envisage the appearance of the countryside, and to a lesser extent the cities, before the Dissolution. Travellers in some remote wilderness would suddenly be confronted by an abbey like Fountains or Rievaulx, clustering round a church of cathedral-like proportions and busy with all the activities of a small township. In the cities the monasteries and friaries were equally centres of activity; while the cathedrals blazed on their outside with painted statues and glowed internally with stained glass, gilding and wall-paintings. But in four years all this splendour was ravaged. Between April 1536 and April 1540 over 800 religious houses were taken over and ransacked prior to demolition; while the cathedrals saw their stained glass smashed, the shrines of their saints destroyed, their organs broken, their statues and tombs mutilated, their vestments pillaged, and their gold and silver treasures stolen or melted down.

So what we still see today is only a fraction of former glories, in spite of the salvaging work of the 17 and 18C, the sweeping and often misguided restoration and rebuilding of the 19C, and the more scholarly, careful and technically skilled renovations of our own day. At the ruined abbeys we have to let our imagination add to what archaeologists and historians have been able to discover. At the still intact abbeys and cathedrals imagination has less work to do. Our sense of wonder takes over, at how artists and craftsmen working with the simplest of tools, and master masons with some sixth sense for the hidden qualities of stone, could construct such buildings over a time-span lasting for centuries, bequeathing them to the present day as symbols of a lost attitude to life and creativity.

The Layout of a Monastery

To Le Corbusier, a house was 'a machine for living in'. To a monk, a monastery was (and still is) a machine for living, dying, working, singing, praying and worshipping in, with emphasis on the last two spiritual aspects. The main feature of any monastery is its church; and the working and domestic buildings are grouped logically round this key element. During the Middle Ages the layout became standardized, so much so that a visitor to the majority of ruined sites can work out the main features, provided there are traceable foundations of the church and its cloister buildings.

Unless the physical nature of the site prevented it, the church stood on the N side of the complex, with its S nave wall forming the N side of the cloister. The cloister's **E Range** abutted against the S transept of the church; its rooms (N to S) were typically as follows. A *Slype* (passageway), leading to the open ground outside the SE corner of the church, where the monks' graveyard was often situated; the end of the slype might be subsequently blocked off at the E end to form a sacristy. The *Library* (in smaller monasteries book-cupboards were usually sufficient). The *Chapter house* where monastic business was conducted and where the abbots or priors of the monastery were buried. The *Parlour*, where talking was allowed.

An *Undercroft*, used as storage space or turned into rooms for various purposes. Over the whole E range was the first-floor *Dorter*

Castle Acre Priory, Norfolk. (Top) A reconstruction by Alan Sorrell, showing the priory before the Dissolution. (HMSO, Crown Copyright reserved). (Bottom) The ruins of the priory as they are today. (Aerofilms)

(dormitory), with *Night-stairs* descending from its N end into the S transept, *Day-stairs* from its W side into the cloister, and a *Reredorter* (lavatory) at its S end above a stream or artificial drain. **S Range**. The main room on this side was always the *Frater* (refectory), large enough for all the monks to eat together, with a pulpit from which texts were read during meals. The frater was flanked by the *Warming-house* where the monks could enjoy a fire on cold days, and the *Kitchen*. **W Range**. Not as constant in its components as the E and S ranges. Normally consisted of: (ground floor) *Undercroft* used as storage and cellars, *Outer parlour* for meeting visitors from outside; (upper floor) *Abbot's* or *Prior's lodgings*, *Guest-rooms*, accommodation of different sorts.

In Cistercian monasteries, the rectangular frater was turned through 90 degrees, with its narrow end to the cloister, so that it extended back considerably S of the kitchen and warming-house. The upper floor of the W range became the *Lay brothers' dorter*, with its own reredorter on the S end.

The layout of the remaining monastic buildings was far more flexible. These normally included: a *Gatehouse*; an *Infirmary*, with its own chapel and cloister like a monastery in miniature; an *Abbot's* or *Prior's lodging* (the head of a monastery soon began to live apart from the rest of the monks, often in considerable style); and a *Guesthouse*.

The Rule of St Benedict

The Rule under which monks were expected to live was compiled by St Benedict c 530. As abbeys grew more prosperous, so the original precepts, especially those enjoining poverty, were forgotten; and the history of medieval monasticism is largely one of attempts to return to Benedict's principles, typified by the Cistercians in the 12C and the Dominicans and Franciscans in the 13C. The following extracts from the chapters of the Rule concerned with administration rather than spiritual matters give an idea of Benedict's practical approach to communal life (translation by Dom Bernard Basil Bolton OSB).

It is called the Rule because it guides straight the life of those who obey. (Preliminary)

An abbot who is worthy to rule over a monastery ought always to remember what he is called and live up to the name of Superior in what he does. Treating one with pleasant humour, another with rebuke, a third with persuasiveness, he must so adapt and fit himself to all that he may suffer no loss in the flock entrusted to him. (Chapter 2)

Because of the holy servitude they [the monks] have professed, as soon as a command has been given by a superior, they may not tolerate any delay in carrying it out, just as if it was a direct command from God. (Chapter 5)

Even in the case of conversing on good, holy and edifying subjects, to perfect disciples let permission be rarely granted because of the importance of keeping silence. (Chapter 6)

The prophet says: 'Seven times a day have I given praise to Thee' (Ps 119). This sacred number seven will be observed by us, if we fulfil the duties of our service in the early morning and the first, third, sixth and ninth hours, in the evening and the close of day. Of the Night Watches the same prophet says: 'At midnight I arose to give Thee praise'. (Chapter 16)

Each monk is to sleep in a separate bed. If possible, they are to sleep all in one room, but if their numbers do not admit of this, then let them take their rest in tens or twenties with older monks to look after them. They are to sleep clothed, with a girdle or cord round their waists. (Chapter 22)

If a brother is convicted of lighter offences he is to be deprived of sharing in the common table. The brother who has incurred the punishment due to a graver fault is to be suspended from both table and oratory. If a brother has often been punished for some offence, if he has even been excommunicated, and still has not amended his ways, then sharper correction must be applied to him and corporal punishment be administered. (Chapters 24, 25, 28)

As Cellarer of the monastery, let one be chosen who is wise, mature in character, temperate; not a big eater, not proud, not one who makes trouble, not harsh, not dilatory, not extravagant. (Chapter 31)

The brethren are to serve one another, and no one is to be excused from the [weekly] kitchen service unless he is either ill or engaged in business of considerable importance. (Chapter 35)

For the sick brethren there should be special quarters set apart, and an infirmarian who is conscientious, diligent and solicitous. The sick may be offered a bath as often as seems desirable, but to those in good health, especially the young, a bath is not to be allowed too easily. So also with the eating of flesh meat; it may be granted to the sick who are very weak to build up their strength, but when they are better again, all must refrain from flesh as usual. (Chapter 36)

Let two cooked dishes suffice for all the brethren, and if there is any fruit or green vegetables available, let a third be added. For bread, one pound full weight should be enough for the day. Taking into account the feebleness of the weak, we consider that half a pint of wine is sufficient for each daily. If the local conditions or the work or the summer heat demand more, it can be left to the judgement of the superior. (Chapters 39, 40)

Idleness is the enemy of the soul. Therefore the brethren ought to be occupied at definite times in the work of the hands, at other set times in holy reading. It is very important that one or two seniors be appointed to go round the monastery during the time when the brethren are supposed to be reading, to keep an eye on them in case somebody may become restless and spend the time in idleness and gossip instead of being intent on his book. (Chapter 48)

All visitors who call are to be welcomed as if they were Christ. It is in the welcome given to the poor and the strangers that special attention should be paid; for in the case of the wealthy the awe they inspire itself ensures respect. On no account may any monk who has not been told to do so associate with guests or enter into conversation with them. (Chapter 53)

On no account may a monk accept letters, pious tokens or small presents of any kind, from his parents or anyone else, or give them himself, nor may the brethren exchange them with one another, without the permission of the Abbot. (Chapter 54)

In temperate regions it will be sufficient for each monk to have a cowl and a tunic, the cowl woolly in winter and thin or worn in summer, and also a belt for work, stockings and boots for footwear. When they receive new things, they must always hand back the old ones, to be put in the clothing store for the poor. For it is enough for a monk to have two tunics and two cowls, allowing for night wear and laundry. For bedding let a straw mattress, a blanket, a coverlet and a pillow suffice. The beds must be often searched by the Abbot, for possible secret hoarding. (Chapter 55)

If there are any craftsmen in the monastery, let them practise their crafts with all humility. But if one of them gets a swollen head because of his skill in his craft, and thinks he is conferring a benefit on the monastery, he is to be taken off that craft, and not allowed to practise it again until his pride has been humbled and the Abbot tells him he may do so. (Chapter 57)

At the monastery gate let a sensible old man be stationed, who will know how to take a message and give the answer, one whose years will not let him wander about. (Chapter 66)

GLOSSARY

To prevent the glossary from becoming too unwieldy, it is divided into three sections: on the main building styles, on the buildings, and on the people who used them.

1. Main Church Building Styles, in chronological order. (Individual terms, e.g. Dogtooth, Lancet, appear in the next section)

SAXON Pre-Conquest building style, smaller in scale and more primitive in detail than Norman, with which it shares many features.

NORMAN On the Continent, the style called Romanesque, introduced into Britain at the Norman Conquest and lasting until c 1150. Characterized by rounded arches, simple vaulting, and vigorous carving of detail.

TRANSITIONAL (TRANS) Usually applied to 12C buildings built in a style which combines Norman and Early English (EE) elements (e.g. round and pointed arches appearing together).

GOTHIC Style of architecture covering most of the medieval period and characterized by pointed arches.

EARLY ENGLISH (EE) First style of English Gothic, c 1150–1250, characterized by lancet windows and dogtooth moulding.

DECORATED (DEC) Second style of English Gothic, c 1250–1350, characterized by elaborate carving on columns and Geometric window tracery.

PERPENDICULAR (PERP) Last phase of English Gothic, c 1350–1540, characterized by large windows and vertical tracery to give a feeling of lightness and space. Vaulting is more complex than in earlier periods.

FLAMBOYANT French Gothic style (14C on), contemporary with English Perp.

BAROQUE Architecture inspired by the buildings of ancient Greece and Rome, looking to Italian models (St Paul's is the main English example).

GOTHIC REVIVAL A movement, combining architectural with religious fervour, which began c 1840, and is characterized by imitations of medieval churches, especially of the EE period.

2. The Buildings

ABBEY Monastic house with an abbot or abbess at its head, which normally had to have at least 12 monks or nuns to qualify for abbey status. Smaller houses were known as *Priories* (q.v.).

AISLE Outer part of church on either side of nave, or chancel, and separated from it by an arcade.

ALIEN PRIORY Priory dependent on a Continental mother house, penalized during wars with France during Middle Ages. Such priories often severed their foreign connections and became denizen or naturalized.

ALMONRY Building or room from which alms were given to the poor and sick.

ALTARPIECE Ornamental panel, often with a painting, behind an altar.

AMBULATORY Processional passageway leading from one side of the church to the other behind the high altar.

APSE (adj. *Apsidal*) Vaulted semicircular or polygonal end to a church or chapel, typical of the Norman period.

ARCADE Row of arches separating nave or chancel from aisle.

ASHLAR Squared block(s) of stone.

AUMBRY Cupboard or recess in wall for sacramental vessels.

BALDACCHINO Large ornamental canopy, supported on columns, usually over an altar or tomb.

BALL-FLOWER Stone ornament of Dec style, consisting of a three-petalled flower enclosing a small ball.

BAPTISTRY The part of a church containing the baptismal font.

BARREL VAULT Vault with semicylindrical roof.

BAY Smallest unit of a building, e.g. a single arch of an arcade or one set of vault ribs.

BELFRY Part of tower where bells are hung.

BLIND ARCADE Line of arches used for decoration, with solid wall-surface behind.

BOSS Piece of wood or stone, often elaborately carved, covering the intersection of two or more vault ribs or roof timbers.

BUTTRESS Masonry or brickwork built against wall for additional strength.

CALEFACTORIUM: see WARMING-HOUSE

CANDELABRUM Multiple candle-holder hanging from ceiling.

CAPITAL Decorated stone at top of column below the arch.

CARREL Seating recess in cloister wall, used by monks for study.

CATHEDRAL The main church of a diocese, containing the bishop's throne (from *kathedra*, Greek for seat or throne).

CELL 1) Daughter house of a larger and more important monastery. 2) Monk's room.

CENOTAPH Empty tomb honouring a person who is buried elsewhere.

CHAMFER Bevelled or mitred angle, without moulding.

CHANCEL The part of a church E of the crossing, in which the main altar is placed.

CHANTRY Small chapel endowed for a priest to say masses for the soul of its founder.

CHAPTER HOUSE 1) Room in which monks met daily for monastic business, after which a chapter (*capitulum*) of the monastic rule would be read. 2) Room in which the dean and canons (forming the chapter) of a cathedral meet for business.

CHEVET E end of church consisting of several apses (French term).

CHEVRON Norman zigzag moulding.

CHOIR (QUIRE) Part of church between presbytery and nave containing stalls where monks sat to sing the offices. In cathedrals, occupied by singing choir.

CHOIR SCREEN: see PULPITUM

CINQUEFOIL Five-leaved.

CLERESTORY Upper story of church, with windows set above line of aisle roofs to provide light for central part of building.

CLOISTER (adj. CLAUSTRAL) Four-sided enclosure, with covered walk all round, usually S (sometimes N) of church and with monastic buildings opening off it.

CLOSE Cathedral precinct, usually a grassy area round the cathedral, surrounded by bishop's palace, deanery etc.

COLLEGIATE Used to describe a church with a college of priests or a chapter, but without a bishop.

CONSISTORY COURT Bishop's court with jurisdiction over church matters.

CONVENTUAL Pertaining to the convent or monastic community.

CORBEL Stone bracket projecting from wall, usually used as support for roof vaulting or beam and often carved with ornamentation, heads, animals etc.

CORNICE Projecting upper part of a wall.

CRENELLATED Battlemented.

CROCKET Small carved and decorated projection, especially on spires and pinnacles.

CROSSING Central space, usually surmounted by central tower, where main E-W axis of church is crossed by N-S transept.

CRUCIFORM In the shape of a cross.

CRYPT Basement of a church, usually at the E end, often vaulted, and used for services and burials.

CUPOLA Small ornamental dome.

CURTAIN WALL Fortified connecting wall between towers, bastions and gates.

CUSP Small projection on underside of window arch dividing it into 'foils' or leaves.

DAY-STAIRS Daytime access from monks' dorter to cloister.

DIAPER Diamond pattern of decoration.

DIOCESE (also SEE) The parishes that come under a cathedral and its bishop.

DOGTOOTH Small pyramid-shaped ornament on EE stonework.

DORTER Monastic dormitory.

EFFIGY Stone or wood statue, usually lying down, on top of a tomb.

FAN VAULT Vaulting in a fan-like pattern that became widely used in the 14C.

FERETORY Ornamental setting behind high altar for main shrine of church (originally a portable shrine, from Latin *feretrum*).

FILLET Narrow flat band between mouldings.

FLÈCHE Small spire (French for 'arrow').

FLUSHWORK Flint used decoratively with dressed stone to form a patterned wall.

FLYING BUTTRESS External buttress, often taking the thrust of a high roof-vault above a lower aisle.

FOLIATE Leaf-like.

FRATER Monastic refectory or dining hall.

FREESTONE Fine-grained stone which can be easily cut and worked.

FRONTAL Covering for front of an altar.

FROSTERLEY MARBLE Dark stone from Frosterley, Co Durham.

GALILEE (also NARTHEX) Porch at W end of church, sometimes enlarged to form a chapel.

GARDEROBE Privy or lavatory.

GARTH Area enclosed by a cloister.

GRANGE Outlying farm, managed from a monastery.

GRISAILLE Greyish patterned glass.

GROIN Intersecting edge between two planes of a vault.

HAGIOSCOPE: see SQUINT

HAMMERBEAM Projecting bracket that supports the main trusses of a roof.

HEART SHRINE Small shrine holding the heart of a saint or notability.

HOOD-MOULD (also LABEL) Weathering or dripstone protecting the upper edge of a door or window.

HORARIUM The timetable of a monk's day, built round seven services or offices, after Psalm 119 verse 164: 'Seven times a day do I

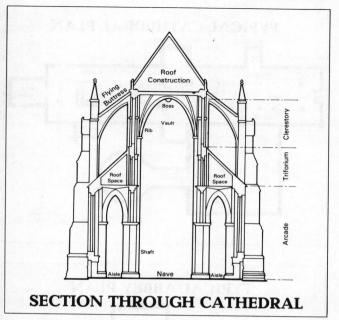

Roof
Construction

Flying
Buttress

Boss

Vault

Rib

Clerestory

Roof
Space

Roof
Space

Triforium

Shaft

Arcade

Aisle

Nave

Aisle

SECTION THROUGH CATHEDRAL

praise thee'. (See also OFFICE)

INFIRMARY Separate part of monastery set aside for sick and elderly monks.

JESSE TREE Family tree showing the descent of Christ from Jesse, father of King David, often found in stained-glass windows.

KEYSTONE Central stone of an arch.

LABEL: see HOOD-MOULD

LADY CHAPEL Chapel dedicated to the Virgin Mary, usually at the E end of a church.

LANCET Narrow window with pointed head, typical of EE period.

LANTERN Circular or polygonal tower with windows all round, usually above the crossing of a church.

LAVATORIUM (also LAVER) Trough with running water, usually outside the frater doorway, where monks washed their hands before meals.

LECTERN Reading-desk on a stand, often in the form of a brass eagle.

LIERNE Tertiary linking ribs in a vault.

LIGHT Subdivision of a complex window.

LOCUTORIUM: see PARLOUR

MINSTER A term with no precise definition, meaning a church of importance, not necessarily a cathedral (and not necessarily a monastic foundation, though the name derives from Latin *monasterium*).

MISERICORD 1) Bracket under hinged choir seat, to give support during long periods of standing; often fancifully carved. 2) Room in a monastery where eating meat was permitted. (From Latin *misericor-*

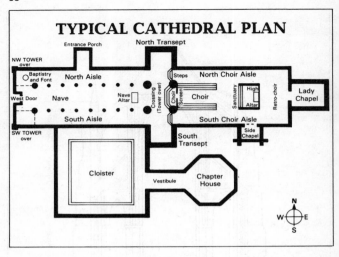

TYPICAL CATHEDRAL PLAN

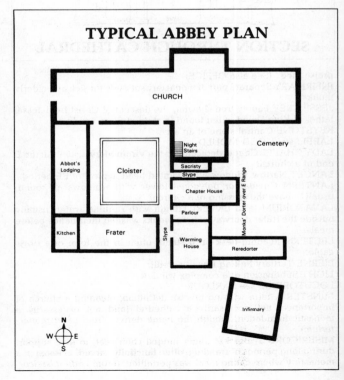

TYPICAL ABBEY PLAN

dia=pity)

MONASTERY Generic name for a community of monks, whether an abbey or a priory.

MOULDING Ornamental contour given to stones of arches, column bases etc.

MULLION Vertical bar dividing the lights of a window.

NARTHEX: see GALILEE

NAVE Part of church extending W from the crossing, separated from the side aisles by pillars and used by the congregation.

NIGHT-STAIRS Access from monks' dorter into church (generally S transept), used by monks for night offices.

NUNNERY Generic name for a community of nuns, whether abbey or priory.

OCTAFOIL Eight-leaved.

OFFICE Monastic church service. There were eight offices altogether, one at night and seven during the day (Nocturns 2 a.m., Matins 5 a.m., Prime 6 a.m., Terce 8 a.m., Sext 12 noon, None 1.30 p.m., Vespers 5.00 p.m., Compline 6.30 p.m.; all times approximate).

OGEE Wave-like shape formed from alternate concave and convex curves, common in Dec arches.

PARCLOSE Screen, usually of wood, shutting off a chapel from the rest of the church.

PARLOUR (also LOCUTORIUM) Room in which conversation was allowed.

PARVISE Room built over a church porch.

PENDANT Roof boss so elongated that it appears to hang down.

PENTISE Penthouse or lean-to, often used as a passage.

PIER Main support for arcade, often square or composite in section.

PILASTER Flattened column projecting from a wall.

PISCINA Small basin in wall-niche beside altar, used for cleaning sacramental vessels.

PLINTH Projecting masonry, often with decorative moulding, at the base of a wall.

PODIUM Base or platform for building, tomb, statue etc.

PRECINCT: see CLOSE

PRESBYTERY Part of church, E of choir, containing main altar and reserved for clergy.

PRIORY Monastic house with a prior or prioress at its head; usually an offshoot from an abbey.

PULPITUM (also CHOIR SCREEN) Partition, normally of stone, between nave and choir (to be distinguished from 'pulpit', the raised platform used for preaching); often has organ over.

PURBECK MARBLE Dark stone from Purbeck in Dorset, much used in the 12 and 13C for the shafts of columns.

QUATREFOIL Four-leaved.

QUIRE: see CHOIR

REBUS Punning visual representation of a name, e.g. the name Bolton, shown as a bolt (arrow) and a tun (barrel).

REFECTORY: see FRATER

REREDORTER Building containing latrines, usually flushed by a channel of running water (literal meaning 'behind the dormitory').

REREDOS (also RETABLE) Ornamental screen behind altar.

RESPOND Half-column or half-capital found where an arch or line of arches joins a wall.

RETABLE: see REREDOS

RETICULATE(D) Like a net (of window tracery).

RETROCHOIR The part of a church immediately behind the choir.

RIB Part of a stone framework supporting a vaulted roof.

ROOD-SCREEN Transverse screen, pierced with tracery and generally of wood, surmounted by a crucifix (rood) and set at the E end of the nave (distinct from *Pulpitum* but often confused with it).

ROSE-WINDOW Round window with stone tracery radiating from the centre.

SACRISTY Room for keeping sacred vestments and vessels.

SANCTUARY The part of a church within the communion rail containing the altar.

SARCOPHAGUS Elaborately carved coffin.

SEDILIA Seats, usually three in number, for officiating priests beside altar; often elaborately carved.

SEE: see DIOCESE

SEXFOIL Six-leaved.

SHAFT Small or subordinate pillar.

SHRINE The container, often elaborate, in which a saint's body or relics were kept.

SLYPE Passageway, often from cloister to monks' cemetery.

SOFFIT Underside of arch or window-head.

SOLAR Upper living-room of medieval house.

SPRINGER Lowest stone of arch or vaulting rib.

SQUINT (also HAGIOSCOPE) Aperture cut slantwise through church stonework to give a view of the high altar (often called 'leper's squint').

STALLS Facing rows of carved and canopied seats lining the walls of choir or chancel.

STELLAR (STELLATE) Of vaulting: with the ribs arranged in a star-like pattern.

STIFF-LEAF Stylized EE foliage carving on capitals.

STOUP Basin for holy water at church entrance.

STRING COURSE Horizontal band of masonry, sometimes projecting from wall.

TESSELLATED Made up of small tiles to form a mosaic.

TIERCERON Secondary rib rising from the base of a vault and reaching the ridge.

TRACERY Stone ribwork in the head of a Gothic window.

TRANSEPT Transverse part of a church, running N-S at right angles to the main E-W axis.

TREFOIL Three-leaved.

TRIFORIUM Gallery between main arcade of church and clerestory (sometimes called *Tribune*).

TYMPANUM Semicircular panel within a Norman door-arch, often decorated with carving.

UNDERCROFT Chamber, usually vaulted, supporting a main chamber such as a frater or dorter.

VAULT Arched work comprising a stone or wood roof.

VESICA Pointed oval.

VESTRY Room where clergy and choir put on their ceremonial robes.

VOUSSOIR Single stone of an arch.

WARMING-HOUSE (also CALEFACTORIUM) Room in a monastery where a communal fire was kept burning in winter; the only room besides the kitchen and infirmary in which a fire was allowed.

3. The People

ABBOT (f. ABBESS) Monastic official at the head of an abbey.

ARCHBISHOP Chief dignitary of a group of dioceses.

ARROUAISIANS Subsection of the Augustinian order, named after Arrouais in Picardy.

AUGUSTINIANS Order of canons who followed precepts laid down by St Augustine in the early 5C, less rigorous than the later Benedictine Rule. Also known as Austin Canons, or Black Canons.

BENEDICTINES Order founded in 529 by St Benedict of Subiaco at Monte Cassino, Italy. Benedict's 'Rule' of monastic regulations was later followed throughout Europe. Also known as Black Monks.

BISHOP (adj. EPISCOPAL) Chief church dignitary of a diocese, with his official seat or throne in a cathedral.

BLACK CANONS: see AUGUSTINIANS

BLACK FRIARS: see DOMINICANS

BLACK MONKS: see BENEDICTINES, CLUNIACS

BRIDGETTINES Order of nuns named after St Bridget, of Sweden.

CANON (also SECULAR CANON) A cathedral dignitary of sufficient importance to have a seat in the choir.

CANON REGULAR A canon living under a monastic rule (Latin *regula*), as opposed to a secular canon attached to a cathedral.

CARMELITES Order of friars named after Mount Carmel in Palestine. Known as White Friars.

CARTHUSIANS Order named after La Grande Chartreuse, in the French Alps, founded in the 1080s by St Bruno. Reviving the hermit ideal, the Carthusians lived in separate cells, only meeting on Sundays and feast days. Their monasteries were known as Charterhouses.

CELLARER Official in charge of monastery provisions.

CHAPTER: see DEAN

CHARTERHOUSE: see CARTHUSIANS

CISTERCIANS An order whose goal was the return to the original austerity of St Benedict's Rule, inspired by St Bernard of Clairvaux (d 1153), and named after the abbey of Cîteaux in Burgundy. The Cistercians frowned on decorative stonework and the arts in general, and were great agricultural innovators, using a labour force of lay brothers (Latin *conversi*). Known as White Monks from their unbleached habits.

CLUNIACS Named after the great abbey of Cluny, in Burgundy, founded in 927 by Odo of Cluny. The Cluniacs concentrated on elaborate ritual, and evolved a highly centralized organization, with 1,500 monasteries eventually controlled from Cluny. Known as Black Monks (like the Benedictines).

CONVERSI: see LAY BROTHERS

DEAN The church dignitary at the head of a cathedral chapter (the administrative body of canons).

DOMINICANS Order of friars founded c 1200 by the Spanish St Dominic (d 1221). Known as Black Friars, they were mainly a preaching order.

EPISCOPAL: see BISHOP

FRANCISCANS Order of friars founded c 1210 by St Francis of Assisi, dedicated to a life of total self-denial. A mendicant (begging) order, known as Grey Friars. Franciscan nuns were called *Poor Clares* (q.v.).

FRIAR Unlike monks or canons regular, the friars were teachers and preachers who mixed with the outside world. The two main orders were the *Dominicans* and the *Franciscans* (both of which q.v.).

GILBERTINES The only religious order of English origin, founded in the 1130s by St Gilbert of Sempringham, in Lincolnshire. Communities were mixed, with both canons and nuns.

GRANDMONTINES A small order, named after the French mother house of Grandmont, near Limoges.

GREY FRIARS: see FRANCISCANS

LAY BROTHERS (also CONVERSI) Monks not in Holy Orders, who carried out manual labour. Mainly employed in agriculture by Cistercian monasteries, and usually occupying the W range of the monastic cloister.

METROPOLITAN Pertaining to an archbishop (of Greek origin).

MINORESSES: see POOR CLARES

MONK The name derives from the Greek *monachos* ('solitary'), and was originally applied to the desert hermits of early Christianity. From about the 4C groups of monks began to live together, and their system of communal life gradually spread from the Near East to Europe.

POOR CLARES (also MINORESSES) Familiar name for order of Franciscan nuns, founded in Italy in 1215 by St Clare, a disciple of St Francis of Assisi.

PRECENTOR Official in charge of monastery's music and singing.

PREMONSTRATENSIANS An order of canons regular established c 1120 at Prémontré, in N France, by St Norbert. An ascetic branch of the Augustinians, known as White Canons.

PRIOR (f. PRIORESS) Monastic official at the head of a priory.

SACRIST Monastic official in charge of church vestments and treasures.

SAVIGNACS Order named after the French monastery of Savigny in Normandy, absorbed by the Cistercians in 1147.

SECULAR CANON: see CANON

TIRONENSIANS Reformed order of Benedictines founded c 1110 at Tiron, near Chartres, by St Bernard of Abbeville (d 1117).

TRAPPISTS Branch of the Cistercian order established in 1664 at the monastery of La Trappe, in Normandy; subject to a rigorous vow of silence.

WHITE CANONS: see PREMONSTRATENSIANS

WHITE FRIARS: see CARMELITES

WHITE MONKS: see CISTERCIANS

Bibliography

Bede, The Venerable. *A History of the English Church and People* (Penguin, 1955)

Butler, Lionel, and Given-Wilson, Chris. *Medieval Monasteries of Great Britain* (Michael Joseph, 1979)

Clifton-Taylor, Alec. *The Cathedrals of England* (Thames and Hudson, 1967)

Cook, G.H. *The English Cathedral through the Centuries* (Phoenix, 1960)

Gilyard-Beer, R. *An Illustrated Guide to the Abbeys of England and Wales* (HMSO, 1976)

Little, Bryan. *Abbeys and Priories in England and Wales* (Batsford, 1979)

Morris, Richard. *Cathedrals and Abbeys of England and Wales* (Dent, 1979)

New, Anthony. *A Guide to the Cathedrals of Britain* (Constable, 1980)
Richards, Ian. *Abbeys of Europe* (Hamlyn, 1968)
Other sources: *England*, *London* and *Wales* in the 'Blue Guide' series;
Pevsner's 'Buildings of England' series; the Pitkin cathedral guides;
the DoE guides to abbeys in its charge.

Opening Times

These have only been given in a few exceptional cases. As a general
rule, cathedrals are open from c 7.30–19.30, though some may close
earlier, while parts may be closed during services. The standard
DoE/Welsh Office opening times are: Mar.–Apr., Wkdays 9.30–17.30,
Sun. 14.00–17.30; May–Sept. Wkdays 9.30–19.00, Sun. 14.00–19.00;
Oct., as Mar.–Apr.; Nov.–Feb., Wkdays 9.30–16.00, Sun. 14.00–16.00.

1. SOUTH-EASTERN ENGLAND

Arundel Cathedral, W Sussex (RC)

Ded: St Philip Neri.

Bulky and spikily pinnacled, the cathedral dominates the view of Arundel from the river, and forms a counterpart to the mock-baronial of Arundel Castle. It was built in 1870–73 by Joseph Hansom (better known as the inventor of the Hansom cab) for the 15th Duke of Norfolk, and until the establishment of the diocese of Arundel and Brighton in 1965 it was the RC parish church. The original intention was to build a spire 280ft high, but this was never undertaken. Inside it is very Gothic in appearance, with a rose-window, an apsidal east end, and a forest of superimposed columns. In the N Transept is the shrine of the Blessed Philip Howard, 13th Earl of Arundel, who died in the Tower of London in 1595, after 11 years of imprisonment for his Roman Catholicism.

Aylesford, Kent: The Friars

Ded: Our Lady.

A medieval Carmelite foundation, dating from 1242, the original friary was dissolved in 1538 and re-established with the return of the dispossessed Carmelites in 1949. It is now a pilgrimage shrine, with a large courtyard for open-air services. Much of the medieval friary has been adapted and restored, including the gateway, part of the cloisters, and the magnificent galleried Pilgrims' Hall, which looks out on the Medway. Among the modern works commissioned by the Carmelites are some fine ceramics by the Polish artist, Adam Kossowski, in the side chapels opening off the courtyard. The Relic Chapel contains the relics of St Simon Stock (d 1265), first Prior of Aylesford, brought back to Aylesford from Bordeaux in 1951.

Battle Abbey, E Sussex

Ded: St Martin.

Grounds and ruins open daily 10.00–16.00 or 18.00.

Now largely occupied by a girls' school, the abbey is approached through the medieval gatehouse that closes off one end of the Market Square. It was founded by William the Conqueror in fulfilment of a vow, immediately after the Battle of Hastings on 14 Oct. 1066; the High Altar was erected where Harold raised his standard and was killed. The Abbey was colonized by Benedictines from Marmoutier,

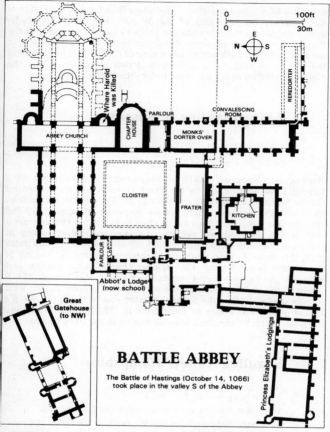

0   100ft

0   30m

Where Harold was Killed

PARLOUR

CONVALESCING ROOM

REREDORTER

CHAPTER HOUSE

MONKS' DORTER OVER

ABBEY CHURCH

CLOISTER

FRATER

KITCHEN

PARLOUR

Abbot's Lodge (now school)

Great Gatehouse (to NW)

Princess Elizabeth's Lodgings

BATTLE ABBEY

The Battle of Hastings (October 14, 1066) took place in the valley S of the Abbey

near Tours, and the church was consecrated to St Martin in 1094. One of the most prosperous abbeys in England, at the Dissolution in 1538 it was granted to Sir Anthony Browne, Master of the King's Horse, who destroyed the church and adapted the monastic buildings to secular use.

The imposing *Gatehouse (1339) is battlemented and turreted with Dec arcading; the E wing is 16C. In front as we enter are the inhabited parts of the abbey, including the Abbot's Lodge, remodelled by Browne, and two towers (1540), all that remains of Princess Elizabeth's Lodgings. Under the terms of Henry VIII's will, Browne was put in charge of the upbringing of the future Elizabeth I and intended her to live at Battle, but he died in 1548, and she never came to live there. The Abbey Church, 224ft long, has practically disappeared, except for part of the undercroft of the 14C eastern extension, which had five chapels. The most impressive remains are those of the monks' Dormitory (dorter), S of the church, with fine S wall and lancet windows. The undercroft is intact, with three beautiful EE vaulted chambers. The lower floor formed the E side of the Cloister; the arcading of the W side with Perp tracery is incorporated into the school house (Abbot's Lodge). Remains of the Parlour can be seen adjoining the dorter to the N. Beyond these, to the right, a broad walk commands a view of the battlefield, including the heights of Senlac and of Telham, across the valley, where the Normans pitched camp the night before the battle.

Bayham Abbey, E Sussex

Ded: St Mary.

Off B2169, 4 miles E of Tunbridge Wells.

Bayham was founded c 1210 for Premonstratensian canons, on a beautiful and remote site by the River Teise. It had an uneventful career, and was dissolved by Wolsey in 1525, a decade earlier than most abbeys, to raise money for his proposed colleges. After the Dissolution it passed through various hands. In the mid 18th century it was much admired by Horace Walpole and other lovers of picturesque Gothic ruins; the Gothic Revival villa W of the site dates from this time. A good deal of the gatehouse survives, looking N across the Teise. Of the 13C apsidal church, long, narrow and aisleless, the roofless E end stands to a considerable height. The E range of the cloister included the sacristy and chapter house, with monks' dorter over; on the S was the frater, and on the W the abbot's hall or guesthouse above an undercroft. In 1982 the first Tridentine Mass since the Reformation was celebrated in the abbey ruins.

Beaulieu Abbey, Hampshire

Ded: St Mary de Bello Loco Regis.

At junction of B3054 and B3056, 6 miles E of Brockenhurst.

Open daily, inclusive ticket to abbey ruins, Palace House and Montagu Motor Museum.

This wealthy and powerful Cistercian house was founded by King John in 1204, on a picturesque site beside the Beaulieu River (the name Beaulieu means 'beautiful place'). It was dissolved in 1538 and bought by Thomas Wriothesley, later Earl of Southampton. The chief survivor of the extensive buildings is the EE refectory, now the parish church, with fine lancet windows, remarkable roof beams and bosses, and a superb reader's pulpit (now used for sermons), from which a monk would read during the otherwise silent mealtimes. (The door into the church from the cloisters is normally kept locked, and entrance is from the Hythe road, on the outskirts of Beaulieu village.)

Little is left of the abbey church, once the largest Cistercian church in England, apart from sections of the S nave aisle and S transept walls; but it is clearly marked out on the ground. Of the cloisters (apart from the refectory already mentioned), only the arcades of the N, E and S sides survive; on the W side, the lay brothers' frater and cellar have been made into a permanent museum of Cistercian monastic life (opened 1977). A plaque (1969) in the cloister commemorates the part played by Beaulieu during World War II, when men and women of the European Resistance movement trained there. The 14C monastic gatehouse forms the nucleus of Palace House, most of which dates from the 19C. The medieval rooms, turned to domestic use, include the vaulted outer porch (now the lower drawing-room), the inner hall (now the dining-hall), and the abbot's chapel (now the upper drawing-room).

Boxgrove Priory, W Sussex

Ded: St Mary and St Blaise.

Off A27, 3 miles NE of Chichester.

A Benedictine priory was founded here from Lessay, in Normandy, about 1117, and the present splendid parish church comprises the chancel, crossing and a small section of the nave of the priory church. The rounded arches and stumpy columns of the Norman building survive in the transepts, together with Trans work of about 1170, with pointed arches, in what is left of the nave. Boxgrove's chief glory lies in its Choir and Chancel, built on the site of the old Norman chancel c 1220, and a textbook of EE style, with every pair of columns different in volume, or in the use of Purbeck marble shafting. The vaulting is of a rare type called 'double-bay vaulting', with four bays in the choir and eight in each of the aisles, and the whole choir recalls the work of Bp Seffrid in Chichester Cathedral. About 1530 the vault was painted with a stylized design of fruit and foliage by Lambert Barnard, who also worked at Chichester. In the south arcade is the De La Warr Chantry, inserted in 1532 for Lord De La Warr and his wife, and carved all over in a fine combination of the dying Gothic period and the blossoming Renaissance.

Outside the church are traces of the monastic buildings on the N side: fragments of the cloister and chapter house, and the remains of the substantial guest house lie beyond.

Canterbury Cathedral, Kent

Ded: Metropolitan Church of Christ.

The mother church of Anglican Christianity and the seat of the Archbishop of Canterbury, Primate of All England, Canterbury Cathedral is a building of a splendour that matches its unique position and history.

History. Canterbury itself has been at the centre of English Christendom since 597 A.D., when Pope Gregory sent St Augustine to Kent to 'recover' the country for Christianity. The following year Augustine founded outside the walls of the city the monastery that still bears his name (see St Augustine's Abbey, below), and about 602 built another church possibly on the site of an earlier, Roman foundation, and possibly somewhere below the nave of the present cathedral. It can be said with certainty that there was a Saxon cathedral on the site, and that this was burnt down in 1067, to be followed by the Norman cathedral begun in 1070 by Lanfranc, William the Conqueror's first archbishop. Lanfranc, also reformed the monastery at Canterbury, with the cathedral as its priory church. Lanfranc's hasty reconstruction proved too small for the monks, and his successor, Abp Anselm (1093–1109), decided to rebuild the E end. Begun under Prior Ernulf in 1096, the work was promoted to a grander scale by Prior Conrad, who nearly doubled the area of the building. The 'glorious choir of Conrad', completed in 1130, stood for little more than 40 years, as the central part burned down in 1174, leaving only the outer aisle walls. Meanwhile the event that was to transform the history of Canterbury in general and the cathedral in particular had recently taken place: the murder on the evening of 29 Dec. 1170, in his own cathedral, of Abp Thomas Becket at the instigation of King Henry II. After Becket's canonization in 1173 the future of Canterbury as a place of pilgrimage was assured, and from that time dates the fame of the miracles wrought at the tomb of the 'holy blissful martyr' about whom Chaucer wrote almost two centuries later. A leading French master mason, William of Sens, was chosen to rebuild the cathedral after the fire, and he started work in 1175. However, three years later, he was crippled by falling from scaffolding and, after directing the work from his bed until he had completed the E transepts, handed over the task to William the Englishman. Working apparently from French William's plans, English William finished St Thomas's Chapel, Becket's Crown and the crypt below (1179–84).

The church remained in this state for nearly 200 years, with Lanfranc's unambitious nave and transepts adjoining the rich and intricate E end. Under Abp Sudbury, Lanfranc's nave was pulled down, and the present magnificently spacious and simple nave built by Henry Yevele (pronounced Yeavely) between 1391 and 1405. Additional chapels were added, and finally, between 1493 and 1505, *Bell Harry, the noblest of Perp towers, was built by John Wastell in place of the original Angel Steeple. The NW tower of Lanfranc was replaced in 1834 by a copy of Thomas Mapilton's SW tower, built 1424–34. The roof of the Trinity Chapel was restored after a fire in 1872.

Thus, though Canterbury Cathedral was begun in 1070 and complete by 1505, it is in fact the work of two detached centuries, as little was done between about 1180 and 1380. Although in area it ranks only ninth, and in length fourth, among English cathedrals, in its majestic proportions and the interest of its detail it stands in the top rank. Externally its character is Perp W of the central tower and early Gothic over a Norman crypt at the E end. The stained glass compares in quality with the best in France.

The principal entrance, the South Porch (1418), probably commemorates the victory of Agincourt in 1415. The old bas-relief over this represents the Altar of the Sword's Point in the Martyrdom, erected where Becket fell. The statues here, as on the W front (1862), replace those destroyed at the Reformation.

Interior. The *Nave* (c 1390) is well lit and stately in design, but unfortunately has lost its fine old original stained glass, except for some fragments collected in the W window. Under the NW tower is a

Canterbury Cathedral, a 17C view of the S side.

memorial to Abp Benson (1882–96). Near the tomb is the so-called 'Corinthian Throne', carved by Grinling Gibbons, presented in 1704 by Abp Tenison. The vista from the W end, closed by the flight of steps ascending to the choir screen, through which can be glimpsed a second flight to the altar, produces an impressively noble effect. The reticulated crosspieces under the lantern are struts to support the piers under the enormous weight of the tower; they bear the initials of Prior Thomas Goldstone, together with his rebus of three golden stones, and the motto *Non Nobis, Domine*. Goldstone was responsible for completing the tower. In the N aisle are the ornate font (1639) and (5th bay) the monument by Nicholas Stone to the organist and composer Orlando Gibbons, who died in 1625 at Canterbury while on his way to Dover with the musicians of the Chapel Royal to welcome Queen Henrietta Maria, bride of Charles I. An elaborate 15C Screen, with six crowned figures (Henry V, Richard II, Ethelbert, Edward the Confessor, Henry IV, Henry VI) and its original iron gates, separates the nave from the choir. The great *Windows in the W transepts are well seen from here: that in the NW transept, with its silvery colouring and its portrait figures of Edward IV (d 1483) and his queen, was presented by Edward; and that in the SW transept has 15C tracery, filled with glass, mostly 15C but with three 12C rows from the choir clerestory.

The *West* or *Nave Transepts*, like the nave, were rebuilt by Yevele, who left little of Lanfranc's work but the rough lower portion of the walls. The NW Transept, or Martyrdom, was the scene of Becket's murder, and the door from the cloisters is in the same position as when the four knights entered by it to cut down the 'turbulent priest', as Henry II called him. The spot where the archbishop is believed to have fallen is marked by a small slab of stone, replacing, according to tradition, a bloodstained fragment of the original pavement cut out and sent to Rome as a relic. An inscribed slab inserted in the pavement recalls that Pope John Paul II and Abp Robert Runcie knelt here together to pray on the occasion of the Papal visit on 29 May 1982. Under the Edward IV window are the tombs of Abp Peckham (1279–92), the oldest effigy in the cathedral, and Abp Warham (1504–32). The Lady Chapel, to the E of this transept, is late Perp (1449–68), with a rich fan vault; it is also called the Deans' Chapel, on account of the tombs it contains. The SW Transept (with the cathedral bookstall) has a corresponding chapel, known as St Michael's or the Warriors' Chapel (Perp, c 1420–28). In the centre stands the tomb erected by Margaret Holand (d 1437) for herself and her two husbands. The N wall is crowded with monuments, mainly good 17C work. At the E end, projecting from the wall, is the stone coffin of Abp Stephen Langton, who in 1215 helped the barons to persuade King John to sign Magna Carta (see also Bury St Edmunds). In this chapel is the Roll of Honour of the Buffs (formerly the East Kent, now the Queen's Own Buffs). The ship's bell of HMS *Canterbury*, just outside, is struck every morning at 11, as a memorial to men of the Navy, and a page of the book containing the Roll is turned over by a representative of the Buffs, prayer then being offered for those who have died in the wars of the 20C. In the 15C All Saints Chapel above, a Norman arch of Lanfranc's church has been exposed.

On entering the *Choir*, one of the longest in England, we notice the strange contraction at the E end. William of Sens drew in his building in this way, so as to preserve the two Norman side chapels of St Andrew (on the N) and St Anselm (on the S). The Trans style of the choir is seen in the juxtaposition of Norman and EE features. The choir of Sens cathedral (SE of Paris), finished in 1168, determined the form of Canterbury choir, which resembles the French model in many particulars; although irregularities, such as the mixture of round and pointed arch forms and of Norman and EE decoration, seem to indicate an attempt at compromise between French innovation and English tradition. The stalls at the W end are by Roger Davis, a London joiner (1682). The diaper work on the S wall, above the lower flight of stairs to the altar, may be part of the shrine of St Dunstan (c 909–88), which ranked second only to Becket's shrine in sanctity; though it is more probably the remnant of sedilia. The beautiful and unusual *Screens between the choir and its aisles (1304–05) alternate with canopied tombs. Behind the High Altar on the platform (which is in fact the floor of the Trinity Chapel) stands the simple but impressive **'Marble Chair', probably dating from the time of Abp Stephen Langton (d 1228), though known often as 'St Augustine's Chair', in which from time immemorial the Primates of All England have been enthroned. It was restored to this place in 1977, after being moved about for 150 years.

The *Choir Aisles* and *East* or *Choir Transepts* are mainly the work of Ernulf and Conrad, altered and enriched by William of Sens. Through the N door of Prior Eastry's screen we enter the N Choir Aisle, in the windows of which is some fine medallion glass of c 1200. On the wall adjoining the NE transept is a 15C fresco of the life of St Eustace; on the S side are the canopy-tombs of Abp Bourchier (1454–86) and Abp Chichele (1414–43), and the neo-Gothic monument of Abp William Howley (d 1848). In the NE Transept the circular window preserves much of its late 12C glass. St Martin's Chapel, on the E side of the transept, contains a restored glass medallion of the saint. Abp

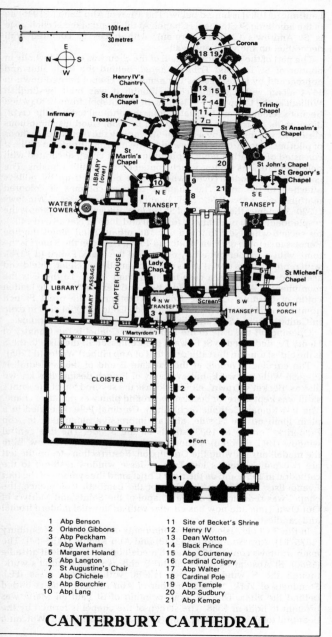

0 ____ 100 feet
0 ____ 30 metres

N E / S W (compass)

Corona — 18 19

Henry IV's Chantry

St Andrew's Chapel

Henry IV's Chantry — 16

13 15 17
12 14
11
7

Treasury

St Martin's Chapel

Infirmary

Trinity Chapel

St Anselm's Chapel

LIBRARY (over)

20

St John's Chapel
St Gregory's Chapel

10

9

8

21

N E TRANSEPT

S E TRANSEPT

WATER TOWER

LIBRARY PASSAGE

CHAPTER HOUSE

Lady Chap.

LIBRARY

6

5

St Michael's Chapel

4 N W TRANSEPT

Screen

S W TRANSEPT

SOUTH PORCH

3

('Martyrdom')

CLOISTER

2

Font

1

1 Abp Benson	11 Site of Becket's Shrine
2 Orlando Gibbons	12 Henry IV
3 Abp Peckham	13 Dean Wotton
4 Abp Warham	14 Black Prince
5 Margaret Holand	15 Abp Courtenay
6 Abp Langton	16 Cardinal Coligny
7 St Augustine's Chair	17 Abp Walter
8 Abp Chichele	18 Cardinal Pole
9 Abp Bourchier	19 Abp Temple
10 Abp Lang	20 Abp Sudbury
	21 Abp Kempe

CANTERBURY CATHEDRAL

Lanfranc (d 1089) is buried below. The ashes of Abp Lang (d 1945) lie in the adjoining St Stephen's Chapel. At the E end of the N choir aisle is St Andrew's Chapel (Norman), with traces of coloured wall decoration on the vault and walls.

The part of the cathedral to the E of the choir was erected wholly in honour of St Thomas. *Trinity Chapel*, behind the high altar and approached by steps, retains the name of a chapel burned down in 1174 along with Conrad's choir, though it was built by English William as the Chapel of St Thomas. In this chapel, from 1220 (when Becket's remains were translated from the original tomb in the crypt) down to its destruction by Henry VIII in 1538, stood his sumptuous shrine, its site marked by a pavement worn by the feet of generations of pilgrims. The shrine was viewed by the pilgrims through a grille; it consisted of a marble table supporting an oak chest, decorated with gold and precious stones, which contained the saint's remains. The chest had a wooden cover, which could be drawn up by pulleys attached to the roof. The chapel's coupled columns of coloured marbles are very fine, and beautiful stained-glass *Windows (1220–30) depict the miracles of St Thomas. Between the N piers is the resplendent tomb of Henry IV (d 1413) and Joan of Navarre (d 1437), his second wife. Next to it is a tiny 18C organ. Then comes the fine Renaissance tomb of Dean Wotton (d 1567). Between the S piers is the tomb with a copper-gilt effigy of Edward the Black Prince (d 1376), with reproductions (1954) of his surcoat, gauntlets, helmet, shield and scabbard (originals in a case in the S choir aisle). To the E is the monument of Abp Courtenay (d 1396), and next to that is the leaden coffin of Cardinal Odet de Coligny, brother of the great French admiral and Huguenot leader Gaspard de Coligny. Odet died in exile in Canterbury in 1571, and his body still awaits return to France.

Opening off the aisle to the N of Trinity Chapel is the Chantry of Henry IV, dedicated to St Edward the Confessor. In the aisle to the S is the oldest tomb in the cathedral, that of Abp Hubert Walter (d 1205).

The circular *Corona*, at the extreme E end of the cathedral, is English William's work, but evidently of French design. It is known also as 'Becket's Crown', either because the severed top of the saint's skull was kept there, or because its ground plan was the same shape. The last Roman Catholic archbishop, Cardinal Pole, is buried in a plain tomb on the N side, and an impressive monument to Abp Frederick Temple (d 1903) stands on the S side. The fine central window (13C, restored) is known as the 'Redemption Window' from the medallions showing the Crucifixion, Resurrection etc; on the left are two panels from a lost Tree of Jesse window restored to the cathedral in 1954, and on the right Christ amid the symbols of the four Evangelists. In 1978, at the close of the Lambeth Conference, the chapel was rededicated as the Chapel of the Saints and Martyrs of Our Own Time and now has an altar with an unusual modern frontal and candlesticks.

In the S Choir Aisle are the monuments of Abp Simon of Sudbury (1375–81), Abp Stratford (1333–48) and Abp Kempe (1452–54). The main windows contain 13C French medallions set in modern grisaille (1960). St Anselm's Chapel, at the E end, is mainly Ernulf's work, though the S window is Dec (1336), with modern glass (H.J. Stammers of York, 1959) in honour of Abp Anselm, who is buried behind the altar. The 12C wall painting of St Paul on Malta was brought to light in 1888. The screen of the chapel is formed by the beautiful tomb of Abp Meopham (1329–33). The so-called 'Watching

Chamber' above this chapel overlooks Trinity Chapel. The four S windows (Erwin Bossanyi, 1960) are highly colourful. The Chapel of St John the Evangelist was restored in 1951 as a memorial to Abp William Temple (1881–1944). The adjoining *Chapel of St Gregory the Great* was restored in 1978 as a memorial to Abp Geoffrey Fisher (d 1972). On the S wall of the aisle is the recumbent figure of Prior Eastry (d 1322).

The spacious *Crypt*, dedicated to the Virgin, is entered from the SW or NW transept. It is mainly the work of Ernulf and Conrad, and the *Capitals of the pillars and some ornamental shafts are vigorous examples of Norman stone-carving. Especially fine is the central pillar of the chapel at the SE corner, dedicated to St Gabriel; the apse preserves its *Paintings of c 1130. A chapel of the S aisle is walled off to form a 'Temple' for French Protestants, who have worshipped in this crypt since 1568 (the notorious Massacre of St Bartholomew, in which many Protestants were murdered in Paris, took place in 1572). Every Sunday at 15.00 a service is held in French in the Black Prince's Chantry (SE transept of the crypt), which commemorates the papal dispensation in 1363 enabling the Prince to marry his beautiful cousin Joan, the 'Fair Maid of Kent'. It seems probable that the Black Prince was also responsible for the exquisite stone screen and other decoration of the adjoining Chapel of Our Lady Undercroft, in which was buried Cardinal Abp Morton (1486–1500) under a long-vanished brass. The lovely 17C Portuguese ivory Madonna and Child, presented in 1948, was stolen in 1981 and has been replaced by a fine bronze statue ('Our Lady of Canterbury') made in 1982 by Sister Concordia, a Benedictine nun from the abbey at Minster-in-Thanet. The graceful late 12C *Crypt* under the Trinity Chapel and Corona includes the site of the chapel where St Thomas was first buried. Here, on 12 July 1174, Henry II completed the penance imposed on him for the death of Becket, spending the night in fasting, and receiving three lashes from each of the monks the following morning. On the W wall are graffiti, showing Christ the teacher, surrounded by the emblems of the Evangelists, and at the side are two 7C columns and (in a case further W) fragments of a Saxon cross from the ruined church at Reculver, on the N Kent coast.

Precincts. On the N side of the cathedral are the extensive monastic buildings. The Benedictine monastery founded by St Augustine was enlarged and converted into a priory by Lanfranc, and much altered and rebuilt by later archbishops and priors.

The *Great Cloister* (1397–1414) is entered from the NW transept. Though mainly Perp, it incorporates some fine Norman work and beautiful EE arcading in the N walk, cut into by the Perp vaulting. The painted vault bosses, which include over 800 shields, are superb; one of them, in the E walk, portrays Henry Yevele, architect of the cathedral nave. Opening off the E walk is the spacious *Chapter House*, the lower part of which is the work of Prior Eastry (1304–20), completed by Chillenden when he began the cloisters, T.S. Eliot's *Murder in the Cathedral* was commissioned for performance here in 1935. To the NE is the rebuilt Chapter Library (1954), replacing a building destroyed during the air raids of 1942. In the Dark Entry, between this and the chapter house, are two fine ranges of pillars of Lanfranc's time, some with incised decoration; these and the pillar bases in the lawn beyond the modern arcade of the library were part of the sub-vault of the Dormitory. We emerge in the Infirmary

Cloister, passing on the right a door into the crypt and a stair to the NE transept. On the left is the elaborate Norman sub-vault of the Water or Lavatory Tower, which formed part of the ingenious water-supply system of Prior Wibert (1151–67), and was built to house the monastery's main water cistern; the upper floor of the tower is Perp. The cloister is continued by the 13C sub-vault of the Prior's Chapel (chapel replaced after 1660 by the brick Howley Library).

The infirmary cloister is prolonged N by a passage below the Wolfson Library (1966) to Prior Sellingegate (c 1480) and the Green Court. On the E side of this square stands the Deanery, mixed medieval and 16C; and in the SW corner is the Archdeaconry with a curious wooden pentice (lean-to) of 1390 in its garden. To the E of this the Larder Gate Building (1951) incorporates a 15C archway and part of the monastic kitchens. This, with all the remaining buildings in the square, is part of the King's School, a monastic foundation of the 7C, installed on this site by Henry VIII as a grammar school for 50 (now 700) boys. Famous pupils include Christopher Marlowe, William Harvey, and Somerset Maugham. The monastic Brewhouse, Bakehouse (1303) and Granary are incorporated in the N range. In the NW corner of the Green Court the exterior *Norman Staircase (by Wibert, 1151–67) leading to the hall is unique and still supremely beautiful, despite the modern roof. Through the adjacent Court Gate we enter the Mint Yard, the former Almonry. Hence the North Gate opens on Palace Street, named from the Archbishop's Palace destroyed by Puritan fanaticism c 1643, in the time of Abp Laud.

Returning to the Prior's Chapel, we turn E where a stately row of Norman arches marks the hall of the Infirmary. The more ornate arches, still further E, are remains of the 14C Infirmary Chapel. On the right of the hall is the arcaded Norman Treasury, while the Choir School on the left incorporates a refectory of 1343. Passing round the unfinished exterior of the Corona, we join the path skirting the S side of the cathedral. This leads across the former lay cemetery, which extended from the South Porch to the exquisitely arcaded *St Anselm's Tower and was there divided by a wall from the monks' cemetery. The grandeur and fine colouring of the SE transept are very striking from this point. Opposite the E end of the cathedral is an old walled garden, now the site of the Kent War Memorial (by Sir Herbert Baker). On its E side is a bastion of the old city wall, transformed into a chapel of silence, with a cenotaph, flags and inscriptions.

Canterbury, Kent: Grey Friars

A pretty little EE building, built on pillars right over a branch of the River Stour (entrance in Stour Street), is all that remains of the monastic buildings of the Grey Friars (Friars Minor), who came to Canterbury in 1224, sent over by St Francis of Assisi. It dates from around 1270, and consists of a large upstairs room, with a smaller room opening off it. In later years it became a refuge for Flemish Huguenot weavers fleeing from the Continent, and was used as a prison.

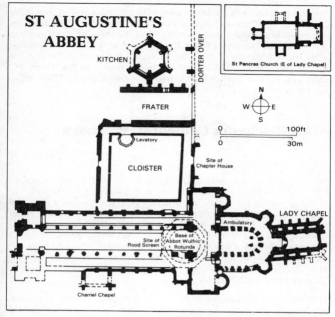

Canterbury, Kent: St Augustine's Abbey

Built just outside the city walls, opposite the E end of the cathedral, the original Abbey of St Peter and St Paul was founded by St Augustine in 598, as accommodation for the monks who came with him from Rome. It stood outside the walls, as the early Church did not allow burial within a city. The abbey was the burial place of the early archbishops, including St Augustine himself. Three separate churches were built on the site in the 7C; the brick-built St Pancras Church, east of the abbey ruins, may have been King Ethelbert's idol-chapel before his conversion to Christianity. In 978 St Dunstan rededicated the abbey to its founder, and in 1049–59 Abbot Wulfric began to link the two W churches by a rotunda, unique in this country, copied from the rotunda of St Bénigne at Dijon. All this work was demolished by Abbot Scotland, the first Norman abbot, who in 1073 started a new church, completed c 1120. The abbey, which until the time of Becket ranked as the second Benedictine house in Europe, was destroyed in 1538 and a royal staging-post built on the site, incorporating the ruins. This was visited by Elizabeth I, Charles I (who received his bride Henrietta Maria here in June 1625), and Charles II (who stayed here on his way to London at the Restoration of 1660).

We approach by the cloister garth. On the right, beneath a low protective roof, lies the N part of the first church (St Peter and St Paul), in which King Ethelbert, Queen Bertha, St Augustine and at least eight of his early successors were buried. The empty tombs of SS Lawrence, Mellitus and Justus have been identified. The massive octagonal foundations of Abbot Wulfric's Rotunda are prominent to the SE. Of the Norman Church the NW wall of the nave still stands, with Tudor additions of the 'King's House', and much of the crypt of the apsidal choir. St Pancras, the easternmost of the three 7C churches, built of Roman bricks, had its E end altered c 1387, using Roman bricks.

Chichester Cathedral, W Sussex

Ded: Holy Trinity.

In 1075 a new see was established in the old Roman town of Chichester, some 8 miles inland from the coastal village of Selsey, site of the previous see (established in the 7C), and the cathedral was begun within the next two decades. It is still predominantly a Norman building, with few, though important, alterations and additions. Unenclosed on the N flank, it dominates West Street, and seen from a distance provides a constant focus to the town. The Bell-tower (c 1400–36) is the only remaining English example of a detached belfry adjoining a cathedral (except for the modern tower at Chester). Visitors enter by the EE west porch.

History. After the transfer of the see from Selsey, the new cathedral was begun after 1091 by Bp Ralph de Luffa on the site of an old collegiate church, and consecrated in 1108. Partly destroyed by fire in 1114, it was at once repaired and was practically finished by 1184. A second fire in 1187 led to the rebuilding of the inside of the clerestory and the addition of stone vaulting and Purbeck marble shafts. The Norman chancel apse was replaced by Bp Seffrid II (1180–1204), who built the present square retrochoir. The three porches and the sacristy are of the EE period. The outer aisles were formed by throwing into one a series of chapels originally added between 1245 and 1280. The upper stage of the central tower, with its plate-tracery windows, belonged to about 1247. The Lady Chapel was completed in 1288–1304. A good deal of damage was done by the Parliamentarians, after Chichester was captured by the Puritans in 1643. The bell-tower, the cloister and the graceful spire (277ft), recalling that of Salisbury and said to be the only cathedral spire in England visible from the sea, were built soon after 1400. The spire collapsed in 1861, possibly because its stone had been weakened by the fire in 1187, and was rebuilt almost at once. The NW tower, which fell in 1635, was re-erected in 1901. Since 1964 the cathedral fabric has been carefully strengthened and repaired, using imported French stone.

Interior. The sober and harmonious proportions are immediately apparent; a low screen separates the nave from the choir. The arcades and gallery of Bp Ralph de Luffa's *Nave* contrast effectively with Bp Seffrid's light and graceful clerestory (in which Purbeck marble is freely used) and with the Dec tracery of the outer aisles. The SW tower preserves its fine Norman base with EE additions, copied in the reconstructed NW tower (now the Sailors' Chapel, dedicated to Sussex men who died at sea during World War II). The Baptistry

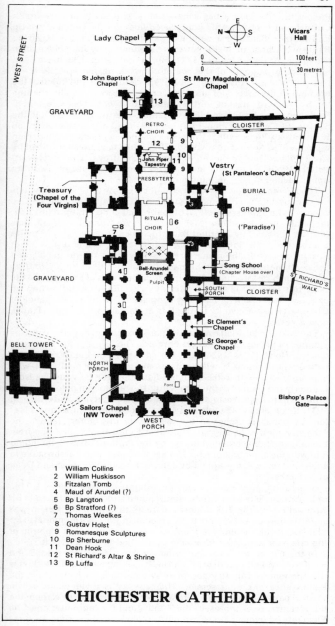

WEST STREET

Lady Chapel

St John Baptist's Chapel

St Mary Magdalene's Chapel

GRAVEYARD

RETRO-CHOIR

CLOISTER

Vicars' Hall

N E S W

0   100 feet
0   30 metres

13

12

9

10

11

9

John Piper Tapestry

PRESBYTERY

Vestry (St Pantaleon's Chapel)

BURIAL

GROUND

('Paradise')

Treasury (Chapel of the Four Virgins)

8
7

RITUAL CHOIR

6

5

Bell-Arundel Screen
Pulpit

Song School (Chapter House over)

GRAVEYARD

4

3

SOUTH PORCH

CLOISTER

ST RICHARD'S WALK

St Clement's Chapel

St George's Chapel

BELL TOWER

2

NORTH PORCH

Font

1

Sailors' Chapel (NW Tower)

WEST PORCH

SW Tower

Bishop's Palace Gate ⟶

1   William Collins
2   William Huskisson
3   Fitzalan Tomb
4   Maud of Arundel (?)
5   Bp Langton
6   Bp Stratford (?)
7   Thomas Weelkes
8   Gustav Holst
9   Romanesque Sculptures
10 Bp Sherburne
11 Dean Hook
12 St Richard's Altar & Shrine
13 Bp Luffa

CHICHESTER CATHEDRAL

(below the SW tower) has a new font (1983) made of dark-green Cornish stone, by John Skelton, placed there for the centenary of Bp Bell (born 1883); and a painting (1952) by Hans Feibusch, of the Baptism of Christ. In the SW tower is a monument by John Flaxman to the poet William Collins (1721–59), a native of Chichester—an outstanding example of this sculptor's work. In the N Aisle are a statue of William Huskisson, the MP knocked down and killed at the opening of the Liverpool and Manchester Railway in 1830; the fine tomb of Richard Fitzalan, Earl of Arundel (d 1376) and his wife; and (E bay) the tomb ascribed to Maud, Countess of Arundel (c 1300). In the S Aisle, St George's Chapel has been restored as a memorial to the Royal Sussex Regiment; St Clement's Chapel has an elegant Flaxman monument to Agnes Cromwell (d 1797), and a modern altar frontal by Cecil Collins. The cantilevered pulpit, by Geoffrey Clarke and Robert Potter (1966), is made of stone-faced reinforced concrete with an upper section of cast aluminium.

The *S Transept* has a fine seven-light window (c 1330). Below it is the canopy-tomb of Bp Langton (1305–37). Opposite, under a fine Dec canopy, is an expressive effigy, probably that of Bp Stratford (d 1362); the tomb-chest dates from 1846. Here also are two unusual paintings (c 1519, restored) by Lambert Barnard, a local artist employed by Bp Sherburne (1508–36); they represent King Ceadwalla of the South Saxons bestowing the monastery of Selsey on St Wilfrid in 680, and the confirmation of this grant made by Henry VIII to Bp Sherburne, above much restored medallion heads of the Kings of England. To the W of this transept is the EE Sacristy, with fine vaulting resting on exquisite corbels. It is now the song-school, with a 15C panelled Chapter House above it. To the E is St Pantaleon's Chapel (Trans), now a vestry.

The *N Transept*, long used as the parish church of St Peter, contains pictures of bishops by Lambert Barnard. The ashes of the composer Gustav Holst (1874–1934) are buried here. On the W wall is a memorial to Thomas Weelkes, the great composer of madrigals, who was organist here in 1602–23. It is adjoined on the E by the *Treasury* (formerly the Chapel of the Four Virgins), with an iron gate of c 1700, brought here from Westgate House, now the County Record Office, in 1951. It contains vestments and other cathedral treasures and silver lent by parish churches in the diocese. In the *Library* (above the Treasury, viewed by special request) are a few books surviving from the pillage of the cathedral library by the Puritans in 1643, including one with the signature of Abp Thomas Cranmer, burnt at the stake in 1556, and three autographed by John Donne, the 17C poet and Dean of St Paul's.

Separating the nave from the slightly raised choir is the Bell-Arundel Screen, a three-aisled vaulted structure attributed to Bp Arundel (1459–78). Taken down in 1860, this fine Perp screen was stored in the bell-tower until its re-erection in 1961 as a memorial to Bp Bell (1929–58), remembered both as a humanitarian and a patron of the arts, whose portrait in bronze is attached to the side of it.

In the *Choir*, the Stalls, partly modernized, date from c 1335 and have well-carved misericords. The most striking feature of the choir is the enormous *Tapestry designed by John Piper, which covers the Renaissance oak altar screen. The tapestry is divided into seven vertical panels, separated by the wooden buttresses of the screen; the three central ones represent the Trinity, and the four outer ones the Elements (above) and the Evangelists (below). In the S choir aisle are

Chichester Cathedral, 12C sculptured stone panel showing the Raising of Lazarus. (A.F. Kersting)

two of the cathedral's greatest treasures—sculptured stone *Panels (c 1140) of most refined workmanship and design. They show Christ arriving at the house of Martha and Mary in Bethany, and the Raising of Lazarus; they would originally have been brightly coloured, with jewels in the eye-sockets. Between them is the tomb of Bp Sherburne (d 1536), and opposite that of Dean Hook (d 1875), a good work by Gilbert Scott. The vista of this aisle is closed by the *Chapel of St Mary Magdalene, with modern altar, rails, candlesticks and bookrest, and with Graham Sutherland's painting 'Noli me tangere' (Christ appearing to Mary Magdalene after the Resurrection) above the altar. Between the choir and the N transept is the fine organ, with decoration on the pipes going back to the 17C.

The *Retrochoir, completed by Bp Seffrid in 1199, is a charming example of the final transition from the massive Norman to the lighter Gothic style. The interval between the fine Purbeck marble piers and their detached shafts is wider than in any other known example. The sculptural decoration in the triforium is noteworthy. On the N side is a window by Chagall (1978), on the theme of Psalm 150. On the S side is the fragment of a 2C Roman mosaic (glassed over), found under the foundations in 1969. The altar in the retrochoir marks the site of the shrine of St Richard of Chichester (d 1253), a much loved bishop, canonized in 1262, whose shrine was a centre of pilgrimage until it was destroyed at the Reformation. Nearby are deposited the ashes of Bp Bell.

The gates of the Lady Chapel are a relic of the grille that surrounded the platform on which St Richard's shrine stood. The two W bays of the long and narrow chapel belonged to the original Norman church, while the three E bays were added between 1288 and 1304. In the first two bays are traces of the paintings by Lambert Barnard which once covered the vaults throughout the cathedral. The simple tomb of Bp Ralph de Luffa (d 1123) is in the first bay.

The *Cloisters*, entered by the beautiful EE S Porch, are 15C and irregular both in position and form. They were not built for monastic purposes, and have no north walk; originally they surrounded the cathedral's 'paradise' or burial ground. From the S walk a passage called St Richard's Walk leads to Canon Lane. In front is the Deanery (1725); to the right the lane ends at the 14C gateway of the Bishop's Palace, half of which is now a theological college. Its chapel and kitchen-walls are of the 13C, the remainder 14–18C. The chapel (entered opposite the cathedral's SW tower) has fine vaulting and corbels, and an exquisite painted tondo (c 1250). At the other end of the lane, beyond the 15C Vicars' Close (built for the vicars choral, responsible for the cathedral's music), is the 16C Canon Gate into South Street. By another entrance to the precincts, a few yards to the left along South Street, is a 12C vaulted undercroft (now a café) below the beamed Vicars' Hall and Parlour.

Chichester, W Sussex: Grey Friars

In Priory Park, NE of the cathedral.

The EE choir of the Grey Friars' church survives, now used as an annexe to the Chichester Museum. The Franciscans settled in Chichester about 1240, and their church was built soon after. It was later used as an assize court; its most famous trial was that of the poet William Blake for sedition, in 1804.

Guildford Cathedral, Surrey

Ded: The Holy Spirit.

Set commandingly on Stag Hill, to the W of Guildford, this is one of the only two Anglican cathedrals in Britain to have been built on a new site since medieval times (the other is Liverpool). Long and narrow, with a central tower 160ft high, it is built mainly of local brick, and represents an austere modern interpretation of the Gothic style. There are no transepts to speak of, due to the nature of the site (a narrow ridge running E-W), and the building is lit by slender, lancet-like main windows.

The need for a cathedral in Guildford arose in 1927, when the old

GUILDFORD CATHEDRAL

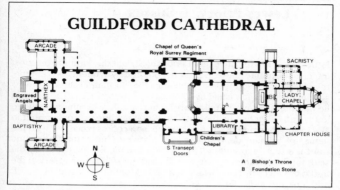

diocese of Winchester was split into three (Winchester, Guildford and Portsmouth); the design was put out to competition, and the winner was Edward (later Sir Edward) Maufe. The foundation stone (directly behind the sanctuary) was laid in 1936 by Dr Cosmo Gordon Lang, Abp of Canterbury; the cathedral was consecrated in 1961 (building had been interrupted by the war) and completed in 1964.

Interior. The simplicity of the exterior is carried over inside the building, which is of light golden-brown stone, with little colour by way of contrast. The wide *Nave*, flanked by tall narrow aisles, focuses attention on the high altar, which has a tall gold brocade reredos behind it and a rose window high above. The wooden cross above the altar is painted in Byzantine style by Brenda Bridge. On the S side of the chancel is the bishop's throne, in simple modern style, and nearer the altar the three-seated sedilia, carved with smiling angels between the arches. A brass stag in the paving of the crossing marks the summit of Stag Hill (so called because it was a hunting-ground of the Norman kings). The nave is enlivened by hundreds of colourful kneelers, each embroidered with a different design. Behind the sanctuary is the angularly apsidal Lady Chapel, featuring a modern lignum vitae carving of the Madonna and Child, by Douglas Stephen.

The narrow N transept is occupied by the Chapel of the Queen's Royal Surrey Regiment, separated from the nave by wrought-iron gates; the regiment was founded in 1661 by Charles II, whose cypher appears in the ironwork. Opposite, on the S side of the cathedral, is the Children's Chapel, with iron gates given by the Girl Guides. Looking back towards the W end of the nave, it is worth noting the pair of angel musicians, engraved by John Hutton on the glass of the bronze entrance doors.

Externally, two massive bronze doors leading to the S transept have low reliefs by Vernon Hill illustrating the traditional occupations of women. There are several modernistic stone sculptures decorating the walls, culminating in the gilded angel on the tower, which can be seen for miles when the sun strikes it. Students of brickwork should note the unusual bond, consisting of two stretchers to one header. The enormous teak cross outside the E end of the cathedral was put up to mark the site in 1933.

Lewes Priory, E Sussex

Ded: St Pancras.

Little remains of the once great Priory of St Pancras, formerly the most important Cluniac house in Britain. Founded by William de Warenne, the Conqueror's son-in-law, soon after the Norman Conquest, it was systematically demolished by Thomas Cromwell in 1537. The remains lie behind St John's, the old parish church of Lewes, among playing fields and cut in two by the railway. When the line was being built in 1845, workmen on the site dug up two lead coffins inscribed with the names of William de Warenne and his wife Gundrada. Beside the ruins is a bronze monument in the form of a medieval helmet, by the sculptor Enzo Plazzotta, commemorating the 700th anniversary of the Battle of Lewes in 1264, when Simon de Montfort defeated Henry III and took him prisoner.

Michelham Priory, E Sussex

Off B2108, 2 miles W of Hailsham.

Adm. daily, April–Oct.

On the site of a Norman manor house beside the River Cuckmere, Michelham Priory was built by the Augustinian canons in the 13–14C. At the Dissolution in 1536 it passed through various hands, before being bought in 1587 by Herbert Pelham, who built a Tudor house on the remains. The gate-tower by the wide moat dates from 1405; of the older, 13C monastic buildings, the vaulted buttery (or parlour), the lavatory arches (on the cloister wall) and the rebuilt refectory survive. The cloister, chapter house and long narrow monastic church have disappeared, but are marked out by stones in the turf to the N of the Tudor building. The exhibits include documents relating to the priory's history, and some fine old furniture.

Minster-in-Sheppey Abbey, Kent

Ded: St Mary and St Sexburga.

On Isle of Sheppey, 3 miles E of Sheerness.

About 670, Sexburga, widow of one of the Kings of Kent, founded a nunnery on high ground on the Isle of Sheppey. Periodically destroyed by the Danes, it was re-established about 1130; the sturdy gatehouse dates from the 15C. The abbey church still contains some Saxon work, notably a window in the N aisle. It is unusual in being a 'double church': the original Nun's Church, and the parish church built against it in the 13C, when arcades were pierced through. The fine monuments, notable for details of armour, include the tomb of Sir Robert de Shurland (d c 1310), who was Lord Warden of the Cinque Ports and features in R.H. Barham's *Ingoldsby Legends* (the legend of the horse called Grey Dolphin); and the *Brasses (c 1330) commemorating Sir John de Northwode and his wife Lady Joan.

Minster-in-Thanet Abbey, Kent

Ded: St Mary.

Off B2048, 5 miles W of Ramsgate.

The grand church (12–13C) survives from the monastic foundation, one of the earliest Christian centres in Kent. It was established as a nunnery in 669 by Domneva, who was succeeded as abbess by her daughter, St Mildred. The church has a fine Norman tower and nave and EE chancel. Nearby is today's abbey (not in fact the original monastic site but medieval farm buildings), which has been occupied by Benedictine nuns since the 1930s. The W range dates from the late 11C or early 12C, and this incorporates the W end of the abbey church (with a spiral staircase in the tower); excavations revealed the plan of the church, which can be seen marked out on the ground. A groin-vaulted passage and chapel are also shown.

Mottisfont Abbey, Hampshire

Ded: Holy Trinity.

Off A3057, 4 miles N of Romsey.

In a beautiful setting by the River Test, Mottisfont was founded in 1201 as a priory of Augustinian canons. It survives today as a Tudor and Georgian country house, adapted from the monastic buildings; unusually, it was the church that was adapted and incorporated into the new structure, rather than the monks' living quarters, which was the normal procedure. The house occupies the nave and south transept of the church and part of the cloister; on the N side the stone buttresses reveal the original structure. Most of the alterations were carried out by Lord Sandys, Henry VIII's Lord Chamberlain, who pulled down the bulk of the cloister, dorter, kitchens and other residential parts of the priory to the south of the church, creating a typical U-shaped Tudor house, with the cloister garth forming the open forecourt. The medieval vaulting of the monks' cellarium (under the SW wing) is still in perfect condition.

Netley Abbey, Hampshire

Ded: St Mary.

Off minor road on N side Southampton Water, S of A3025.

A Cistercian abbey, founded in 1239 in the reign of Henry III, Netley was one of the last Cistercian foundations in England. It was first occupied by monks from Beaulieu, across the Solent. The name was originally Letley, later corrupted into Netley, and in the Middle Ages it became Laetus Locus, the 'happy place', from its beautiful riverside setting. At the Dissolution the abbey buildings were adapted to form a Tudor manor-house, with the cloister garth turned into a central courtyard. Much of the church and cloister buildings still remain, in a ruined and roofless condition, including the chapter house, the reredorter, and an isolated building to the E of the main block, which was probably the abbot's lodging. The room below the reredorter may have been the infirmary or 'seyny hall', where the monks were bled at regular intervals for the good of their health. During the heyday of the Romantic period, Netley came to symbolize the perfection of Gothic ruinousness, and in the 1790s there was even an 'operatic farce' named after it and performed at Covent Garden.

Portsmouth Cathedral, Hampshire

Ded: St Thomas of Canterbury.

Formerly the parish church of Portsmouth, St Thomas's attained cathedral status when the diocese of Portsmouth was established in 1927. A strange hybrid of a church, it is a mixture of 12C, 17C and 20C elements: the transepts and sanctuary of the medieval church, built 1188–96; the nave and tower, rebuilt c 1693 after being damaged by cannon fire in the Civil War, with the cupola added in 1703; and the modern nave and aisles, begun in 1935 by Sir Charles Nicholson, and still incomplete. In effect, the old church is embedded in the recent one, as the outer walls of the 17C rebuilding were pierced with arches when the 1935 additions were built; and the tower is now central to the church, instead of being at the W end, as it was before the westward extension of the nave.

Portsmouth's connection with England's maritime history is emphasized in the Navy Aisle (to the right of the entrance), or south choir aisle, dedicated in 1938; it contains a piece of Nelson's flag from Trafalgar, and the monument to Admiral Sir John Kempthorne (d 1679), together with a wooden model of his ship the *Mary Rose*, in which he defeated the Algerian pirates in 1669. To the E is the Martyrs' Chapel, dedicated in 1196 to various martyrs, and now a memorial to members of Portsmouth Civil Defence who died during World War II. The Choir, with a W gallery of 1708, contains the Corporation Pew of 1693 with the seat of the Lord Mayor of Portsmouth; and the pulpit, also of 1693, reconstructed in 1902–04. In the S Sanctuary Aisle is a monument by Nicholas Stone to George Villiers, Duke of Buckingham, the favourite of James I and Charles I, who was assassinated in Portsmouth in 1628 (buried in Westminster Abbey). The Retrochoir, behind the High Altar, contains the tomb of the Rev. Benjamin Burgess (d 1673), the only Presbyterian minister to be buried in an English cathedral. An interesting architectural feature of the sanctuary aisles is the construction of the arcading, which consists of double pointed arches within large semicircular outer arches, similar to those at Boxgrove (see above), and probably the work of the same architect. On the NE wall of the N transept are the remains of a wall painting of the Last Judgement (c 1250).

Of the Nave, which dates from 1939, so far only three of the proposed seven bays have been completed. It contains the 'Golden Barque', a gilded ship which acted as the weather vane on the tower from 1710–1954, when it was blown down by a gale. The plinth is made of oak from the *Victory*. The N Tower Transept (baptistry) contains a fine majolica plaque of the Virgin and Child, made in Florence by Andrea della Robbia c 1500. In the S Tower Transept are a fine bronze statue of St John the Baptist (1951), by David Wynne, and a 'Stars and Stripes' flag presented by Washington Cathedral.

Portsmouth Cathedral, Hampshire (RC)

Ded: St John the Evangelist.

This austere building, of dark-coloured brick and Portland stone, was begun in 1880 and mainly completed during the 1890s, to the designs of John Crawley, followed by Joseph Hansom. It was designated a cathedral in 1882. After bomb damage in 1941, large-scale repairs were undertaken; and much of the decoration and furnishings are modern. The interior is spacious and open, with transepts the same width as the aisles, and side chapels (St Patrick off the north aisle, and the Last Supper S of the Sanctuary). There is some striking modern stained glass by Arthur Buss.

Quarr Abbey, Isle of Wight

Ded: St Mary.

Off A3054, 2 miles west of Ryde.

Quarr was a Cistercian house founded by Baldwin de Redvers for monks from Savigny, in Northern France, in 1131. The name comes from the nearby quarries of fine limestone, used in Winchester and Chichester Cathedrals. Little survives of the medieval abbey; but in 1907 the estate was bought by Benedictines from Solesmes, who built a new abbey in Gothic-inspired brickwork. The architect was Dom Paul Bellot, a member of the Quarr community. The refectory and other monastic buildings have a genuinely medieval atmosphere, with their brick-built pointed arches; while the church (open to visitors) is highly original in design, with a stumpy tower over the sanctuary, and a strange but effective turret at the SW corner.

Rochester Cathedral, Kent

Ded: Christ and the Blessed Virgin Mary.

Comparatively modest in size, Rochester Cathedral makes an admirable foil to the massive square keep of the castle nearby. It dates mainly from the 11–15C, and resembles Canterbury Cathedral in having double transepts, a raised choir and presbytery, forming a

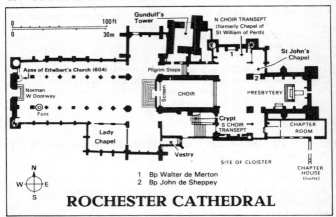

1 Bp Walter de Merton
2 Bp John de Sheppey

ROCHESTER CATHEDRAL

relatively long E arm, and a large crypt under the presbytery. The Norman West Front, with its elaborate recessed mid 12C *Doorway, perhaps the finest of its kind in England, is the most striking feature of the exterior. The tympanum and the figures on the shafting of the door (Solomon and the Queen of Sheba) were added c 1175. The figures of Bp Gundulf and John of Canterbury, to either side of and above the arch, are early 20C.

History. By 604, only seven years after St Augustine landed in Thanet, a missionary monk called Justus was appointed first bishop of Durobrivae (the Roman name for Rochester), and established a church in the same year; it is thus the oldest bishopric in the country after Canterbury. Of the original Saxon church, 42ft long and with an apse at the E end, nothing remains except the foundations, discovered in 1889. Its Saxon successor, though probably stripped of all adornments at the Norman Conquest, no doubt continued to be used for some years after 1066. Gundulf, the second Norman bishop (who also built the White Tower of the Tower of London), began a new church c 1080 and replaced the secular clergy by Benedictine monks. His work may be traced in the S nave aisle wall, in the arches of the nave arcade (S side), in the crypt, and in the partially demolished N tower, originally detached, which was probably built for defence in the early years of the Conquest, and is the earliest Norman development on the site. The completed Norman church was consecrated in 1130.

After 1200, a rebuilding in the pointed style was begun, coinciding with the influx of pilgrims to the shrine of St William of Perth (see below). The EE presbytery and the E transepts were erected round the Norman presbytery, which was then partly demolished; the choir, separated from the aisles by blank arcades incorporating the Norman walls, was remodelled by Sacrist (later Prior) William de Hoo, and the whole covered with fine sexpartite vaulting (1227). The N main transept (EE) dates from c 1235, and the S transept (Early Dec) and the two E bays of the nave from c 1320. The central tower and spire were completed c 1343. Late in the 15C the great Perp window was inserted in the W front. In 1904 the central tower, rebuilt in the 19C, was replaced by the present tower and spire (156ft high), completed in accordance with the 14C originals.

Interior. The six W bays of the soberly massive *Nave* are Norman. Lines on the pavement at the NW angle mark the site of the apse of the first Saxon church. The elaborately decorated triforium passage opens on both nave and aisles. At the same level, the junction with the 14C work (E bays and tower arch) is remarkable, as the later builders rebuilt a triforium arch on each side in the Norman style. The clerestory windows are Perp. Off the S aisle is the Lady Chapel of c 1490, its great arch into the transept now closed by a modern screen. In the *S Transept* are a brass memorial to Charles Dickens (1812–70), several of whose novels (*Pickwick Papers*, *Great Expectations*, *Edwin Drood*) are set in and around Rochester; and the monuments of Richard Watts (d 1579), a Rochester philanthropist, and Dean Hole (Samuel Reynolds Hole, Dean of Rochester, and founder of the National Rose Society, d 1904). The *N Transept* was the entrance lobby of approach through the choir aisle to the shrine of St William.

A peculiarity of the raised EE *Choir* is the absence of aisle arcades. The figures on the Choir Screen are a memorial to Dean Scott (1811–87), one of the compilers of the famous lexicon of Ancient Greek known as 'Liddell and Scott'. The details of the corbels and the shafts of Purbeck and Petworth marble are noteworthy. The Stalls and *Monks' Benches (with modern book desks) are early 13C and probably the oldest work of this kind in England (even older than those in Winchester Cathedral); they were incorporated in the stalls when these were re-ordered in the 16C and again in the 19C. Opposite the bishop's throne (19C) is part of a mural painting of the 'Wheel of Fortune' (13C). The *N Choir Transept* was formerly the Chapel of St William of Perth, a Scottish baker who was murdered in Rochester in 1201 when on a pilgrimage to the Holy Land. The shrine became so popular that the rebuilding of the choir is said to have been defrayed by the offerings of the pilgrims who visited it. A slab believed to have come from his shrine, and his probable tomb, stand against the N wall of the N choir transept. Between them is the much restored tomb of Bp Walter de Merton (d 1277), founder of Merton College, Oxford, with an Elizabethan effigy in alabaster. To the E is St John the Baptist's Chapel. In the arch between this chapel and the presbytery is the tomb, with coloured effigy, of Bp John de Sheppey (d 1360), discovered in the wall in 1825. The S Choir Transept contains the remarkable Dec *Doorway (c 1340) leading to the Chapter Room, which contains the Library. The figures (carefully restored in 1825) represent the Synagogue and the Church, the four great Church Fathers, and a soul (of the donor, perhaps Bp Hamo de Hythe) rising from Purgatory. The apparent oak carving of the door itself is a lead casting (c 1826). To the E of the choir is the Presbytery, with tombs of medieval bishops, including the reputed tomb of Gundulf.

From the S Choir aisle a flight of steps descends to the *Crypt, which is one of the largest and most beautiful in England; it has fine EE vaulting, with great variety of spans, and some medieval graffiti scratched into the piers. The two W bays, with piers of tufa and a white stone believed to be Barnack, and ribless quadripartite vaulting, date from the early Norman period. The fragments of medieval glass in the E windows came partly from Canterbury and were put together by a Victorian collector.

To the SE of the choir are the ruins of the Chapter House and remains of the Norman cloister, built by Bp Ernulf (1115–24). The ruined 14C Bishop's Gate was the W entrance to the cloister.

Romsey Abbey, Hampshire

Ded: St Mary and St Ethelfleda.

The superb abbey church survived the Dissolution of the Monasteries, as it was bought by the town; the rest of the abbey buildings were destroyed. It presents the aspect of a Norman conventual church more completely than any building of equal size in England (263ft long, 75ft across nave and aisles, 127ft across transepts). The first nunnery was founded here in 907 by King Edward the Elder (son of Alfred the Great) for his daughter Elfleda. It was enlarged on Benedictine lines in 967 by King Edgar the Peaceful, with Morwenna and later St Ethelfleda as abbesses. A stone Saxon church was built on the site in about 1000, with its eastern apse where the Norman crossing now is, and its nave stretching half-way down the present nave; the foundations of part of the apse can be seen through a trap door in the N transept.

There is no W door, and the church is entered through a porch (1908) on the N side. Internally it is mainly Norman, with rounded arches, except for the three W bays, which are EE. Approximate dates of building are: choir and transepts, 1120–40; four Norman bays of nave, 1150–80; EE bays of nave, 1230–50. The choir aisles end in apses (square externally); and the E sides of the transepts are adjoined by circular chapels. Originally the building continued beyond the E wall to form a Lady Chapel (foundations can be seen outside the church). The two great E windows are 14C insertions. The N aisle and transept were long used as the parish church, and the reredos here preserves notable paintings on wood (c 1500) of the Resurrection and saints. The beautiful mouldings and original Norman triforium and clerestory of the choir are worth special attention. The church's treasures include a superb carved Saxon rood or crucifix (E end of S choir aisle), dating from c 940; a display case containing a magnificent psalter (same aisle); and medieval floor tiles (E end of N choir aisle). Among the monuments are (S transept) the simple floor slab to Earl Mountbatten of Burma (1900–79), and an elaborate memorial (1650s) to John St Barbe and his wife Grissell, with an inscription that is an anagram of their names ('be in shares in blest glorie'). Outside the S or abbess's door, on the W (external) wall of the S transept, is the famous Romsey Rood (a stone carving of a crucifix with the Hand of God above, probably made in the first half of the 11C).

St Augustine's Abbey, Ramsgate, Kent

Dating from the revival of Roman Catholicism in the 1840s, St Augustine's church is the work of the architect Augustus Welby Pugin (1812–52), who lies buried inside it. After his death it was handed over to a group of Benedictine monks, who built the conventual buildings and the abbey school from the 1860s on. Pugin intended his church to have an enormous spire, which would have been visible far out to sea; but he ran out of money before it could be built. The church is much as Pugin left it, with glass, wood carvings and metal screens from the early Victorian period. Pugin's monument, with its recumbent effigy, is in its own chantry off the main body of the church.

St Hugh's Charterhouse, Cowfold, W Sussex

By A281, 8 miles S of Horsham.
Visits by arrangement with the Prior.

Known also as Parkminster, St Hugh's is the only functioning charterhouse (Carthusian monastery) in the British Isles. It was built in 1877–83, and its vast spire, 200ft high, is one of the landmarks of the Weald. Each monk has his own cell or cottage, built round a central garth or orchard 3½ acres in extent; the sides of this huge cloister measure 440ft by 380ft, making it one of the largest in the world.

St Radegund's Abbey, Bradsole, Kent

On minor road between A20 and B2060, 5 miles W of Dover.

This abbey was founded by White Canons (Premonstratensians) in 1191. During the 13C a large church and extensive monastic buildings were built; the main survival is the tower of the church, which was turned into a gatehouse after the Dissolution, when a Tudor manor-house was built on the site. The present Elizabethan farmhouse was adapted from the monks' refectory, which was on the S side of the cloisters.

St Hugh's Charterhouse, a view showing the enormous area covered by the cloister. (Aerofilms)

Shulbrede Priory, Linchmere, W Sussex

On minor road off B2131, 4 miles SW of Haslemere.
Visit by arrangement with owner.

A small Augustinian priory, founded c 1200. The church, on the N side of the cloister, has disappeared; the vaulted parlour and buttery survive downstairs, as does the prior's chamber upstairs. At the Dissolution the priory became a farmhouse, and the chamber was decorated with mural paintings, including animals announcing the Nativity (the cock crows 'Christus natus est'; the duck quacks 'Quando, quando?'; the rook caws 'In hac nocte'; the ox bellows 'Ubi, ubi?'; and the sheep bleats 'In Bethlehem').

Titchfield Abbey, Hampshire

Ded: St Mary and St John the Evangelist.
On N side of A27, 3 miles E of Fareham.

Founded in 1232 by Peter des Roches, Bishop of Winchester, for White Friars (Premonstratensians), Titchfield was the last abbey of this order to be built in England. In the Middle Ages it was of considerable importance, being near Portsmouth and thus on one of the main sea routes to France; it was probably in the abbey church that Henry VI was married in 1445 to Margaret of Anjou, who had just landed in England. At the Dissolution in 1536, it came into the hands of Thomas Wriothesley, later Earl of Southampton (see also Beaulieu above), who turned it into a substantial Tudor mansion called 'Place House', using the cloister garth as the inner courtyard. The chief survival is Southampton's great four-storey gatehouse, formed from the central bay of the aisleless monastic church; the rest of the nave was turned into a Tudor range, with mullioned windows and battlemented parapet. The square-ended church, with three transeptal chapels on each side, is marked out on the ground.

Southampton built his hall on the N side of the cloister, on the site of the frater, but nothing of this survives beyond the cloister wall, since most of the Tudor mansion was demolished in 1781. Of the medieval abbey church, everything E of the nave has disappeared, except for part of the N transept wall backing on to the cloister. Best preserved is the 13C triple entrance arch (blocked up) to the chapter house, on the same (E) side of the cloister. The cloister contains a number of medieval floor tiles, with floral, geometric or heraldic patterns, dating from c 1300.

Waverley Abbey, Surrey

Ded: St Mary.
Off B3001, 2 miles SE of Farnham.
In private grounds, not open to the public.

Sir Walter Scott is said to have taken the name of *Waverley*, his first novel, from this abbey, whose ruins lie in the beautiful valley of the

River Wey. It was the first Cistercian monastery in England, founded in 1128 by the Bishop of Winchester for monks from Aumône in Normandy. Of the two successive churches on the site, one 12C, the second begun in 1203 and finished in 1278, hardly anything survives, save parts of the S transept. There are also fragments of the 13C cellarium and monks' dorter.

West Malling Abbey, Kent

Ded: St Mary.

Restricted visiting, by arrangement with the Abbess.

An abbey of Benedictine nuns was founded here in 1090 by Gundulf, Bishop of Rochester. It was dissolved in 1538, and in the 18C the conventual buildings were adapted to form a country house. In 1916 an Anglican community of Benedictine nuns returned to West Malling; their main buildings now consist of a fine 15C gatehouse, the 18C house, and an austere modern church, completed in 1966 on the site of the crossing of the medieval church. Of the medieval abbey church, part of the S transept survives, and the lower stage of the Norman W tower, which has a later (15C), octagonal upper stage.

Wilmington Priory, E Sussex

Off A27, 6 miles NE of Eastbourne.

Adm. daily, Sun. from 14.00.

Founded soon after the Conquest by Benedictines from the abbey of Grestain in Normandy, Wilmington was never a prosperous house, and had decayed long before the Dissolution, by which time it had become a farmhouse. There was no abbey church as such; the few monks made do with the parish church next door to the priory. The main survival consists of the corner turrets and part of the shell of the 14C hall; beside it is an older (13C) porch or gatehouse, with well-carved vaulting. A small museum upstairs has a collection illustrating Sussex rural life.

Winchelsea Abbey, E Sussex

When 'New' Winchelsea was built at the end of the 13C, the Grey Friars (Franciscans) moved there from the old, derelict town. Of their church, built 1310–20, only the ruined choir and chancel arch survive.

Winchester Cathedral, Hampshire

Ded: Holy Trinity, St Peter and St Paul, and St Swithun.

For almost 250 years, from 829 until the Norman Conquest, Winchester was the capital of England, and the city's successive cathedrals bear witness to its importance. The cathedral we see today is a building of high architectural interest, though disappointing at first sight owing to its unimposing W front and the absence of a lofty tower. It is the longest medieval cathedral church in Europe (556ft) and is made to seem even longer by the modest height (78ft) of the nave. The best view of it, which emphasizes its setting in the heart of the city, is from Magdalen Hill, the approach road to Winchester from the E.

History. Christianity was introduced into Wessex, of which Winchester (Saxon Wintanceaster) was the capital, by St Birinus in 634, and the bishopric was established 40 years later. Excavations begun in 1961 to the N of the cathedral located the Saxon Old Minster, built by King Cenwalh of Wessex in 643–48 on the site of the Roman forum, and the cathedral of all Wessex. Outside the W door of this

Winchester Cathedral, the Izaak Walton window.

church, St Swithun (always spelt thus in Winchester, never Swith*i*n) Bp of Winchester, was buried in 862. On 15 July 971 his remains were transferred to a shrine inside the church; as soon as the grave was opened, rain began to fall and continued for 40 days, from which derives the supposed control of St Swithun over the English summer climate. Under St Ethelwold, Bp of Winchester 963–86, the church was extended W to honour the original shrine; Ethelwold also greatly improved the monastic buildings. A leading administrator, together with St Dunstan (Abp of Canterbury), he reorganised the secular clergy into an established Benedictine Order. In 980–94 the Old Minster was further extended to the E. To the N of the Old Minster was the New Minster, an abbey founded by King Alfred and built by Edward the Elder in 903. To the W lay the royal palace. Nothing of this complex is now visible.

Exterior. The present fabric was begun by Bp Walkelin 'from the foundations' in 1079 and consecrated in 1093. Walkelin's superb Norman building received additions in the EE style from Bp Godfrey de Lucy (1189–1204). Bp William Edington (1346–66) rebuilt the W front, including the magnificent W window, and began the transformation of the nave from Norman to Perp. To Edington is due the famous remark that 'Canterbury was the higher rack, but Winchester was the richer manger'. His work was carried on by the great Bp William of Wykeham (1367–1404) and his master mason William Wynford, and was completed by Bp William Waynflete (1447–86). Winchester Cathedral was the scene of royal weddings: Henry I and Matilda in 1100, and Philip of Spain and Mary Tudor in 1554. Later centuries were more concerned with beautifying the interior than with altering the exterior. A major constructional task was to underpin the foundations, which the original builders had not carried down to sufficiently firm ground; this was successfully carried out in 1905–12 by Sir T.G. Jackson and Sir Francis Fox, who also built the ten flying buttresses supporting the S wall of the nave.

The W (entrance) front is approached by a fine avenue of lime trees. Opposite is a war memorial (by Herbert Baker), incorporating a stone from the Cloth Hall at Ypres.

Interior. The core of the nobly imposing *Nave, with its thick walls and massive piers, is substantially the work of Bp Walkelin. The two W bays on the N side and the W bay on the S side were rebuilt by Bp Edington (see above), and the remainder, including the arcades, was transformed by Bp Wykeham into the new Perp style. This was done without pulling down the old 11C work: the Gothic mouldings of the S piers are simply cut in the Norman stones. The main arcade and clerestory were greatly enlarged, while the triforium was reduced to the present beautiful little balcony. Most of the windows are very graceful. Fragments of 14C glass, surviving from the Cromwellian destruction of 1642, remain in the aisles and clerestory, and in the great W window. The magnificent lierne vault bears the arms of Edington and Wykeham on the ceiling bosses, which are of high quality throughout the cathedral (there are some 1,100 altogether). Against the W wall are statues of James I and Charles I by Hubert Le Sueur. In the S arcade of the nave are the two earliest of an unsurpassed series of Chantries, illustrating the development of architecture from 1366 to 1555. Bp Edington's Chantry is near the E end. Succeeding it in date, and far surpassing it in splendour, is Bp

Wykeham's Chantry, in the fifth bay from the W end, with the effigy of the great builder, statesman, and founder of Winchester College and New College, Oxford (d 1404); the three little monks carved at his feet may be his secretaries, or his master mason, master carpenter and clerk. At the W end of the N aisle is a stone Cantoria or minstrels' gallery, in which is displayed notable silverware from the treasury. On the wall of this aisle (which is covered with memorials to members of the Rifle Brigade), opposite the Wykeham Chantry, are a brass tablet and a window to Jane Austen (1775–1817), who lies under the pavement at this spot. Five bays to the E is a memorial to Field-Marshal Lord Wavell (1883–1950), one of the greatest leaders of World War II.

In the N aisle is the *Font (12C), carved with scenes from the life of St Nicholas of Myra. Made of black marble (or basalt) from Tournai, it has rich carvings of Belgian workmanship. In 1979, for the 900th anniversary of the founding of the cathedral, the nave was decorated with a series of 16 coloured banners illustrating the Creation. Designed and created by Thetis Blacker, they are hung in the nave for festivals and celebrations.

The massive *Transepts* remain much as Walkelin left them (1079–98), and typify the grand scale of his design. Later Norman work (distinguished by finer masonry) is the rebuilding of Walkelin's central tower, which fell in 1107, popularly because of the burial beneath it of the heretical king William Rufus in 1100. Under the organ loft of the N transept is the Chapel of the Holy Sepulchre (12C), with superb *Wall Paintings (c 1170–1205) of the Life and Passion of Christ. The W aisle was screened off in 1908 as the Epiphany Chapel (Burne-Jones windows). Among the monuments in this transept is a memorial plaque to the composer Samuel Sebastian Wesley (1810–76), who was cathedral organist 1849–65. The S transept is made less impressive than the N arm by the enclosure of the aisles, forming (E) Prior Silkstede's Chapel (1524) and the Venerable Chapel (note the elaborate ironwork), and (W) the Treasury of Henri de Blois (1129–71). In the Silkstede Chapel is buried Izaak Walton (1593–1683), author of the *Compleat Angler*, who died in Winchester. The chapel window was the gift in 1914 of the fishermen of England; in the bottom right-hand corner is a portrait of Walton beside the River Itchen. Entrance to the S choir aisle is through a 12C iron *Grille that possibly came from St Swithun's shrine, which stood in the retrochoir (see below).

The *Choir* is separated from the nave by an oak screen designed by Sir Gilbert Scott. The excessive stoutness of the tower piers is the result of their being strengthened after the fall of the tower in 1107. Under the tower is a marble tomb traditionally that of William Rufus. The magnificent *Stalls (1305–10), with their vigorous misericords carved with human, animal and monster motifs, are the oldest cathedral stalls except for some fragments at Rochester (see above); the desks of the block on the E date from 1540. The pulpit was given by Prior Silkstede (c 1520) and is carved with skeins of silk forming a rebus on his name; the bishop's throne is modern. The piers, arches and clerestory of the Presbytery (prolonging the choir towards the E) were rebuilt early in the 14C. Bp Fox (1501–28) rebuilt the outer walls of the presbytery aisles, inserted the tracery of the clerestory and E window, and put up the wooden lierne vault, with its superb roof bosses. To him are due also the screens between the presbytery and the aisles, which now bear six painted and gilded mortuary chests (four of 1525 and two copied in 1661), made to contain the bones of Egbert, Canute and other pre-Conquest monarchs. The E window is filled with glass of the 15, 16 and 19C. The great Reredos, almost certainly dating from c 1480, was mutilated at the Reformation, but was restored and furnished with statues in 1884–91. There is, however, some fine original work in the spandrels of the doors. On the E side of the reredos is the Feretory, a place for the *feretra* or shrines for the relics of saints. To the N of the feretory is the Chantry of Bp Gardiner (1555); and to the S, the Chantry of Bp Fox (1528), with a remarkable *memento mori* carving of a decomposing corpse.

To the E is the large *Retrochoir* of three bays, with the Lady Chapel

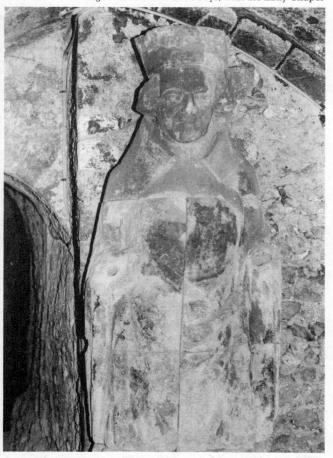

Winchester Cathedral, medieval relief carving in the crypt.
(K. Spence)

beyond. With the exception of the 15C rebuilding of the Lady Chapel, the work is by Bp de Lucy (1189–1204) and, together with the Chapel of the Holy Sepulchre, is the earliest Gothic work in the cathedral; except for the choir of Lincoln Cathedral (see below), it is perhaps the earliest purely Gothic work in England. In the centre of the retrochoir stood the shrine of St Swithun. Here, above 13C encaustic floor tiles, now stands a new shrine (1962) of the saint, by Brian Thomas, an iron framework supporting a canopy with medallions of the saint's consecration and his teaching of Prince Ethelwulf and, at the W end, a relief figure of St Swithun in brass, with the first bridge over the Itchen. On the E wall of the feretory, at the W end of the retrochoir, are nine exquisite niches, and below is the entrance to the 'Holy Hole', or vault under the feretory. In the retrochoir on either side are (N) the Chantry of Bp Waynflete (1486) and (S) the Chantry of Cardinal Beaufort (1447); against the NE pier is a wooden figure, by Sir Ninian Comper, of St Joan of Arc, who was condemned to the stake by Cardinal Beaufort and the French bishops. The late 12C Chapel of the Guardian Angels (N), with painted *Roof bosses (c 1240), contains the effigy of Richard Weston, Earl of Portland (d 1635), a masterpiece attributed to Francesco Fanelli. The E window contains 13C grisaille glass from Salisbury, mixed with 14C glass. The admirable woodwork and the mural paintings from the Life of the Virgin in the Lady Chapel (restored by Prof. Tristram in 1933–36) are late 15C work. Also in the Lady Chapel is the chair on which Mary Tudor sat for her wedding to Philip II of Spain in 1554. The chapel to the S, fitted up as a chantry by Bp Langton (1501), has remarkable woodwork. At its entrance (left) is a statuette by Sir Charles Wheeler (1962), commemorating William Walker, the diver who saved the cathedral in 1906–12 by underpinning it with thousands of concrete blocks and bricks (though it is now thought to be a likeness of William West, his mate, or of Sir Francis Fox); and (right) a fine headless statue of c 1235.

The impressive *Crypt* (subject to flooding and only open in the dry summer months), entered from the N transept, is in three parts. The first two are Norman, of the same date and character as the transepts. In the first and larger, under the high altar, is a well, which would have been outside the original Saxon church and was probably the ancient Holy Well. The rectangular E crypt, below the Lady Chapel, is EE (1189–1204).

Over the passage between the S transept and the Norman arches of the old Chapter House is the Library (12C, reconstructed in 1668), containing 4000 printed books and some rare MSS. Its chief treasure is the *Winchester Bible (12C), a magnificent illuminated Vulgate (Latin bible) in four volumes, rebound in 1948.

From the SW corner of the nave we reach the close through the Slype, a passage constructed in 1636 as a substitute for the right of way through the cathedral. The beautiful and spacious *Close* is partly surrounded by the ancient monastery walls. The Norman *Arcade of the demolished chapter house links the S transept to the Deanery, which is approached by a vestibule of three arches (c 1225–50). The Pilgrims' Hall (c 1295), with an early hammerbeam roof, adjoins the main buildings of the Pilgrims' School (1687), where classrooms occupy the picturesque 16C priory stables. We leave the close by the 13C King's Gate, leading into Kingsgate Street, over which is the church of St Swithun (rebuilt in the 16C).

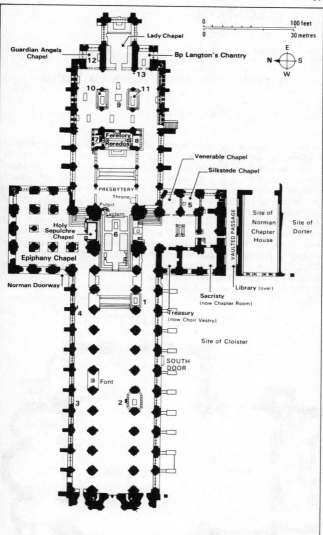

Guardian Angels Chapel
Lady Chapel
Bp Langton's Chantry
12
13
10 11
9
Feretory Reredos
7 8
Venerable Chapel
Silkstede Chapel
PRESBYTERY
Throne
Pulpit
Lectern
5
Holy Sepulchre Chapel
6
Epiphany Chapel

Site of Norman Chapter House
Site of Dorter

VAULTED PASSAGE

Norman Doorway

Library (over)

Sacristy (now Chapter Room)

Treasury (now Choir Vestry)

1

4

Site of Cloister

SOUTH DOOR

Font

3 2

N E S W

0   100 feet
0   30 metres

1   Bp Edington
2   Bp William of Wykeham
3   Jane Austen
4   Field-Marshal Lord Wavell
5   Izaak Walton
6   William Rufus
7   Bp Gardiner
8   Bp Fox
9   Shrine of St Swithun
10 Bp Wayneflete
11 Cardinal Beaufort
12 Earl of Portland
13 William Walker, the Diver

WINCHESTER CATHEDRAL

2. LONDON

Greek Cathedral (Greek Orthodox)

Ded: Aghia Sophia (Holy Wisdom).

In Moscow Road, W2.

With its shallow green copper dome and horizontally striped brickwork, the Greek cathedral is an oddity among the plain Victorian buildings of Bayswater. Its comparative external austerity gives no hint of the neo-Byzantine splendours of the interior, whose gold mosaics, hanging lamps and iconostasis (icon-covered wooden screen shutting off the body of the church from the sanctuary) would not seem out of place in Athens or Thessaloniki. The architect was John Oldrid Scott; the foundation stone was laid in 1877, and consecration took place in 1882. It was in fact the fourth Greek church in London: the first was a chapel built in Soho in 1677; then came a chapel at Finsbury Circus; followed in 1849 by a church in London Wall, superseded in its turn by the present building, which was promoted to cathedral status in 1922.

The main doors, on the S side of the church facing Moscow Road,

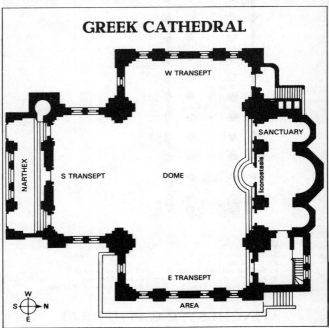

open into a Narthex or vestibule, which in turn leads into the S transept. (Visitors normally enter through a small door at the back of the cathedral, approached by a path along the W side.) On the wall of the narthex is an inscribed stone that stood above the front door of the first (1677) Greek church, and the silver trowel with which Lady Ralli laid the foundation stone of the cathedral exactly 200 years later. The interior of the church is dominated by the mosaic in the dome of the Pantokrator (Christ in Glory), designed in naturalistic style by A.G. Walker, who was influenced by the Pre-Raphaelites. The more austere, authentically Byzantine-looking mosaics, round the arches and above the sanctuary are by Boris Anrep and were added in the 20C. In the centre of the inlaid floor is the double-headed eagle of the Byzantine emperors.

The two-tiered Iconostasis is made of walnut, and the icons, painted on canvas, depict angels, saints and the Virgin Mary. The most striking of the interior furnishings is a huge *Double Greek Cross, silver-plated and fitted with ruby-coloured glass lamps, which are lit at major church festivals. The sanctuary treasures include a number of precious objects from Russia, notably the crucifix behind the altar.

St Bartholomew's Priory, Smithfield

The church survives from the priory of Augustinian canons, founded in 1123 by Rahere, a courtier of Henry I, who also founded St Bartholomew's Hospital near by. It is the oldest church in London, after the chapel in the White Tower (Tower of London). At the Dissolution of the Monasteries, the conventual buildings and much of the church were pulled down or alienated. Of the original priory church only the choir, built by Rahere, still stands, together with the crossing and one bay of the nave, added before 1170 by his successor. The restoration of the church was begun in 1863, and resumed in 1886 with Sir Aston Webb as architect.

The church is approached from the E corner of Smithfield (to the N of the hospital) through a small gateway, which once formed the W entrance to the S nave aisle. Above the gateway is a house, with an Elizabethan half-timbered facade which was brought to light in 1915, when a bomb dropped by a Zeppelin loosened the tiles that concealed it. The site of the nave, which was completed in the 13C, is now occupied by the churchyard. We enter the church by a modern porch beneath a brick tower, built in 1628 to take the place of the tower over the crossing. The five bells date from 1510, and the church is noted for the quality of its music.

The interior of the church (the choir of Rahere's priory church) is most impressive, with its heavy columns, piers and round arches in the pure Norman style. The clerestory was rebuilt early in the 15C, and the Norman triforium is interrupted on the S side by *Prior Bolton's Window, a beautiful oriel which once communicated with the prior's house; it was added by Prior Bolton (1506–32) and is carved with his rebus (a bolt or arrow, and a tun or barrel). The apsidal ending of the choir, with its stilted arches, was built between 1886 and 1910 by Sir Aston Webb in place of the previous square ending, which is supposed to have been an innovation of the 15C. On the N side of the sanctuary is the *Tomb of Rahere (d 1143), with a coloured effigy beneath a rich canopy (c 1400, perhaps by Henry Yevele, architect of the nave of Canterbury Cathedral).

In the S Transept stands the 15C font at which the artist William Hogarth was baptized in 1697. In the S Ambulatory is the alabaster tomb of Sir Walter Mildmay (d 1589), founder of Emmanuel College, Cambridge. The Lady Chapel, rebuilt in 1896 and retaining little of the original fabric of the 14C, is separated from the E end of the choir by a fine modern iron screen. It was at one time used as a printing office, and then as a factory for making cloth fringes. The Chapel of the Imperial Society of Knights Bachelor is at the E end of the S aisle. The N Transept was at one time occupied by a blacksmith's forge. The stone screen at its S side dates from the beginning of the 15C. The screen below the organ has painted panels (1932) illustrating the life of Rahere. A Norman doorway, with 15C oaken doors, leads to the E walk of the old Cloister, built c 1405 and reconstructed in 1905–28. The arches in the wall mark the entrance to the former chapter house.

St Paul's Cathedral

St Paul's Cathedral, the largest and best-known church in the City of London, stands at the top of Ludgate Hill. The cathedral of the Bishop of London, it is the masterpiece of Sir Christopher Wren—a soberly dignified building in a Renaissance style, dominated by the famous dome. The Portland stone of which it is built used to be picturesquely bleached and stained by the London climate and smoke, but successive cleanings since 1960 have disclosed its golden colour and the beautiful detail of the carved stonework. Since the marriage at St Paul's of the Prince of Wales and Princess Diana on 29 July 1981, it has become one of the most-visited of all our churches.

History. The tradition that a Roman temple dedicated to Diana stood on the cathedral's commanding site was denied by Wren, and there is no evidence to support it. A Christian church, said to have been founded here in the 7C by Bp Mellitus and endowed by Ethelbert, King of Kent, was burned down in 1087, and its Norman successor was partly destroyed by fire in 1136 but immediately restored. In the 13C the steeple was rebuilt and the choir extended eastwards. This was the noble church of Old St Paul's, in which John Wyclif was tried for heresy in 1377, and William Tyndale's English translation of the New Testament was publicly burned in 1527. It was the longest cathedral in England (600ft). The central tower was surmounted by a steeple, which at the lowest estimate was 460ft high; but this was destroyed by lightning in 1561 and never re-erected. For a long period St Paul's was sadly neglected, but restorations were begun under Charles I. Inigo Jones added a classical portico to the W front, one of his objects being to offer an alternative meeting place to the miscellaneous Londoners who for over a century had used the middle aisle of the nave (known as 'Paul's Walk') for carrying on both business and intrigue.

In 1666 the cathedral was practically burned down in the Great Fire of London, and Wren (1632–1723) was commissioned to design its successor. He planned an entirely new cathedral (in fact, he produced three plans, of which the third was accepted by the royal commissioners responsible for the project); building was begun in 1675; the first service was held in the choir in 1697; and the last stone was placed in position in 1708—42 years after the fire. Wren began his task when he was 34, and completed it when he was 76; he lived on until 1723, and lies buried in the crypt of his greatest building. (Also in the crypt are a model of Old St Paul's, and Wren's 'Great Model'.) The building cost about £748,000, most of which was raised by a tax on sea-borne coal entering London. Wren's original design, in the form of a Greek cross, was modified at the demand of the Court party, some of whom may have looked forward to the eventual restoration of Roman Catholicism, whose ceremonies call for a long nave and side chapels. For over two centuries the cathedral survived unaltered; then, during the height of the German air attacks on London in 1941, it received two direct hits from high-explosive bombs, and was also hit by incendiary bombs, which were put out by the cathedral's 'Night Watch' before they could do any serious damage.

Exterior. The lower order is Corinthian, the upper Composite. On the N and S sides the upper order is merely a curtain wall, not corresponding with the height of the aisles and concealing the flying buttresses that support the clerestory of the nave. The balustrade along the top was added against the wishes of Wren, who cynically remarked of it that 'ladies think nothing well without an edging'. The W Front, approached by a broad flight of steps and flanked by towers, has a lower colonnade of 12 columns and an upper one of eight columns. In the NW tower is a peal of 12 bells, and in the SW tower are the clock and 'Great Paul', a bell weighing nearly 17 tons (hung in 1882), which is rung daily for 5 minutes at 1 p.m. In the pediment of the S Front is a Phoenix, symbolizing the rise of new St Paul's from the ashes of the old. It also recalls the incident when Wren, looking for a stone from the ruins to mark the centre of the new dome-space, was presented by a workman with a stone carved with the Latin word *Resurgam* ('I shall rise again'). The 18C sculpture in the W Pediment and Portico and the statues above the N Pediment are by Francis Bird.

The famous •Dome lifts its cross 365ft above the City below. The outer dome is of wood covered with lead, and does not bear the weight of the elegant lantern on the top, which rests upon a cone of brick rising between an inner brick dome and the outer dome. The Ball and Cross date from 1721.

Interior. Although 'classical' in detail, the general ground plan is of a Gothic church: nave and aisles with triforium and clerestory, transepts and choir, with the great dome-space at the crossing. Against the massive piers rise Corinthian pilasters, and stone enrichments relieve the wall-spaces. Wren no doubt contemplated the use of colour in the decoration, but, though Sir James Thornhill's paintings in the dome were finished in 1720, nothing more was done until the dome and choir mosaics were added in 1863–97.

The *Dome*, the inner cupola of which is 218ft overhead, rests on 12 massive supports, of which the four chief ones, at the angles, afford room in their interiors for the vestries and the library staircase. In the spandrels of the dome are 19C mosaics executed by Antonio Salviati of Venice. Those on the W, completed in 1864, were designed by Alfred Stevens and partly executed by W.E.F. Britten. They represent (from S to N) Isaiah, Jeremiah, Ezekiel and Daniel; the others

represent SS Matthew and John (by G.F. Watts) and SS Mark and
Luke (by Britten). In the quarter-domes, at a lower level, are more
recent mosaics by Sir W.B. Richmond (d 1921).

Above the arches is the Whispering Gallery, above which again are
recesses with marble statues of the Fathers of the Church. The cupola
above was decorated by Thornhill with eight scenes in monochrome
from the life of St Paul. The gallery, open to the public except on
Sundays, is entered by a staircase at the SW corner of the dome.

Returning to the W end of the cathedral by the *N Nave Aisle*, we can
now begin to look at the monuments, eloquent of British history. In
the first recess, 'Two Angels at the Gate of Death' by C. Marochetti, in
memory of Viscount Melbourne (1779–1848) and his brother. On the
wall, Lord Roberts (1833–1914), bust by John Tweed. In the next
recess, General Gordon (1833–85), and in the last recess Lord
Leighton (1830–96), the painter. Beneath the arch opposite Gordon's
monument is the massive *Monument to the Duke of Wellington
(1769–1852), by Alfred Stevens.

At the W end of this aisle beyond St Dunstan's Chapel is All Souls'
Chapel, now the Kitchener Memorial Chapel, with a recumbent
figure of Field-Marshal Lord Kitchener (1850–1916) by Sir William
Reid Dick, and a roll of honour of Kitchener's regiment, the Royal
Engineers.

S Nave Aisle. The chapel at the W end has been since 1906 the
Chapel of the Most Distinguished Order of St Michael and St George,
with the banners of the Knights Grand Cross (GCMG). The order,
instituted in 1818, is conferred for distinguished service in foreign,
and formerly colonial, affairs. The prelate's throne is in memory of
Lord Forrest (d 1918), of Bunbury, Western Australia, the first
Australian peer. On the fourth pier in the S aisle hangs 'The Light of
the World', the best-known painting by William Holman Hunt
(1827–1910). At the E end of the aisle is the ticket-office for the
galleries (see below).

S Transept. In the W aisle are monuments to the Scottish general Sir
Ralph Abercromby (1734–1801), and to Sir John Moore (1761–1809),
who died at Corunna during the Peninsular War. To the left, above, is
a memorial designed by Princess Louise to the Colonial Troops who
fell in the South African War. On the W wall of the transept is the
*Monument of Lord Nelson (1758–1805) by John Flaxman; the reliefs
on the pedestal represent the Arctic Ocean, the North Sea, the Nile
and the Mediterranean. On the S wall of the E transept aisle, J.M.W.
Turner (1775–1851), the painter, and Lord Collingwood (1750–1810),
Nelson's second-in-command at Trafalgar. On the E wall, another
great admiral, Lord Howe (1726–99), by Flaxman. On the left, further
on, a military commander, Sir Henry Lawrence (1806–57), who was
killed during the Indian Mutiny. Opposite is the entrance to the
Crypt, beyond which, at the angle of the dome-space, is a statue of
John Howard (1726–90), the prison reformer, the first monument
allowed in the new St Paul's.

We now enter the *Choir*, at the end of the S choir aisle, with fine
wrought-iron gates by Jean Tijou, the French master craftsman who
worked in St Paul's from 1691 to 1709. On the right side of this aisle,
beyond the monument of Dean Milman (1791–1868), a noted church
historian, is the figure, clad in a shroud, of *John Donne (1573–1631),
poet and Dean of St Paul's. This is the only comparatively uninjured
monument that survived the destruction of Old St Paul's, and it still
shows traces of fire. Entering the choir proper, above the High Altar is

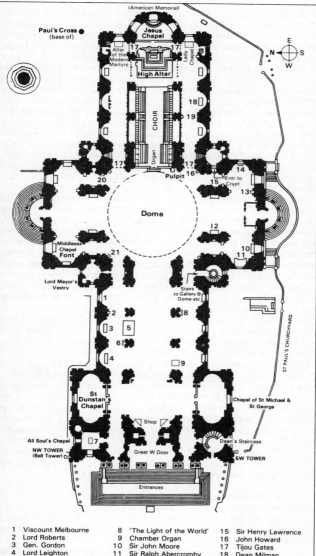

Paul's Cross (base of)

(American Memorial)

Jesus Chapel

N E S W

Altar of the Modern Martyrs

17 17

High Altar

Lady Chapel

CHOIR

18

19

Organ

17 17 14

Pulpit 16

20

Entr to Crypt

15

13

Dome

12

10

11

Middlesex Chapel Font

21

Lord Mayor's Vestry

Stairs to Gallery & Dome etc

1

2

5 8

3

6

4

9

St Dunstan's Chapel

Chapel of St Michael & St George

ST PAUL'S CHURCHYARD

All Soul's Chapel

7

Dean's Staircase

NW TOWER (Bell Tower)

Shop

Great W Door

SW TOWER

Entrances

1	Viscount Melbourne	8	'The Light of the World'
2	Lord Roberts	9	Chamber Organ
3	Gen. Gordon	10	Sir John Moore
4	Lord Leighton	11	Sir Ralph Abercromby
5	Duke of Wellington	12	Lord Nelson
6	Field-Marshal Lord Slim	13	J.M.W. Turner
7	Lord Kitchener	14	Lord Howe

15	Sir Henry Lawrence
16	John Howard
17	Tijou Gates
18	Dean Milman
19	John Donne
20	Dr Johnson
21	Sir Joshua Reynolds

ST PAUL'S CATHEDRAL

a carved and gilded baldacchino (canopy) of marble and oak, by Godfrey Allen and S.E. Dykes Bower, which replaces the reredos damaged in 1941 and serves as a memorial to the Commonwealth people of all creeds and races who lost their lives in the two World Wars. The tall bronze Candlesticks in front are copied from four now in St Bavon's, in Ghent, Belgium, which were made by Benedetto da Rovezzano for the tomb of Henry VIII at Windsor, but were sold under Cromwell. The beautiful carved Choir Stalls and the Organ Case are by Grinling Gibbons. The organ was originally built in 1694–97 by Bernard Smith ('Father' Smith) to specifications by the composer John Blow (1648–1708), who was in charge of the music at St Paul's, and Jeremiah Clarke played at its inauguration. In 1872 it was largely rebuilt by 'Father' Henry Willis; and after damage during World War II, it was reconstructed in 1973–77 by Noel Mander. Although a bomb struck the east end of the choir, bringing down tons of masonry on to the sanctuary, the priceless carvings of the stalls and organ case escaped almost undamaged.

Behind the High Altar is the Jesus Chapel, which occupies the eastern apse of the cathedral. It is the memorial to America's fallen in World War II, with a roll of honour containing the names of 28,000 Americans who died in operations based on Britain. A replica book can be consulted by relatives on application to a verger. The Mosaics that decorate the choir vaulting were designed by Sir William Richmond and were executed in 1891–1912. The stained glass windows are also by Richmond. In the central panel of the great apse is Christ in majesty, seated upon the rainbow. In the shallow cupolas above the choir proper are (from W to E) the Creation of the Beasts, the Birds and the Fishes.

In the N choir aisle is the Altar of the Modern Martyrs, which commemorates all known Anglican martyrs since 1850. On our right, through another superb set of gates by Tijou, is a statue of Dr Johnson (1709–84) in a Roman toga, by John Bacon. The choir screen, formed of the original altar rails, is also by Tijou. On the right is a carved wooden pulpit (1964), designed by Lord Mottistone (John Seely).

N Transept. This transept was severely damaged by a heavy bomb in April 1941, when the transept dome and the whole of the N Porch, with the famous inscription from Wren's tomb, *Lector, si monumentum requiris, circumspice* ('Reader, if you seek his monument, look around you'), fell into the crypt below. Here are monuments to the composer Sir Arthur Sullivan (1842–1900), the naval commander Lord Rodney (1718–92), and the artist Sir Joshua Reynolds (1723–92), the last by Flaxman. The W aisle of this transept is now the Baptistry; the massive font, by Francis Bird, was finished in 1727.

The *Crypt* (entrance in the S transept, fee) corresponds in size with the upper church, and has recently been restored. It now includes a new treasury and an audio-visual lecture room, as well as Wren's Great Model of 1673–74, which is 20ft long and made of oak, and took nine months to make.

We first reach the crypt below the S choir aisle. At the foot of the staircase is (right) a bust of Sir John Macdonald (1815–91), premier of Canada. In the second bay (right) monuments to the artist Sir Edwin Landseer (1802–73) and the hymn-writer Reginald Heber (1783–1826), by Sir Francis Chantrey. In the pavement is the tomb of the painter Sir Lawrence Alma-Tadema (1836–1912). In the next bay is the tombstone of Sir Christopher Wren (1632–1723), above which is the original tablet with its famous epitaph (see above). This bay and the one to the N constitute Painters' Corner, for here are buried Lord Leighton (1830–96), Benjamin West (1738–1820), Sir Thomas Lawrence (1769–1830), Landseer (1802–73), Sir John Everett Millais (1829–96), Turner (1775–1851), Reynolds (1723–92), John Opie (1761–1807) and Holman Hunt (1827–1910). On the walls are memorials to the illustrator Randolph Caldecott (1846–86), William Blake (1757–1827), Sir Anthony Van Dyck (1599–1641), John Constable (1776–1837), Wilson Steer (1860–1942), the architect Sir Edwin Lutyens (1869–1944) and Muirhead Bone (1876–1953). John Singer Sargent (1856–1925) is commemorated by a relief group of the Redemption, designed by himself.

St Faith's Chapel, at the E end of the crypt, was rededicated in 1960 as the Chapel of the Order of the British Empire, an order instituted by King George V in 1917. It was designed by Lord Mottistone, Surveyor to the Fabric of St Paul's 1957–63. Further W, a wall-tablet marks the grave of Sir Alexander Fleming (1881–1955), the discoverer of penicillin.

Passing through the gates to the W portion of the crypt, we see the colossal sarcophagus of the Duke of Wellington, surrounded by tablets to the 12 Field-Marshals of World War II. On the left, further on, is a memorial to Florence Nightingale (1820–1910). In recesses to the S: three admirals, Lord Beatty (1871–1936), Lord Jellicoe (1859–1935) and Lord Keyes (1872–1945); the son of the last-named, Lt-Col Keyes VC (1917–41); and Lord Napier of Magdala (1810–90), one of the heroes of the Indian Mutiny. To the N, three famous soldiers: Lord Wolseley (1833–1913), Lord Roberts (1832–1914), and a bust of Lawrence of Arabia (1888–1935). A plaque commemorates nearly 6,000 men of the garrison of Kut, in Iraq, who died in 1916. In the adjoining recess: R.J. Seddon (1845–1906) and W.M. Hughes (1864–1952), both prime ministers of New Zealand; and a fine bust by Epstein of Sir Stafford Cripps (1889–1952). Opposite is a bust of George Washington, near a tablet to Pilot Officer William Fiske, RAF, who lost his life in the Battle of Britain, 'an American citizen who died that England might live'. Here too are memorials to the caricaturist George Cruikshank (1792–1878), and a *Bust by Rodin to the poet and critic W.E. Henley (1849–1903). In the nave are: Wilson Carlile (1847–1942), founder of the Church Army; R.H. Barham (1788–1845), author of the *Ingoldsby Legends*; Sir W. Besant (1836–1901) and Charles Reade (1814–84), the writers; and Sir Alfred Duff Cooper (1890–1954), the politician and diplomat.

In a sculpture bay are memorials to General Sir Charles Napier (1782–1853), the conqueror of Sind, and his brother Sir William Napier (1784–1860), and mutilated monuments from Old St Paul's. Next, a monument to the historian Henry Hallam (1777–1859); opposite is one to the naval commander Lord St Vincent (1735–1823).

The *Upper Parts* of the cathedral are closed to the public; the fine Library is for researchers only. A staircase (SW corner of dome) leads to the Whispering Gallery, 112ft in diameter, within the lower dome, where words whispered near the wall on one side can be distinctly heard at the other side. This gallery is the best point from which to see Thornhill's paintings on the dome.

The Stone Gallery (the exterior gallery round the base of the dome) commands a fine *View over London, which is still more extensive from the Golden Gallery, at the base of the lantern above the dome.

The churchyard (now a public garden) surrounding the cathedral is enclosed by massive railings, reputed to be among the latest examples of charcoal-smelted ironwork from the Weald of Kent and Sussex. In the NE angle are the foundations of Paul's Cross, an open-air pulpit where sermons were regularly preached. On the S side of the church are a few fragments of the cloisters and chapter house, destroyed in 1666. The street skirting the S side of the cathedral is likewise called St Paul's Churchyard. In Dean's Court, leading S, is the Deanery, built by Wren c 1670, and adjoining it, in Carter Lane, is the Choir House, with the old Choristers' School (now a youth hostel). E of the cathedral, the tower and restored spire of St Augustine's has been incorporated in the Cathedral Choir School, designed in 1962 by Leo de Syllas and built after his death, with four linked buildings. The church was rebuilt by Wren in 1683 and destroyed in 1941. The area to the N of the cathedral was devastated by fire in 1940; only the Chapter House by Wren (reopened in 1957) survived. New buildings lacking individual distinction now tower above the chapter house to form Cathedral Place and Paternoster Square. The raised piazzas (underground car park), with shops, restaurants and pubs, afford good views of St Paul's.

(Advance notice of services and concerts, and tickets to events where space is limited, can be obtained from the Friends' Office, in the Chapter House.)

Southwark Cathedral

Ded: St Saviour and St Mary Overie.

A fascinating little cathedral, for its architecture, its monuments and its historical associations, Southwark Cathedral now lies hemmed in between the railway and Borough Market. Officially the Cathedral and Collegiate Church of St Saviour and St Mary Overie, Southwark, it has been the seat of a bishop since 1905. Often rebuilt and repaired, it remains the finest Gothic building in London after Westminster Abbey.

Southwark Cathedral, 17C monument to Lionel Lockyer, a maker of patent medicines.

History. During Roman times there was a flourishing settlement at Southwark, which grew up at the southern end of the Romans' London Bridge. According to legend, a nunnery was founded where the cathedral now stands by a ferryman's daughter called Mary: hence the former title of the church, St Mary Overie, which has been explained as 'St Mary over the Ie' (water). In c 860 this nunnery was changed by St Swithin, Bp of Winchester, into a house for canons regular of the Augustinian order. For centuries after St Swithin's time, Southwark was closely associated with the bishops of Winchester. In 1106 a new church, of which few traces survive, was founded by two Norman knights; from this time too dates the founding of a hospital, run by the Augustinians, which in the 13C was dedicated to St Thomas of Canterbury and became the ancestor of the present St Thomas's Hospital (now in Lambeth). In 1206 the Norman church was badly damaged by fire, and the following year Peter des Roches, Bp of Winchester, built the present choir and retrochoir in the new Gothic style. In the 15C the stone vaulting of the nave roof collapsed and was rebuilt in wood, and the transepts were remodelled. The noble tower over the crossing, 164ft high, also dates from the 15C. In the years round 1600 Southwark saw a period of prosperity, with the building of successive Globe Theatres on Bankside; Shakespeare's brother Edmond (d 1607) was buried in the church, but the whereabouts of the grave are unknown. During the 18C Southwark declined and the church decayed with it; the nave collapsed in 1838, and there were proposals to demolish the entire building. Fortunately these were not carried out, and the late 19C saw the complete rebuilding of the nave by Sir Arthur Blomfield in 1890–96.

Interior. *Nave*. In the SW corner is a portion of 13C arcading; and in the NW corner a case of splendid wooden bosses from the 15C roof, including the head of a king, and the devil swallowing Judas Iscariot. At the W end of the nave is a modern bronze group of the Holy Family, by Robert Hughes. Most of the stained glass is modern (the old glass was mainly destroyed in 1941). Below the 6th window is the sumptuous *Tomb of John Gower (1330–1408), the friend of Chaucer, and a poet who wrote in Latin, French and English. Just to the E is a door that marks the Norman entry to the cloister; the jambs and a holy-water stoup still survive.

Transepts. In the N Transept is a dresser given to the church in 1588. The monuments here include one to Lionel Lockyer (d 1672), a maker of patent pills; the amusingly flattering inscription includes the lines:

> His virtues and his PILLS are soe well known
> That envy can't confine them under stone.

To the E of this transept is the Harvard Chapel, restored and decorated in 1907 in memory of John Harvard, founder of Harvard University, Massachusetts, who was born in the parish and baptized in this church (1607). During the restoration a Norman shaft (left of the altar) was discovered. The stained-glass window (restored 1948) was presented in 1905 by Joseph H. Choate (d 1917). On the right a tablet commemorates the playwright and lyricist Oscar Hammerstein (1895–1960).

The S Transept was rebuilt in the 15C by Cardinal Beaufort, whose niece, Joan Beaufort, was married to James I of Scotland in this church (1423). Beaufort's painted coat of arms, surmounted by the red cardinal's hat, is on the shaft of the vaulting. On the W wall is a monument in miniature to William Emerson (d 1575), a supposed ancestor of the American writer and philosopher Ralph Waldo Emerson. Above, John Bingham (d 1625), saddler to Queen Elizabeth I and King James I. Near by is a touching inscription to Mistress Margaret Maynard, who d 1653 aged 13.

Under the crossing is a splendid brass *Candelabrum, presented to the church by Dorothy Appleby in 1680.

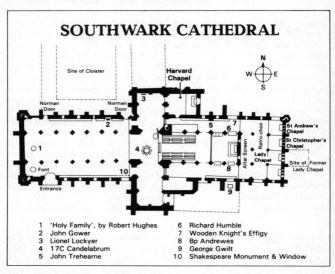

SOUTHWARK CATHEDRAL

1 'Holy Family', by Robert Hughes	6 Richard Humble
2 John Gower	7 Wooden Knight's Effigy
3 Lionel Lockyer	8 Bp Andrewes
4 17C Candelabrum	9 George Gwilt
5 John Trehearne	10 Shakespeare Monument & Window

Choir. This and the retrochoir represent perhaps the earliest Gothic work in London. The *Altar-screen, erected by Bp Fox in 1520, is a magnificent piece of work, though much mutilated and restored. The statues in the niches date from 1905. There are fine tombs in the choir aisles. N Choir Aisle: handsome Jacobean monuments to John Trehearne (d 1618), gentleman-porter to James I, and Richard Humble (d 1616), alderman; and the wooden effigy of a knight (late 13C), thought to be one of the earliest such effigies in England. S Choir Aisle: fine canopied tomb of Lancelot Andrewes, Bp of Winchester (1555–1626), restored in 1930 by Sir Ninian Comper.

The beautiful aisled *Retrochoir*, with its superb blind arcading on the W side, behind the High Altar, is now used as the parish church. A monument to the 19C architect George Gwilt (tomb outside in churchyard) commemorates the man who saved the retrochoir in 1838. The Lady Chapel, which extended to the E, was pulled down in 1830. In the northernmost of the four chapels opening on to the retrochoir (St Andrew's Chapel) Stephen Gardiner, Bp of Winchester in the time of Queen Mary, held his consistory (diocesan) court, which condemned seven men accused of heresy to the stake, including John Hooper, former Bp of Gloucester.

In the S aisle of the nave, below a memorial window to Shakespeare (by Christopher Webb, 1954) is a recumbent alabaster figure of the playwright (1911).

Southwark Cathedral (RC)

Ded: St George.

In Lambeth Road, SE1.

Built on a triangular island site between St George's Circus and the Imperial War Museum, the cathedral forms part of a compact group of ecclesiastical buildings that includes the Archbishop's Palace. It was completed, as St George's Church, in 1848, and became a cathedral in 1850 with the restoration of the Catholic Hierarchy—the first Roman Catholic cathedral in England since the Reformation. The design was by Augustus Welby Pugin, but the cathedral was virtually destroyed during the blitz of 1941, and the present building, which dates from the 1950s, consists largely of restoration work by Romilly Craze.

Externally the cathedral, which faces on to Lambeth Road, is of yellow brick; internally it is of stone, built in a simple neo-Gothic style. The main colour comes from the glowing dark blue glass of the E and W windows. The most notable monuments are in the N aisle: Thomas Doyle (d 1879), who came to St George's as Father Doyle in 1829 and died there as Provost Doyle 50 years later, aged 86; and Abp Peter Amigo (1864–1949). There are no transepts; but the light and airy Lady Chapel is where one might expect the south transept to be. The statue of the Virgin came from the original Catholic chapel in Bandy Leg Walk, London Road, near by. At the E end of the S aisle is the English Martyrs' Chapel, dedicated to Roman Catholics who were martyred and later canonized for their beliefs.

Westminster Abbey

Ded: St Peter

Westminster Abbey, more officially the Collegiate Church of St Peter in Westminster, holds a unique position in English history as both the crowning place and the burial place of most English sovereigns. Though built at different periods, it is (with the exception of Henry VII's magnificent Perp chapel at the E end, Abbot Islip's chapel and the 18C W towers) in the EE style, of which it is one of the most beautiful and best-preserved examples.

History. According to tradition, a church built on Thorney Isle (Isle of Thorns) by Sebert, King of the East Saxons, was consecrated by Mellitus, first bishop of London, in 616. However, there is no authentic record of any earlier church than that of the 10C Benedictine abbey, which was dedicated to St Peter and received the name West Minster ('western monastery'), probably from its position two miles W across the fields from the City of London. Edward the Confessor (d 1066, canonized 1163) rebuilt the abbey on a larger scale; his Norman church was consecrated in 1065, and he was buried there and later translated after his canonization in 1163. In this church, or its successor, every English sovereign since Harold (except Edward V and Edward VIII) has been crowned.

In 1220 a Lady Chapel was added at the E end, and in 1245 Henry III decided to honour St Edward by rebuilding the entire church in a more magnificent style, which we see today. The architects were Henry de Reyns (1245–53), John of Gloucester (1253–60) and Robert of Beverley (1260–84). The influence of French cathedrals such as Reims and Amiens, and of the Sainte Chapelle in Paris, can be seen in the height of the nave and the arrangement of the radiating chapels round the apse. In 1269 the new church was consecrated. From this time until the reign of George III (1760) the abbey became the royal burial church. About 1378 Henry Yevele began to rebuild the nave with money given by Cardinal (formerly Abbot) Simon Langham, and the work was continued after 1400 by William of Colchester; the design of Henry III's time was followed with even the details little changed. The nave vault was completed by Abbot Islip in 1504–06. The new nave was hardly finished when the Lady Chapel was pulled down to make way for the magnificent Chapel of Henry VII (built 1503–19), attributed to Robert Vertue. In 1560 Queen Elizabeth I made the church a 'Royal Peculiar' under an independent Dean and Chapter, whose successors rule it today. The extant monastic buildings date mainly from the 13C and 14C, but there is Norman work in the Chamber of the Pyx and the adjoining Undercroft.

Exterior. The lower part of the W façade dates from c 1390, but was altered by Hawksmoor in the 18C; the towers (225ft high) were added by Hawksmoor c 1735. The whole of the exterior was restored by Wren and Wyatt in 1697–1720. In 1875–84 the façade of the N transept was entirely remodelled by Sir Gilbert Scott and J.L. Pearson. The light and delicately shaped walls of Henry VII's Chapel remain the most pleasing part of the solemn, heavily buttressed exterior.

Interior. Entering by the W Door, the visitor should allow the beautiful interior of the church to make its impact, before turning to the monuments. The architectural and sculptural details can be fully appreciated since the interior cleaning was completed in 1965. The height of the nave is at once striking; separated from the aisles by a tall arcade supported on circular columns round each of which are grouped eight slender shafts of grey Purbeck marble, it is the loftiest Gothic nave in England (102ft; compare York Minster at 100ft). Above the arches runs the double triforium with exquisite tracery and diaperwork, and still higher, the tall clerestory.

Nave. All the extant nave monuments are post-Reformation; and many monuments throughout the church commemorate men and women who are not buried in the abbey. A few paces from the W door in the middle of the nave a slab of green marble is simply inscribed 'Remember Winston Churchill'. Immediately to the E, surrounded by poppies, is the tomb of the Unknown Warrier, brought from France and buried here on 11 Nov. 1920 (Armistice Day), as representative of all the nameless British dead in World War I. He rests in earth brought from the battlefields. In contrast, a florid monument by Westmacott to William Pitt (1759–1806), Prime Minister during the Napoleonic Wars, crowns the W door. On the SW pier hangs a *Portrait of Richard II, the oldest contemporary portrait of any English monarch (reigned 1377–99).

At the foot of the W piers are two fine bronze candelabra (1940) by Benno Elkan, representing the Old and the New Testaments.

A stone NE of the Unknown Warrior's tomb marks the spot where the remains of George Peabody (1795–1869), the American philanthropist, lay for a time before being removed to Massachusetts.

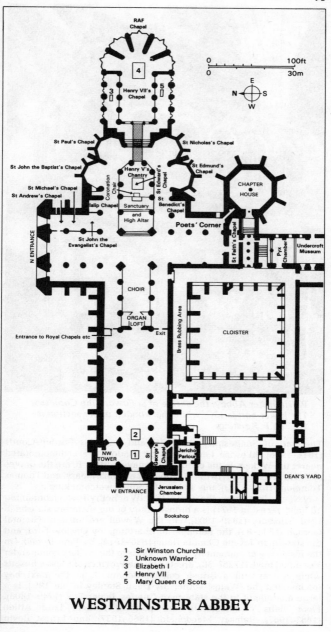

RAF Chapel

0 ———————— 100ft
0 ———————— 30m

N
W — E
S

4 Henry VII's Chapel

3   **5**

St Paul's Chapel

St John the Baptist's Chapel

St Michael's Chapel

St Andrew's Chapel

Islip Chapel

St Nicholas's Chapel

St Edmund's Chapel

Coronation Chair

Henry V's Chantry

St Edward's Chapel

St Benedict's Chapel

CHAPTER HOUSE

Sanctuary and High Altar

Poets' Corner

St John the Evangelist's Chapel

N ENTRANCE

St Faith's Chapel

Pyx Chamber

Undercroft Museum

CHOIR

ORGAN LOFT

Exit

Brass Rubbing Area

CLOISTER

Entrance to Royal Chapels etc

NW TOWER

2

1

St George's Chapel

Jericho Parlour

DEAN'S YARD

W ENTRANCE

Jerusalem Chamber

Bookshop

1   Sir Winston Churchill
2   Unknown Warrior
3   Elizabeth I
4   Henry VII
5   Mary Queen of Scots

WESTMINSTER ABBEY

*Westminster Abbey, the shrine of St Edward the Confessor.
The lower part is 13C, while the wooden upper section is
16C. (A.F. Kersting)*

The Earl of Shaftesbury (1801–85) and Baroness Burdett-Coutts
(1814–1906), likewise benefactors of London, are commemorated
nearer the W door. In the centre of the nave, further E, are the graves
of David Livingstone (1813–73), traveller and missionary, and Thomas
Tompion (1639–1713), the 'father of English watchmaking'.

N Nave Aisle. Across the front of the NW or Belfry Tower (containing
10 bells, recast in 1971) is a bronze effigy of the Victorian statesman
Lord Salisbury (1830–1903). On the W wall are busts of General
Gordon (1833–85), the defender of Khartoum, by Onslow Ford, and
the statesman Joseph Chamberlain (1836–1914), by John Tweed. On
the E side is a monument by Scheemakers to the military commander
Viscount Howe (1725?–58), erected by the Province of Massachusetts
while it was still a British colony. Behind it, in the next bay
(nicknamed the 'Whigs' corner' by Dean Stanley in the 19C), is a
large monument to the statesman Charles James Fox (1749–1806).
Floor slabs commemorate the political leaders Lord Attlee
(1883–1967), Ramsay Macdonald (1866–1937) and Ernest Bevin

(1881–1951), and the social reformers Sidney Webb (1859–1947) and his wife Mary (1858–1943). On the wall is a monument to the Liberal prime minister Sir Henry Campbell-Bannerman (1836–1908).

In the 3rd bay, a small stone in the pavement, inscribed 'O Rare Ben Jonson', marks the grave of the poet and playwright Ben Jonson (1573?–1637); the original stone is at the foot of the adjoining wall, below the monument to Thomas Banks (1735–1805), the sculptor. In the 4th bay is one of the earliest monuments in the nave, of unusual design, to Mrs Jane Hill (d 1631). In the 5th bay, at the foot of the window, is a monument to Spencer Perceval (1762–1812), Prime Minister, shot by a madman in the lobby of the House of Commons; a relief by Westmacott depicts the murder. A slab in the 7th bay marks the grave of the astronomer Sir John Herschel (1792–1871); near by is a memorial to his father, Sir William Herschel (1738–1822), also an astronomer.

The choir screen (1828, since regilded) is the work of Edward Blore. Set in to the W side are two impressive works by Rysbrack and Kent commemorating Sir Isaac Newton (1642–1727), discoverer of the law of gravity, and Earl Stanhope (1673–1721), soldier and politician. Beside Newton's grave is that of Lord Kelvin (1824–1907), mathematician and physicist.

S Nave Aisle. Several of the bays have interesting old coats of arms. To the left, in the 7th bay, is a memorial to Major John André (1751–80), hanged by George Washington as a spy during the American War of Independence; the bas-relief shows Washington receiving André's vain petition for a soldier's death. Floor slabs in front of the next bay (usually covered by stalls) mark the graves of Andrew Bonar Law (1858–1923) and Neville Chamberlain (1869–1944), prime ministers. The 5th bay has unusual monuments with trilingual inscriptions including Hebrew, Coptic and Greek. Above the W cloister door is a dramatic monument by Roubiliac to Field-Marshal George Wade (1673–1748), who built roads and bridges in the Scottish Highlands in 1720–30. In the last bay is a small gallery of oak called the Abbot's Pew, erected by Abbot Islip (16C), and below, William Congreve (1670–1729), the playwright.

The SW Tower, or Old Baptistry, is now the Chapel of St George, dedicated to all who gave their lives in the World Wars and containing a tablet to the million British dead. In the wrought-iron screen is the trophy sent by the French town of Verdun to the Lord Mayor of London. Below is a tablet to Lord Baden-Powell (1857–1941), founder of the Scout movement. In the floor, slabs mark the graves of two generals, Lord Plumer (1857–1932) and Lord Allenby (1871–1936). On the south wall is an oak screen in memory of Henry Fawcett (1833–84), the blind statesman, and his wife Dame Millicent Fawcett (1847–1929). Outside on the W wall is a plaque in memory of President Franklin D. Roosevelt (1882–1945).

To see the rest of the abbey, including the royal tombs, Shrine of King Edward, Henry VII's Chapel and Poets' Corner, it is necessary to buy a ticket at the entrance to the N Choir Aisle (except on Wed. evenings, when the whole building is free).

The *N Choir Aisle* has fine examples of early heraldry on the N wall. A series of medallions under the organ (right) commemorate famous scientists, among them Charles Darwin (1809–82), who developed the theory of evolution (his tomb is in the N nave aisle), and Lord Lister (1827–1912), pioneer of antiseptic surgery. Matching diamonds in the pavement honour four of our greatest composers, Sir Edward Elgar (1857–1934), Sir Charles Villiers Stanford (1852–1924), Ralph Vaughan Williams (1872–1958) and Benjamin Britten (1913–1976). In the next bay William Wilberforce (1759–1833), opponent of the slave trade, and Sir Stamford Raffles (1781–1826), founder of Singapore, sit pensive in effigy above the tomb of Henry Purcell (1659–95), composer and organist of the abbey. Beyond, a bust of Orlando Gibbons (1583–1625) faces the tomb of John Blow (1648?–1708), both, like Purcell, composers and abbey organists. Near by is a memorial to Dr Charles Burney (1726–1814), historian of music. At the entrance to the transept (right) is the monument to William Hesketh (d 1605), with bright Jacobean decoration.

Sanctuary. The 18C roof of the lantern, destroyed by incendiary bombs in May 1941, was replaced soon afterwards. The Sanctuary, or raised space within the altar-rails, has a fine old pavement, laid by Master Odericus in 1268 (protected by carpets). On the left are the three most beautiful architectural •Tombs in the abbey, dating from between c 1298 and 1325, commemorating: Aveline, Countess of Lancaster (d c 1273), first wife of Edmund Crouchback; Aymer de Valence, Earl of Pembroke (d 1324); and Edmund Crouchback, Earl of Lancaster (d 1296), second son of Henry III and founder of the House of Lancaster. On the right side of the Sanctuary are sedilia dating from the time of Edward I, with paintings (1308) of King Sebert, St Peter and King Ethelbert, and an ancient tapestry. On this is hung a Florentine triptych, by Bicci di Lorenzo (1373–1452), of the Madonna between two pairs of saints; it was given to the abbey in 1948 by Lord Lee of Fareham. Below is the tomb of Anne of Cleves (d 1557), fourth wife of Henry VIII. The 17C pulpit, replaced in 1935, is matched by a lectern (1949) in memory of William Carey (1761–1834), the missionary. The choir fittings were designed by Edward Blore in 1830.

Transepts. The uniformity and proportions of the architecture have been upset by a host of monuments. In the N transept the E aisle is partly closed off, while in the S transept the E walk of the cloister takes up the space of the W aisle. Each transept is lit by a large rose-window (the glass in the N transept is the oldest in the Abbey, dating from 1721–22), below which are exquisitely carved angels holding censers, perhaps sculpted by Master John of St Albans c 1250. The S transept also retains two figures below the window.

In the *N Transept* several famous statesmen are remembered. In the W aisle is a delicately carved monument to Jonas Hanway (1722–86), the philanthropist, and busts of Richard Cobden (1804–65), the apostle of free trade, and of Warren Hastings (1732–1818), Governor-General of India. On the wall behind, in the nave, is a huge monument to William Pitt, Earl of Chatham (1708–78), and statues of Lord Palmerston (1784–1865) and Lord Castlereagh (1769–1821). In the pavement are the graves of Henry Grattan (1746–1820), the Irish patriot and orator, and Charles James Fox (1749–1806). Towards the E wall, statues of: George Canning (1770–1827), by Sir Francis Chantrey; Benjamin Disraeli, Earl of Beaconsfield (1804–81), by Sir Edgar Boehm; William Ewart Gladstone (1809–98), by Sir Thomas Brock; and Sir Robert Peel (1788–1850), by John Gibson.

The three chapels (usually closed) of St John the Evangelist, St Michael and St Andrew occupy the E aisle of the N transept. At the entrance to the first chapels is an overwhelming monument to General Wolfe (1727–59), of Quebec fame. To the left, as we enter, Sir

Westminster Abbey, the nave.

John Franklin (1786–1847), lost in the search for the North-West Passage, with a fine inscription by Tennyson; to the right, *Sir Francis Vere (1560–1609) and Lady Elizabeth Nightingale (d 1731), a theatrical sculpture by Louis Roubiliac. The large tomb in the next chapel is that of Lord Norris (1525?–1601) and his wife, neither buried here. On the N wall: Sir James Young Simpson (1811–70), who first used chloroform as an anaesthetic; Mrs Siddons (1755–1831) as the Tragic Muse, by Chantrey after the painting by Reynolds; Sir Humphry Davy (1778–1829), inventor of the miner's safety lamp; John Kemble (1757–1823), actor, designed by Flaxman, Thomas Telford (1757–1834), engineer and bridge-builder. On the right, Admiral Kempenfelt (1718–82), by John Bacon.

(S Transept, see below).

Choir Chapels (N). The choir apse is rounded and contains the Chapel of St Edward, so that the high altar is placed fairly far forward, and the ritual choir extends into the nave. In the ambulatory are two fine brasses for Abbot Estney (1498) and Sir John Harpedon (1457). The three tombs in the Sanctuary (see above) are well seen from here.

The two-storied Chapel of Abbot Islip (lower storey not shown) contains the grave of Adm. Sir Charles Saunders (d 1775), who shared with Wolfe the glory of taking Quebec. On the carving appears the abbot's rebus: an eye with a slip of a tree, or a man slipping from a branch. The upper chapel (adm. on application) is now the Nurses' Memorial Chapel.

The Chapel of St John the Baptist is entered through the tiny Chapel of Our Lady of the Pew. At the entrance is a delicately carved alabaster niche from the demolished Chapel of St Erasmus (15C). Traces of the painted vault remain from the late 14C; an alabaster statue of the Madonna by Sister Concordia was placed in the niche in 1971. To the right in the polygonal Chapel of St John the Baptist are several 15C tombs of abbots, notably William de Colchester (d 1420). The huge tomb of Lord Hunsdon (d 1596) is a masterpiece of Elizabethan bombast. The plain tomb by the NE wall of Hugh and Mary de Bohun dates from 1304–05. Behind is a monument to Col. Popham, who fought for Cromwell; the inscription was removed because of his Parliamentarian activities. In the centre is a large monument to Thomas Cecil, Earl of Exeter (1543–1623), son of Lord Burghley, with his effigy and that of his first wife. His second wife refused to accept the less honourable position on his left-hand side and was buried in Winchester Cathedral.

From the ambulatory opposite the chapel, the mosaics on the tomb of Henry III (see below), can be clearly seen. The well-lit Chapel of St Paul is the easternmost chapel of the N Ambulatory and contains (right) the repainted tomb of Lord Bourchier (d 1430), which forms part of the screen. On the monument of Lord Cottington (d 1652) is a bust of his wife (d 1633) by Le Sueur. On the site of the altar, Frances Sidney, Countess of Sussex (d 1589), founder of Sidney Sussex College, Cambridge. Beyond fine monuments to Dudley Carleton (d 1632), by Nicholas Stone, Sir Thomas Bromley (1530–87) and Sir James Fullerton (d 1631) is one to Sir John Puckering (1544–96), Speaker of the House of Commons. In the centre, Sir Giles Daubeny (d 1508) and his lady, in fine contemporary costume. To the right of the exit, bust of Sir Rowland Hill (1795–1879), champion of penny postage. In the ambulatory opposite the exit from this chapel, the *Grille of Queen Eleanor's tomb, a superb example of English wrought-iron work by Thomas of Leighton (1294). Beneath are traces of paintings by Walter of Durham. Above can be seen the Chantry of Henry V, forming a bridge over the ambulatory.

We now climb the flight of steps leading to the Chapel of Henry VII, entered appropriately through a spacious barrel-vaulted vestibule, decorated with bright roof panelling. (With the current, 1984, order of visiting the abbey, the nave is seen after the N Aisle, see below.)

**Chapel of Henry VII. Built in 1503–19, this chapel is the finest example in England of late Perp or Tudor Gothic. Henry ordered it to be 'painted, garnished and adorned in as goodly and rich a manner as such work requireth and as to a king's work apperteyneth'. The glory of its profuse decoration is the superb fan-tracery vaulting, hung with pendants in the nave, and stretched like a canopy to accommodate the bay windows in the aisles. The beautiful tall windows, curved in the aisles and angular in the apse, are particularly ingenious. The carving throughout is of the highest quality, and includes a series of 95 (originally 107) statues of saints popular at the time, with a frieze of angels and badges below. The chapel was begun as a shrine for Henry VI, murdered in 1471 and remembered as the 'royal saint' after his death. Since 1725 it has been the chapel of the Knights of the Bath; their carved stalls separate the nave from the aisles, which have separate entrances at the W end.

N Aisle of Henry VII's Chapel. The tall canopied *Tomb in the centre of the aisle was erected by James I to Queen Elizabeth I (1533–1603), who lies here in the same grave as her half-sister Queen Mary I (1516–58). The E end of this aisle was called 'Innocents' Corner' by Dean Stanley. Here are commemorated two infant daughters of James I (both d 1607), Princess Mary, and Princess Sophia, represented in a cradle which is her actual tomb; her effigy is reflected in a mirror on the wall behind. In a small sarcophagus by the E wall are some bones, reinterred as those of Edward V and his brother Richard Duke of York, the young sons of Edward IV, murdered in the Tower of London c 1483. (Edward V was born when his mother was in sanctuary in the Abbey.)

Nave of Henry VII's Chapel. The beautiful oak doors plated with bronze at the entrance date from the 16C. The heraldic devices that appear on them and recur elsewhere in the decoration of the chapel refer to Henry VII's ancestry and his claims to the throne. The Welsh dragon indicates his Tudor father; the daisy-plant (marguerite) and portcullis refer to the names of his Lancastrian mother, Margaret Beaufort; the falcon was the badge of Edward IV, father of Elizabeth of York, Henry's wife; the greyhound that of the Nevilles from whom she was descended. The crown on a bush recalls Henry's first coronation on Bosworth field (1485); while the roses are those of Lancaster and York united by his marriage. Other emblems are the lions of England and the fleur-de-lys of France.

On each side of the nave are the elaborately carved stalls of the Knights of the Bath, each with the arms of its successive holders emblazoned on small copper plates and the banner of the current holder hanging above. The lower seats are those of the esquires (no longer used as such) with their coats of arms. Beneath the seats are a number of grotesquely carved misericords, one of which (8th stall on S side) dates from the 13C. At the W end is the naval sword of George VI, with which he conferred the accolade. The altar (1935) is a reproduction of the original, with a 15C altarpiece by Bartolommeo Vivarini.

Under the pavement between the door and the altar lies George II (1683–1760), the last king to be buried in the abbey, with Queen Caroline and numerous members of his family. Below the altar is the grave of Edward VI (1537–53). Behind is the beautiful *Tomb of Henry VII (1457–1509) and Elizabeth of York (d 1503), an admirable work by the Italian Pietro Torrigiani, completed c 1518. The noble effigies of the king and queen rest on a black marble sarcophagus, with a carved frieze of white marble and adorned with gilt medallions of saints. The fine 16C bronze grille, Gothic in feeling and 9ft high, is the work of Thomas Ducheman. James I (1566–1625) is buried in the same vault as Henry VII and his queen.

Apse Chapels (clockwise N–S). In the first chapel is the large tomb by Le Sueur of George Villiers, Duke of Buckingham, assassinated in 1628, the favourite of James I and Charles I, with statues of his children by Nicholas Stone. The low stone screen preserved here is in keeping with the originality of the design of the outer walls of the chapel. In the next chapel is a vault (usually covered by a portable organ) with the graves of Anne of Denmark (1574–1619), queen of James I, and Anne Mowbray, the child wife of Richard, Duke of York, reburied here in 1965.

The E chapel is now the Royal Air Force Chapel. The window by Hugh Easton, commemorating the Battle of Britain (July–Oct. 1940), incorporates in the design the badges of the 68 fighter squadrons that took part. The chapel keeps the roll of honour of the 1,497 airmen of Britain and her allies who fell in the battle. Near by is the grave of Lord Dowding (1882–1970), who commanded the air defence of Great Britain, and on the S side that of Lord Trenchard (1873–1956), 'father' of the RAF. In this chapel were buried Oliver Cromwell (1599–1658), tablet on floor, and three of his leading supporters, Henry Ireton (1611–51), John Bradshaw (1602–59) and Admiral Blake (1599–1657). At the Restoration of Charles II in 1660 all were removed from the abbey; Blake was reinterred in the churchyard of St Margaret's, outside the abbey, but the bodies of the others were treated with ignominy, their heads being struck off at Tyburn (now Marble Arch) and afterwards exposed at Westminster Hall.

In the next chapel is buried Dean Arthur Stanley (1815–81), the most famous 19C Dean of Westminster, with a fine effigy by Boehm. Here too is buried the Duc de Montpensier (1775–1807), brother of the French ruler Louis-Philippe. The last apse chapel on the S is filled by Le Sueur's monument to Ludovick Stuart, Duke of Lennox and Richmond (1574–1624), with a gilt canopy.

Returning down the nave of Henry VII's chapel, we cross a reinforced glass bridge (1971) past the tomb and beneath the Chantry of Henry V (1387–1422). His despoiled effigy rests on a slab of marble and was originally covered with silver-gilt plates, stolen together with the solid silver head in the reign of Henry VIII. In 1971 the head was replaced in polyester resin, by Louisa Bolt. In the chantry (no adm.) Katherine of Valois (d 1437), Henry's 'beautiful Kate', lies beneath the altar; she was originally buried in the old Lady Chapel. On display are a shield, saddle and helmet, probably made for Henry's funeral.

Chapel of St Edward the Confessor. The most sacred part of the church, and in former times the most glorious. In the middle stands the mutilated *Shrine of St Edward the Confessor (1003?–66), erected in the late 13C for Henry III by Peter of Rome, probably the son of Master Odericus (see under Sanctuary above), and showing traces of the original mosaics. The upper part, now of wood (1557), was originally a golden shrine decorated with jewels and gold images of saints, all of which disappeared at the Dissolution in Henry VIII's reign. Sick people used to spend the night in the recesses of the base, in hope of a miraculous cure. Roman Catholic pilgrims visit the shrine on St Edward's Day (13 Oct.).

On the N side of the shrine are three royal tombs. First come the beautiful Gothic *Tombs of Eleanor of Castile (d 1290), wife of Edward I, and her father-in-law Henry III (1207–72). Henry's tomb was designed by Peter of Rome, and Eleanor's was executed by Richard Crundale with paintings by Walter of Durham; but both the beautiful bronze effigies, the earliest cast in England, are by William Torel, a London goldsmith. The canopy over Eleanor's tomb dates from the 15C, when the old one was destroyed by the building of Henry V's Chantry. Next to them is the plain altar-tomb, without effigy, of Edward I (1239–1307); in 1744 the tomb was opened, and his body, 6ft 2in tall, was found to be in good preservation, dressed in royal robes with a gilt crown.

At the W end of the Chapel is a beautiful screen (mid 15C) with 14 scenes of the life of Edward the Confessor. In front are the remains of the medieval pavement, and the *Coronation Chair, made in oak by Walter of Durham c 1300–01. It has left the abbey on only three occasions: first in 1653, when Cromwell was installed as Lord

Protector in Westminster Hall, and next for safety during the two World Wars. It shows traces of its original painting, and is liberally carved with the initials of Westminster schoolboys of past centuries. Below the seat is placed the famous Stone of Scone, carried off from Scotland by Edward I in 1297 and used for all subsequent coronations of English monarchs. Beside it are the State Sword (7ft long) and Shield of Edward III.

The Stone of Scone, on which the Scottish kings were crowned from time immemorial down to John de Baliol in 1292, was regarded as the sacred guarantee of Scottish independence, and its character was supposed to have been vindicated when James VI of Scotland became also James I of England in 1603. A long but mythical history attaches to this block of reddish sandstone from central Scotland. It is traditionally identified with Jacob's Pillow at Bethel, afterwards the Lia Fail or 'Stone of Destiny' on the sacred hill of Tara, in Ireland. Historically, it is recorded as being used for the enthronement of Macbeth's stepson at Scone in 1057, and was certainly in use there earlier. On 25 Dec. 1950, it was stolen by Scottish Nationalists and taken to Arbroath; it was replaced on 13 April 1951.

On the S side of the shrine, nearest the Coronation Chair, is the tomb of Richard II (d 1400) and his first wife Anne of Bohemia (d 1394). It is profusely decorated with delicately engraved patterns, among which are the broom-pods of the Plantagenets (*Planta genista* in Latin), the white hart, rising sun etc; the beautiful paintings in the canopy represent the Trinity, the Coronation of the Virgin, and Anne of Bohemia's coat of arms. Next comes the elaborate tomb of Edward III (d 1377). In the niches were statuettes of his 14 children, six of which remain (see from S ambulatory; see below); the contemporary wooden canopy is very fine. Beyond this is the tomb of Edward's wife, Philippa of Hainault (d 1369), with an alabaster effigy of the queen by Hennequin of Liège, sculptor to the King of France.

S Aisle of Henry VII's Chapel. At the end of this aisle are memorials to the statesmen Lord Cromer (1841–1917), Lord Curzon (1859–1925), Viscount Milner (1854–1925) and Cecil Rhodes (1853–1902). In the centre is the tomb of Margaret, Countess of Lennox (d 1578). Her son, Henry Darnley, was husband of Mary, Queen of Scots, and father of James I of England; and his figure among the effigies on both sides of the tomb may be identified by the crown over his head (if he had ever been crowned, he would have ruled as Henry I of Scotland). Next, under a tall canopy, is a recumbent *Figure of Mary, Queen of Scots (1542–87), whose remains were removed here from Peterborough Cathedral in 1612 by order of her son, James I. The work of Cornelius and William Cure (1605–10), this was the last royal tomb erected in the abbey.

The next *Tomb is that of Margaret of Beaufort, Countess of Richmond (1443–1509), mother of Henry VII, patroness of the printer Wynkyn de Worde, and foundress of Christ's and St John's Colleges at Cambridge. The beautiful recumbent figure in gilt-bronze, the masterpiece of Pietro Torrigiani of Florence, is noted for the delicate modelling of the hands. It is surrounded by a contemporary screen. On the wall to the N is a fine bronze bust of Sir Thomas Lovell (d 1524), also by Torrigiani. The statue of a Roman matron beside it, by Valory, commemorates Catherine Lady Walpole (d 1737).

The incongruous monument to General Monk, Duke of Albemarle (1608–70), restorer of the Stuart dynasty in 1660, covers a vault containing the remains of King Charles II (d 1685), Queen Mary II (d

1694), her husband King William III (d 1702), Queen Anne (d 1714), and her husband Prince George of Denmark (d 1708).

Choir Chapels (S). The Chapel of St Nicholas, off the S ambulatory, has a fine stone screen. On the right of the door, the tomb of Philippa, Duchess of York (d 1431). In the centre is the fine tomb of Sir George Villiers (d 1606) and his wife (d 1630), parents of the Duke of Buckingham. The large monument on the S wall to the wife and daughter of Lord Burghley (c 1588), and that on the E wall to the Duchess of Somerset (d 1587), are good examples of the Renaissance period. Below this chapel is the vault of the Dukes of Northumberland, the only family with the right to be buried in the abbey. In the ambulatory opposite this chapel is an oak *Retable (decorated panel), a rare example of French or English painting of c 1255, with rich decorations.

The Chapel of St Edmund and St Thomas the Martyr is separated from the ambulatory by an ancient oak screen. Inside, to the right, the *Tomb of William de Valence, Earl of Pembroke (d 1296), half-brother of Henry III, consists of an oak coffin and effigy of the earl, plated with Limoges enamel, traces of which can still be seen. The handsome Jacobean tomb of Edward Talbot, Earl of Shrewsbury (d 1617) and his wife was only accommodated by destroying some of the arcading. Also in this chapel, Sir Richard Pecksall (d 1571) and Sir Bernard Brocas (d 1395). Beyond the large monument to Lord John Russell (d 1584) with his infant son, is the seated figure of his daughter, Lady Elizabeth Russell (1576–1601), the earliest non-recumbent statue in the abbey. In the floor is the grave of Edward Bulwer Lytton (1803–73), author of *The Last Days of Pompeii*. In the centre of the chapel are the tombs of Robert Waldeby, Archbishop of York (d 1397), with a brass representing him in full vestments, and of Eleanor de Bohun, Duchess of Gloucester (d 1399), in conventual dress, the largest and finest brass in the abbey.

Near the E wall of the chapel is the tomb of Frances, Duchess of Suffolk (d 1559), mother of Lady Jane Grey. Adjoining are the finely modelled but mutilated effigies of two children of Edward III (1340). Beside the door is the *Tomb of John of Eltham (1316–37), second son of Edward II; the alabaster effigy, the earliest in the abbey, is especially interesting for the careful carving of the prince's armour. Opposite the entrance we see the outer side of Edward III's tomb (see above), with beautiful little brass *Statuettes of his children, with enamelled coats of arms. Between this chapel and the next (St Benedict) a small altar-tomb covers the remains of four children of Henry III and four of Edward I.

The Chapel of St Benedict (no adm.) is best seen from the S transept. Beside the railing on this side is the alabaster tomb of Simon Langham (d 1376), Abbot of Westminster and afterwards archbishop and cardinal. In the ambulatory is the so-called tomb of Sebert and his wife; then a tablet to Anne Nevill (1456–85), queen of Richard III. Above is the back of the sedilia in the sanctuary, with 14C paintings of Edward the Confessor and the Annunciation (mutilated). Outside the gate (right) is a monument to Dr Richard Busby (1606–95), a famous Head Master of Westminster School.

S Transept and Poets' Corner. Poets' Corner, originally taking its name from the tombs of Geoffrey Chaucer and Edmund Spenser, is strictly speaking the S end of the E aisle of this transept; but the tombs of the poets have overflowed into the S end of the central aisle also. On the end wall of the transept are two magnificent *Wall-paintings of St Christopher and Doubting Thomas. Uncovered in 1936, they are ascribed to Walter of Durham (c 1280), and are outstanding examples of the Westminster school of painting.

On the left side of the E aisle as we enter is a bust of John Dryden (1631–1700); on the pier opposite (right) William Blake (1757–1827), by Epstein; by the next pillar (left) Henry Longfellow (1807–82), placed by English admirers of the American poet in 1884. Below the next window is the Gothic *Tomb of Geoffrey Chaucer (1340?–1400), erected 155 years after his death. The space at the end of the altar-tomb is perhaps a prayer recess. Further on, Michael Drayton (1563–1631). Below the pavement in front of Chaucer's tomb are the graves of Robert Browning (1812–89) and Alfred Lord Tennyson (1809–92); and memorials to T.S. Eliot (1888–1965), Lord Byron (1788–1824), Henry James (1843–1916), George Eliot (1819–80), Gerard Manley Hopkins (1844–89), John Masefield (1878–1967), W.H. Auden (1907–73), and Dylan Thomas (1914–53).

At the SE angle are two doorways. Outside that in the E wall is an ancient pathway going straight to the Palace of Westminster, and a tablet on the left marks the approximate site of Caxton's original printing press (1477). In the S wall is the entrance to the Chapter House Crypt (no adm.), an eight-sided undercroft (1248) with a massive central column, once used as the royal treasury.

On the S wall, above the door to the crypt, is a medallion of Ben Jonson (1573?–1637), buried in the nave (see above). Further on, monuments to Edmund Spenser (1552?–99)—a copy (1778) of the original—and John Milton (1608–74), a memorial delayed for over 60 years after Milton's death, because of political feeling over his Cromwellian sympathies. Below, Thomas Gray (1716–71). On the partition wall, the remarkable monument to Matthew Prior (1664–1721), designed by Gibbs, executed by Rysbrack, with a bust by Coysevox. On the next pier, beyond a bust of Tennyson, monuments to Adam Lindsay Gordon (1833–70), Australian poet, and Thomas Campbell (1777–1844). In the floor a little to the N, the gravestone of Thomas Parr (1483?–1635), known as 'Old Parr', said to have lived 152 years and under ten sovereigns, while further S are those of Dr Samuel Johnson (1709–84), compiler of the great dictionary, with a bust by Nollekens above, and the actors David Garrick (1717–79) and Sir Henry Irving (1838–1905).

On the W side of the partition wall: William Wordsworth (1770–1850); Samuel Taylor Coleridge (1772–1834); Robert Southey (1774–1843), epitaph by Wordsworth. On the monument to William Shakespeare (1564–1616), by Scheemakers, erected in 1740, are carved some lines from *The Tempest*, and at the corners of the pedestal are carved heads representing Elizabeth I, Henry V and Richard III. John Keats (1796–1821) and Percy Bysshe Shelley (1792–1822) are commemorated above. James Thomson (1700–48), author of 'Rule Britannia'. Above, Robert Burns (1759–96). Below, the Brontë Sisters (Anne, 1820–49; Charlotte, 1816–55; Emily, 1818–48), with a line by Emily: 'with courage to endure'. Above the door to the Chapel of St Faith, Oliver Goldsmith (1728–74), with an epitaph by Dr Johnson.

The Chapel of St Faith (restored 1972) is now reserved for private prayer.

To the right of the chapel, Sir Walter Scott (1771–1832); above, John Ruskin (1819–1900), author and art critic. The monument to John Campbell, Duke of Argyll (1680–1743) is a fine work by Roubiliac; as is the monument (above on the W wall) to George Frederick Handel (1685–1759), inscribed with some bars from the *Messiah*. A slab on the floor marks his grave, and one beside it that of Charles Dickens (1812–70). In the floor are a tablet commemorating Thomas Hardy (1840–1928) and the grave of Rudyard Kipling (1865–1936). By the pier, William Makepeace Thackeray (1811–63); Joseph Addison (1672–1719), the essayist; Lord Macaulay (1800–59), the historian.

S Choir Aisle. Opposite the E door into the cloisters are two good monuments, to William Thynne (d 1584), and to Sir Thomas Richardson, in black marble, by Le Sueur. To the left in the next bay is a pompous monument to Admiral Sir Cloudesley Shovel (1650–1707), between memorials to Admiral Blake (1599–1657) and Robert Clive (1725–74), 'Clive of India'. Above is a monument to Sir Godfrey Kneller (1646–1723), the only painter commemorated in the abbey. In the 3rd bay (right) the tomb of Thomas Owen, with a fine painted alabaster figure. On either side of it: the tomb of General Pasquale Paoli (1725–1807), the Corsican patriot who died as a refugee in England, and a tablet to William Tyndale (1490–1536), translator of the Bible. Opposite, medallions to the Nonconformist leaders John Wesley (1703–91) and his brother Charles (1707–88). H.F. Lyte (1793–1847), author of the hymn 'Abide with me', and below, Dr Isaac Watts (1647–1748), the hymn writer. Under the organ loft is a monument to Thomas Thynne (1648–82), with a bas-relief depicting his assassination.

Exits from the chapels and transepts section of the abbey are at the W end of the S Choir Aisle into the nave, and through the door from the same aisle into the cloisters.

Precincts. The earliest parts of the present *Cloisters* date from the mid 13C, the remainder from 1344–70. The cloisters are connected with the church by two doors in the S nave aisle, forming convenient exit and entrance routes for religious processions. The door to the E gives access to the cloisters at their NE angle, the earliest and finest part. The external carving on the doorway is of fine quality. In the E Walk a tablet on the wall in the second bay carries the touching inscription 'Jane Lister, dear Childe' and the date 1688. We pass the entrances to the Chapter House and the Chamber of the Pyx (see below), administered by the DoE; between them is the entrance to the Library and Muniment Room. The S Walk (14C) was the burial place of the abbots for nearly 200 years after the Conquest. The three effigies below the wall seat are of Abbots Laurence (d 1173), Gilbert Crispin (d 1117) and William de Humez (d 1222). The recesses in the wall beside the old entrance to the Refectory served as towel-cupboards. The W Walk (14C) was used as the monastery school. On the wall is a memorial, by G. Ledward, to the members of the submarine branch of the Royal Navy who lost their lives in the two World Wars, and to the members of the Commandos, the Airborne Forces and the Special Air Service killed in 1939–45. The N Walk (14C) is now used as a brass-rubbing centre, with kits available to buy or hire. General Burgoyne (1722–92), who surrendered to the American General Gates after the Battle of Saratoga in 1777, is buried here.

The *Chapter House* (fee) is entered from the E Walk. Visitors are provided with felt overshoes, to avoid damaging the original tiled *Pavement. Over the entrance are sculpted figures, much mutilated, of the 13C. The vaulted vestibule has fine bosses. At the top of the stairs are memorials to James Russell Lowell (1819–91), the American writer, and Walter Hines Page (1855–1918), American ambassador. Opposite, the coffin lid, with a cross in relief, is perhaps the only extant relic of Sebert's 7C church; the Roman sarcophagus was buried in the green N of the abbey. The chapter house is a beautiful octagonal room, 56ft in diameter, built c 1245–55. On the left is the Roll of Honour of the Royal Army Medical Corps. The lofty roof is supported by a single central shaft, 35ft high, and is lit by six huge windows. These were destroyed by bombing in 1941 and reset in 1950 with some of the original glass; they show scenes from the abbey's history and the arms of benefactors. The tracery, like the roof, is modern, though copied from the blank window which escaped wartime damage. The arcading on the walls is adorned with paintings (partly restored) of the life of St John and of the Last Judgement, with a frieze of animals below, presented by a Westminster monk, John of Northampton (1372–1404). The beautiful Madonna and angel above the door date from 1250–53).

The Chapter House is memorable as the 'cradle of representative and constitutional government throughout the world'. Here the early House of Commons, separated from the House of Lords in the reign of Edward III, held its meetings from 1376 down to 1547, when it moved to St Stephen's Chapel. From c 1550 to 1865 it was used as a State muniment room; and it is still in the charge of the government (the DoE), not the abbey authorities.

The *Pyx Chamber* (for adm. apply to Chapter House custodian), entered from the E walk by a Norman archway and massive doors with seven locks, is part of the Confessor's building. Originally a chapel, it was afterwards used as the abbot's treasury and contained many sacred relics. It subsequently became the depository of the pyx, or chest containing the Exchequer trial-plates of gold and silver used as standards of reference at the periodical tests of coins of the realm ('Trial of the Pyx'). The altar here is the oldest in the abbey.

The E walk of the cloisters is continued to the S by the Dark or Norman Cloister (11C), from which the *Norman Undercroft* (fee) is entered. It is laid out as a museum illustrating the history of the abbey, and contains a number of effigies carried at royal funerals, made of wood, plaster or wax. Notable among the wooden effigies or heads are those of Edward III (perhaps the oldest in Europe) and Henry VII, both death-mask portraits. Of the 11 wax figures, the oldest is that of Charles II, the one of Elizabeth I having been remade in 1760; others represent William III, Mary II and Queen Anne. The portrait figures of Nelson and Chatham are not funeral effigies but were put there to attract visitors.

Further on, an arched passage on the left leads to the Little Cloister, on the site of the monks' infirmary, a quiet and attractive spot, restored after damage in 1940–41. In the E walk is the 14C doorway of St Catherine's Chapel (1165–70), the infirmary chapel, whose ruined arcades can be seen through a doorway on the left. In the S walk a door leads to College Garden (open Thurs. 12–4 or 6). The Dark Cloister ends at the yard of Westminster School.

From the junction of the W and S walks of the Great Cloister a corridor leads W to Dean's Yard. Near its W end, on the right, is a passage admitting to the Abbots' Courtyard, lying between the Deanery, formerly the Abbots' Palace, on the right, and the College Hall, on the left. The steps at the end climb to the Jericho Parlour, the panelled ante-room to the Jerusalem Chamber (14C), the abbots' retiring room, now used as the chapter room and shown only by special permission of the Dean. Henry IV died in this chamber in 1413, having had a stroke while praying at the Confessor's shrine. As Shakespeare makes the king say (*2 Henry IV*): 'It hath been prophesied to me many years/ I should not die but in Jerusalem'.

The Library and Muniment Room (adm. by special permission only), occupying part of the monks' dormitory, above the chapter house vestibule and the Pyx Chamber, is entered from the E walk of the cloister by the original day stairs. The library was founded c 1623 and contains contemporary book presses, as well as priceless books, charters etc.

The usual entrance to the abbey is through the West Door, outside which is the Abbey Bookshop. It is advisable to avoid peak hours, especially in summer (10.00–12.00 and 14.00–15.30). Conducted tours are escorted by abbey vergers; unauthorized conducted tours are not allowed.

Westminster Cathedral (RC)

Ded: The Most Precious Blood of Our Lord.

The seat of the Cardinal Archbishop of Westminster, and the most important Roman Catholic church in England, Westminster Cathedral was built in 1895–1903. It was designed by John Francis Bentley (1839–1902) in an early-Christian Byzantine style, and the alternate narrow bands of red brick and Portland stone of the exterior (best seen from the piazza opening from Victoria Street) add to its exotic appearance. It has been called the last great building in this country to be almost entirely brick-built, with no steel reinforcement in its construction. The church is oriented NW to SE. The square campanile, 284ft high, commands an extensive *View over London (entrance to lift in vestibule, fee). The NW façade is richly articulated in three receding stages. In the tympanum of the main entrance is a mosaic by Anning Bell (1916), showing Christ, St Peter, Edward the Confessor, our Lady and St Joseph. The detail of the dark interior is hard to see, except when lit during services.

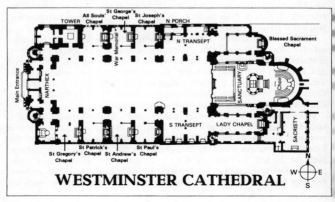

WESTMINSTER CATHEDRAL

Interior. The brick walls are still partly bare, but the vast size and beautiful proportions of the church are remarkably impressive, especially when seen from the W end, from between the two great columns of red Norwegian granite (symbolizing the Precious Blood to which the cathedral is dedicated). The church has the plan of a basilica, roofed with four domes (three nave and one sanctuary). In the apse beyond the raised Sanctuary at the E end is the still higher retrochoir; the Lady Chapel lies at the end of the S aisle.

When the decorative scheme is completed, the walls and piers up to the height of about 30ft will be covered with coloured marble, while the upper walls and the domes will be lined with mosaics. The total length is 342ft; the height of the main arches is 90ft, while the domes are 109ft above the floor. The *Nave* is the widest in England (60ft, or 149ft including aisles and side chapels). On the piers are 14 Stations of the Cross, carved in stone in low relief by Eric Gill (1882–1940). The great *Rood hanging from the arch at the E end of the nave is 30ft long; it is painted with figures of Christ and (on the back) the Mater Dolorosa, by Christian Symons. The elaborately decorated marble pulpit was enlarged in 1934 by Cardinal Bourne, to commemorate his 30 years as archbishop here. Near the pulpit, below the 12th Station of the Cross, is the tomb of Cardinal Heenan (d 1975).

The side *Chapels* are richly decorated with marbles and mosaics. The Baptistry (right of main entrance), with its huge green marble font, is divided from the Chapel of St Gregory and St Augustine by a bronze and marble screen. The chapel was designed by J.F. Bentley, and contains mosaics referring to the conversion of England (by St Augustine, sent by St Gregory) at the end of the 6C. Here is the tomb of Richard Challoner (1691–1781), Bishop of Debra and Vicar-Apostolic of the London district, the most prominent Roman Catholic ecclesiastic of 18C England. Next is the Chapel of St Patrick and the Saints of Ireland, a memorial chapel to the 50,000 Irishmen who fell in the 1914–18 war. Each regiment (Connaught Rangers, Royal Dublin Fusiliers etc) has its own marble tablet and *Liber Vitae*. The gilded bronze statue of the saint is by Arthur Pollen. In the pierced marble screen near the aisle appear the shamrock of St Patrick and the oak leaves of St Bridget. Next comes the chapel, in a faithful Byzantine style by Robert Schultz Weir, dedicated to St Andrew and the Saints of Scotland. Scottish marbles and stone are largely employed in the decoration, with sculpture by Stirling Lee. The fine inlaid ebony choir stalls (c 1912) are the work of Ernest Gimson. The Chapel of St Paul has mosaics (by Justin Vulliamy assisted by Boris Anrep) illustrating the conversion and life of the saint, and a mosaic floor based on a design by the Roman marble workers known as 'Cosmati'.

We now cross the South Transept, passing an early 15C alabaster figure of the Virgin Mary, modelled on Our Lady of Pewe, made by one of the Nottingham school of carvers; above, on the pier, is a bronze panel of St Teresa of Lisieux by Giacomo Manzù. Beyond is the Lady Chapel, richly decorated with mosaics, including the altar piece of the Madonna by Anning Bell. The mosaics of the walls and vault, by Gilbert Pownall, show among other things Tower Bridge, the Tower of London, and Westminster Cathedral itself. Pownall also carried out the mosaics in the sumptuous Sanctuary. Here the altar, flanked by double arcades of coloured marble, consists of a solid block of Cornish granite, weighing 12 tons. Above it rises a white marble baldacchino, with eight monolithic columns of yellow Verona marble on pedestals of verde antico. The throne of the archbishop, to

Westminster Cathedral, the high altar and baldacchino. (A.F. Kersting)

the left, is a reduced copy of the papal chair in St John Lateran, Rome.

On the left of the Sanctuary is the Chapel of the Blessed Sacrament, sumptuously decorated with mosaics (1956–62) by Boris Anrep, symbolizing the Trinity and the Blessed Sacrament. Immediately to the left of it is the small Chapel of the Sacred Heart. Opening off the N Transept is the Chapel of St Thomas of Canterbury, or Vaughan Chantry, in which is a recumbent statue of Cardinal Herbert Vaughan (1832–1903), buried at Mill Hill, who was archbishop during the building of the cathedral. There are three chapels on this side of the nave, as we return towards the exit. The Chapel of St Joseph (corresponding to the Chapel of St Paul opposite) contains the tomb of Cardinal Arthur Hinsley (1865–1943). Next comes the Chapel of St George and the English martyrs, emphasizing England, as the chapels on the opposite side emphasize Ireland and Scotland. It contains the shrine of St John Southworth (1592–1654), a secular priest who was hanged, drawn and quartered under Cromwell, to whose remains have been added a silver face mask and silver hands. Figures of St John Fisher and St Thomas More are carved in the altarpiece by Eric Gill. Lastly, the Chapel of the Holy Souls, designed by J.F.

Bentley, contains mosaics by Christian Symons. The background is silver for mourning, as opposed to the exuberant gold elsewhere in the cathedral.

The *Crypt* is not open to the public and may be visited by previous arrangement only. In the S wall of the semicircular crypt, or Chapel of St Peter, are four relic chambers, in which are preserved fragments of the True Cross and other relics. A floor slab at the E end marks the tomb of Cardinal Griffin (1899–1956), and against the N wall is the tomb of Cardinal Godfrey (1889–1963). Off the W side of the crypt opens the Shrine of St Edmund, a small chapel situated directly beneath the High Altar of the cathedral and containing an altar under which is preserved a relic of St Edmund (displayed on the saint's day, 16 Nov.). In this chapel are the tombs of Cardinal Wiseman (1802–65) and Cardinal Manning (1808–92), the first two archbishops of Westminster, both of whom were originally buried at Kensal Green.

3. SOUTH-WESTERN ENGLAND

Abbotsbury Abbey, Dorset

On B3157, between Weymouth and Bridport.

The most substantial remains at Abbotsbury are those of the magnificent stone barn, at 270ft long by 30ft wide one of the largest in England, and built about 1400. The roof is later (17C), and is still largely thatched. Founded in the 11C by the Benedictines, Abbotsbury was destroyed at the Dissolution, and little remains, apart from a portion of the N wall of the church, which lay S of the present parish church.

Today, Abbotsbury is best known for its swannery, which lies off a by-road S of the abbey. First mentioned at the end of the 14C, it consists of a large pond, roughly square in shape. An estimated 800 birds live and breed there.

Abbot's Fish House, Meare, Somerset

On B3151, 3 miles NW of Glastonbury.

This graceful little stone building, isolated in the middle of a field, was built about 1330, and was used by the abbots of Glastonbury either for storing and drying fish, or as the house of the official in charge of the mere or 'meare' after which the village gets its name. In the 16C the largest of the fish lakes was calculated at 1 mile long and ¾ mile wide.

Bath Abbey, Avon

Ded: St Peter and St Paul.

The last of the great pre-Reformation churches, Bath Abbey stands in the centre of the town, near the Roman Baths and the Pump Room. It is a cruciform building, in a consistent late Perp style, with a central tower 162ft high, and oblong in shape, due to the fact that the crossing is considerably wider N-S than it is long E-W. Its most unusual and fascinating feature is the W front, which has a magnificent window, seven lights wide, flanked by turrets on which are carved ladders with angels ascending and descending.

History. Known to the Romans as Aquae Sulis (after a local deity called Sul), Bath had an elaborate system of bath houses built round its hot springs soon after the Romans conquered Britain in the 1C. The town was captured in 577 by the Saxons, who called it Hat Bathu ('at the baths'); in 676 Osric, a local king, endowed a religious foundation which was both a monastery and nunnery combined. By the 10C Bath had become so important that Edgar was crowned King of England there in 973, and little more than a century later the Normans began to build a cathedral on the site of the abbey church. Little of the Norman building, begun by Bp John de Villula, now remains, apart from an arch in the SE corner of the present building, which led from the Norman S aisle to the S transept. Bp de Villula transferred the seat of the bishopric from Wells (see below) to Bath; in the 13C the title of 'Bishop of Bath and Wells' was ratified by the Pope; and the rivalry between the two places finally came to an end in 1539, when Bath Abbey was dissolved and Wells became the only bishopric in Somerset (though the bishop continued to use the double name).

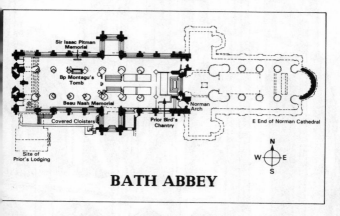

BATH ABBEY

After de Villula's death in 1122 the abbey gradually fell into decay, punctuated by occasional repair works. In 1499 Bp Oliver King began a completely new church on the site, on a far smaller scale: the present E end is where the W arch of the Norman crossing once stood, making the present building little more than half the length of de Villula's cathedral. Bp King was inspired to begin the rebuilding by the vision of angels commemorated on the W front; he was a friend of Henry VII, and had as his architects the king's master masons, the brothers Robert and William Vertue. The Dissolution delayed the completion of the church, which was not finally consecrated until 1616. The interior was largely restored by Sir Gilbert Scott in 1864–74, and further extensive restoration took place in the 1950s.

Interior. The spacious church is remarkable for the size and number of its windows, which have earned for it the title of 'Lantern of the West'. The glass is nearly all modern; there is no triforium; and the clerestory windows are unusually high. The fan-tracery roof is very fine: the Vertues promised Bp King vaulting of such quality that 'ther shal be noone so goodly in england nor in fraunce', and it lives up to their claim. There is no chancel screen to break the continuous majestic line of nave and choir. At the SE angle of the choir is the small chantry of Prior William Bird, begun in 1515 but completed only in recent years; it is notable for its carving. There are no big monuments, apart from the massive altar-tomb of Bp James Montagu

Bath Abbey, the N transept.

(d 1618), on the N side of the nave. Most of the smaller wall tablets commemorate the fashionable society who came to Bath to take the waters in the 18C.

Their uncrowned king, 'Beau' (James) Nash (d 1762), is commemorated by a tablet in the S aisle, which refers to him as *Bathoniae Elegantiae Arbiter* ('Bath's Arbiter of Elegance'). Among the other notables commemorated are: James Quin (d 1766), the Shakespearian actor and comedian, with a poem by David Garrick (N choir aisle); Sir Isaac Pitman (d 1897), inventor of modern shorthand; and Thomas Robert Malthus (d 1834), prophet of the population explosion (in porch).

The covered cloisters built against the S side of the nave were added in 1923.

Bindon Abbey, Dorset

Ded: St Mary.

On by-road E of the village of Wool, 4 miles W of Wareham.

On private property, and not open to the public.

Little is left of the ruins of Bindon, Dorset's only medieval Cistercian abbey, which was founded by Robert de Newburgh in 1172 in watermeadows by the River Frome. The ivy-clad lower stages of the W end of the monastic church survive, as do part of the chapter house and the undercroft of the dormitory. The outline of the cloister is still easy to follow.

The village of Wool was Thomas Hardy's Wellbridge, where Tess of the D'Urbervilles and Angel Clare passed their wedding night. Bindon Abbey features as the scene of the macabre nocturnal episode where the sleep-walking Clare lays Tess in 'the empty stone coffin of an abbot, in which every tourist with a turn for grim humour was accustomed to stretch himself'. The coffin is still to be seen in the ruined chancel.

Bristol Cathedral, Avon

Ded: Holy Trinity.

Originally the church of an abbey founded in 1140 for Augustinian canons by Robert Fitzhardinge, Provost of Bristol, Bristol Cathedral stands on the traditional site of Augustine's Oak, where St Augustine is said to have conferred with the British Christians in 603. It is a rare

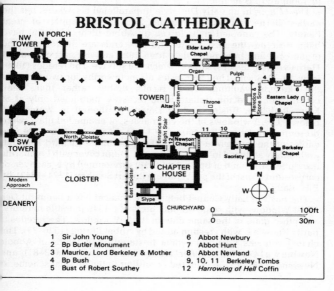

1   Sir John Young
2   Bp Butler Monument
3   Maurice, Lord Berkeley & Mother
4   Bp Bush
5   Bust of Robert Southey
6   Abbot Newbury
7   Abbot Hunt
8   Abbot Newland
9, 10, 11   Berkeley Tombs
12   *Harrowing of Hell* Coffin

example of a 'hall-church'—that is, the aisles, nave and choir are the same height, without triforium and clerestory, and the pier arches rise the full height of the building.

History. Of the Norman buildings, the chief relics are the chapter house and the two precinct gateways. The choir was rebuilt in 1298–1363, mainly by Abbot Knowle (1306–32), who connected his choir with the previously detached Elder Lady Chapel (c 1215), erected by Abbot David. The transepts were mainly rebuilt after 1463, on the model of the older work. The Norman nave, which was still being rebuilt in 1539 when the monastery was dissolved, was allowed to fall into ruin, and the church remained naveless until 1868–88 when the present nave, with its two W towers, was built by G.E Street, on the line of Knowle's choir, with slight modifications. The central tower dates from c 1450. After the Dissolution, the abbey church became the cathedral of the new see of Bristol, created in 1542. From 1836 to 1897, this see was united with that of Gloucester.

Interior. There are a number of remarkable features, notably the choir vault, which has no ridge-rib but centres instead on a series of open 'compartments' (though Street used the ridge-rib in his 19C nave); the star-shaped tomb-niches; and the unusual stonework used to carry the thrust from the centre of the building to the outer buttresses. At the W end of the Nave is the tomb of Sir John Young (d 1603) and his wife Joan, with the arms of Wadham College, Oxford, which was founded by her family. The N transept, with rich lierne vaulting probably due to Abbot Newland or Nailheart (1481–1515), contains a beautiful window and a monument to Bp Butler (d 1752), with an inscription by Southey. The *Elder Lady Chapel is pure EE in style, with Dec vaulting and E window and a beautiful arcade with grotesque carvings. On the S side is the tomb of the 9th Lord Berkeley (d 1368) and his mother.

The *Choir, in an early Dec style unparalleled elsewhere, has the earliest lierne vaulting in England, and foliage capitals of great beauty. The canopied stalls (given by Abbot Elyot, 1515–26) have been restored; the misericords and pew-ends are interesting. The organ case and front pipes date from 1685 and are part of Renatus Harris's organ, the best stops of which still survive. The reredos (1899) is by J.L. Pearson. The choir aisles are noteworthy for two features: the skeleton vaulting, which recalls timber rather than stone construction; and the stellate tomb-recesses, paralleled only at St Mary Redcliffe, Bristol, and St David's Cathedral in Wales (see below). The E windows of the choir aisles, of enamelled glass, were presented by Dean Glemham (1661–67). In the N choir aisle (the earlier of the two) are a tablet to the geographer Richard Hakluyt prebendary at Bristol in 1586–1616; a 13C coffin cover with Lombardic inscription; the tomb of Bp Bush (d 1558) surmounted by a 'cadaver' or corpse; and a bust of the poet laureate Robert Southey (1774–1843), by E.H. Baily.

The Eastern Lady Chapel behind the chancel has a beautiful Dec *East Window, with some original glass of c 1340 (notable heraldry) and other glass of the same date in the SW window. The reredos is partly Knowle's, with cresting added by Abbot Burton (1526–71). The chapel contains beautiful sedilia (restored), and tombs of Abbots Newbury (1428–73), builder of the tower, Hunt (1473–81) and Newland (1481–1515), coloured according to the original scheme. A tablet marks the grave of Bp Butler. In the S choir aisle, with Berkeley monuments in the tomb-recesses, is the beautiful Dec entrance to the monastic Sacristy, with detached vaulting and fine bosses, a recess for banner-staves, and a hearth for baking the sacramental bread. From it opens the Berkeley Chapel, which contains a gilt brass *Chandelier (1450); the only medieval candelabrum in England, it came from Bristol's Temple Church, destroyed by bombs in 1940. The entrance-arch is decorated with ammonites (fossils) and medlars. The Newton Chapel, entered from the W end of the S choir aisle, is late Dec in style and contains 17–18C tombs of the Newton family.

The S Transept, with a groined roof by Abbot Hunt (1473–81), contains a sculptured coffin lid (c 1000) of the Hereford School, found under the chapter house floor in 1831 and depicting the Harrowing of Hell. In the Norman S wall is the entrance to the night stair which descended from the monks' dorter.

A door in the W wall of the S transept leads to the scanty remains (restored) of the Cloisters (c 1480). Off the E walk (with fragments of old glass, documents etc) opens the *Chapter House*, a relic of Fitzhardinge's building, late Norman in style. Entered through a vaulted vestibule, it is rectangular, like other early chapter houses, and is enriched with zigzag and cable mouldings and interlaced arches. The E wall was rebuilt after a mob broke in during the 'Reform Riots' of 1831, when the library collection, kept in the chapter house, was destroyed. The series of vestries etc, built in 1923 as a memorial to H.O. Wills, the tobacco tycoon who founded Bristol University, occupy the site of the monastic dorter. The doorways of the slype and the day stair are preserved. At the end is the 14C doorway of the former bishop's palace (no adm.).

To the W of the cathedral, leading from College Green to College Square, is the late Norman Abbey Gateway, with receding orders enriched by zigzag mouldings. The upper part of the gate is Perp, by Abbot Elyot. In Cloister Court, to the left within the gate, a 13C gateway was the entrance to the Refectory, now part of the Cathedral School (refounded 1542); and lower down, in College Square, is another Norman gateway which led to the abbot's lodgings.

Buckfast Abbey, Devon

Ded: St Mary.

Off A38, on outskirts of Buckfastleigh.

Standing by the River Dart, on the southern edge of Dartmoor, Buckfast was founded by Canute in 1018; it soon fell into decay, and was refounded for the Cistercians by King Stephen in 1147. After the Dissolution in 1539 it was abandoned, until in 1882 a group of exiled French Benedictine monks colonized it once more and rebuilt it over the next half-century. Nothing remains of the original building but a 12C undercroft and the 14C Abbot's Tower. The present cruciform church (adm. daily), modelled on Kirkstall and Fountains, with a square central tower, was built by the monks with their own labour in 1907–38, on the old foundations. The dignified interior has a magnificent mosaic pavement; an altar and font modelled on German

Romanesque work; a giant candelabrum modelled on the one given by the Emperor Barbarossa to the Cathedral of Aix-la-Chapelle; and a bronze plaque by Benno Elkan to Abbot Anscar Vonier (d 1938), who was in charge of the rebuilding. The Blessed Sacrament Chapel, at the extreme E end of the church, is lit by glowing stained glass made in the abbey's own workshops.

Buckland Abbey, Devon

On minor road W of A386, 6 miles N of Plymouth.

Built in 1278 above the River Tavy, west of Dartmoor, by Cistercian monks, Buckland is now chiefly famous for its connection with Sir Francis Drake, who bought it in 1581 and lived there until his death in

Buckland Abbey, the crossing arch, filled in during the 16C to form the wall of a house. (K. Spence)

1596. In 1576 it had been converted into a country house by Sir Richard Grenville, who sold it to Drake. The house incorporates much of the monastic church, including the tower, and inside it is easy to see the Elizabethan and later additions to the medieval structure. Outside, the tower still shows the outline of the roof gable of the S transept; while the transept arch has been blocked in, to form part of the external wall of the house. The magnificent tithe barn, 160ft long and 40ft high, survives intact. The nearby village keeps its medieval name of Buckland Monachorum ('of the monks').

Cerne Abbas, Dorset

On A352, 7 miles N of Dorchester.

Well known for its turf-cut figure, the Cerne Giant, Cerne Abbas takes its name from the Benedictine monastery founded here towards the end of the 10C. The beautiful 15C gatehouse survives, together with a few other remains including a porch and some fragments of walling. The abbey church stood on the site of the present graveyard.

Christchurch Priory, Dorset

Now the longest parish church in England (312ft), this magnificent building gives its name to the town of Christchurch, which was formerly known as Twineham. The late 15C W tower is 120ft high, and offers a fine view from the top. There is beautiful Norman work (c 1090–1120) on the exterior of the N transept. We enter by the North Porch (c 1300), the largest in the country; under the tower is a monument to the poet Shelley by H. Weekes (1854). The *Nave, built by Bp Flambard of Durham about 1093, is a magnificent example of Norman architecture, especially the triforium; the clerestory is EE, and the vaulting is by William Garbett (1819). The aisles are Norman, re-cast in the 13C. The 14C rood-screen was radically restored in 1848. The Choir is for the most part late 15C; the stalls have fanciful misericords (1200–1500); but the chief feature is the superb stone *Reredos (Dec), representing the Tree of Jesse. Well worth looking at are the Chantry of the Countess of Salisbury (who was beheaded in 1541), the Lady Chapel (c 1405), St Michael's Loft, the Draper Chantry (1529) at the E end of the S aisle, and the typical sculptured monument by John Flaxman, commemorating Viscountess Fitzharris (d 1815). High up on the wall S of the Lady Chapel is the so-called 'miraculous beam', which was cut too short by a workman but lengthened the following night by divine agency.

Cleeve Abbey, Somerset

Ded: St Mary.

Off A39, just S of Washford.

Beautifully sited among water-meadows, the remains of Cleeve include a good deal of the monastic living quarters, excellently preserved. It was founded for Cistercian monks in about 1190, by

William, Earl of Roumare, and dissolved in 1537. The abbey is entered through a well-preserved gatehouse, built in the 13C but much altered later, especially in the 16C; the name of the last abbot, Abbot Dovell, is carved in stone above the entrance. Of the EE church, not much survives, apart from the S wall of the nave, and the S wall of the S transept. The cloister buildings give the visitor a clear idea of life in a small, fairly prosperous monastery. On the E side, the EE dorter range is virtually complete. On the ground floor are the sacristy, library, chapter house and parlour; above is the monks' dorter, lit by a long row of lancet windows. Much of the S range was built later, in the 15C; it consists of a row of small chambers on the ground floor, and the frater on the first floor, lit by graceful traceried windows, and with a superb timber roof. An upper room in this range has late 15C wall-paintings, including representations of St Catherine and St Margaret; while the gallery preserves an example of medieval caricature: the tonsured head of a monk, with the name 'Thomas' in Gothic script. Especially noteworthy at Cleeve are the fine doorways and tiled pavements.

Clifton Cathedral, Avon (RC)

Ded: St Peter and St Paul.

An uncompromisingly modern building of the early 1970s, this reinforced concrete cathedral is designed as an uninterrupted open space, with the congregation seated around the sanctuary. The plan is in the form of an irregular hexagon, and the decoration is austere, with little colour apart from the stained glass. The cathedral is largely lit from above, with light entering from the tall shafts which are an arresting feature of the external appearance.

Downside Abbey, Somerset

Ded: St Gregory the Great.

By A367, in Stratton-on-the-Fosse.

In 1793 a community of Benedictine monks, expelled by French Revolutionary forces from Douai in Flanders, took refuge in England, and in 1814 acquired the site at Downside. Here they established a boys' public school, and built the enormous neo-Gothic basilica, begun in 1874 and not completed until 1938. The original design was by Edward Hansom, but much of the work is by later architects, notably Sir Giles Gilbert Scott, who designed the nave. The interior, which is open to the public, contains a number of Old Master paintings, some fine examples of medieval wood carving, and modern works such as ceramic panels (1956) by Adam Kossowski. On the N side of the church is the shrine of St Oliver Plunkett, Archbishop of Armagh, the last Roman Catholic martyr to be executed for his beliefs, who died in 1681.

Edington Priory, Wiltshire

Off B3098, 4 miles E of Westbury.

On the northern edge of Salisbury Plain, Edington was probably the Saxon Ethandune, where c 878 King Alfred defeated the Danes. During the 1350s a priory of an order known as Bonshommes was established here, one of only two such houses in England. The Bonshommes were not monks, but regular clergy following the Augustinian rule. Their priory church, c 1350–70, survives little altered except for the addition of an early 16C choir screen, and is a beautiful example of the transition from Dec to Perp. Among the monuments are two from the abandoned church at Imber, now in the military zone of Salisbury Plain. An annual festival of church music is held at Edington in August.

Exeter Cathedral, Devon

Ded: St Peter.

One of the most attractive of all our cathedrals, Exeter is a comparatively small building, with nave and choir of almost equal lengths. It is mainly of the Geometric Dec period, built between about 1270 and 1370, with towers from the earlier Norman period.

History. Exeter was the Isca Dumnoniorum of the Romans, known to the Saxons as Escancestre. A monastery with a Saxon abbot existed there by 680. In 932 a conventual church was founded by Athelstan a little to the W of the cathedral; it was damaged by the Danes in 1003 and re-endowed by Canute in 1019. In 1050 the bishoprics of Devon and Cornwall were united, and the see was transferred from Crediton to Exeter, which was a walled city and hence more secure. The first bishop was Leofric (d 1072). The Saxon church was superseded by a Norman building (1112–1206); of this the only important remains are the massive twin towers, to which battlements and corner turrets were added in the 15C. The extension and transformation of the Norman church, starting from the E end, was begun c 1270 by Bp Bronescombe (d 1280) and was continued by Bps Quivil (d 1291), Bitton (d 1307), Stapeldon (d 1326) and Grandisson (d 1369). The W facade is decorated with sculptured figures, carved from soft Beer stone and greatly weathered. The central subject is the Coronation of the Virgin, or the Enthronement, flanked in the upper tier by Apostles, Evangelists, Patriarchs and Prophets, while in the lower tier the figures are kings, possibly the royal line of Judah. The lower figures appear to belong to the time of Bp Grandisson, but the upper figures are later (possibly late 15C). The numerous flying buttresses contrast effectively with the solid austerity of the Norman towers. The curfew is rung from the N Tower on 'Great Peter', a bell of over 4 tons.

Interior. The most striking characteristic is the uniformity of design, each detail marked by purity of style (Dec) and answering to its counterpart with unfailing symmetry. The unbroken stretch of vaulted roof, over 300ft in length and the longest continuous stretch of Gothic vaulting in the world, is a *tour de force*; and the roof bosses

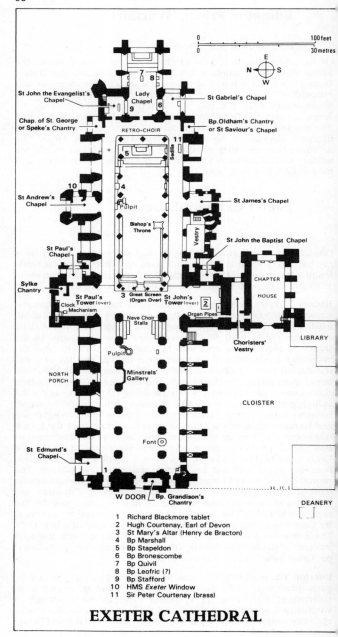

0   100 feet
0   30 metres

N E
W S

St John the Evangelist's Chapel

7 **8**

Lady Chapel

9 **6**

St Gabriel's Chapel

Chap. of St. George or Speke's Chantry

RETRO-CHOIR

Bp.Oldham's Chantry or St Saviour's Chapel

11

Sedilia

5

St Andrew's Chapel

10

4

Pulpit

St James's Chapel

Bishop's Throne

Vestry

St John the Baptist Chapel

St Paul's Chapel

Sylke Chantry

St Paul's Tower (over)

Clock Mechanism

3 Great Screen (Organ Over) **St John's Tower** (over)

2

Organ Pipes

CHAPTER HOUSE

LIBRARY

Nave Choir Stalls

Pulpit

Choristers' Vestry

NORTH PORCH

Minstrels' Gallery

CLOISTER

Font ⊙

St Edmund's Chapel

1

W DOOR **Bp. Grandison's** Chantry

DEANERY

1   Richard Blackmore tablet
2   Hugh Courtenay, Earl of Devon
3   St Mary's Altar (Henry de Bracton)
4   Bp Marshall
5   Bp Stapeldon
6   Bp Bronescombe
7   Bp Quivil
8   Bp Leofric (?)
9   Bp Stafford
10 HMS *Exeter* Window
11 Sir Peter Courtenay (brass)

EXETER CATHEDRAL

are of the highest quality. There is a lofty clerestory, but the triforium is represented by a small blank arcade. At the W end of the N aisle is the Chapel of St Edmund, dedicated to the Devonshire Regiment; adjoining it is a tablet to Richard Blackmore (1825–1900), author of *Lorna Doone*. To the S of the central door is a chapel constructed for Bp Grandisson (begun c 1360).

The most notable single feature of the *Nave*, with its fine Purbeck marble pillars, is the *Minstrels' Gallery (by Bp Grandisson) on the N side, with angels playing harp, bagpipe, trumpet, hand organ and other instruments. On the N wall near by are memorials to the cathedral's organists, including Samuel Sebastian Wesley (1810–76). Near the W end of the S wall is the sledging flag of Captain R.F. Scott (1868–1912), given by his mother in 1922.

The *Transepts*, with their beautiful window tracery and exquisite triforium gallery, were reconstructed by Bps Bronescombe and Quivil under the Norman towers. In the N transept are the Sylke Chantry, founded in 1508; a 15C wall painting of the Resurrection; a statue of the painter James Northcote (1746–1831) by Chantrey; and a fascinating 15C *Clock, which shows the Earth at the centre of the dial, with the Moon and the Sun revolving round it. The S transept contains the tomb of Hugh Courtenay, Earl of Devon (d 1377) and his wife. In the SW corner is the entrance to a vestry, beyond which is the Chapter House (EE and Perp; ceiling of 1465–78). The niches on the N and S sides of the chapter house are filled by a remarkable series of statues (1974), made of polyester resin, by the sculptor Kenneth Carter; the theme is that of creation through the Old and New Testaments, from Genesis to the Resurrection.

Exeter Cathedral Chapter House, with polyester statues by Kenneth Carter. (K. Spence)

The *Choir* is separated from the nave by a triple-arched stone screen erected by Bp Stapeldon (d 1326), with paintings of the 17C. Henry de Bracton or Bratton, who has been called the 'Father of English Common Law', was buried near here in 1268. Above the screen towers the magnificent organ case, made in 1665 by John Loosemore; the bass pipes of the organ are placed at a distance, in the S transept. Noteworthy monuments in the choir are those of Bp Marshall (d 1206) and Bp Stapeldon. The Stalls and Reredos are of the 19C, but the former have EE misericords, and the oaken *Bishop's Throne and stone Sedilia are exquisite works of the early 14C. The E window (Perp) contains glass of the 14C. Three of the small chapels opening off the choir aisles are closed by early 15C stone screens; the others have 16C screens. St James's Chapel (S), destroyed by a German bomb in May 1942, has been beautifully rebuilt; following medieval practice, the corbels, carved by George Down, the master mason after the War, are topical, and include a cat, a Rugby forward and a self-portrait of Mr Down. St Andrew's Chapel (N) has a memorial window (1948) to the men of HMS *Exeter*, sunk in the Java Sea in 1942. Bp Oldham's Chantry (1519), in the SE corner, is decorated with owls, in punning reference to the founder's name (presumably pronounced 'Owldham'). At the S side of the Lady Chapel entrance is a *Wall-painting of the Assumption and Coronation of the Virgin (c 1500).

The *Lady Chapel* is mainly of the time of Bps Bronescombe and Quivil, with four interesting episcopal tombs, notably the late 13C effigy of Bronescombe himself, intricately decorated, with the gilding and colour well restored. In a niche on the S side is a stone effigy, possibly that of Leofric (d 1072), the first Bp. A charming 15C woodcarving, representing the shepherds and their flocks at the time of the Nativity, was made by Devon craftsmen.

On the S side of the cathedral, part of the Cloister has been rebuilt in the original (Dec) style, to form a 'cloister room'. A wing of the Bishop's Palace (rebuilt) is occupied by the Cathedral Library (entrance in Palace Gate), which includes some Anglo-Saxon charters, the Exeter Domesday MS and the 10C 'Exeter Book of Poetry', a famous Anglo-Saxon collection. The former palace chapel (partly 13C) is now used as vestries.

Exeter, Devon: St Nicholas Priory

In a lane called The Mint, not far from the cathedral, the guest wing of a Benedictine priory has been turned into a small museum containing medieval and Tudor furniture and other artefacts. In 1070 a group of monks from Battle Abbey, in Sussex, founded a priory in Exeter; the original Norman undercroft survives, as does the kitchen (13C and 15C). On the first floor is the Guest-Hall (15C), where the prior would have entertained important guests; it retains its 15C oak screen. Next to it is the Prior's Solar, with considerable remains of Tudor plasterwork. In the garden is a 7C Celtic cross, attached for 200 years to a pier of the Exe bridge. The Mint takes its name from the small assay-furnaces formerly in the undercroft.

Forde Abbey, Dorset

Ded: St Mary.

On back road, 3 miles SE of Chard.

Privately owned, open May–Sept., Wed. and Sun. p.m.

Founded by the Cistercians in 1141, Forde lies in the depths of the countryside beside the River Axe. It is an intriguing combination of monastic and domestic architecture, and has been little altered since the mid 17C. The last of the abbots, Abbot Thomas Chard, who was in charge at the Dissolution in 1539, virtually reconstructed the medieval abbey in the new Tudor style, building the great hall, the ornate tower over the main entrance, and what remains of the cloister. Forde was turned into a country mansion by Edmund Prideaux, Attorney-General to Oliver Cromwell, who bought it in 1649, and during the next ten years built the grand staircase and a series of sumptuous state rooms.

The original abbey church, which has completely disappeared, stood S of the domestic buildings, where there is now a large lawn. The chief survival of medieval Forde is the long narrow 13C range, running N from the E corner of the abbey; this was originally the monks' dormitory, and was built above an undercroft. The vaulted 12C chapter house, on the E side of the cloister garth, is now a chapel.

Glastonbury Abbey, Somerset

At Glastonbury, ancient tradition and legend mix inextricably with fragmentary ruins, creating an atmosphere unique among the country's monastic remains. The abbey, entered by the Abbot's Gate in the market place, represents the earliest Christian foundation in England. Surviving the storms of Saxon, Danish and Norman conquest, it presents an unparalleled continuity of religious life.

According to the romantic legend, in about A.D. 60 St Joseph of Arimathea with 11 companions brought to Glastonbury the chalice of the Last Supper (or, according to another tradition, the phials that held the blood of the Crucifixion). Here, in the Druidic Isle of Avalon or

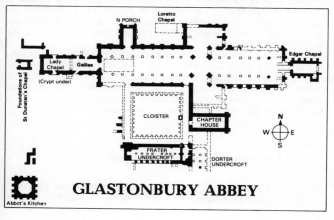

GLASTONBURY ABBEY

Ynyswytryn, the 'Blessed Isle', they were granted land by the British chief Arviragus and built the Vetusta Ecclesia ('old church'), a primitive building of wood and wattle. Refounded by Pope Eleutherius in 166, the settlement was visited by St Patrick (who according to one legend died here in 463) and by St Bridget (488). Larger churches, always carefully including the Vetusta Ecclesia, were built successively by Ine, King of the West Saxons, in 708; by St Dunstan (d 988), who was born and educated at Glastonbury; and by Thurstin and Herlewin, the first Norman abbots after the Conquest. Under Dunstan, who became abbot about 940 and introduced the Benedictine rule, the abbey became a centre of learning and gave England many great churchmen. The Saxon kings Edmund the Magnificent (d 946), Edgar (d 975) and Edmund Ironside (d 1016) were buried in this sacred spot. Until 1154, when precedence was given to St Albans, the mitred abbot of Glastonbury was the premier abbot of England. The remains of King Arthur and Queen Guinevere, reputed to have been discovered here in 1191, were reinterred in front of the high altar in 1276, in the presence of Edward I.

In 1184 the whole abbey, including the Vetusta Ecclesia, was burnt to the ground. Rebuilding was begun at once and was completed in 1303, except for a few later additions. The first part to be finished was the Lady Chapel (often called St Mary's Chapel), built on the site of the old wooden chapel and, so it is said, in strict fidelity to the ancient plan. The abbey was suppressed in 1539, when the last abbot, Richard Whiting, was executed on Glastonbury Tor, on a trumped-up charge. After the Reformation the buildings were neglected, and until about 1830 they were used by the local inhabitants as a stone-quarry. The ruins were bought for the Church of England in 1908.

Of the vast church, the sole remains are the two E piers of the central tower, with parts of the transeptal walls attached; one of the N transeptal chapels with groups of floor tiles; parts of the S aisle walls of the nave and choir; and the W door. This leads into the 13C Galilee or vestibule connecting the church with the *Lady Chapel (walls still standing), a jewel of late Romanesque architecture, with rich carvings and interlacing arcades. Beneath is a 15C Crypt connecting with a well of unknown antiquity. The length of the whole range of buildings was proved to be c 590ft by the discovery in 1909 of the apsidal Edgar Chapel, built by Abbot Bere, at the extreme E end. The foundations of St Dunstan's Chapel, at the extreme W, and of the N Porch and the Loretto Chapel (N side of nave) are marked on the ground, as are the sites of the Chapter House, Cloisters and the sub-vaults of the Refectory and Dormitory.

Within the abbey enclosure is the excellently preserved *Abbot's Kitchen (14C), which has a high octagonal stone roof and lantern, and contains display panels illustrating monastic life. In Bere Lane, to the NE, is the superb stone-built Abbot's Barn (late 14C), decorated with symbols of the Evangelists, and with a fine collarbeam roof. It now forms part of the Somerset Rural Life Museum.

Lacock Abbey, Wiltshire

Lacock is a unique amalgamation of three architectural periods—medieval monastic, Tudor and Gothic Revival. Founded in 1232 for

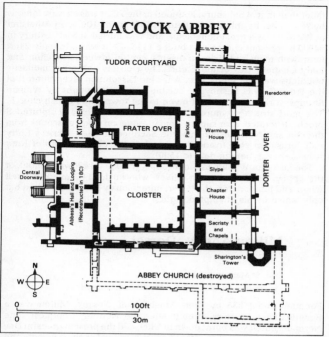

LACOCK ABBEY

TUDOR COURTYARD

Reredorter

KITCHEN

FRATER OVER

Parlour

Warming House

DORTER OVER

Central Doorway

Abbess's Hall and Lodging (Reconstructed in 18C)

Slype

Chapter House

CLOISTER

Sacristy and Chapels

Sharington's Tower

ABBEY CHURCH (destroyed)

N / W / E / S

0 ___ 100ft
0 ___ 30m

Augustinian canonesses by Ela, Countess of Salisbury, who was also
the first abbess, it was dissolved in 1539, when it was bought by Sir
William Sharington. Sharington kept very much to the medieval plan,
preserving the cloisters, turning the upper storey with its refectory
and dormitory into Tudor galleries, with rooms opening off them, and
building a tower at the SE corner of the abbey. The hall and
dining-room on the W side were built in the 1750s, in the 'Gothick'
style. The 13–14C cloisters are still largely complete, with good roof
bosses. The abbey church, which lay on the S side of the cloisters, has
disappeared, except for its N wall, which now forms the S wall of the
house. The medieval sacristy, chapter house and warming-house
survive on the E side of the cloister. A tombstone in the cloister is said
to be that of Ela, Countess of Salisbury (d 1261).

In the 1830s and '40s William Henry Fox Talbot, the owner of
Lacock, carried out some of the earliest photographic experiments
there. The superb medieval barn at the abbey gates is now a museum
illustrating the history of photography.

Malmesbury Abbey, Wiltshire

Ded: St Peter and St Paul.

Only the nave survives of Malmesbury's mighty Benedictine abbey
church, which was once of near-cathedral size, with a spire that was

taller than that of Salisbury. Founded in the 7C, it was already famous by 700, under its abbot St Aldhelm (d 709). In the 10C King Athelstan of Wessex was a great benefactor, and was buried at Malmesbury in 940. The present church was built c 1115–40; it was originally 240ft long, with nave and aisles, transepts, central tower, large choir and Lady Chapel (13C) at the E end. The cloisters and other monastic buildings were on the N side. After the Dissolution, everything E of the crossing was destroyed; but the nave was bought by William Stumpe, a rich clothier, and given to the town as its parish church. The most striking feature of the abbey is the richly sculptured S porch, decorated with superb Romanesque carvings of scenes from the Old and New Testaments (the Sacrifice of Isaac, Christ's Entry into Jerusalem etc). Inside the church is the alleged tomb of King Athelstan, very late in date (c 1500).

The historian William of Malmesbury (c 1090–1143) was a monk of the abbey, as was a certain Oliver, who in the 11C made himself wings and jumped from the tower; miraculously he was not killed but only lamed by his attempted flight.

Milton Abbey, Dorset

Ded: St Mary and St Michael.

On minor road off A354, 6 miles SW of Blandford.

Founded about 935 by King Athelstan of Wessex, Milton was a Benedictine monastery, rebuilt after the Norman Conquest. The Norman church was burnt down in 1309, and the present graceful Dec building was begun soon after. It consists only of choir, transepts and crossing, as the nave was never built; the Lady Chapel at the E end has disappeared. The pinnacled tower is later (15C). After the Dissolution the church became the parish church of Milton Abbas, but the village was destroyed by the Earl of Dorchester in the late 18C, and the church became the private chapel of his new country house, designed by Sir William Chambers. Chambers incorporated in the house the stately Abbot's Hall, late Gothic in style and dated 1498. Church and mansion now form a boys' public school.

Inside the church are a rich altar screen of 1492, an elaborate wooden tabernacle (15C), some medieval tiles, interesting tombs, and a brass (1565) of Sir John Tregonwell, who got possession of Milton after the Dissolution.

Muchelney Abbey, Somerset

2 miles S of Langport.

A Benedictine monastery, established about 700 by Ine, King of Wessex, Muchelney was the oldest monastic foundation in Somerset after Glastonbury. The large apsidal Norman church, later Lady Chapel and most of the monastic buildings have disappeared, apart from their foundations. What survives is the abbot's house, built in late Gothic style at the beginning of the 16C. This solid stone building shows the comfort in which Muchelney's abbot lived in the years before the Dissolution: it has a guest room with tall mullioned windows; the abbot's chamber or parlour, with a fireplace carved with stone lions; and a number of smaller rooms. Part of the S cloister walk survives on the N side of the house, as does the monks' reredorter, in a small building to the E.

Old Sarum Cathedral, Wiltshire

Ded: The Blessed Virgin Mary.

2 miles N of Salisbury, on A345.

Old Sarum, on a low chalk hill above the valley of the Wiltshire Avon, was the site successively of an Iron Age British hill-fort known to the Romans as Sorviodunum, of a Saxon town (Searoburh), and of a Norman fortress and cathedral. About 1078 the Normans transferred the bishopric of Sherborne to Sarum. The cathedral was begun by Bp Herman and continued by Bp St Osmund, whose Ordinal of Offices for the Use of Sarum (the 'Sarum Use') became the ritual of all South England until 1550; it was consecrated in 1092 and subsequently enlarged by Bp Roger, Osmund's successor. As completed by Roger about 1130, it had three towers (one over the crossing and a pair at the W end), wide transepts and S porch, with a cloister, bishop's palace and other buildings at its NE corner.

Friction between the bishop and the military authorities in the castle led to the transference of the see to Salisbury in 1219, where the new cathedral was begun the following year (see below). Among the reasons advanced for the transfer were the hostility of the garrison, the noise caused by the wind whistling round the cathedral, the scarcity of water, and the fact that 'the whiteness of the chalk causes blindness'. The cathedral at Old Sarum fell into decay, and it was finally razed in 1331 to provide building materials for Salisbury cathedral close. The foundations of the cathedral have been marked out on the site; these show that the E end of Bp St Osmund's church, which terminated in three apses, was greatly extended by Bp Roger, and by the middle of the 12C had been provided with straight outer walls.

Plymouth Cathedral, Devon (RC)

Ded: St Mary and St Boniface.

In Wyndham Street West.

The cathedral's needle-like, Gothic Revival spire, over 200ft high, is a landmark on the N side of the city. The building, designed by Joseph A. Hansom, was opened in 1858; its gaunt interior is dominated by a huge hanging crucifix. In the S transept is a brass to Bp William Vaughan (1814–1902), the cathedral's first bishop.

St Germans Priory, Cornwall

5 miles W of Saltash, 1 mile S of A38.

An immediately arresting church, with its oddly matched pair of W towers, one square and one octagonal, St Germans has its origins in the earliest days of Christianity in Cornwall. Until the 9C, the Cornish church was independent of the Saxon church established elsewhere in England, and it was not until c 830 that Cornwall was subdued by the Saxon King Egbert. In 926 King Athelstan set up a Cornish diocese, with St Germans as its cathedral; the Cornish bishopric lasted until 1050, when Bp Leofric, who was bishop of the joint sees of Cornwall and Crediton, moved his cathedral to Exeter (see above).

During this period there was a secular canonry attached to St Germans; but in the 12C this was turned into a priory of Augustinian canons. They pulled down the old Saxon church, and c 1160 began the Norman church of which a good deal still survives. The most striking of the Norman remains is the superb W door, with seven concentric arches of decoration, much eroded by the weather. The towers were completed after the main body of the building; the octagonal N tower is 13C, while the S tower is 15C Perp. Inside, the Norman arches under the towers survive, together with Trans arches in the S aisle. The Norman N aisle was demolished in 1802. Alterations were made in the 14C, when the E end of the S aisle was rebuilt in Dec style, and in the 15C, when there was considerable Perp rebuilding, including the porch on the S side. After the Dissolution, the choir fell into decay and a new E wall was built, utilizing the magnificent E window from the old choir. The glass in the E window is by Burne-Jones. The priory buildings have disappeared; they were N of the church, on the site now occupied by the house called Port Eliot.

St Germans Priory, an 18C engraving by S. and N. Buck.

St Michael's Mount, Cornwall

In Mount's Bay, 3 miles E of Penzance.

One of the landmarks of the southern coast of Cornwall, St Michael's Mount is a steep 200ft outcrop of slate and granite that looks like a smaller version of Mont St Michel, in Normandy. It is connected to the shore by a 500yd causeway, uncovered at low tide for 3 hours. The Mount has been identified with the island known to the Greeks and Romans as Ictis, from which tin was exported to the Mediterranean. Its connection with Christianity began in 495, when some fishermen saw the Archangel Michael standing on a rock high above the sea. Two early Celtic saints, St Keyne and her nephew St Cadoc, have legendary associations with the Mount. In 1047 King Edward the Confessor established a chapel here, placing it under the Benedictine abbey of Mont St Michel. Between c 1135 and 1150 Abbot Bernard of Mont St Michel built a priory on the Mount; the church was destroyed by an earthquake in 1275 and rebuilt in the 14C. Fortified during the Middle Ages, the Mount was much fought over in the Wars of the Roses and the Civil War. In 1659 it was bought by the St Aubyn family, who turned the priory and fortifications into a private house.

The priory remains include the refectory (now the 'Chevy Chase Room'), the small church, and the Lady Chapel (converted in the 18C into Gothic Revival drawing-rooms).

Salisbury Cathedral, Wiltshire

Ded: The Blessed Virgin Mary.

Salisbury's majestically elegant spire, rising above the water-meadows beside the Avon, is still very much as John Constable painted it, and is the perfection of English cathedral architecture. The most striking approach is through St Ann's Gate, which leads to the N Walk of the precincts and gives us our first complete view from the NE. The tranquil *Close, with its spacious expanse of grass, noble trees and dignified old houses, forms a charming setting for the great church. The Avon marks the W limit of the precincts, the other three sides being bounded by a wall built in the 14C of stone from Old Sarum (see above). At the SW angle is Harnham Gate, and to the NW is the North or High Street Gate.

History. The cathedral was begun by Bp Richard Poore in 1220 on land he himself owned, and consecrated in 1258 by Bp Giles de Bridport. As mentioned under Old Sarum, the cathedral there had become untenable by about 1200, and the bishop and clergy were only too pleased to leave that bleak upland site, to 'descend joyfully to the plains, where the valley abounds in corn, where the fields are beautiful and where there is freedom from oppression' (from the papal bull authorizing the change of site). Alone among English cathedrals, it is of uniform design (EE), for though the graceful spire (at 404ft the loftiest in England) was the daring addition of a century later (c 1320), it is the consummation of the original pyramidal conception. The building was supervised by Elias de Dereham, a canon of the cathedral, while the master mason was Nicholas of Ely. The apex of the spire is 2½ft out of the perpendicular, and the immense weight of the stonework of tower and spire (more than 6,400 tons) puts such a strain on the four bearing columns that they are slightly bent. A traditional rhyme claims that:

> As many days in one year there be,
> So many windows in this church we see.
> As many marble pillars here appear
> As there are hours throughout the fleeting year.
> As many gates as moons one year does view—
> Strange tale to tell! yet not more strange than true.

Exterior. Perfectly proportioned, restrained in ornament, of exquisitely precise workmanship, built of material so well chosen that seven centuries have merely added a little beauty of tint to the stone (from the Chilmark quarry, 12 miles from Salisbury), Salisbury Cathedral is a classic of architecture. It expresses the renewal of national spirit realized in the 13C, and its square E end, following the model of the later church at Old Sarum (one of the earliest instances of the departure from the Norman tradition of the apsidal end), became the norm for future English choirs. The W front, contemporary with the spire, seems to have been intended to present a great drama of sculpture (compare Exeter, above, and Wells, below); its present sculptures, representing the 'Te Deum', are mid 19C. The detached bell-tower, similar to that still in existence at Chichester (see above), which stood about 200ft N of the nave, was removed in the 18C by James Wyatt. Salisbury was not a monastic foundation, and so it never had any of the ancillary monastic buildings associated with most other cathedrals. The cloisters and chapter house were built c 1260–80. The administration of Salisbury followed rules laid down by St Osmund, bishop at Old Sarum, towards the end of the 11C: the cathedral was run by a Brotherhood of Canons, led by four *Personae* (the Dean, the Precentor, the Chancellor and the Treasurer).

Interior. In spite of its fine proportions and the harmony of its design, the interior is less satisfying than the exterior. The chilliness of effect has been increased by the ruthless way in which Wyatt (1788–89) removed screens and chapels and rearranged the monuments in tidy rows. The restoration, begun by Sir Gilbert Scott in 1859, has tried to minimize the damage done by Wyatt, and recent repainting of the tombs has restored some colour to the aisles. Colour has also been added by new embroideries, altar frontals and hangings in various parts of the cathedral. The usual entrance is by the N porch.

The *Nave* is divided into ten bays by clustered columns of polished Purbeck marble. The fine triforium has characteristic EE plate tracery. In the W triple lancet window is a patchwork of 13–15C glass, some of it from Dijon; and the 3rd window from the W in the S aisle contains a 14C *Tree of Jesse. At the W end of the aisles is some 13C grisaille glass of lovely quality. The *Clock Movement at the W end of the N aisle, probably the oldest surviving mechanism in Europe (c 1386), was restored to working order in 1956. Nearly above it hang colours of the Wiltshire Regiment.

Among the monuments may be mentioned the following (beginning at the W end of the S aisle). Oldest monument in the church, brought from Old Sarum (possibly Bp Herman, d 1078). Bp Roger of Old Sarum (d 1139). Bp Jocelin of Old Sarum (d 1184). Bp Beauchamp

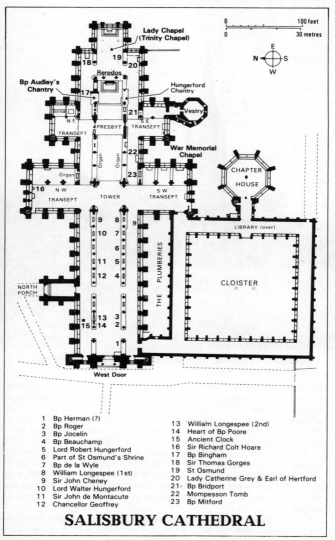

1 Bp Herman (?)
2 Bp Roger
3 Bp Jocelin
4 Bp Beauchamp
5 Lord Robert Hungerford
6 Part of St Osmund's Shrine
7 Bp de la Wyle
8 William Longespee (1st)
9 Sir John Cheney
10 Lord Walter Hungerford
11 Sir John de Montacute
12 Chancellor Geoffrey
13 William Longespee (2nd)
14 Heart of Bp Poore
15 Ancient Clock
16 Sir Richard Colt Hoare
17 Bp Bingham
18 Sir Thomas Gorges
19 St Osmund
20 Lady Catherine Grey & Earl of Hertford
21 Bp Bridport
22 Mompesson Tomb
23 Bp Mitford

SALISBURY CATHEDRAL

(d 1482). Robert, Lord Hungerford (d 1459, elaborate effigy). Base of the 13C Shrine of St Osmund (the holes are the foramina or kneeling-holes for sick pilgrims). Bp de la Wyle (d 1271). William Longespée (d 1226), 1st Earl of Salisbury and son of Henry II (the earliest English military effigy, once brilliantly coloured). Crossing to the N aisle. *Sir John Cheney (d 1509), a gigantic knight of the bodyguard of Henry VII, who fought at Bosworth against Richard III.

Salisbury Cathedral, soaring above water-meadows beside the Avon. (A.F. Kersting)

Walter, Lord Hungerford (d 1449), a hero of Agincourt, and his wife. Sir John de Montacute (d 1390), a hero of Crécy, wearing elaborate gauntlets. Chancellor Geoffrey (d 1558). William Longespée, 2nd Earl of Salisbury, killed by the Saracens near Cairo (1250). Diminutive effigy, traditionally that of a 'boy bishop' but now thought to be a heart shrine, probably that of Bp Poore (d 1237).

The *W Transepts* resemble the nave; the Perp arches at the crossing were inserted by Bp Beauchamp (1450–81) to strengthen the original arches against the lateral thrust of the tower and spire. In the NW arm are a 14C cope-chest, and a bust of Richard Jefferies (1848–87), the Wiltshire-born naturalist and writer; in the SW arm is a war memorial chapel.

In general design the *Choir* and *Presbytery* differ little from the nave; they suffered from the drastic clearing of Wyatt, who was intent on obtaining a vista from end to end of the church. The paintings on the vault are repaintings (c 1870) of defaced 13C originals. The stalls have been freely restored. The throne is by Scott, but most of his furnishings were replaced in 1959 by Lord Mottistone. In front of the altar are buried the Earls of Pembroke. On the N side of the 2nd bay from the E is the fine late Perp Chantry of Bp Audley, and opposite it is the Hungerford Chantry (c 1429), an important example of early ironwork.

In the *NE Transept* are portions of the original screen (13C) and the unusual 14C •Brass of Bp Wyville (d 1375), over 7ft long and showing the bishop in a fortified tower. In the aisle, near Audley's chantry, is the cenotaph of Bp Bingham (d 1246), and further E is the lavish monument to Sir Thomas Gorges (d 1610) and his wife. The lancet window behind, with glass by Christopher Webb, commemorates the poet George Herbert (1593–1633).

The *Lady Chapel* (more correctly the Trinity Chapel, as the whole cathedral is dedicated to Our Lady) was completed in 1225 and was the first part of the building to be finished. It is divided into nave and aisles by graceful clustered shafts and slender single pillars; some of the glass is 13C and 14C. The lancets at the E end contain glowing modern glass (1980) made by Gabriel Loire, of Chartres, commemorating Prisoners of Conscience in the 20C. In the centre of the chapel stood the Shrine of St Osmund (d 1099), Bp of Old Sarum; his grave-slab, on the S side, marks the spot where his body was first reburied after the building of the cathedral. At the E end of the S aisle is the imposing monument of Edward, Earl of Hertford (d 1621) and his wife Lady Catherine (d 1568), sister of Lady Jane Grey. Also in the S choir aisle are the finely sculptured tomb of Bp Bridport (d 1262) and the brightly painted Mompesson tomb (1627); two windows here are of the Pre-Raphaelite school, and in the SE transept is some 13C grisaille glass. The tomb of Bp Mitford (d 1407), further W, also has some delicate sculpture.

From the SW transept we enter the well-preserved •*Cloisters* (c 1270), begun by Bp de la Wyle, unusually large for a non-monastic church, which are separated from the cathedral itself by a passage known as the Plumberies. Above the E side is the Library, built in 1445. It contains almost 200 ancient MSS, including an Anglo-Saxon liturgy with finely drawn capitals, and a late 11C St Augustine, perhaps written by St Osmund. There is also a collection of early scientific books collected by Bp Seth Ward (d 1689), who was a founder member of the Royal Society, and called in Sir Christopher Wren to advise on repairs to the cathedral. The octagonal •Chapter House, 52ft high, entered from the E walk, was built a little after the cloisters. Above the niches of the seats is a frieze of fine late 13C sculpture, illustrating scenes from Genesis and Exodus, including the Six Days of Creation and the Giving of the Ten Commandments. Many of the cathedral's treasures are on display in the chapter house, including one of the four original copies of Magna Carta, documents and books from the archives and library, and silver lent by parishes in the diocese.

The walled close is calm and spacious, with some superb buildings, among them •Mompesson House (National Trust), which has fine panelling and exquisite interior decoration, and the old Bishop's Palace (13–18C), now the Cathedral School. Just south of the close, towards Harnham Bridge, is St Nicholas' Hospital, said to be the original of Hiram's Hospital in Anthony Trollope's *The Warden*.

Shaftesbury Abbey, Dorset

Open Easter–Sept. only.

Dramatically sited on a spur 700ft high, Shaftesbury is one of the oldest towns in England. In 880 King Alfred founded an abbey for Benedictine nuns, which in the Middle Ages was the largest and richest nunnery in England. Hardly anything survives of this great establishment; the church plan can be followed on the ground, but the cloisters and other monastic buildings have disappeared. The empty tomb of King Edward the Martyr, murdered in 978, was found in 1861 on the N side of the altar, and in 1931 a casket was unearthed near by containing bones which may be those of Edward, whose relics were kept at Shaftesbury and highly venerated. There is a small museum on the site.

Sherborne Abbey, Dorset

Ded: The Blessed Virgin Mary.

This magnificent church, the largest in Dorset, is as much a historical document in stone as a noble building. As it now stands, it is one of the finest extant examples of the Perp style, but there are considerable remains of earlier periods incorporated in it. In 705 King Ine of Wessex established a new bishopric at Sherborne, and appointed St Aldhelm, Abbot of Malmesbury, as the first bishop. This Saxon bishopric (divided in 909 into the sees of Crediton and Wells) lasted until after the Norman Conquest, when in 1078 the bishop's seat was transferred to Old Sarum (see above). An abbey was attached to the cathedral from early times, occupied first by secular canons, then, after 998, by Benedictine monks. From the Conquest until the Dissolution in 1539 the church was a monastic building; and since 1539 it has been the parish church.

Remains of the Saxon church can still be seen at the W end, where an 11C doorway is preserved, and in the four piers that support the crossing. After 1122 this building was largely demolished, and a Norman church built in its place; of this, there survive the S porch, the crossing archway and considerable amounts of the N and S transepts. The Lady Chapel and further additions followed in the 13C; then, in the 15C, came an almost total rebuilding in Perp style, beginning with the choir and continuing with the nave, both of which have fan vaulting of exceptional richness. Meanwhile, late in the 14C, the parish church of All Hallows had been added at the W end in early Perp style. Having parishioners and monks under one roof led to conflict, culminating in 1437 when the priest of All Hallows set the monks' part of the church on fire. All Hallows itself was demolished in the 1540s; the lower courses of its N wall can still be seen to the W of the church. A further alteration took place in 1560, when the E bays, including the Lady Chapel, were turned into a house for the headmaster of Sherborne School, complete with fireplaces and domestic-looking windows.

Inside the church, the most notable feature is the superb 15C fan vaulting. There are a number of striking monuments. In the Wykeham Chapel, off the N transept, is the tomb of Sir John Horsey (d 1546), who sold the church to the town at the Dissolution, and of his son (d 1564); and in the N transept a stone marks the probable grave of the poet Sir Thomas Wyatt (d 1542). The 13C Lady Chapel was restored and enlarged by W.D. Caroë in 1921–34; the engraved glass reredos, by Laurence Whistler (1968), depicts the symbolic attributes of the Virgin Mary. The ambulatory W of the Lady Chapel is dedicated to the Dorset Regiment. In the S transept is the vast Baroque memorial (1698), by John Nost, to John Digby, 3rd Earl of Bristol, and his two wives; while St Katherine's Chapel, on the W side, contains the imposing tomb to John Leweston (d 1584), and some good 15C heraldic glass. The peal of eight bells in the tower is said to be the heaviest in the world: the average weight is just under 1 ton.

Stogursey Priory, Somerset

Ded: St Andrew.

N of A39, 3 miles N of Nether Stowey.

Only the Norman church survives of this Benedictine priory, which was founded c 1075, soon after the Conquest. Long and narrow, and without aisles, it has a splendid Norman arch at the crossing. The apsidal E end was rebuilt on a much grander scale in the late 12C, with the transepts continued E, forming side chapels. In 1414 the priory's revenues were sequestered to the Crown by Henry V and in 1440 they were given to Eton College. Thereafter, the priory church became the parish church. There is a Norman font in the N transept chapel, and a number of good memorials in the Verney Chapel opposite.

Stoke-sub-Hamdon Priory, Somerset

1 mile W of Montacute, just N of A3088.

In 1304 John de Beauchamp founded a collegiate chantry for a provost and four chaplains, whose duty was to offer masses for the souls of members of the Beauchamp family. The private chapel in which they officiated has long since disappeared. The surviving buildings date from the 15C; they include a great hall and screens passage (passage between kitchen and hall), with a bay opening off it. (This is the only section open to the public, as the rest is privately occupied). Associated with the domestic buildings are two barns, an open shed and a circular dovecote, making an attractive medieval picture. The chantry survived the Dissolution of the Monasteries, but was finally suppressed under Edward VI in 1548.

Tavistock Abbey, Devon

Ded: St Mary and St Rumon.

Between 974 and 981 Ordulf, Earl of Devon, built a large Benedictine monastery on the western edge of Dartmoor, beside the fast-flowing

River Tavy. Burnt by the Danes in 997, it was soon rebuilt on a grander scale; during the Middle Ages its lands included the whole of the Scilly Isles, and it was famous for the relics of St Rumon, a 7C Irish missionary. The present remains are of the 12C and later; they are hard to trace, as most of the buildings, including the abbey church, were demolished after the Dissolution, and only fragments remain. The most substantial of these is the battlemented wall on the S side, beside the Tavy; the pinnacled Court Gate (12C with 15C additions); and the so-called Abbey Chapel, which was the monks' Misericord, or dining-hall for the sick. The cloisters have disappeared under the Plymouth Road, apart from one EE arch now half-buried in the parish churchyard. The Bedford Hotel stands roughly on the site of the chapter house. On the W side is the gateway to the abbot's lodging, known as Betsy Grimbal's Tower; below it is a sarcophagus, possibly that of Ordulf, founder of the abbey.

Torre Abbey, Torquay, Devon

Standing a short way back from Torquay's sea-front, Torre is one of the few English abbeys built beside the sea. It was established in 1196 for Premonstratensian canons. Dissolved in 1539, it was saved from complete decay in the 18C, when it was partly turned into a country house; it is now an art gallery run by the Torquay Corporation. Of the original buildings, built round the cloister garth, the W side (abbot's apartments) and S side (refectory) are still largely intact. Little of the church (on the N side) survives, apart from large blocks of masonry from the fallen central tower, and sections of the chancel and S transept. The lidless stone tomb in the chancel is probably that of William de Brewer (d 1232), son of the founder of the abbey. The fine Norman doorway, with windows on either side, originally led from the cloister garth to the chapter house. There is a spacious undercroft below the abbot's apartments. The massive gatehouse was built c 1330, and the nearby tithe barn dates from soon after the foundation of the abbey in 1196. Nicknamed the 'Spanish Barn', from the prisoners kept there in 1588 after the Spanish Armada, it has been converted into a theatre.

Tresco Abbey, Scilly Isles

Only a few walls remain of the priory, founded at Tresco in 964 and attached to Tavistock Abbey. They now form a backcloth for the climbing and hanging plants of Tresco's famous Abbey Gardens.

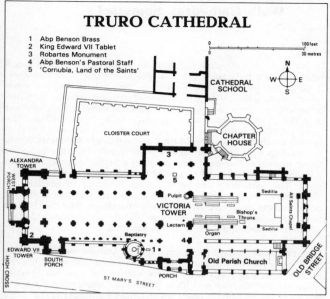

TRURO CATHEDRAL

1 Abp Benson Brass
2 King Edward VII Tablet
3 Robartes Monument
4 Abp Benson's Pastoral Staff
5 'Cornubia, Land of the Saints'

CATHEDRAL SCHOOL

CLOISTER COURT

CHAPTER HOUSE

ALEXANDRA TOWER

WEST PORCH

Pulpit

VICTORIA TOWER

Lectern

Baptistry

EDWARD VII TOWER

SOUTH PORCH

Sedilia

Bishop's Throne

Organ

Sedilia

All Saints Chapel

PORCH

Old Parish Church

OLD BRIDGE STREET

ST MARY'S STREET

HIGH CROSS

Truro Cathedral, Cornwall

Ded: The Blessed Virgin Mary.

The centre of Truro is dominated by this spiky, Gothic Revival building with its three spires, which has been compared with 'a great church in Brittany rather than Britain'. Until 1877 Cornwall formed part of the bishopric of Exeter, but in that year it became a separate diocese (in spite of the earlier opposition of Mr Gladstone, who saw no reason for the change, 'bearing in mind the greatly increased facilities recently created of communication by the penny post, and of moving from one part of the country to another by the railroad, that render it easier now than formerly for a bishop to look after a diocese of large extent'). The architect chosen was J.L. Pearson, who designed a building in uniform EE style; the foundation stone was laid in May 1880, and the building was consecrated in 1887. The two western towers, named after King Edward VII and Queen Alexandra, were completed in 1910, while the cloisters and chapter house were built in 1935–67. The cathedral stands largely on the site of Truro's 16C parish church, whose graceful S aisle was incorporated in the new building, where it now forms the S choir aisle. The enormously tall circular *Baptistry, beside the S transept, is a memorial to the missionary Henry Martin (1781–1812), who was born in Truro. In the N aisle is a tablet to Sir Arthur Quiller-Couch (1868–1944), known as 'Q', the writer and anthologist. In the N transept, a large panoramic painting, 'Cornubia, Land of the Saints', by John Miller, shows all of Cornwall's 248 churches; this was unveiled by Prince Charles as Duke of Cornwall on 20 May 1980, to commemorate the centenary of the laying of the foundation stone.

Wells Cathedral, Somerset

Ded: St Andrew.

In Wells, town, cathedral and bishop's palace form a harmonious whole, closely integrated yet clearly separate one from the other. Beyond the moat on the S side of the palace lies the open countryside, while N of the cathedral are the soberly dignified houses of the clergy, now occupied by the cathedral school, together with the unique street of small buildings called Vicars' Close. The close (at Wells not called by this name but known as Cathedral Green) is reached from the Market Place through Penniless Porch, where alms were once distributed. However, the entrance in Sadler Street known as Browne's Gate provides a better approach, as then the whole astonishing W facade of the cathedral bursts upon the view. The cathedral, one of the most beautiful in England, is complete in all its parts. As it was not a monastic foundation, it never had the usual ancillary monastery buildings; thus the cloisters have no buildings opening off them, not even the chapter house, which is on the opposite side of the cathedral.

History. Tradition says that a church of St Andrew was founded by King Ine of Wessex c 705 near the springs which have given the city its name. In 909 Wells became the seat of the new bishopric of Somerset, but Bp John de Villula (1088–1122) transferred the see to the walled town of Bath (see above). Under Bp Savary (1192–1205) the title of the see was 'Bath and Glastonbury'. Bp Jocelin (1206–42) returned to Wells and in 1219 surrendered the claim to Glastonbury, retaining the title 'Bath'. His successors ever since 1244 have been bishops of 'Bath and Wells', and the monks of Bath and the canons of Wells had equal voices in the election of bishops until the suppression of Bath Abbey in 1539.

The present cathedral was begun under Bp Reginald de Bohun (1174–91) c 1180. The three W bays of the choir, the transepts and the E bays of the nave were probably finished soon after 1200. The N porch was built in the time of Bp Jocelin, who also saw completed the nave, and the famous W front designed by Thomas Norreys (fl 1229–49). The church was consecrated in 1239. To the Dec style belong the chapter house (c 1290–1306), with its staircase and earlier undercroft (begun c 1230, work resumed 1286), and the central tower, built to its present height in 1321, but probably topped by a lead-covered wooden spire, burnt down in 1438. The present 'Lady Chapel behind the high altar' (as it was called to distinguish it from an earlier 'Lady Chapel next to the cloister'), the three E bays of the choir, and the retrochoir were rebuilt under Dean Godelee and completed c 1325. The Perp W towers, probably designed by William de Wynford (d 1405), were largely paid for by two bishops: Bp Harewell (d 1386), the SW tower, in his lifetime; Bp Bubwith (d 1424), the NW tower, by legacy. The cathedral suffered from Puritan vandalism and from damage done by Monmouth's West Country rebels in 1685. Restoration was carried out in the 19C by Benjamin Ferrey (1842), who substituted Kilkenny marble for the blue lias shafts on the W front, and by Anthony Salvin, who restored the choir in 1848–54. In 1975 the W facade was covered in scaffolding, so that many of the statues could be preserved by 'lime-poulticing', and the masonry could be repointed and replaced where decayed. The work is due to be completed by 1986–87.

Exterior. The ˙˙W *facade*, of pure EE work, can challenge the finest French facades such as those at Reims and Amiens. The W towers, Perp in their upper parts, are not continuations of the aisles but—unusually for England—stand out beyond them. The result is a vast screen, 147ft wide and divided vertically by six buttresses, which provides the framework for an astonishing display of stone-carving. The superb ˙˙Statues and exquisite sculptural detail were created by a local school of craftsmen. There were originally over 400 figures in full colour, a summing-up of sacred and profane history, carried in six tiers across the whole facade and round the sides of the W towers. Over 300 remain, about half of them life-size or larger, to form the finest collection of medieval sculpture in England. The statues have suffered from weather and iconoclasm, and identification in many cases is doubtful. In the tympanum above the main doorway are the

Wells Cathedral, two of the three scissors arches built to strengthen the crossing. (K. Spence)

seated Virgin and Child; in the niche above, the Coronation of the Virgin. In the gable are the nine orders of angels, the 12 Apostles and the Saviour (highest of all, the figure mutilated).

On the N side of the nave, the Gothic walls have an elegant Dec parapet (c 1326) and Perp window tracery. The *North Porch was built c 1206–08. The capitals on the E side are exquisitely carved with the Martyrdom of St Edmund. Outside the N transept, which is similar in style, is the 19C replacement dial of the 14C clock (see below), with two *Figures in armour striking the quarters with their battle-axes, probably the oldest clock-jacks in the country (c 1475).

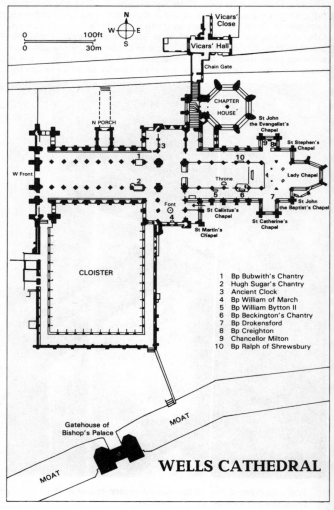

0   100ft
0   30m

Vicars' Close
Vicars' Hall
Chain Gate
CHAPTER HOUSE
St John the Evangelist's Chapel
St Stephen's Chapel
N PORCH
Lady Chapel
Throne
St John the Baptist's Chapel
W Front
Font
St Calixtus's Chapel
St Catherine's Chapel
St Martin's Chapel

CLOISTER

1   Bp Bubwith's Chantry
2   Hugh Sugar's Chantry
3   Ancient Clock
4   Bp William of March
5   Bp William Bytton II
6   Bp Beckington's Chantry
7   Bp Drokensford
8   Bp Creighton
9   Chancellor Milton
10   Bp Ralph of Shrewsbury

Gatehouse of Bishop's Palace
MOAT
MOAT

WELLS CATHEDRAL

The Chain Gate, an elegant Perp bridge built for Bp Beckington (1443–65), connects the chapter house with Vicars' Close.

Interior. As we enter from the W end, our eye is at once attracted to the remarkable 'scissors arch', one of three such arches erected to redistribute the weight of the tower soon after its completion (c 1322). Over this arch stands the Rood, replaced in this position in 1920, 400 years after the original Rood was destroyed at the Reformation. The rich carving of the *Nave* makes it look higher than it is (67ft), and the unbroken row of lancets in the triforium greatly increases its apparent length. The chief decorations are the elaborate *Capitals, and the medallions and carvings in the lancet spandrels. In the S clerestory is a Perp gallery (c 1450), probably made for 'angels' in Nativity and Easter plays, and below the triforium are carved brackets, probably supports for an early organ. On the N side is the hexagonal Perp chantry of Bp Bubwith (d 1424), with an alabaster panel of the Ascension, and opposite is that of Treasurer Hugh Sugar (d 1489), with a stone pulpit of c 1545 attached. In the W window the side-lights contain remains of enamel-painted glass (1670–72) presented by Bp Creighton.

The aisled *Transepts* with their carved capitals date from c 1190. In the N transept is the *Clock (after 1386 and before 1392), which retains its contemporary astronomical indications (a 2 × 12hr dial giving hours, minutes and the days of the lunar month) and tournament of knights; the original works are in the Science Museum in London. Below is an impressive Crucifixion in yew by E.J. Clack (1955). The space beneath the tower, which is EE with fan-tracery vaulting, bounded on three sides by the scissors arches already mentioned. On the fourth (E) side is the screen (14C), altered by Salvin to carry the organ. In the S transept are the Chapel of St Calixtus, containing a tomb of c 1440, with unique representations of medieval choir vestments and alabaster *Panels of the Annunciation and the Trinity; and the Chapel of St Martin, refitted as a war memorial by Sir Charles Nicholson (1922), with the tomb of Chancellor William Biconyll (d 1448). By the S wall of the transept are a 19C copy of the brass of Viscountess Lisle (d 1464) and the tomb of Bp William of March (d 1302). The Saxon font (10 or 11C, with Jacobean cover) may have come from the earlier cathedral, which lay S of the present building.

In the S choir aisle are the tombs of Bp Wm Bytton II (1267–74), which has the oldest incised slab in England, and in the Middle Ages became famous for curing toothache, and Bp Beckington, with an exquisite canopy and iron screen, and a *memento mori* effigy. The effigies of the earlier bishops in the choir aisles were probably set up c 1205 to vindicate the priority of the see of Wells over that of Bath. Both aisles retain some 14C glass, while the SE transept contains glass (c 1510) from Rouen, by pupils of Arnold of Nijmegen, acquired in 1812 and 1953, and also the painted effigy of Bp John Drokensford (d 1329). In the SE chapel is the chantry-like tomb of an unknown cathedral dignitary.

Of the *Choir*, the first three bays (Trans, end of 12C) formed the original presbytery, the ritual choir then occupying the space below the tower and the first bays of the nave. The E portion of the choir is in a rich Dec style (Geometrical). The lierned stone vaulting recalls in its form a type of wooden roof common in Somerset. The stalls of c 1335 incorporate 64 lively *Misericords and are backed by an over-

Vicars' Close, Wells, built in the 14C for the Vicars Choral of the cathedral. (K. Spence)

elaborate Victorian stone canopy; they have been enlivened by heraldic needlework seat coverings (1937–48). The E end of the choir is formed by three arches surmounted by the *E Window, known as the 'Golden Window', which was inserted c 1340 and depicts the Tree of Jesse. Behind the altar is a low screen, over which we obtain a charming vista of the retrochoir and Lady Chapel. The *Retrochoir, which is Dec throughout (c 1330) unites the Lady Chapel with the presbytery, by four supporting pillars and highly ingenious vaulting. The Dec *Lady Chapel, an irregular octagon, was completed before 1326; the large windows, with Geometrical tracery, are filled with superbly coloured fragments of stained glass (c 1325). The imposing lectern (1661) was the gift of Bp Creighton.

The NE Transept contains a sculpture of the Ascension and the monuments of Bp Creighton (d 1672) and Chancellor Milton (d 1337). In the N choir aisle is the fine alabaster effigy of Bp Ralph of Shrewsbury (d 1363). An exquisite early Dec staircase leads from the E aisle of the N transept to the octagonal **Chapter House, which is in the full Dec style and the finest of its date in England. Probably completed c 1306, it has no fewer than 32 vaulting ribs springing like a fountain of stone from the central pier. Spacious and full of light, it has a double-arched doorway, old glass in the upper lights of its beautiful windows, and delicately carved corbels and arcading above the 51 stalls for the members of the chapter. The staircase continues up and over the Chain Gate (see above).

From the S Transept a staircase climbs the Central Tower (182ft), from which there is a fine view. Another doorway leads to the Chapter Library, built over the E walk of the cloisters in 1425; it contains 6,000 books, original charters from 958 onwards, and a crozier decorated with 13C Limoges enamelling. The three-sided Cloisters, entered from the S transept, were rebuilt c 1425–1508. The walls are lined with tablets removed from the cathedral, including one (E side) to the Wells-born composer Thomas Linley (1732–95) and his two daughters, one the wife of the playwright Sheridan. The central space is known as the 'Palm Churchyard',

probably after the Palm Sunday procession which passed through
it.

The *Bishop's Palace*, S of the cathedral, was built by Bp Jocelin c
1230–40, with walls and moat added by Bp Ralph of Shrewsbury
(1329–63). Swans in the moat have by long tradition been trained to
pull on a bell-rope when they wish to be fed. Beyond the massive
14C gatehouse are the ruins of the magnificent Great Hall, built by
Bp Burnell (c 1280–90) and dismantled in the 16C. Rounding the S
side of the moat a path leads back to the road, and gives an
excellent view of the finest E end in England, with the Dec central
tower, octagonal chapter house (good gargoyles), and octagonal
Lady Chapel standing clear of the choir. N of the cathedral,
looking across Cathedral Green, are several fine buildings: the 15C
Deanery; the Tudor Chancellor's House, rebuilt in the 19C and now
a museum; and the Music School of the Cathedral School, dating
from c 1280 but modernized. Just to the E, and connected to the N
side of the cathedral by the bridge over the Chain Gate (see
above), is the unique 14C *Vicars' Close, built by Bp Ralph and his
successors for the College of Vicars Choral, who were the deputies
of the cathedral canons. It consists of two facing rows of 21 houses
(c 1360), altered but retaining their medieval charm. Between the
Chain Gate and the Close is the Vicars' Hall or refectory
(completed 1348), where the members of the College ate together.

Witham Friary, Somerset

Ded: St Mary, St John the Baptist and All Saints.

E of A359, 5 miles S of Frome.

The church incorporates part of the monastic church of the first
English charterhouse (Carthusian monastery), founded in 1178–79.
The third prior was St Hugh of Lincoln, who was probably responsible
for the building; it may have been the lay brothers' chapel.

Woodspring Priory, Avon

Ded: Holy Trinity, St Mary and St Thomas the Martyr.

Near Kewstoke, 5 miles N of Weston-super-Mare.

The remains of Woodspring are incorporated into a farm beside the
coast, on land owned by the National Trust. In c 1210, William
Courtenay, the grandson of Reginald Fitzurse, one of the murderers
of St Thomas Becket, founded a small priory of Augustinian canons
(known as Victorines, after St Victor) to expiate his grandfather's
crime. A phial of the saint's blood was kept at Woodspring and made
it a goal of West Country pilgrims. At the Dissolution in 1536 the
church was turned into a private house. All that survives are the 15C
central tower and nave, a chapel on the N side, the priory infirmary,
and a grand stone-built tithe barn, which is bigger than the church.

4. EASTERN ENGLAND

Beeleigh Abbey, Essex

1 mile W of Maldon.

The Tudor house (built c 1536) incorporates the vaulted chapter house and dormitory vaulting of a Premonstratensian abbey. Originally founded near the coast, the abbey was transferred to its present inland site c 1180.

Binham Priory, Norfolk

Ded: St Mary and the Holy Cross.
Off B1388, 5 miles SW of Blakeney.

The extensive remains of this remote Benedictine priory are reached through the ruins of a medieval gatehouse, which also gives access to a farmyard. Founded in 1091 by Peter de Valoines, nephew of William the Conqueror, it was the most important priory in Norfolk after Castle Acre (see below) and Thetford (see below); it was dissolved in 1540. As with other Benedictine priories, the nave was (and still is) used as the parish church, and this survives, though without its aisles. During the building of the church over a period of 150 years the rounded Norman arch gave way to the pointed EE arch, and the magnificent W front was built c 1230 in ornately decorated EE style. The great W window fell into disrepair and was bricked up at the beginning of the 19C. At the back of the church are four panels from the medieval rood-screen, on which traces of the original paintings of saints can be seen, overpainted with Biblical texts at the Reformation. To the E, much of the rubble core of the crossing piers, together with some of the facing stonework, survives to a considerable height, and the outlines of the original E apses and later squared presbytery and Lady Chapel can still be traced. A large proportion of the walls of the chapter house, parlour, refectory and other monastic buildings survives to a height of 6ft or so.

Brentwood Cathedral, Essex (RC)

Ded: The Sacred Heart and St Helen.

This small cathedral is an enlargement and transformation, carried out in 1972–74, of a church dating from c 1860; the first bishop was appointed in 1917. The Victorian exterior gives no idea of the modernity of the interior, with its abstract stained glass, its stone altar carved with the Last Supper, and its uncluttered, spacious atmosphere.

Broomholm Priory, Norfolk

Off B1159, 3 miles SE of Mundesley.

Founded by William Glanville in 1113, as a cell of Castle Acre Priory (see below), the remains are now incorporated in a farm. These consist of a fine medieval gateway, together with parts of the N transept and the chapter house. During the Middle Ages, Broomholm was famous for having a part of the True Cross, said to have the power to bring the dead back to life and to cure leprosy. It was well enough known to have been mentioned by Chaucer in the *Canterbury Tales*: in the Reeve's Tale the miller's wife calls on the 'hooly croys of Broméholm' for help. In 1233 King Henry III spent some time there with his court. In the 16C the soothsayer Mother Shipton prophesied that 'Bacton Abbey shall be a farm', correctly as it turned out.

Bury St Edmunds Abbey, Suffolk

All roads in Bury St Edmunds lead down to the huge precinct of the abbey, entered by a splendid pair of tower gateways. The town (also called St Edmundsbury) gets its name from the shrine of St Edmund, the last King of East Anglia, who was murdered by the Danes in 870. In 903 his remains were brought to Bury, then called Bedericsworth, where there was already a religious community with a timber church; a new stone abbey, financed by Canute, was dedicated in 1032. Building on a large scale began soon after the Conquest, c 1090, and was more or less complete by c 1210. The Benedictine abbey church was enormous, the largest in East Anglia, with a length of over 500ft (50ft more than Norwich Cathedral) and a great west front almost 250ft wide. Throughout the Middle Ages the abbey was extremely prosperous, and was often visited by the reigning monarch; when it was dissolved in 1539 it had a gross income of over £2,300 a year—a vast sum for those days—and distributed almost £400 a year to the poor. Its greatest historical moment came in November 1214, when the English earls and bishops met at St Edmund's altar in the church to hear Archbishop Langton read Magna Carta, ratified by King John at Runnymede the following year.

Most of the abbey church and the monastic buildings have disappeared, and what remains is hard to follow on the ground, as much of the precinct is a public park with tennis courts etc, and there has been later building on the site. The finest of the survivals are the two gateways: the free-standing Norman Tower and Gateway, directly opposite the west front of the abbey and just south of the cathedral (see below); and the later Great Gate (facing up Abbeygate Street), built after a rebellion by the townspeople in 1327, in which an earlier gate was destroyed. The Norman tower (St James's Gate), built by Abbot Anselm (1121–48), was both the main entrance to the abbey and the bell-tower for St James's Church, now the cathedral. The Great Gate was the entrance to the Great Court, which stretched almost down to the river, and to the abbot's palace. The outlines of the

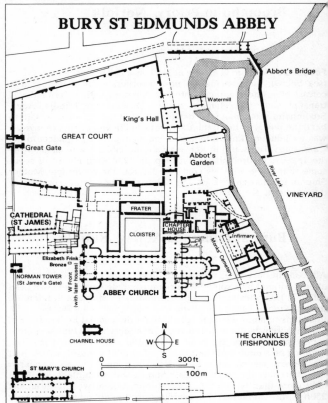

BURY ST EDMUNDS ABBEY

Abbot's Bridge

Watermill

King's Hall

GREAT COURT

Great Gate

Abbot's Garden

VINEYARD

CATHEDRAL (ST JAMES)

FRATER

CLOISTER

CHAPTER HOUSE

Infirmary

Monks' Cemetery

Elizabeth Frink Bronze

NORMAN TOWER (St James's Gate)

W Front (with later houses)

ABBEY CHURCH

River Lark

N
W—E
S

CHARNEL HOUSE

THE CRANKLES (FISHPONDS)

0   300 ft
0   100 m

ST MARY'S CHURCH

abbey church, with its apsidal E end and side chapels, are reasonably clear; on one of the piers are two plaques, set up in 1847, celebrating the reading of Magna Carta. At the other end of the church the lower levels of the west front have survived, in a strange amalgam of medieval stonework and houses built into the façade in the 17–19C. The cloister and monastic buildings lay N and E of the church; on the floor of the chapter house, which opened off the E side of the cloister, are the graves of six early abbots of Bury. Apart from the gateways already mentioned, the best medieval survival is the Abbot's Bridge, in the NE corner of the precinct, which originally led to the abbey vineyard on the other side of the River Lark.

Bury St Edmunds Cathedral, Suffolk

Ded: St James.

In 1913 the diocese of St Edmondsbury and Ipswich was created, and the parish church of St James was raised to the status of a cathedral

Bury St Edmunds Abbey, the ruined W front with later houses incorporated. The bronze statue of St Edmund is by Elizabeth Frink. (K. Spence)

When it was built in the 15C, it would have been dwarfed by the mighty abbey looming behind it; and it stills seems hardly larger than a substantial parish church. It is entered through the west front, which faces directly on to the street and is decorated with the emblems of St James (staff, wallet and scallop shell), the patron saint of pilgrims. Inside, the impression is of brilliance and light; the Perp nave, built mainly by John Wastell, one of the greatest church architects of the period around 1500, was begun in 1502 and has tall, slender shafts and graceful arcading. The church was restored in the 1860s by Sir George Gilbert Scott (who was responsible for the hammerbeam roof, brightly painted in 1948–49). The new chancel and crossing blend harmoniously with the older work; designed by Stephen Dykes Bower, they were consecrated in 1970. The most striking of the furnishings is the painted and gilded font with its tall pinnacled canopy, decorated in 1960. The only monument of any consequence is by the W door; it commemorates James Reynolds (d 1738), Chief Baron of the Court of the Exchequer. In the N choir aisle a set of nine bold tapestries, worked by school-children of West Suffolk, show scenes from the martyrdom of St Edmund; they were made in 1970, to commemorate the 1,100th anniversary of Edmund's death. In the forecourt SE of the cathedral is a striking bronze by Elizabeth Frink.

Bury St Edmunds, Suffolk; St Mary's Church

Though neither a cathedral nor an abbey, St Mary's forms an integral part of the abbey precinct (at its SW corner), and could almost be considered a twin of the cathedral (see above). Most of the building is light and airy 15C Perp (apart from the chancel, which is Dec of c 1300, and the squat tower, which is c 1400). Its most striking feature is the superb double row of carved wooden angels on the hammerbeams of the nave roof. The monuments include the tomb (with skeleton effigy) of John Baret, a wealthy local clothier (d 1467), in the S nave aisle; above it is an elaborate chantry ceiling painted with Baret's mottoes 'God me gyde' and 'Grace me governe'. In the NE corner of the sanctuary, beside the altar, is the grave of Mary Tudor (1496–1533), sister of Henry VIII.

Butley Abbey, Suffolk

On minor road off B1084, between Woodbridge and Orford.

On private property, but visible from the road.

All that survives of the 12C Augustinian priory is the magnificent gatehouse, built c 1320–25 and a superb example of flushwork decoration.

Cambridge: Jesus College

Founded in 1496 by John Alcock, Bp of Ely and Comptroller of Works to Henry VII, Jesus incorporates much of the 12C Benedictine nunnery of St Radegund, which originally stood outside the town. The chief survival is the chapel, which is in fact only part of the conventual church, as the W end of the nave was turned by Alcock into the Master's Lodge of his new college. The chapel is entered by the S side of the nuns' cloister. On the E side are the exquisite EE arches that led into the chapter house, rediscovered in 1840 after being hidden for more than 300 years by Alcock's alterations. The chapel is a fascinating and unusual mixture of Norman (notably in the N transept), EE (the chancel) and Pre-Raphaelite (ceilings painted by William Morris, stained glass designed by Burne-Jones and Ford Madox Brown). It underwent two phases of restoration in the 19C, under the influence of the Gothic Revival: first after 1845, by Anthony Salvin, who restored the choir roof, and Augustus Welby Pugin, who put in a new E window containing some medieval glass from Chartres cathedral, and designed the heavy wooden screen which cuts off the choir from the nave; and secondly after 1864, when the Pre-Raphaelite decoration was carried out.

Castle Acre Priory, Norfolk

4 miles N of Swaffham, off A1065.

Among the finest and most extensive monastic remains in Norfolk, the Cluniac priory of Castle Acre was founded c 1090 by William de

Warenne, 2nd Earl of Surrey, and dissolved in 1537. The approach is through a fine two-storey gatehouse (late 15C or early 16C), which still has its porter's lodge. Of the priory church, the chief survival is the elaborately moulded 12C W front, which was pierced in the 15C with a large window, obliterating much of the Norman arcading; the S tower still stands to a height of four storeys. The apsidal E end was enlarged and squared off in the early 14C; the position of the nave piers is marked out in the turf, and much of the masonry of the crossing survives. Of the 12C buildings surrounding the cloister, the best preserved are those on the E side: the chapter house, abutting on to the S transept of the church, and next door to it the long undercroft of the monks' dorter, with the remains of the staircase that led up to the dorter. At right angles to the dorter is the reredorter, over 90ft long and built over a stream. The 12C prior's chapel and lodging, on the W side of the cloister, were remodelled during the 15C and turned into a comfortable house, with a porch, guest-chamber, study with oriel windows, and long gallery. After the priory was dissolved, the lodging was still lived in, and further alterations were made.

Chelmsford Cathedral, Essex

Ded: St Mary the Virgin, St Peter and St Cedd.

Chelmsford became the see of a bishop in 1914, when the parish church was promoted to the status of a cathedral. A fine airy building, it was completed in 1424, but was largely rebuilt after a disaster in 1800, when two of the nave pillars collapsed, bringing down the S arcades, clerestory and roof. This accounts for the most unmedieval though attractive nave roof, put in after the disaster by John Johnson, who was in charge of the rebuilding; it was painted in 1961. The chancel was not affected by the collapse, and remains mainly in its original form, though a new E window was inserted in 1878. The main monuments are on the N side of the choir, to members of the Mildmay family: a sumptuous memorial to Thomas Mildmay (d 1566) and his wife Avice (d 1557), carved with their eight sons and seven daughters; and a classical urn commemorating Benjamin Mildmay, Earl Fitzwalter (d 1756). The tower has an unusually large peal of 13 bells, and is surmounted by a graceful 18C spire, originally lead-covered but clad with copper in 1932. Outside, on the south-east buttress, is a modern sculpture of St Peter by T.B. Huxley-Jones (d 1968), showing the saint dressed in fisherman's boots and holding a gigantic Yale key.

Clare Priory, Suffolk

Just S of A1092, 6 miles W of Long Melford.

Founded by Richard de Clare in 1248, Clare was the first Augustinian friary in England. Most of the monastic ruins are now on private property and cannot be visited, but the remains of the cloister can be seen from the public path. The priory was suppressed in 1538 but rededicated in 1954; a small RC church, open to the public, has been formed from the medieval infirmary.

Colchester, Essex: St Botolph's Priory

The ruins of St Botolph's are in the heart of Colchester. Built in a mixture of flint, carved stone and brick from Roman Camulodunum, the priory was founded before 1100, and was the first house of Augustinian canons in England. The chief remains (12C) are those of the nave of the church and the W front, which originally had a round window—the earliest such feature in the country. Part of the church served as the parish church, and after the priory was dissolved in 1535 the congregation continued to use it. In 1648 the church was destroyed by Cromwellian cannon fire, and it has been in ruins ever since.

Colchester, Essex: St John's Abbey

On St John's Green.

Of the Benedictine abbey founded by Eudo Dapifer in 1096, all that remains is a magnificent 15C gatehouse, restored in the 19C. Battlemented and flanked by octagonal turrets, it is a fine example of flushwork. The last abbot of St John's was hanged in 1539, and St John's, apart from the gatehouse, was destroyed.

Creake Abbey, Norfolk

Ded: The Blessed Virgin Mary.

2 miles S of Burnham Market, E of B1355.

In a pastoral setting beside a farm, the ruins of Creake are not very substantial but extremely attractive. It was founded for Augustinian canons in 1206, under the name of Sancta Maria de Pratis ('St Mary of the Meadows'), and began its life as a priory-hospital for 13 poor men, with a Master, four chaplains and a body of lay brothers. In 1231 it was raised to the status of an abbey and reached its peak in the 14C; in the early 16C it was ravaged by an epidemic (possibly the plague), which carried off all the canons one by one, until only the prior was left. When he too died in 1506, the abbey reverted to the Crown and was allowed to decay. The central section of the church has disappeared, but the graceful pointed arches of the 13C transepts survive, together with fragments of a 14C chapel on the N side.

Crowland (Croyland) Abbey, Lincolnshire

Ded: St Guthlac.

Off A1073, 7 miles N of Peterborough.

The broad tower of Crowland, topped by a stumpy spire, is one of the landmarks of the flat fenlands on the Lincolnshire–Cambridgeshire border. The abbey was founded by King Ethelbald of Mercia c 716, on the site of the cell of the hermit Guthlac, who had retired to what was then an island in the Fens. During Saxon times Crowland became a centre of learning, and is said to have supplied some of the earliest teachers at Cambridge. It was sacked by the Danes in 870, and after being rebuilt was burned down by a disastrous fire in 1091. A great Norman church was built in the early 12C by Abbot Joffrid (1109–70); of this church the chief survival is the gigantic arch which stood below the vanished central tower. The present church is in fact the N aisle of the Norman church, given a Perp facelift in the first half of the 15C. The abbey was dissolved in 1539, and the E end (choir, transepts and central tower) were demolished soon after. In 1643 the nave and S aisle were bombarded by Cromwell's troops and subsequently pulled down; the nave, open to the sky, is now a garden. Among the statues on the W front is one of Guthlac scourging the Devil, and the supposed site of his cell is marked by a plaque on the SW corner of the church.

Denny Abbey, Cambridgeshire

On E side of A10, 6 miles N of Cambridge.

Denny is unique in England, since it is the only surviving substantial remains of a house of the Order of St Clare (Poor Clares). As originally established c 1160, it was a priory of Benedictine monks and a cell of Ely; but in 1170 it was transferred to the Knights Templars, who kept it until their order was suppressed in 1308, using it as a hospital for their sick and elderly members. During the 1340s it was converted into a priory for the Poor Clares (Franciscan nuns or minoresses) by the Countess of Pembroke, who also founded Pembroke College, Cambridge. It was dissolved in 1539, when most of the buildings were demolished, apart from the church, later converted into a farmhouse, and the 14C refectory, turned into a barn. The external appearance of the church is an odd combination of Norman arches and 18C brickwork; inside, it is possible to trace the nave, crossing and transepts of the Templar church, greatly altered by the Countess, who seems to have adapted them to domestic use.

Dunwich Friary, Suffolk

2 miles E of B1125, between Aldeburgh and Southwold.

For millennia the sea has been eating away at the coast round Dunwich, drowning a Saxon city and Norman port beneath the waves.

The friary was built out of reach of the sea after 1290; little remains apart from the ruins of the gatehouse and crumbling stretches of wall.

Ely Cathedral, Cambridgeshire

Ded: Holy Trinity.

The name Ely means 'Eel Island'; and though the 'island' on which the little city is built stands less than 70ft above the black earth of the Fens, it is high enough to give prominence to the extraordinary cathedral from whichever direction it is approached. One of the longest (517ft) and most varied churches in England, it is a huge cruciform structure representing an architectural history of four centuries.

History. The first building at Ely was a Benedictine abbey for both monks and nuns, established by St Etheldreda (or Audrey), Queen of Northumbria (d 679), who retired from the world here to the home of her girlhood and became abbess in 673. Soon after her death miracles were being reported from the shrine set up to her, and Ely became a goal of Saxon pilgrimage. In 870 the Danes sacked the abbey; but in the 10C it was refounded by King Edgar (959–75) as a Benedictine monastery. A century later it was used by Hereward the Wake as the headquarters of his last-ditch stand against the Normans (1070–71). William the Conqueror appointed as abbot a Norman, Simeon, who began the present structure in 1083; the transepts and E end were completed by 1106, and three years later the church became the cathedral of a new diocese. The Norman nave seems to have been finished c 1189, and the Galilee (W porch) was added by Bp Eustace (1198–1215). Bp Hugh of Northwold (1229–54) lengthened the choir by six exquisite bays in the EE style, which provided a worthy setting for St Etheldreda's shrine. In 1322 the collapse of the central tower wrecked the Norman choir and gave the sacrist Alan de Walsingham and his team of craftsmen the chance to build the lovely and original Dec octagon and the three W bays of the present choir; at the same time work began on the building of the Lady Chapel, which was not completed until after 1350. The chantry chapels at the E end of the church belong to the Perp period (1486–1533). The incomplete, asymmetrical appearance of the W front is due to the fall of the NW tower in a storm in 1701.

Exterior. A walk round the outside of the cathedral gives a constantly changing vista of shapes and surfaces, from the forthright Norman style of most of the building, to the fanciful pinnacles of the octagon and the graceful lines of the Lady Chapel. The most prominent part is the W Front, including the castellated W tower, the Galilee porch, and the SW transept. Except for the octagonal top storey and corner turrets, which are Dec, the whole of the striking tower (215ft) belongs to the Trans Norman period (1174–89), though the lack of the NW transept robs the facade of its full dignity. The unique Central Octagon is one of the marvels of medieval building; the timber lantern was restored in the 19C by Sir George Gilbert Scott.

Interior. The EE *Galilee Porch consists of two simply vaulted bays, with blind arcades; the doorway leading from the porch into the nave is richly moulded. From the W entrance there is an impressive vista of the full length of the church. The architecture increases in richness as the eye travels on to the stained glass of the E end lancets. The interior of the W Tower, with its arcaded galleries, has a 19C painted roof. The *SW Transept, in the Norman Trans style, has richly arcaded walls, triforium and clerestory. It is adjoined by the semicircular St Catherine's Chapel (rebuilt 1848).

The narrow *Nave*, nearly 250ft long and consisting of 12 bays, is an imposing example of late Norman work almost contemporary with the nave of Peterborough (see below). The triforium arcade is nearly equal in height to the main arcade, both in nave and transepts. Massive though the piers are, they are light in comparison with the earlier work of the transepts, or of Durham or Gloucester (see below). The old unadorned roof has been replaced by a 19C painted ceiling, but the S aisle vaults in the four E bays retain their original 12C colouring. The windows in the N aisle are Perp insertions, and those in the S aisle have been restored to their original Norman form. In the S aisle is the Prior's Doorway (c 1140), normally kept closed in winter; on the outside it is richly carved on the tympanum with Christ in Majesty, and on the pilasters with fanciful figures of men and beasts.

Ely Cathedral, the 14C Lady Chapel. (K. Spence)

Near the door is the base of a Saxon Cross, called 'Ovin's Stone', erected to Ovinus, a leading East Anglian thane and a vassal of Queen Etheldreda. The inscription on the pedestal reads: *Lucem tuam Ovino da Deus et requiem amen* ('O God, grant Ovinus thy light and rest, amen'). The S Doorway, also richly decorated outside, at the E end of the S aisle, was the monks' entrance from the cloisters. Near the W end of the nave lies Alan de Walsingham, builder of the octagon, under a marble slab from which the brass has disappeared.

The lower parts of the *Great Transepts*, which have aisles on both sides, display the oldest work in the cathedral (1083–1107). In the E aisle of the N arm is St Edmund's Chapel, with a 14C screen and a 12C wall painting of St Edmund's martyrdom at the hands of the Danes (see also Bury St Edmunds, above). The adjoining St George's Chapel was restored as a war memorial by Sir George Dawber (1922). The bronze group, 'Christ and Mary Magdalene', in the S arm is by David Wynne (1963). The hammerbeams of the transept ceilings are adorned with brightly painted carved angels (15C).

The great **Central Octagon**, with its lantern that seems to be poised in space, has been called 'perhaps the most beautiful and original design to be found in the whole range of Gothic architecture'. As Nikolaus Pevsner writes, in *The Buildings of England*, 'the basic emotion created by the octagon as one approaches it along the nave is one of spaciousness, a relief, a deep breath after the oppressive narrowness of the Norman work'. Looking up at the lantern, the effect is of some giant eight-armed starfish, with the body formed by the light-filled space of the lantern itself, and the arms made up of the vaulting that descends from each side of the lantern to the widely spaced supporting columns. The wooden lantern, set with its angles opposite the faces of the stone octagon below, weighs 400 tons, and all England was searched to find oaks large enough for the corner posts, which are 63ft long. The weight is distributed by a wooden framework, on the principle of the hammerbeam, out of sight behind the vaulting. The master carpenter of the octagon—the inspiration of Alan de Walsingham (see above)—was almost certainly William Hurle or Hurley, who was the most famous carpenter of his age, and worked at Westminster and Windsor on the royal palaces. High up on the arches of the octagon are stone carved heads, including those of King Edward III and Queen Philippa, Alan de Walsingham, Prior Crauden and Bishop Hotham. (Pevsner recommends taking field-glasses to study the octagon details.)

The *Choir* is separated from the octagon by a 19C screen. There is a clear division between Hugh of Northwold's EE bays and the three Dec ones built by de Walsingham adjoining the octagon. The vaulting has some superb carved bosses. Of the choir stalls, the upper ones are 14C with some lively carved misericords, but the other furnishings are 19C. On the high altar a cross (1964) by Louis Osman stands between candlesticks of 1661. The most interesting monuments include: (S choir aisle) tomb-chest of Bp Hotham (d 1337); canopied tomb of John Tiptoft, Earl of Worcester (beheaded in 1470 during the Wars of the Roses), between his two wives; Bp William de Luda (d 1298); Sir Robert Steward (d 1570), wearing armour; Sir Mark Steward (d 1603), recumbent effigy. (N choir aisle) Bp Hugh de Northwold (d 1254), elaborately canopied; Bp William of Kilkenny (d 1257); Bp Redman (d 1506); Dean Caesar (d 1636). The monument next to Bp Northwold's tomb is probably the canopy from the tomb of Bp Hotham in the S choir aisle. An inscribed slate slab in front of the high altar marks the

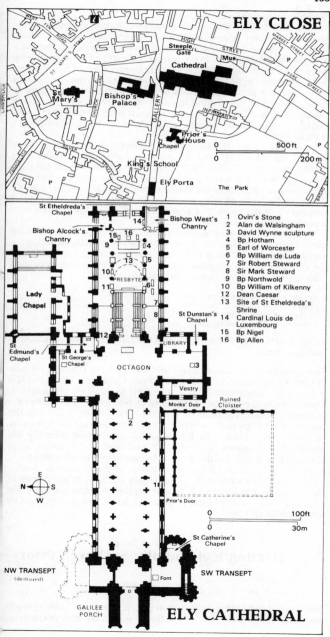

ELY CLOSE

WEST FEN ROAD
ST MARY'S STREET
HIGH STREET
MARKET STREET
Steeple Gate
Mus
Cathedral
FORE STREET
P
CHURCH LANE
GALLERY
St Mary's
Bishop's Palace
INFIRMARY
CAMBRIDGE
RIVER
Prior's House
Chapel
King's School
0 500 ft
0 200 m
P
Ely Porta
The Park
P
BROAD

ELY CATHEDRAL

St Etheldreda's Chapel

Bishop Alcock's Chantry

Bishop West's Chantry

14

15 16
9
4
13
10 5
PRESBYTERY
11 6
Lady Chapel
7
St Dunstan's Chapel
8
12
St Edmund's Chapel
St George's Chapel
LIBRARY
3
OCTAGON
Vestry
Monks' Door
Ruined Cloister
2
Prior's Door
1

N E S W

0 100 ft
0 30 m

St Catherine's Chapel

NW TRANSEPT (destroyed)
Font
SW TRANSEPT

GALILEE PORCH

1 Ovin's Stone
2 Alan de Walsingham
3 David Wynne sculpture
4 Bp Hotham
5 Earl of Worcester
6 Bp William de Luda
7 Sir Robert Steward
8 Sir Mark Steward
9 Bp Northwold
10 Bp William of Kilkenny
12 Dean Caesar
13 Site of St Etheldreda's Shrine
14 Cardinal Louis de Luxembourg
15 Bp Nigel
16 Bp Allen

site of St Etheldreda's shrine.

At the E end of the N aisle is the intricately fretted stonework of Bp Alcock's Chantry; Alcock (d 1500) founded Jesus College, Cambridge (see above), and the chantry is decorated with his rebus of a cock standing on a globe. In the corresponding position to the S is Bp West's Chantry (West d 1534), a graceful combination of classical and medieval styles. In St Etheldreda's Chapel, between the chantries, is the monument of Cardinal Louis de Luxembourg (d 1443), Abp of Rouen and Bp of Ely. Behind the altar screen are the black marble tomb-slab of Bp Nigel (d 1174) and the tomb of Bp Allen (d 1845), with a slab of Alexandrine mosaic, originally intended for Napoleon's tomb in Paris.

To the NE of the N transept is the elegant and spacious *Lady Chapel*, started c 1321 and completed c 1353, which served as a parish church from 1566 to 1938. It is elaborately decorated, but most of the statuettes are badly damaged, mainly due to the clunch (soft limestone) of which they are made, though they also suffered at the hands of the Duke of Somerset, Lord Protector during the reign of Edward VI, in the 1540s. The complex lierne vault, which spans 46ft, is the widest medieval vault in England.

The *Cloisters* are now represented mainly by the E walk, which forms the S entrance to the nave. A tombstone to William Pickering and Richard Edger (both d 1845 in an accident during the building of the local railway) is inscribed with a delightfully naive poem called 'The Spiritual Railway', which includes the lines:

All you who would to glory ride,
Must come to Christ, in him abide,
In First and Second and Third Class,
Repentance, Faith and Holiness.

To the E of the S transept are parts of the Infirmary (fine examples of Norman work).

The remains of the Conventual Buildings, S of the cloisters, include the Prior's House and the exquisite Prior Crauden's Chapel (1324, with a 13C undercroft), built for the prior by Alan de Walsingham. These now form part of the King's School, refounded in 1541 after the monastery was dissolved as 'The King's New College at Ely' and the successor to the monastic school at which King Edward the Confessor (d 1066) was a pupil. The Deanery was constructed from the old guest-hall and retains some of its 13–14C work and remains of the 12C monks' kitchen. On the S side of the precinct is an attractive park, from which Ely Porta (the great gateway of the monastery, built c 1394) leads into a street called The Gallery and back to the W front of the cathedral. The Bishop's Palace facing the cathedral is mainly late 17C, but retains wings built by Bp Alcock and a long gallery built by Bp Goodrich (d 1554).

Herringfleet, Suffolk: St Olave's Priory

On N side of A143, 5 miles SW of Great Yarmouth.

Not much is left of this Augustinian priory, founded c 1216 on a site above the River Waveney. Part of the W wall of the church survives, together with the bases of some of the piers, and the refectory undercroft.

Isleham Priory, Cambridgeshire

Ded: St Margaret of Antioch.

On B1104, 8 miles SE of Ely.

At first sight, the little Norman church of Isleham's Benedictine priory looks like a barn, and in fact it was used as one for centuries. Built c 1100, it has an apsidal E end, with a single round arch between the aisleless nave and the chancel. Isleham was administered at long range from the Breton monastery of St Jacut-de-la-Mer, and was too small to have a cloister or other monastic buildings. In 1414 it was seized by the King and granted to Pembroke College, Cambridge, who cut a wide entrance door on the S side and turned it into a barn. (Key kept in village.)

Ixworth Abbey, Suffolk

5 miles NE Bury St Edmunds.

Remains of an Augustinian priory, founded c 1170, are incorporated in a later (mainly Georgian) country house, now privately owned. Foundations of the Norman church survive, as does the 13C dormitory undercroft.

Leez Priory, Essex

On minor road between A131 and B1417, 5 miles SW of Braintree.

Grounds only open, Easter–late Sept., Wed. and Sat. p.m.

The strange-looking name is presumably a phonetic spelling derived from Little Leighs, the nearest village. The Augustinian priory founded here in the 13C was dissolved in 1536 and taken over by Lord Rich, who built himself a redbrick Tudor mansion on the site, with two impressive gatehouses. Little survives of the priory, though the cloister was turned into an inner courtyard and the priory foundations were largely used.

Leiston Abbey, Suffolk

Ded: The Blessed Virgin Mary.

On W side of B1122, 1 mile N of Leiston.

In 1182 Ranulf de Glanville, Henry II's Lord Chief Justice, founded an abbey of Premonstratensian canons at Minsmere, near the Suffolk coast. In 1363 it was moved to its present site a mile inland, and though a fire in 1389 severely damaged the domestic buildings, a good deal of the abbey survives. The S transept wall still stands to a considerable height, as does the pointed window of the refectory and parts of the chapter house, sacristy and reredorter. Dissolved in 1535, the abbey became a farm; in recent years the Lady Chapel has been reroofed, and the farmhouse inside the ruins is now used as a religious retreat.

Lincoln Cathedral

Ded: The Blessed Virgin Mary.

Lincoln has the most commanding situation of any cathedral in England, soaring high on a rock ridge above the surrounding countryside. Unusually harmonious in design, it was praised by William Cobbett as 'the finest building in the whole world', while John Ruskin called it 'out and out the most precious piece of architecture in the British Isles'. Due to its exposed position it is subject to erosion from wind and rain, and to air-borne pollution from the industrial Midlands; and so it is undergoing a major repair programme.

History. In the 1C the Romans occupied a British site called Lindum, which became a colony (Lindum Colonia) for ex-soldiers. Christianity must have been introduced by the 3C, as in 314 the Bp of Lincoln attended the Council of Arles. The next historical evidence dates from c 630, when St Paulinus conducted a mass baptism in the River Trent. Until the 11C Lincoln was in the diocese of Dorchester; but in 1072, at the order of William the Conqueror, the first Norman bishop, Remigius, transferred the see from Dorchester-on-Thames to Lincoln, which at the time of the Conquest was the fourth city in England, after London, Winchester and York. Of Remigius's early Norman church, consecrated in 1092, there remain the central portion of the W front, with its three deep recesses, and part of the first bay of the nave. The three W doorways (with the intersecting arcade above), the three lower stages of the W towers and their N and S gables are ascribed to the late Norman restoration of Bp Alexander after a fire in 1141. The Norman cathedral was shattered by an earthquake in 1185, and Bp Hugh of Avalon (1186–1200), later St Hugh of Lincoln, at once began to restore and extend it, with Geoffrey de Noiers in charge of the building operations. The choir and E transepts were their work, and the four-part vault of St Hugh's Choir is the earliest example of the use of ribs for purely decorative purposes. As the whole cathedral, apart from the Angel Choir and part of the W transepts, is mainly of St Hugh's inspiration, he deservedly ranks as one of the greatest names in the history of English architecture. By c 1250 the nave and W transepts were completed, and the Chapter House, Galilee Porch and upper part of the W façade were added. The Angel Choir belongs to the period between 1258 and 1280, and the cloisters are late 13C. The upper part of the central tower dates from 1307–11 (Geometric Dec), while the W towers are late Dec (c 1420). The only Perp work in the cathedral is the W window of the nave (1436–49) and the chantry chapels (c 1425–1550).

Exterior. The precincts are entered through the 14C Exchequergate. The imposing *W Front consists, roughly, of a block of Norman work encased in a larger surface of EE lancet work. Above the richly moulded central doorway are 11 statues of kings. The much weathered frieze of carved panels (c 1145) is very similar to a series at Modena Cathedral in Italy. Those on the S have Old Testament scenes (the expulsion of Adam and Eve from Eden, Cain killing Abel, Noah building the Ark, Daniel in the Lions' Den etc), while those on the N are from the New Testament (Dives and Lazarus, the Harrowing of Hell etc). The SW turret is surmounted by a statue of St Hugh, and on the NW turret is the so-called 'Swineherd of Stow', who gave all his savings to St Hugh as a contribution to the new building.

The W Towers are 206ft high; the magnificent *Central Tower, in which hangs 'Great Tom of Lincoln', a bell weighing almost 5½ tons, is 271ft and commands a panoramic view. On the S side is the Galilee Porch, which leads into the S transept. Further to the E, between two Perp chantries, is the Judgement Porch, whose deeply recessed arch has a remarkable representation of the Last Judgement, and other rich carvings (the head of Christ and the figure of the Madonna are modern). Among the interesting gargoyles on this part of the building is one known as 'the Devil looking over Lincoln'. The figures on the buttresses are believed to represent Edward I and his two wives: Queen Eleanor of Castile, who died near Lincoln in 1290, after which the progress of her body south to Westminster was marked by the series of 'Eleanor Crosses' ending at Charing Cross; and Queen Margaret, the head of which is 19C. The open space beyond gives a good view of the E end of the cathedral, with its noble window, deep buttresses, lines of arcading, enriched gable and crocketed pinnacles. At the top of the gable is a group of the Virgin and Child. To the N is the Chapter House, with its great flying buttresses, and the building further W is the Library (over the cloisters).

Interior. The *Nave* is striking for its unusual width and for the correspondingly wide spacing of the arcades. The view from the W

Lincoln Cathedral, an early 18C engraving of the S side.

end is truncated by the stone rood-screen, with the tall 19C organ pipes and casing above it. The general proportions of the nave, with its clustered columns and beautiful triforium, are harmonious and impressive. The Morning Chapel (St Mary Magdalene, N side) and the Consistory Court (S side) open off the W end of the nave. The chapel below the SW tower (closed to the public) is known as the Ringers' Chapel and has the names of many bellringers, dating back to 1614, painted on its walls. The fine late Norman font (S side of nave), carved with fabulous beasts, is made of marble from Tournai in Belgium and is similar to the font in Winchester Cathedral (see above).

The Central Tower is supported by four massive piers bearing lofty arches. The *Great or W Transepts* were begun by St Hugh and completed between 1200 and 1235. The beautiful circular windows still retain medieval stained glass: the N window, known as the Dean's Eye, is EE c 1220 and contains its medieval glass more or less complete; and the S window, called the Bishop's Eye, is Dec of c 1325–50, with gracefully flowing tracery. There are six transeptal chapels: those on the N, with modern stained glass by Harry Stammers, Christopher Webb and Archibald Nicholson, are devoted to (from the left, facing) Airmen (St Michael), Seamen (St Andrew) and Soldiers (St George). In the Airmen's Chapel are books containing the names of 22,000 men of Nos 1 and 5 Bomber Groups and the 9th Training Group killed in World War II. The Soldiers' Chapel and the Works Chantry have unusual double arcading. In the S transept is a vigorous statue of Bp King (1885–1910), who is buried in the cloister. The N and S lancets of the great transepts and the windows at the E end of both choir aisles contain medieval stained glass of high quality.

The fine EE *Choir*, begun in 1192, is separated from the nave by a Dec stone Screen (c 1300), richly decorated by diaper work and flanked by elaborately carved doorways. We enter the choir by the door of the S aisle, in which are the remains of the shrine of Little St Hugh, once said to have been ritually murdered by the Jews in 1255. The magnificent canopied *Choir Stalls (early Perp, c 1380), with elaborately carved bench-ends and misericords, are among the finest in England. The subjects range from Alexander the Great carried up to heaven by griffins, to scenes from Arthurian legend, as well as more strictly Christian carvings, and medieval parables such as the fox preaching to the geese (W end of N range). On the left of the high

Lincoln Cathedral, 14C misericord in the choir stalls.

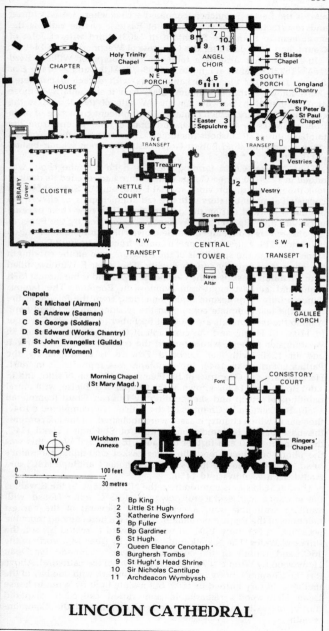

CHAPTER HOUSE

Holy Trinity Chapel

N E PORCH

ANGEL CHOIR

8 7
9 10
11

St Blaise Chapel

SOUTH PORCH

Longland Chantry

Vestry

St Peter & St Paul Chapel

6 4 5

Easter Sepulchre 3

N E TRANSEPT

S E TRANSEPT

Vestries

Treasury

LIBRARY (over)

CLOISTER

NETTLE COURT

Vestry

2

Screen

A B C

N W TRANSEPT

D E F

S W TRANSEPT

CENTRAL TOWER

Nave Altar

Chapels

A St Michael (Airmen)
B St Andrew (Seamen)
C St George (Soldiers)
D St Edward (Works Chantry)
E St John Evangelist (Guilds)
F St Anne (Women)

GALILEE PORCH

Morning Chapel (St Mary Magd.)

Font

CONSISTORY COURT

Wickham Annexe

Ringers' Chapel

N
E   S
W

1

0   100 feet
0   30 metres

1 Bp King
2 Little St Hugh
3 Katherine Swynford
4 Bp Fuller
5 Bp Gardiner
6 St Hugh
7 Queen Eleanor Cenotaph
8 Burghersh Tombs
9 St Hugh's Head Shrine
10 Sir Nicholas Cantilupe
11 Archdeacon Wymbyssh

LINCOLN CATHEDRAL

altar is the Easter Sepulchre (canopied arches where Christ's burial and resurrection were symbolized at Easter); on the right is the monument to Katherine Swynford (d 1403), third wife of John of Gaunt, and their daughter the Countess of Westmorland (d 1440).

In the N choir aisle is a tablet to the composer William Byrd (1543–1623), organist at Lincoln in 1563–72. At the angles of the *E or Lesser Transepts* are remarkable piers with detached crocketed shafts, known as the 'Trondheim Pillars' from their similarity to those at Trondheim, in Norway. On the W side of the N arm is the cathedral Treasury, which contains a magnificent collection of plate from churches in the diocese, and chalices and patens from the tombs of three 13C bishops (including Grosseteste). In the S arm is a stone commemorating Robert Grosseteste, the great scholar-bishop (1235–53).

The *******Angel Choir*, forming the five E bays of the choir, was added in 1255–80, when Gothic architecture had reached its peak. It took the place of the previous apsidal E end, built by St Hugh, which consisted of an ambulatory with five radiating chapels, or *chevet*; the outline is marked out on the present floor. The new choir became necessary after Bp Hugh of Avalon was canonized by the Pope, as the *chevet* was too cramped for the crowds of pilgrims that thronged his shrine. The Angel Choir gets its name from the beautifully carved stone angels in the spandrels of the triforium, and all the carving in the choir is of equally superb quality. The great E Window, filled with Victorian glass, is in the Geometric style, and is the largest (57ft high) and earliest eight-light window in England. The famous 'Lincoln Imp' (a grotesque figure emerging from the foliage at the top of the last complete column on the N side) can be found here. Among the monuments are those of Bp Fuller (d 1675), Bp Gardiner (d 1705), St Hugh, and the cenotaph of Queen Eleanor (buried in Westminster Abbey), who attended the consecration of the new E end in 1280, with her husband Edward I; destroyed by the Parliamentarians in 1644, the cenotaph was reproduced in 1891. Here too are the Chantries of Bp Fleming (1425), on N side; and (S side) Bp Russell (1490), known as the Chapel of St Blaise, with mural paintings of sheep and shepherding by Duncan Grant (completed 1958). Bp Longland's Chantry, off the S aisle, was completed c 1547, the year in which chantry masses were abolished. At the NE corner is the base of the battered stone Shrine of St Hugh's Head (14C, despoiled in 1540 and further damaged in the Civil War); this was the plinth on which stood the silver casket containing the saint's head. Opposite are the tombs of Sir Nicholas Cantilupe (14C) and Archdeacon Wymbyssh (d 1460).

The 13C *Cloister* is entered from the NE transept. In the E walk is the entrance to the graceful polygonal 13C *Chapter House*, with vaulting springing from a central shaft. Several of the earliest meetings of the English parliament took place here; among them the occasion, in February 1301, at which Edward I created his son the Prince of Wales. The N walk (pulled down by Dean Macworth in the 15C, and rebuilt in the form of a Doric colonnade for Dean Honywood by Wren c 1674) gives fine views of the cathedral. Above it is the Chapter Library (entrance in NE corner), with one bay of the medieval library burned in 1609, but mainly built by Wren to house Dean Honywood's remarkable and varied collection, acquired during his exile in the Netherlands at the time of the Commonwealth.

The Galilee Porch takes us out of the cathedral into the Close or Minster Yard. At the corner nearly opposite is the 14C Cantilupe Chantry House; and below and behind this is the arched entrance to the Old Bishop's Palace (founded 12C, with 13–15C additions). Next comes the gatehouse of the Vicars' Court, built 1300–80 for a college of priest-vicars. To the E of the cathedral are the Chancery (14–15C) and the Choristers' House, and further N is the Priory Gate, an arch on the site of an old gateway destroyed in 1815. On the green stands a statue of Tennyson, by G.F. Watts. On the N side are several old houses, including the present Bishop's House.

Ludham, Norfolk: St Benet's Abbey

Ded: St Benedict.
On banks of River Bure, 1½ miles S of A1062.

Reached down a farm track and set in water-meadows, this is an oddity among abbeys, as little more than the ruined gatehouse survives, with the redbrick conical base of an 18C windmill poking out of it. The abbey was originally founded c 1020, in the reign of Canute, but nothing of the original foundation is left. The Bp of Norwich—the only abbot in the Church of England—takes the title 'Abbot of St Benedict' from this abbey.

North Elmham Cathedral, Norfolk

On B1110, 5 miles N of East Dereham.

The substantial remains of a Saxon cathedral, surrounded by a grassy moat, lie in a field N of the parish church. In the late 7C a bishop's seat

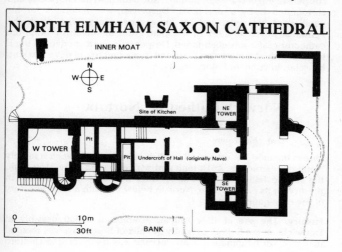

North Elmham, the massive walls of the Saxon cathedral. (K. Spence)

was established at North Elmham, and from c 955 to 1075 it was the only see in East Anglia. In the latter year the see was moved to Thetford, and finally, in 1095, to Norwich. The cathedral dates from the late 10C or early 11C; the stone walls are massive, and show it to have been a small building, little more than 100ft long, without aisles and terminating in an E transept with a single apse opening off it. The cathedral was greatly altered in the late 14C, when Henry le Despenser, Bp of Norwich, turned it into a fortified hunting lodge and surrounded it by a dry moat. Despenser was notorious for his flamboyant life style, and for his savagery in putting down the Peasants' Revolt of 1381 in his area. After his death in 1406, the cathedral-castle was abandoned. Despenser's work survives in the E tower beside the main doorway, and in walling in the nave marking his solar, kitchen and other rooms.

Norwich Cathedral, Norfolk

Ded: Holy Trinity.

One of the most majestic of all English cathedrals, Norwich is mainly Norman in structure, 461ft long and with a soaring spire 315ft high, the second tallest in the country, after Salisbury. It is unusual in preserving its eastern apse, Norman below but with a Dec clerestory of great elegance above.

History. The see of East Anglia, established c 630 possibly at Dunwich, on the Suffolk coast, by St Felix of Burgundy, was merged in that of North Elmham (see above) c 955 and transferred to Thetford (see below) in 1075. It was not until 1094 that it was permanently fixed at Norwich by Bp Herbert de Losinga (d 1119), following the Norman practice of moving bishops' seats to important fortified towns. Losinga commandeered and destroyed much of Saxon Norwich to build his cathedral; he laid the foundations in 1096 and lived to complete the choir, transepts, E end of nave and lower stage of the tower. Bp Eborardus (Everard de Montgomery), his successor, finished the long nave c 1145. In 1272 the townsfolk rose against the cathedral clergy and burnt the interior fittings and most of the domestic buildings. In 1362 a gale brought down the spire, which destroyed the Norman clerestory of the presbytery and apse as it fell; the clerestory was rebuilt in Dec style by Bp Percy (1355–69). Bp Alnwick (1426–36) altered the W front and completed the cloisters, which had been begun 130 years earlier. After a fire in 1463 the stone vaulting of the nave was built by Bp Lyhart (1446–72); while his successor, Bp Goldwell (1472–99), was responsible for the stone vault of the presbytery and the splendid stone spire. The cathedral suffered greatly at the hands of the Puritans; an eyewitness alludes to 'what clattering of glasses, what beating down of walls, what tearing down of monuments, what pulling down of seats, and wresting out of irons and brass from the windows and graves, what defacing of arms, what demolishing of curious stonework'. The cathedral was repaired after the Restoration in 1660; and in 1930–32 the new E chapel (St Saviour's) was added, on part of the site of the 13C Lady Chapel.

Exterior. The cathedral is approached through the Erpingham Gate (c 1420), with beautifully preserved sculpture; it was built by Sir Thomas Erpingham (d 1428), who fought at Agincourt and is addressed in Shakespeare's *Henry V* as 'Good old knight' (IV. i). The spacious close has many fine trees. The most striking features of the exterior are the apsidal E end, with its beautiful flying buttresses, the Norman arcading on the E wall of the S transept, and the Norman •Tower, surmounted by its 15C spire, the whole set off by the long unbroken line of the nave and chancel roof. The pinnacles are contemporary with the spire. The large Perp window in the W front is flanked by pseudo-Norman turrets.

Interior. In plan and structure the cathedral is still practically identical with Losinga's building. Viewing the finely proportioned church from the W door, the eye is at once caught by the majesty of the continuous lierne-vaulted 15C roof. The •Bosses tell the story of the Bible (both Testaments), and are well worth studying with binoculars; the Crucifixion and Harrowing of Hell in the 12th bay are outstanding. (There are mirror trolleys both in the nave and cloister for easier viewing.) The *Nave* consists of 14 bays, supported by massive Norman columns; its rhythmic unity is accentuated by the light colour of the stone and the absence of monuments. The arches of the triforium are most unusual in being practically the same size as those of the main arcade. The clerestory, set back within a wall passage, has Norman lights. The circular opening in the roof, which takes the place of one of the bosses, was used for letting down a model angel with a thurible or censer, and possibly for releasing a white dove at Whitsun. The Aisles also are Norman. Two bays of the S aisle (beside the pulpit) were converted into a Perp chantry by Bp Nykke (d 1535). There is Norman painted vaulting in the S aisle, near the screen. The Monks' Door and the Dec •Prior's Door lead from the S

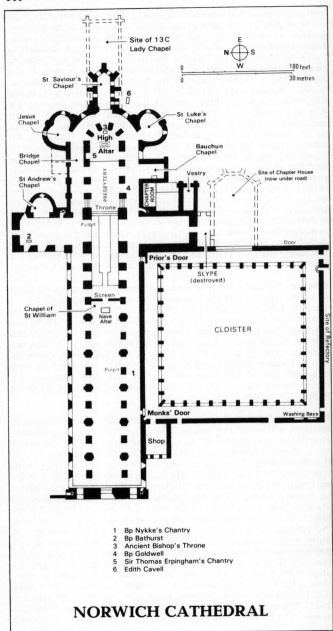

Site of 13C Lady Chapel

E
N — S
W

0   100 feet
0   30 metres

St Saviour's Chapel

St Luke's Chapel

Jesus Chapel

High Altar

Bauchun Chapel

Bridge Chapel

Vestry

Site of Chapter House (now under road)

St Andrew's Chapel

PRESBYTERY

CHAPTER ROOM

Throne

Door

Pulpit

Prior's Door

SLYPE (destroyed)

CLOISTER

Screen

Chapel of St William

Nave Altar

Site of Refectory

Pulpit

Monks' Door

Washing Bays

Shop

1   Bp Nykke's Chantry
2   Bp Bathurst
3   Ancient Bishop's Throne
4   Bp Goldwell
5   Sir Thomas Erpingham's Chantry
6   Edith Cavell

NORWICH CATHEDRAL

aisle to the cloisters. The two E bays of the nave are included in the ritual choir and contain the fine 15C stalls with their lively misericords. The lower stage of the Central Tower is Losinga's work, while the upper storeys are Norman of later date.

The *Transepts* resemble the nave in architectural style. Off the N arm is the apsidal St Andrew's Chapel with 15C stained glass from the Deanery and a statue of Our Lady by John Skelton (1960). The monument in the N transept to Bp Bathurst (d 1837) is by Sir Francis Chantrey. In the S transept is an effigy originally placed above the N transept door in 1100, representing possibly Bp Losinga.

The *Choir*, beginning W of the central tower, terminates on the E in a semicircular apse with ambulatory and radiating chapels—a French arrangement fairly unusual in English churches. The Presbytery, to the E of the central tower, has been considerably altered, though the Norman ground-plan remains unchanged. The notable early 15C lectern has a pelican instead of the usual eagle and is made of latten (a brass-like metal). The ivory chair (1512) near the high altar may have belonged originally to the Abp of Bavaria. The Bishop's Throne behind the altar is of the greatest interest, as, with its surroundings, it preserves the plan of the Christian sanctuary normal until c 1100. This plan probably goes back to the beginnings of Christianity and may have been derived from the Roman lawcourts, with the judge sitting on a throne in the centre of the apse and his officials ranged round the apse on either side of him. The chair itself is 8C or earlier and may have come originally from the Saxon cathedral at Dunwich (see 'History' above). Bp Herbert de Losinga (d 1119) was buried before the high altar, and the top slab of a new monument erected to him in 1682 is let into the pavement. The beautiful clerestory was rebuilt after 1362 in a style transitional between Dec

Norwich Cathedral, seen from the W. (Aerofilms)

and Perp; the stone vaulting was added between 1472 and 1499, and at the same time the main arches were redesigned in the current style.

In the S aisle of the presbytery is the tomb of Bp Goldwell (d 1499), the builder of the vault and the stone spire of the cathedral. On the S side of this aisle is the Bauchun Chapel of Our Lady of Pity, founded in 1330 and restored in 1968 as the chapel of the Friends of Norwich Cathedral; it was vaulted in 1450 and has remarkable roof bosses. The window, by Moira Forsyth (1964), represents the Benedictine Order; and there is a sculpture of Our Lady of Pity, by John Skelton. The Chapter Room (restored in 1961), W of this, contains Renaissance panelling, probably from St Benet's Abbey, Ludham (see above). At the E end of the choir aisles are two chapels (Jesus Chapel on the N and St Luke's Chapel on the S) which have a most unusual ground-plan formed of intersecting segments of circles.

At the E end of the cathedral is St Saviour's Chapel, built in 1930–32 as a war memorial. This is entered by two fine EE arches, a relic of the Lady Chapel built by Bp Walter de Suffield (d 1257). Furnished in 1963 as the regimental chapel of the Royal Norfolk Regiment, it contains superb 14C painted panels from the Norwich church of St Michael-at-Plea. Even finer is the *Retable in St Luke's Chapel, probably presented by Bp Despenser (d 1406) as a thank-offering for the suppression of the Peasants' Revolt in 1381 (see also North Elmham, above). Together they form a rare survival of masterpieces of the East Anglian school, which are as fine as anything being produced in Italy at the same period. The 15C Bridge Chapel spanning the N aisle was probably used for exhibiting relics and formed an antechapel to the now-destroyed reliquary chapel; it now houses the Treasury presented by the Worshipful Company of Goldsmiths in 1972. The paintings of the vault above are of c 1300. A window in the N aisle was filled in 1963 with medieval Norwich glass.

In May 1919 the body of Nurse Edith Cavell, shot by the Germans in 1915, was brought from Brussels and buried outside the cathedral, just E of St Luke's Chapel.

The splendid *Cloisters, the only two-storeyed monastic cloister in England, were built in the 12C, rebuilt from 1300 to 1430, and restored in 1935–38. The vault bosses, some with charming contemporary scenes, are even better than those in the nave. Notable also are the tracery of the cloister windows, the monks' hand-washing troughs (SW corner), and on the E side the beautiful Dec entrance of the vanished chapter house. Ruins of the infirmary and refectory (S side) and guest-hall (W side) can be seen from the close.

To the E of the cloisters, a road now covers the site of the parlour, chapter house and dormitory. Across the road is the Deanery, which before the Dissolution was the Prior's Lodging (partly 13C).

Norwich Cathedral, Norfolk (RC)

Ded: St John the Baptist.

Above inner ring road, W of city centre.

The Roman Catholic diocese of East Anglia dates from 1976; previously the cathedral was the parish church. A vast stone building looming above the town, it was built 1882–1910 by the Duke of Norfolk, to designs by George Gilbert Scott jr and his brother John Oldrid Scott. In style it is consistently EE, with good stained glass in the lancet windows. Worth seeing are the statue of St John, carved by F. Stufflesser, opposite the entrance doorway, and the ornate Walsingham Chapel in the N transept.

Norwich, Norfolk: St Andrew's Hall

Now used as a civic centre for a wide range of concerts and other activities, St Andrew's Hall was originally the Norwich church of the Dominicans or Black Friars. It is a unique survival, as it is the only friary church in England which has survived complete (though minus its octagonal tower, which collapsed in 1712). The Dominicans' first church on the site was built c 1300, but the present building is mainly 15C (1440–70). After the friary was dissolved in 1538 the buildings were kept in use for a variety of purposes; and in the 1860s the church was thoroughly restored. It now forms two separate halls: St Andrew's Hall, the aisled nave, which was the friars' preaching hall and is a spacious hall with graceful arcading and a hammerbeam roof; and Blackfriars' Hall, formerly the friars' chancel, smaller and flooded with light from the tall windows. An earlier, pre-Dominican crypt (13C) is now a coffee bar; and a 13C church known as 'Becket's Chapel' is at present being excavated.

Peterborough Cathedral, Cambridgeshire

Ded: St Peter, St Paul and St Andrew.

Known to the Saxons as Medeshamstede, the city of Peterborough grew round a great monastery founded c 655 and has been a bishop's see since 1541. The cathedral is one of the most important Norman buildings in England, with a notable 13C W front.

History. Peterborough Cathedral belongs to that splendid series of Saxon foundations, the monasteries of the Fenland, which include Ely Cathedral (see above) and Crowland Abbey (see above). Founded by Peada, King of Mercia (d 656), the monastery with its first church was destroyed by the Danes in 870. A second Saxon church, built in the 10C, was burnt down in 1116, and the present building was begun the following year. Before 1155 the E limb had been completed, the transepts and tower piers carried some way up, and the nave begun. In that year William de Waterville took up the work, completing the transepts, the piers and arches of the central crossing, and the central tower; he also did a good deal of work in the nave, especially on the S side. Except for the tower, all this grand early Norman work remains. In 1177 Abbot Benedict added two W bays, making ten in all, completed the aisles, vaulted all but the tenth bay of the aisles, and probably constructed the nave ceiling. This work, finished in 1199, completed the original design which was kept to by successive builders.

In the W Transept, which Benedict began, pointed arches show the departure from the old style. This transept was finished by Benedict's successor, Abbot Andrew (1195–1200). The next abbot, Acharius (1200–10), probably designed the unique and splendid *W Front, with its three great pointed arches; this is the most striking feature of the exterior, though it masks the Norman front. (The delicate little central porch with its Dec window, which sits somewhat uneasily in the enormous central arch, was added in the late 14C.) The NW tower was completed c 1270; the corresponding SW tower remains incomplete. A magnificent Lady Chapel was added c 1270, but was pulled down in 1651–52. In the 14C the central Norman tower was replaced by a lower and lighter one (rebuilt on the original lines by J.L. Pearson in 1884–86), and the elegant SW spire was added. In the 13C and 15C larger windows were substituted for the Norman ones. The fan-vaulted retrochoir was built c 1496–1509. As at Norwich, the interior—glass, woodwork, sculpture and monuments—suffered wholesale sacking by Cromwell's soldiers: an observer wrote how 'in a short time, a fair and goodly structure was quite stript of all its ornamental beauty, and made a ruthful spectacle, a very chaos of desolation and confusion, nothing scarce remaining but only bare walls, broken seats, and shatter'd windows on every side'. At the Restoration the cathedral was patched up, but there has been little rebuilding since apart from Pearson's work in the 1880s. In the 19C the presbytery was repaved. In 1958–63 the W front was restored, and in 1974–75 a number of statues by Alan Durst replaced the decayed originals.

Interior. The magnificent Norman *Nave* is entered from the parvise porch, a rich early Perp addition of c 1370, with a remarkable central boss of the Trinity. The upper floor of the porch, originally the Trinity Chapel, is now the cathedral treasury and library. On either side is a chapel, with noble pointed arches under the W towers. Other impressive features of the nave are the finely vaulted aisles, the dignified triforium and clerestory, and the expanse of wooden painted ceiling, dating from c 1220, repainted c 1750 and 1834. Unique to England, the ceiling is divided into lozenge-shaped compartments painted with bishops, saints and mythical beasts. The 13C font, with a bowl of local marble, stands in the NW transept chapel. The SW chapel, now the Chapel of St Sprite, contains a beautiful double piscina. To the N of the W door is an 18C copy of a naive portrait of Robert Scarlett ('Old Scarlett'), sexton and gravedigger, who d 1594 aged 98; a poem tells how:

> He had inter'd two queenes within this place
> And this towne's householders in his live's space
> Twice over; but at length his own turne came....

(For the queens he buried, see below.) On the 6th S pier of the nave a tablet commemorates Nurse Edith Cavell, shot by the Germans in 1915, who was at school in Peterborough (see also Norwich, above). High above the nave is a large (15ft high) rood or crucifix, installed in 1975, with cross by George Pace and aluminium figure of Christ by Frank Roper.

In the S transept wall is a tombstone of two Saxon bishops, discovered in 1888 in the foundations of the early Saxon church which may be seen beneath the S transept. The NE chapel of the S transept (St Oswald's Chapel) may once have contained a shrine to the saint, whose arm was one of Peterborough's most treasured relics. The

*Peterborough Cathedral, the Norman nave with its unique
13C painted ceiling. (A.F. Kersting)*

screens on the E side of the transepts are 15C. The timber ceilings of
the transepts are original Norman work; the nave ceiling was given
its sloping sides in the 14C. The choir furnishings are Victorian,
except for the late 15C brass lectern.

The *Sanctuary* is the oldest part of the building; however, the
wooden roof is Perp, with groining ribs springing from the Norman
shafts, except over the apse, where the flat roof is retained (painted in
1855). This apse stands within the so-called 'New Building'—the
square-ended processional path and chapels added at the E end in
the late 15C. The intricate fan vaulting, in contrast to the plain
ceilings elsewhere in the church, was restored in 1936; it may be the
work of John Wastell, who designed similar vaulting for the chapel of
King's College, Cambridge. In the N choir aisle is the fine tomb-slab
of Abbot Benedict (d 1192), builder of the nave; and further E, below
the banners of England and Spain, is a memorial stone to Catherine of
Aragon, whose elaborate tomb was demolished by the Puritans. At
the end of the S choir aisle is the Hedda Stone or Monks' Stone carved
with five robed figures; said to be the memorial to the monks of
Peterborough slaughtered by the Danes in 870, it is certainly not less
old than that date, and may even be a century older. The effigies of

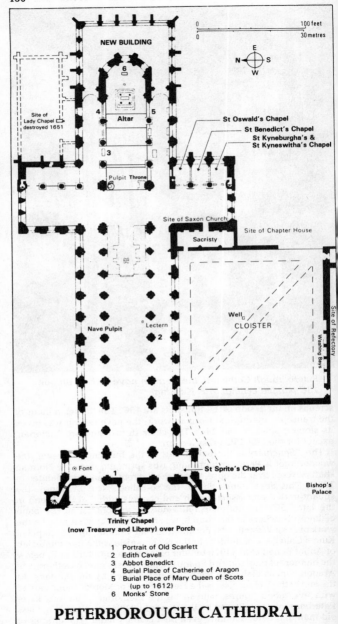

NEW BUILDING

0 · · · · · 100 feet
0 · · · · · 30 metres

N
E
W — S
W

Site of
Lady Chapel
destroyed 1651

6

4 Altar **5**

St Oswald's Chapel

St Benedict's Chapel

**St Kyneburgha's &
St Kyneswitha's Chapel**

3

Pulpit Throne

Site of Saxon Church

Site of Chapter House

Sacristy

Nave Pulpit

Lectern

2

Well
CLOISTER

Site of Refectory

Washing Bays

⊙ Font

1

St Sprite's Chapel

Bishop's
Palace

Trinity Chapel
(now Treasury and Library) over Porch

1 Portrait of Old Scarlett
2 Edith Cavell
3 Abbot Benedict
4 Burial Place of Catherine of Aragon
5 Burial Place of Mary Queen of Scots
  (up to 1612)
6 Monks' Stone

PETERBOROUGH CATHEDRAL

12–13C abbots, removed here from the ruins of the chapter house, are claimed to be the finest series of Benedictine memorials in England. To the right, a slab beneath the Scottish flag marks the supposed burial place of Mary, Queen of Scots, buried in the church in 1587 but in 1612 transferred by her son, James I, to a more stately tomb in Westminster Abbey (see above). Tablets to the two queens, paid for by 'Catherines' and 'Marys', have been placed near their graves.

On the S side of the cathedral are the ruins of the *Cloister*, with 14C washing-bays on the S side. From the SE corner a passage with a blind arcade, once vaulted, leads to the two fine EE arcades of the *Infirmary* (now incorporated in more recent buildings). To the NE a spirelet, blown down by a hurricane in January 1976, has been set up on the grass.

Prittlewell Priory, Essex

Ded: St Mary.

In Southend-on-Sea, 1½ miles inland from sea-front.

Closed Wed. and Sun.

Set in a delightful park, the refectory and prior's house of a 12C Cluniac priory are now used as a museum. Founded about 1100 by Robert of Essex, Prittlewell was dissolved in 1536, when most of the monastic buildings were demolished. What survives is a noble stone refectory (late 12C) with a magnificent 15C roof; and at right angles to it a building whose half-timbered upper floor is known as the 'Prior's Chamber'. The foundations of the cloister and church are marked out in the turf of the surrounding garden.

Ramsey Abbey, Cambridgeshire

In Ramsey, 12 miles SE of Peterborough.

An important Benedictine abbey was founded here in 969; of the buildings on the site, the 13C Lady Chapel is incorporated in a school (not open to visitors). The ruined base of the 15C gatehouse belongs to the NT and can be visited. The parish church outside the gatehouse began its life as a large guest-house for the abbey, and was converted into a church probably during the 13C.

St Osyth's Priory, Essex

Off B1027, 10 miles SE of Colchester.

Gatehouse and gardens open May–Sept.

Osyth was an East Anglian princess and abbess, who was martyred by the Danes in 653. In the early 12C a priory for Augustinian canons was founded here by the Bp of London. During the Middle Ages it was much visited for its relics of St Osyth, including her arm, and her skull set in silver. By the end of the 12C St Osyth's had been raised to the rank of abbey; dissolved in 1539, it was turned into a country mansion. The chief monastic survival is the magnificent late 15C *Gatehouse, which is a remarkable example of flushwork. The abbey church, now vanished, lay between the gatehouse and the later mansion, where there is now a topiary garden. The most substantial remains apart from the gatehouse are those of a 13C chapel.

Thetford Priory, Norfolk

Ded: St Mary.

Beside A11, near station, on W outskirts of town.

The extensive remains of this Cluniac priory are hard to find, as they are tucked away between a new housing estate and the river. It was founded at the beginning of the 12C by Roger Bigod, an old soldier and counsellor of William the Conqueror; the monks' original church was in the town, in the building that had been the cathedral of the East Anglian diocese until 1094, when the bishopric was moved to Norwich (see above). Bigod died a week after laying the foundation stone, in 1107; the church was completed in 1114, and the monastic buildings date mainly from 1120–40. Early in the 13C a large Lady Chapel was built to house a miraculous statue of the Virgin. The priory was dissolved in 1540 and quickly became ruinous.

Though the remains do not survive to any great height (apart from the 14C gatehouse in a garden to the N), they are easy to follow on the ground. The Norman church ended in an E apse, squared off and extended in the 13C. In front of the high altar is the Tomb of Thomas Howard, 2nd Duke of Norfolk (d 1524), who defeated the Scots at Flodden in 1513. The cloister was on the S side of the church, with the sacristy and chapter house on the E side, the frater on the S, and guest-rooms with cellar under on the W. To the W of the main complex, a long narrow building called the Prior's Lodging survives up to first-floor height. A charming feature of Thetford is the Infirmary, with its own small cloister like a monastery in miniature.

About 2 miles from the priory and W of the Brandon road (B1107) is *Thetford Warren Lodge*, a small fortified stone tower-house of c 1400, almost certainly occupied by the prior's gamekeeper and an indication of the importance of the chase to medieval churchmen.

Thorney Abbey, Cambridgeshire

Ded: St Mary and St Botolph.

Off A47, 5 miles E of Peterborough.

About 670 a monastery was founded here on what was then an island in the Fens (Thorney means 'thorn island'). Sacked by the Danes in 870, it was refounded in 972 as a monastery for Benedictine monks; in 1085 Abbot Gunter pulled down the Saxon church and began a vast

Norman building, completed in 1108. It was five times larger than the present church, with a central tower said to have been higher than Boston Stump. The abbey was dissolved in 1539 and mostly demolished; but a century later, in 1638, what remained was restored as a church for the families of men employed on draining the Fens. The present church consists only of five bays of the Norman nave, without aisles (pulled down) and with the aisle arches blocked in; the transepts and chancel are 19C in the Norman style. The central section of the Norman W front survives, with twin octagonal turrets; the large W window is Perp. The church was restored in 1977–80.

Thornton Abbey, Humberside

Ded: The Blessed Virgin Mary.

On minor road 2 miles E of Thornton Curtis (A1077).

A remote abbey lost among the fields S of the Humber, Thornton was founded as a priory of Augustinian canons in 1139 and raised to abbey status in 1148; it was dissolved in 1539. The most impressive of the remains is the grand *Gatehouse (late 14C), imposing enough to have been the abbot's lodging. Built mainly of brick and one of the earliest large-scale brick structures in the country, it has a lofty entrance archway, a first-floor chamber 48ft long by 20ft wide with a fine oriel window, and another room the same size on the floor above. Several of the niches still have their statues of saints. The abbey was largely rebuilt in the late 13C and early 14C; the church was uncomplicated and square-ended, with a Lady Chapel added to the E (late 14C), and a chapel to St Thomas of Canterbury on the N side of the chancel. Of the monastic buildings, the finest survival consists of two sides of the octagonal chapter house (early 14C), where the graceful blank arcading still stands almost to full height. Thornton has its own legend: the story of a mummified canon, walled up with book, pen and ink, and only discovered when the wall was knocked down. (The DoE's official handbook pours cold water on the tale.)

Walsingham Priory, Norfolk

Ded: Our Lady of Walsingham.

In Little Walsingham, on B1105, 5 miles N of Fakenham.

According to legend, in about 1060 Walsingham's lady of the manor, Richeldis de Favarques, had a vision of the Virgin Mary who took her in spirit to Nazareth and told her to build a wooden chapel similar to the house where the Annunciation had taken place. A priory of Augustinian canons followed in the mid 11C, and Walsingham quickly became a centre of pilgrimage, popularly called 'England's Nazareth'. Long after the Dissolution Walsingham's fame lived on, as in Sir Walter Raleigh's poem:

As you came from the holy land
Of Walsinghame,
Met you not with my true love
By the way as you came?

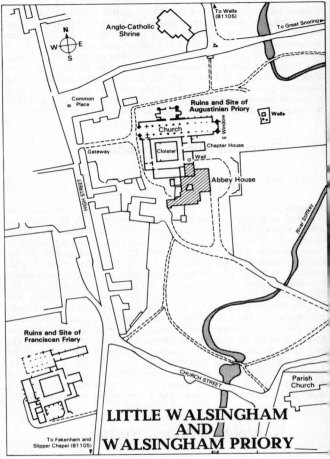

To Wells (B1105)

To Great Snoring

Anglo-Catholic Shrine

N

W E

S

Common Place

Ruins and Site of Augustinian Priory

Wells

Church

E Window

Gateway

Chapter House

HIGH STREET

Cloister

Wall

Abbey House

River Stiffkey

Ruins and Site of Franciscan Friary

CHURCH STREET

Parish Church

LITTLE WALSINGHAM AND WALSINGHAM PRIORY

To Fakenham and Slipper Chapel (B1105)

A medieval gateway (c 1440) in the High Street still gives access to the priory grounds; but little survives of the great church apart from the magnificent E wall (late 14C), without its window but still standing to full gable height. The cloister was on the S side of the church, and part of the refectory survives on its S side. On this side also is the healing well for which the priory was famous. In the 1920s pilgrimages to Walsingham were revived, and today's pilgrims congregate in the modern (1930s) Anglo-Catholic shrine to the N of the priory.

Also in Little Walsingham: *Franciscan Friary*, on S side of village beside Fakenham road. Considerable remains of the friary, founded in 1347, can be seen from the road. (Privately owned and not open to the public.) *Slipper Chapel*, 1 mile S of village, on lane off Fakenham road. This tiny 14C chapel, dedicated to St Catherine of Alexandria,

Walsingham Priory, the remains of the 14C E end. (K. Spence)

was the last stop for pilgrims on their way to Walsingham, and is so called because it was where they left their shoes and proceeded barefoot. Even Henry VIII is said to have done this. Beside it is the new (1982) Roman Catholic *Chapel of Reconciliation*, red-roofed and looking like an enormous tithe barn.

Waltham Abbey, Essex

Ded: The Holy Cross and St Lawrence.

The present church is hardly more than a quarter of the length of the enormous medieval building, which was over 300ft long and the largest Augustinian church in England. Founded c 1030, the abbey was originally a college of secular canons, and was rebuilt by King Harold and consecrated in 1060. The church consists of the massive *Nave begun by Harold, the Lady Chapel of 1316, and a W tower of 1556–58. The mighty columns of the nave, deeply channelled with chevrons and spirals, recall Durham Cathedral, which Waltham must have resembled before Henry II's vast E extensions of c 1180 were demolished after the Dissolution. The composer Thomas Tallis was organist here until 1540. The E end, filled in during the 19C, is where the Norman crossing began; the fine windows are by Burne-Jones. On the S the raised 14C chapel has a 'Doom' painting of the Last Judgement (c 1430), and a large W window with delicate tracery. The nave ceiling, painted in lozenges and reminiscent of the medieval ceiling at Peterborough, was in fact painted by Edward (later Sir Edward) Poynter in 1860. The church has two remarkable tombs: to Sir Edward Denny (d 1600) and his wife, with painted effigies; and to Captain Robert Smith (d 1697), ornately carved with 'the Ship of Industry dodging the Rock of Sloth'.

Outside the church, in the garden to E and N, the transepts, apse and cloister are marked out on the ground. A stone at the E end of the Norman apse marks the site of the grave where Harold was buried, after his death in 1066 at the Battle of Hastings (see also Battle Abbey, above). To the N is a monastic gateway (c 1370), and an ancient bridge known as 'Harold's Bridge'.

Weybourne Priory, Norfolk

Ded: The Blessed Virgin and All Saints.

On A149, 3 miles W of Sheringham.

A priory of Augustinian canons was founded at Weybourne early in the 13C. They originally used an existing Anglo-Saxon church, whose nave became the N aisle of the present (late 13C) parish church. The W tower is 15C. The most prominent of the ancient remains is the tall fragment of the Saxon tower, which was the central tower of the original church. The cloister and monastic buildings lay to the N of the priory church, on what is now private land.

Wymondham Abbey, Norfolk

Ded: St Mary and St Thomas of Canterbury.

Off A11, 8 miles SW of Norwich.

Open daily, Easter–Oct. 10.00–18.00, Oct.–Easter 11.00–15.00.

With its two mighty towers, one at each end, Wymondham (pronounced 'Windham') abbey church has an extraordinary and striking silhouette, which derives from an eventful history. A Benedictine priory was founded here in 1107 by William de Albini (d 1155), 1st Earl of Arundel and Chief Butler to Henry I, as a cell of St Albans Abbey; it was raised to full abbey status in 1448. The church was shared from the outset by the monks and the local parishioners, which led to frequent squabbles. The original building consisted of a large nave with N and S aisles, a presbytery with chapels at the E end, a central tower over the crossing, and a pair of towers at the W end. In 1249 the Pope decreed that the parishioners should have the nave, N aisle and NW tower, while the monks were allocated the choir, transepts, S aisle and SW tower.

During the 14C the central tower became unsafe, and c 1390 the monks built the graceful octagonal tower two bays to the W and supported it by an immense wall right across the W arch, cutting the church completely in two and depriving the parishioners of access to the high altar. Quarrels over where the bells should be hung, as well as questions of access to the church, led to full-scale rioting by the townspeople; but by the 1440s matters were settled, and the parishioners built the present magnificent W tower, rivalling the monks' octagonal one. The N porch, superb Perp N aisle and clerestory also date from this period. At the Dissolution in 1540 the monastic buildings were demolished, as was the church E of the octagonal tower; only the lofty chapter house arch survives to remind us of Wymondham's monastic glory.

Inside the church, the nave is the original Norman (except for the clerestory). The 15C hammerbeam roof is decorated with angels and elaborate bosses. There is an outstanding terracotta Renaissance monument to the last abbot, Elisha Ferrers (d 1548), on the S side of the altar; and a large and elaborate reredos (c 1935) by Sir Ninian Comper.

5. CENTRAL ENGLAND

Abingdon Abbey, Oxfordshire

Ded: St Mary.

Buildings open daily, except Mon. during winter.

Standing on the N side of the Thames, E of Abingdon's main square,
the remains of the abbey are so closely integrated with later buildings
that it is hard to distinguish them. The first monastery was founded
here in 675 by Hean, a Saxon nobleman; devastated by the Danes in
the 10C, it was refounded as a Benedictine house c 955 by S
Ethelwold. At the beginning of the 12C, under Abbot Fabritius, it
became one of the most prosperous abbeys in the country, and
remained so until it was dissolved in 1538. The way into the abbey is
through the impressive 15C Gatehouse, which adjoins the medieval
St Nicholas' Church. The enormous abbey church has disappeared;
the overgrown fragments in the public gardens W of the gateway
were put together as a folly in the 19C. The main survivals are a range
of ancillary buildings to the S, beside the mill stream, which are
owned and maintained by the Friends of Abingdon. The large square
14C hall, known as the 'Checker' (an abbreviation of Exchequer, as
the abbey accounts were dealt with there), was fitted up in 1953 as an
Elizabethan theatre (the Unicorn Theatre); and adjoining it is the fine
early 16C Long Gallery, facing N, which was originally subdivided
into rooms and used as accommodation for guests, or offices for
clerks.

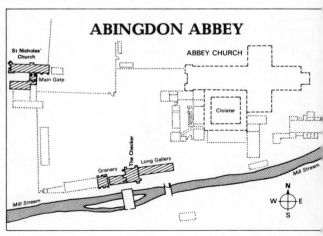

Birmingham Cathedral, W Midlands

Ded: St Philip.

This classical-style building stands on the only green oasis left in the heart of Birmingham. Designed by Thomas Archer, it was built for a parish called into being by the early 18C expansion of the town, and was consecrated in 1715. It was completed ten years later, with the help of a grant of £600 from King George II; and in 1884 it was enlarged one bay to the E. In 1905 the diocese of Birmingham was formed, and St Philip's was raised to cathedral status.

Externally the chief feature is Archer's concave-sided Baroque tower, topped by a dome and cupola; inside the church is sober and dignified, with Corinthian columns at the chancel end, and galleries at the sides and W end. In contrast to the white paint and gilding are the glowing *Stained-glass Windows (1884–90) by the Pre-Raphaelite artist Burne-Jones, three at the E end (left to right, Nativity, Ascension and Crucifixion) and one at the W end (Last Judgement). At the E end of the S aisle is a colourful tapestry by Carole Raymond (1975), on the theme of God's creativity. Among the monuments is a tablet (N aisle column) to Peter Oliver (d 1791), Chief Justice of Massachusetts, who remained loyal to Britain during the American War of Independence.

Birmingham Cathedral, (RC)

Ded: St Chad.

The redbrick Roman Catholic cathedral, with its lofty nave and pair of W towers topped by needle-sharp spires, is sundered from the centre of Birmingham by the hurtling traffic of the city's inner ring road. Designed by Augustus Welby Pugin in the Gothic style and built in 1839–41 (except for the SW spire, completed in 1856), it was the first Catholic cathedral designed and built in England since the Reformation. In 1850 Catholic bishoprics were officially recognized, and the Vicar Apostolic of the Midland District became the Catholic Bishop of Birmingham; in a papal reorganization of 1911, Birmingham was made an archbishopric. The cathedral's interior gives an impression of overwhelming height, due to the narrow pillars and enormously tall arcades. The sanctuary ceiling is sumptuously painted and gilded, and there is plenty of colour elsewhere in the church, notably in the glass at the apsidal E end, and in the naturalistic Stations of the Cross, by John Hardman (1875). The chief monument is the stone-canopied tomb in the N aisle to Bp Walsh (d 1849), designed by Pugin in medieval style.

Bisham Abbey, Berkshire

Off A404, 2 miles SW of Marlow.

Standing by a beautiful stretch of the Thames, Bisham (pronounced Bizzum) is a Tudor mansion incorporating the remains of an

Augustinian priory. At the time of Domesday (1086), Bisham belonged to the Ferrers family, who c 1140 handed it over to the Knights Templars. When the Templars were suppressed in 1307 it passed through various hands, and in 1337 was owned by the Earl of Salisbury, who in that year founded a priory of Augustinian canons there. When it was dissolved in 1536, the church and most of the conventual buildings were demolished; the last prior, William Barlow, subsequently married and was the father of five daughters, all of whom married Elizabethan bishops. The medieval survivals are of Templar, not monastic origin. The Templars' great hall, over 50ft long, is used as a dining-room by those attending the National Sports Centre, of which the old mansion is now the headquarters.

Blyth Priory, Nottinghamshire

Ded: St Mary and St Martin.

5 miles NE of Worksop, on A634.

A Benedictine priory was founded at Blyth in 1088, and the present noble parish church dates back to that foundation. It originally consisted of a nave with two aisles, transepts, and chancel with five radiating chapels; c 1290 the Norman S aisle was pulled down and the present wide S aisle was built. The Dec W tower dates from c 1400, as does the chancel screen painted with saints on its panels. Some time during the Middle Ages a wall was built across the church, at the E end of the nave (now the E end of the church), to separate the monks from the lay congregation; when the priory was dissolved in 1535, the (monks') E section was demolished, leaving the church shorn of its transepts and chancel.

Buildwas Abbey, Shropshire

Ded: Our Lady and St Chad.

On B4378, 2 miles N of Much Wenlock.

Standing on the south bank of the Severn, Buildwas is near the birthplace of British industry, at Coalbrookdale and Ironbridge, with the vast cooling towers of a power station across the road to the E. It was founded in 1135 by Roger de Clinton, Bp of Coventry and Lichfield, for monks of the Order of Savigny (Savignacs), an austere order which in 1147 was merged with the Cistercians. Its history was uneventful, apart from raids by Welsh marauders in 1350 and 1406; it was dissolved in 1536. The buildings were probably all completed by 1200, and so the abbey ruins are consistent Norman or Trans in style. Much of the church remains intact though roofless, with massive columns, very slightly pointed arches, and clerestory above; the presbytery has three lancet windows at the E end; and the later chapel on the S side (c 1400) has tomb-slabs of the abbey's lay benefactors. The monastic remains are on the N, towards the river; best-preserved is the elegant chapter house, with four columns supporting the vaulting, and some medieval floor tiles still in position.

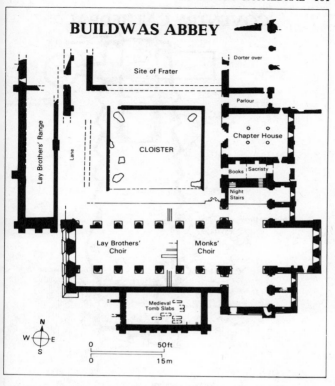

To the N, the abbey is on private ground and is unexcavated; to the S, there are remains of fishponds on the other side of the railway.

Coventry Cathedral, W Midlands

Ded: St Michael.

On the night of 14 November 1940, a devastating air raid gutted the centre of Coventry, destroying the cathedral (apart from the tower and spire), but in the process providing the opportunity to build one of the largest and most imaginative churches of the post-war period.

History. Coventry's history begins with the foundation of a Benedictine priory (St Mary's) in 1043 by Leofric, Earl of Mercia, and his wife Godgyfu (better known to legend as 'Lady Godiva'). After the Norman Conquest the lordship of Coventry passed to the Earls of Chester, and in the 12C the priory church was for a time the cathedral of the joint diocese of Coventry and Lichfield. At the Dissolution in 1539 the priory church was largely destroyed, though fragments of it survive in Priory Row, W of today's cathedral. In 1918 Coventry was

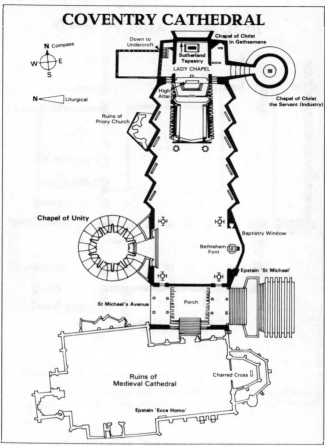

COVENTRY CATHEDRAL

N Compass

N Liturgical

Down to Undercroft

Chapel of Christ in Gethsemane

Sutherland Tapestry

LADY CHAPEL

High Altar

Chapel of Christ the Servant (Industry)

Ruins of Priory Church

Chapel of Unity

Baptistry Window

Bethlehem Font

Epstein 'St Michael'

St Michael's Avenue

Porch

Ruins of Medieval Cathedral

Charred Cross

Epstein 'Ecce Homo'

made a diocese in its own right, and St Michael's parish church became the cathedral. Its splendid steeple, tower, octagon and spire, 295ft high, survived the firestorm of 1940; and its ruined shell has been rededicated as a memorial shrine and vestibule to the new cathedral. The moving desolation of its 14C walls is heightened by two crosses on the altar at the E end, one made of charred roof beams (now a replica, as in 1978 the original was moved to the cathedral undercroft), and one of three 14C hand-forged nails, which fell from the roof during the fire of 1940. Set against the S wall is Sir Jacob Epstein's monumentally brooding figure of Christ, 'Ecce Homo' (1935), bearing a strong resemblance to an Easter Island statue. As a gesture of reconciliation (the theme of the new cathedral) the vestries were rebuilt as an international centre by German students and apprentices.

The new cathedral, designed by Sir Basil Spence in modern idiom and materials and built in 1954–62, extends towards the N at right angles to the old. (Thus the 'E end' of the cathedral is in fact N-facing; for clarity, the liturgical as opposed to the geographical points of the compass will be put in inverted commas.) Benjamin Britten's 'War Requiem' was written for the rededication of the cathedral, and received its first performance there in May 1962.

Exterior. The arrangement of an alternating screen of wall (in uncoursed pink sandstone) and window, set saw-toothed to the line of the building, gives marked contrasts according to one's viewpoint. The roof is topped by a gilded bronze flèche or spirelet (locally nicknamed 'Radio Coventry'), which was lifted into place by helicopter. Old and new are linked by a boldly designed Porch, whose extended roof binds the two together. The enormous glass screen, by John Hutton, engraved with translucent figures of saints and angels, which takes the place of the cathedral's 'W wall', further emphasizes the unity of the new and the old. The porch is crossed by a ceremonial way (St Michael's Avenue), so that entrance can be made from either side independently of the old cathedral. On the nave wall facing Priory Street, at the head of a great flight of steps, is Epstein's bronze of 'St Michael Subduing the Devil', 25ft high and far more naturalistic in style than his 'Ecce Homo' in the old cathedral.

In the angle of the old and new buildings, and connected with the latter by a short cloister, stands the *Chapel of Unity*, an undenominational place of worship for all Christians. It has the form of a crusader's tent with heavy buttresses, symbolizing Christianity as a crusade against the forces of evil. The mosaic floor was designed by the Swedish artist Einar Forseth; and the narrow stained-glass windows, by Margaret Traherne, were paid for by donors in the German Federal Republic.

Interior. Since the side windows are hidden from view when the cathedral is entered from the 'W end', the attention is immediately drawn towards the altar by the immensity of Graham Sutherland's tapestry (see below). The *Nave*, 270ft long and 80ft wide, has a floor of polished black and white marble contrasting with the plain plastered walls. The ceiling is carried on two rows of slender concrete columns and is made up of concrete ribs, forming an unbroken diamond pattern that extends to the chancel and is filled in with wooden louvres; the weight of the roof above is wholly carried by the outer walls. To the right, the *Baptistry* takes the form of a shallow alcove bounded by an immense stained-glass *Window, designed by John Piper and carried out by Patrick Reyntiens, extending from floor to ceiling. The 198 lights, set in a checker-board pattern between deep mullions, represent in abstract form the light of the Holy Spirit shining through the life of man. On a marble step in the centre of the alcove stands an unwrought sandstone boulder from the valley of Barakat, outside Bethlehem, in which a scallop-shaped hollow serves as a font.

As we advance towards the 'E end', passing the carved stone *Tablets of the Word, designed by Ralph Beyer, at the foot of each section of wall, each pair in turn of the ten *Nave Windows* comes into view. They throw their light in the direction of the altar. The windows were designed by Lawrence Lee, Geoffrey Clarke and Keith New, and made in London. Each pair has a predominant colour and theme but an abstract form. The first pair (green) represents Beginnings; the second (red), God's intervention in the world; the third (multicoloured), Conflict; the fourth (blue and purple), Maturity; and the

Coventry, Epstein's 'Ecce Homo' in the ruins of the old cathedral. (K. Spence)

fifth (silver and gold), the Ultimate Realities.

The *Chancel* is not distinguished structurally from the nave but formed by the traditional placing of lectern (cast-bronze eagle by Elizabeth Frink), pulpit and stalls. These and the bishop's throne (on the left) have canopies which suggest (not too happily) flocks of doves in flight. The uncased organ is built on either side against the end walls of the aisles. The stone altar, 15ft long and unadorned, stands alone in front of a huge (¼ ton) silver-gilt cross by Geoffrey Clarke, which cradles another Cross of Nails (see above). Below the altar, work during the building uncovered the apse of the 12C cathedral (St Mary's). Between the high altar and the 'E wall' is the *Lady Chapel*, its structural simplicity forming a foil for the vast tapestry, by Graham Sutherland, which fills the whole of the wall.

The *Tapestry*, woven in one piece at Felletin, near Aubusson, in Australian wool, is the largest in the world, measuring 72ft by 38ft. On a green background is displayed a figure of Christ in glory, with Man between his feet. The composition was inspired by St John's vision in Revelation (iv. 2–3): 'And, behold, a throne was set in heaven, and one sat on the throne. And he that sat was to look upon like a jasper and a sardine stone: and there was a rainbow round about the throne, in sight like unto an emerald'. On either side of Christ are the four beasts of Revelation (iv. 6–8), linked with the four evangelists (Matthew, man; Mark, lion; Luke, bull; and John, eagle). A lower panel (Christ crucified) gives the effect of a reredos to the Lady Chapel altar and, when seen from the nave, to the high altar, 50ft further forward.

To the right of the Lady Chapel is the dramatic *Chapel of Christ in Gethsemane*, separated from the aisle only by an iron screen in the form of a crown of thorns, designed by Sir Basil Spence, and wrought and presented by the Royal Engineers. Behind the asymmetrically placed altar a kneeling angel in bronze relief, holding a cup, is silhouetted against a rich gold mosaic (by Stephen Sykes). A short passage leads to the *Chapel of Industry* (Chapel of Christ the Servant), a separate circular structure, which from outside provides a graceful foil to the massive chancel. It combines the functions of the former guild chapels, and has windows of plain glass giving glimpses of industrial Coventry.

To the left of the Lady Chapel, steps lead down to an *Undercroft*, opened in 1983 as a Visitors' Centre. This includes a historical exhibition, displays of cathedral treasures, an audio-visual theatre, and a 'walkway' of holograms (three-dimensional light images) by Malcolm Woodward.

John F. Kennedy House, a residential youth centre in the precincts, was opened in 1965 by Herr Willy Brandt, then Chief Burgomaster of Berlin and later Chancellor of West Germany.

Coventry, W Midlands: Whitefriars

SE of cathedral, down Whitefriars Street and under ring road.

A Carmelite friary was founded here in 1342; and the E and W walls of its enormous church, 303ft apart, were discovered as recently as 1962. The E cloister walk, chapter house and dormitory survive; the dormitory was opened in 1970 as a museum of Coventry history displaying local finds, chiefly of medieval date.

Croxden Abbey, Staffordshire

Ded: St Mary.

On minor road between A50 and B5032, 5 miles NW of Uttoxeter.

Few monastic remains evoke the plain austerity of the Cistercians better than the ruins of Croxden, in quiet countryside hardly more than ten miles from the Potteries. The abbey was founded in 1176 by Bertram de Verdun, for Cistercian monks from Aunay in Normandy. The church and E cloister range were completed by c 1250, while the W range was finished some 40 years later. Croxden subsisted from agriculture, mainly sheep farming; it was dissolved in 1538. Unfortunately, the road now cuts diagonally across the nave, which means that the ruins have to be seen in two sections. Of the church,

Croxden Abbey, the austere W end. (K. Spence)

the chief survival is the magnificent W end, with its three narrow lancets and austere absence of decoration. Similar lancets appear in the S transept. The E end (across the road) had five radiating circular chapels (forming a *chevet*), and an ambulatory behind the high altar. Of the cloister buildings, the chapter house has been recently discovered to be rectangular, resting on two rows of four columns each, instead of square as was previously thought. Between the S transept and the chapter house is a narrow sacristy; and S of the chapter house come the parlour, a slype, and the undercroft of the monks' dormitory. On the S side are the remains of the warming-house, frater and kitchen. A Georgian farmhouse now occupies a good deal of the S and W (lay brothers') ranges.

Dale Abbey, Derbyshire

In Dale village, on minor road off A6096, 8 miles NE of Derby.

A single gaunt arch, standing forlornly in the corner of a field, is all that survives of Dale's Premonstratensian abbey. Near the arch (? the E window) are the bases of a few columns and a number of overgrown mounds which look as though they would repay excavation.

Darley Abbey, Derbyshire

Off A6, on N outskirts of Derby.

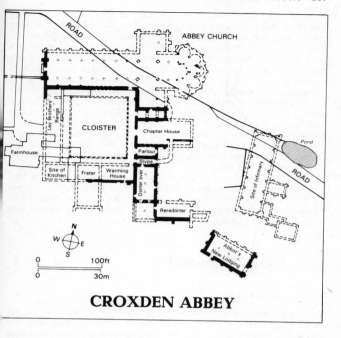

CROXDEN ABBEY

The old village of Darley Abbey lies at the bottom of a hill beside the Derwent. Nothing remains of the medieval abbey except for a small building which looks as though it was at one time a chapel or infirmary, and has now been turned into a pub.

Deerhurst Priory, Gloucestershire

Ded: St Mary.

On minor road off B4213, 3 miles SW of Tewkesbury.

Though Deerhurst is today only a hamlet, in Saxon times it was one of the most important townships of Hwicce, a kingdom of the lower Severn, and the site of its chief monastery. By the 6C this part of the country was Celtic Christian, and the original monastery may well date from this early period. It reached its greatest prosperity c 800; but thereafter it declined, and before the Conquest was given by Edward the Confessor to the abbey of St Denis, near Paris. In the 15C it was successively taken over by the Crown, given to Eton College and made a cell of Tewkesbury; and after the Dissolution the church became the parish church.

The building is largely Saxon, with a core that may go back to the 7C. The lower half of the tower is Saxon, and later herringbone work can be seen in many parts of the external walls. The Saxon nave, pierced with EE arcades, incorporates the original choir, which was 20ft long; the Saxon apse was destroyed by a fire in the 15C and not rebuilt, but can still be traced outside. In the E wall of the tower, looking down into the nave, is a strange two-light triangular-headed window, which may contain reused Roman stones, and below it is a triangular opening (like others in the N and S walls), and a blocked door that once led to a W gallery. The ancient *Font has spiral decoration, probably pre 9C, and the hood-moulding of the blocked-in chancel arch is carved with typically Celtic semi-stylized animal heads. In the N choir aisle is the 15C brass to Sir John and Lady Cassey, which has the only named figure of a dog found on any brass; inscribed with his name 'Terri', he lies at his mistress's feet.

Such monastic buildings as survived are now incorporated in a private house on the S side of the church. The door that led into the cloister can still be seen.

About 200 yards away, across the road and attached to a fine half-timbered house, is the so-called *'Odda's Chapel', dating from 1056, according to a dedication stone now in the Ashmolean Museum, Oxford. Odda was a friend of Edward the Confessor, and built the chapel in memory of his brother Aelfric.

Derby Cathedral

Ded: All Saints.

The magnificent Perp tower is all that survives of the medieval All Saints, one of Derby's six original parish churches. Raised to the status of a cathedral in 1927, it is an extraordinary and successful amalgam of three separate centuries of building: the early 16C tower, the early 18C body of the church, and the 20C E end, completed as recently as 1972. (For a photograph, taken from the E, see front cover.)

A church has stood on the site since Saxon times. Little is known of the original medieval church, built mainly in the 14C. The present splendid *W Tower, 212ft high to the summit of the pinnacles, was rebuilt c 1510–30 in elaborate late Perp style; it now carries the oldest ring of ten bells in the country (the tenor was cast in the 15C and is thus older than the tower). The words 'young men and maidens' are carved fairly low on the S wall, which may mean that the young

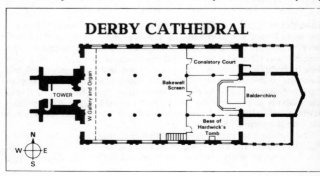

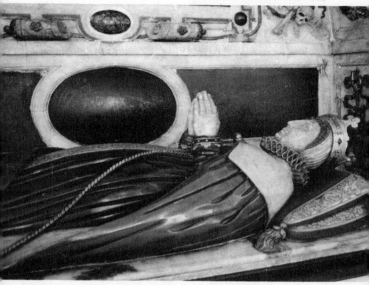

Derby Cathedral, the tomb of 'Bess of Hardwick' (d 1608). (K. Spence)

people of Derby paid for the lower stage of the tower. The present classical-style nave is due to a high-handed action by the vicar of the day, Dr Michael Hutchinson. Before dawn one morning in 1723 he sent workmen with pickaxes into the old Gothic church, and they soon demolished it, leaving only the tower. The replacement nave (1723–25) was designed by James Gibbs, architect of London's St Martin-in-the-Fields; after its completion the church remained unaltered for almost 250 years. By the mid 20th century, because of the church's recent promotion to cathedral status, a new and expanded E end had become necessary. In 1965–72 this was built to a restrained design by Sebastian Comper (son of the famous church architect Sir Ninian Comper), echoing the rounded windows and overall simplicity of Gibbs's 18C work.

The Interior, painted mainly in white and gold, astonishes the visitor by its Rococo impression of lightness and space. The chief feature is the elaborate wrought-iron *Screen that stretches from one side of the church to the other; the work of Robert Bakewell, of Derby (d 1752), it bears the Hanoverian coat of arms. Beyond the screen is Sebastian Comper's baldacchino over the high altar, supported on four massive Corinthian columns, with an upper storey resembling a small Greek temple. A gallery and organ loft runs across the W end of the church. The windows are of plain glass, except for the two on either side of the baldacchino; designed by the painter Ceri Richards (d 1971) they represent in abstract form the concepts of All Souls (left) and All Saints (right). Against the N wall, E of Bakewell's screen, is furniture made in 1634 for the consistory court that decided affairs that fell within church jurisdiction. The bishop's throne was brought from Constantinople when the diocese was formed, and originally came from a Greek church. There are a number of fine monuments, notably the effigy tomb of 'Bess of Hardwick' (Elizabeth, Countess of Shrewsbury; d 1608) in the S choir aisle. Next to it is the reclining figure of Caroline, Countess of Bessborough (d 1760), by Rysbrack.

Dorchester Abbey, Oxfordshire

Ded: St Peter and St Paul.

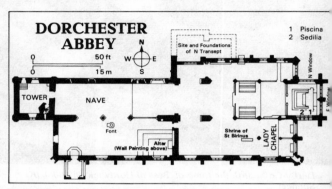

Now little more than a village on the River Thame (a tributary of the Thames), Dorchester was a Roman military centre and later an important Saxon town. From 634 to 705 it was the cathedral city of Wessex, and from 869 to 1072 that of Mercia; in the latter year the see was transferred to Lincoln. A priory of Augustinian canons was founded here c 1140; of the original Norman church, probably begun before the abbey and completed c 1180, the nave and W end of the choir survive. The S nave aisle, and the S and N choir aisles, are built in the Geometric Dec style (1280–1320); while the E end of the church, with its three superb windows, dates from the close of the Dec period. At the Dissolution the church remained intact. The low W tower and round transept arches were added in the 17C.

The interior of the church is full of interesting features. The moulded leaden font (1170–80), one of only 30 such fonts surviving in England, is decorated with figures of the Apostles. The three *Sanctuary Windows (c 1340) are of unique design, as they are fully traceried, without the usual vertical mullions. The E window, divided in two by a massive buttress, contains much 14C glass, including a panel showing St Birinus, who converted Wessex to Christianity, preaching to King Cynegils. The N window takes the form of a 'tree of Jesse', growing from a stone figure of Jesse on the windowsill. Below the window on the S are beautiful canopied sedilia and piscina, with 12C glass in the small window openings behind. The wide S choir aisle (Lady Chapel) terminates at its E end in twin altars, in front of which are a number of fine brasses and tombs, including one with the effigy of a cross-legged knight, and a conjectural reconstruction (1964) of the Shrine of St Birinus.

The abbey cloisters lay N of the church, where an 'Anglo-American' garden has been laid out. The cross in the garden (1960) commemorates the abbey's benefactors; and a plaque in the garden is in memory of American airmen who lost their lives in World War II. The American connection is further recalled by a portrait head (on the buttress at the SW corner of the abbey) of Edith Stedman, who founded the American Friends of the Abbey.

Dunstable Priory, Bedfordshire

Ded: St Peter.

In the 1130s Henry I founded a priory of Augustinian canons at Dunstable. During the Middle Ages the church was used by the parishioners as well as the monks, and after the Dissolution it remained in use instead of being demolished. The magnificent Norman nave and great doorway survive, as does the EE W front. It was in St Peter's that, in 1533, Abp Cranmer pronounced the sentence of divorce between Henry VIII and Catherine of Aragon.

Evesham Abbey, Hereford and Worcester

Of the once large and rich Benedictine abbey, founded by Bp Egwin of Worcester in 714, all that survives is the Norman and Tudor gateway of the churchyard, and a superb detached 16C *Bell-Tower. Built in the 1530s by Clement Lichfield, the last abbot, it is an example of the best and most ornate Perp style, 110ft high and elaborately pinnacled. As Pevsner says of it: 'It is astonishing how unaware England's abbots were of the gathering storm. If they had not been, how could they indulge in such conspicuous display?' The abbey precinct contains two parish churches: St Lawrence (now redundant), a Perp building of c 1470; and All Saints, the present parish church, which is Norman greatly altered in the Perp period. St Lawrence seems to have been used by pilgrims, many of whom were diseased; so the parishioners kept to their own All Saints. The pilgrims were housed in the Almonry, now a small museum (open Good Fri.–end Sept., exc. Mon. and Wed).

Flaxley Abbey, Gloucestershire

Off A48, 10 miles W of Gloucester.

A Cistercian monastery founded in the 12C, Flaxley lies on the edge of the Forest of Dean, in iron-working country, and had its own substantial forge. The present house (not open), partly Jacobean with additions of 1780, preserves the refectory (c 1148) and abbot's hall (c 1350). Part of the S wall of the nave now serves as the backing wall of an 18C greenhouse.

Gloucester: Blackfriars

W of Southgate Street, S of Cathedral.

A Dominican friary was built in Gloucester in the 13C. Of the church, much of the E end survives; at the Dissolution the friary, including the church, was turned into a private house and factory by a wealthy cloth-manufacturer. The upper floor of the S cloister range was probably the Dominicans' library, to judge from the recesses in the walls, which may have been used as desk-spaces. The church is at present being restored.

Gloucester Cathedral

Ded: St Peter and the Holy Trinity.

Gloucester's elegantly fretted tower is a great landmark in the surrounding countryside. Once the church of a Benedictine abbey, the cathedral is a noble building, and the city's most magnificent feature. The King's School and other surrounding buildings make it impossible to walk round it in a complete circuit, and it is best viewed from the W and S, from College Green. Elsewhere the visitor has to be content with partial glimpses over walls, along paths and through gateways. In 1981 the cathedral celebrated the 1,300th anniversary of its original monastic foundation.

History. The character of the foundation has varied. In 681 Osric, a prince of Mercia, founded a monastery within the diocese of Worcester for both men and women; deserted after about a century, in 823 it was refounded as a college for secular priests. In 1022 King Canute established a Benedictine abbey dedicated to St Peter; and soon after the Conquest, William I appointed one of his chaplains, Serlo, to be the first abbot of a new foundation. The Benedictines held the abbey until the Dissolution in 1540, when Henry VIII raised it to cathedral rank, severing its connection with Worcester. The existing building was begun by Serlo (d 1104) in 1089, and dedicated in 1100. Soon afterwards the Norman nave was built, thus completing the present plan of the church, except for the Lady Chapel. In 1216 the nine-year-old Henry III was crowned at Gloucester; and in 1327 the body of Edward II, murdered at Berkeley Castle and refused burial at Bristol and Malmesbury, was enshrined there. After his death the king's feebleness and irresponsibility were forgotten, and his shrine soon became a focus of miracles and pilgrimage. From the income that accumulated, and from gifts sent by the young Edward III, the monks largely rebuilt both the church and the abbey. It seems likely that the king sent his own master mason, William Ramsay, to take charge of the work, which was in the new Perp style, then being developed in London; thus Gloucester became the first major success of Perp architecture. As a result the exterior is largely Perp, and in the choir a Perp casing effectively disguises the Norman core. The choir vault dates from 1337–51 and the cloisters from c 1370–1410; the W façade and S porch (much restored) were built in 1420–37; the stately central tower (225ft high), with its austerely fine decoration, replaced

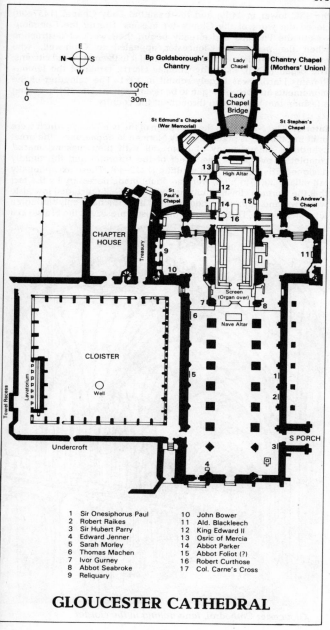

Bp Goldsborough's
Chantry

Lady
Chapel

Chantry Chapel
(Mothers' Union)

Lady
Chapel
Bridge

St Edmund's Chapel
(War Memorial)

St Stephen's
Chapel

N
E
W
S

0 ___ 100ft
0 ___ 30m

High Altar

St Paul's
Chapel

St Andrew's
Chapel

CHAPTER
HOUSE

Treasury

Screen
(Organ over)

Nave Altar

CLOISTER

Lavatorium

Well

Towel Recess

Undercroft

S PORCH

1   Sir Onesiphorus Paul
2   Robert Raikes
3   Sir Hubert Parry
4   Edward Jenner
5   Sarah Morley
6   Thomas Machen
7   Ivor Gurney
8   Abbot Seabroke
9   Reliquary
10 John Bower
11 Ald. Blackleech
12 King Edward II
13 Osric of Mercia
14 Abbot Parker
15 Abbot Foliot (?)
16 Robert Curthose
17 Col. Carne's Cross

GLOUCESTER CATHEDRAL

the 13C tower in 1450; and the beautiful Lady Chapel (1457–98) closed the work of the Gloucester masons. During the Commonwealth the Puritans had already begun their work of destruction when the people of Gloucester appealed to Cromwell, who guaranteed its safety and in 1657 granted it to the mayor and citizens. The organ (1665), made by Thomas Harris, father of the famous Renatus Harris, was largely rebuilt in 1971. The colouring of the monuments and bosses began to be restored in the late 1940s, setting a fashion that was copied throughout the country.

Interior. The *Nave*, with the exception of the two W bays which were built in 1420–37, is predominantly Norman in appearance; the great cylindrical pillars, many of them still with their masons' marks, completely overpower the effect of the triforium and the timidly designed EE clerestory and vaulting (1242–45). These exceptionally tall pillars, 30ft 7in high, were no doubt made necessary by the fact that the Norman cloister built against the N wall precluded low aisle windows, and high-set windows could light the nave only through a lofty pier arcade. The support of the cloister preserved the N aisle at a

Gloucester Cathedral, fan-vaulting in the cloister.

time when the S aisle became unsafe and had to be revaulted (c 1318), the period also of the ball-flowered Geometric tracery of the S aisle windows. In the N aisle the Norman vaulting and carved capitals are noteworthy, as is the fine Perp doorway to the cloisters at its E end. In the S aisle are monuments to Sir Onesiphorus Paul (d 1820), the prison reformer, and Robert Raikes (1735–1811), the pioneer of Sunday Schools; at its W end is a tablet to Sir Hubert Parry (1848–1918), the composer. Near the W door is a statue to Edward Jenner (1749–1823), the discoverer of vaccination, who was a Gloucestershire man. In the N aisle is a graceful memorial by Flaxman to Mrs Morley (d 1784); the elaborate family monument of Alderman Thomas Machen (d 1614) and his wife; and (by the steps) a small memorial to the composer and poet Ivor Gurney (1890–1937). The third and fifth windows from the W end on this side contain old glass (restored).

The *Choir (which projects one bay into the nave and is separated from it by a screen of 1820, with organ above) is usually entered from the S aisle, at the E end of which is Abbot Seabroke's Chantry, an elegant Perp chantry with an alabaster effigy of the abbot (d 1457). Choir and *Transepts* look pure Perp, as the walls were veiled with tracery and the massive piers of the choir were pared down, when the dimly lit old Norman choir was transformed in the mid 14C. The latest part is the N transept (restored 1368–74). On its E side is St Paul's Chapel, with a fine (restored) altar screen; and against its N wall is a beautiful EE arcaded structure, known as the Reliquary. It now forms the entrance to the Treasury (1977), which is entered through a door cut in the N wall of the transept; the treasury is housed in a long, narrow room that opened off the cloisters and was originally either a slype or the monks' *locutorium* (a place where they were allowed to talk). On the W wall is a monument to John Bower (d 1615) and his wife, inscribed with the words 'Vayne, Vanytie, All is but Vayne'. The similar S transept, remodelled in 1331–37, forestalls by some 20 years the evolution of the Perp style elsewhere in England. On the E wall is a carved bracket nicknamed the Prentice Bracket, on which venerated carvings originally stood; in the form of a mason's square, it is said to commemorate a young mason who was killed by falling from the vault. Beside it is St Andrew's Chapel (the Scouts' and Guides' chapel), with a huge diagonal strut. On the S wall is the twin effigy tomb of Alderman Abraham Blackleech (d 1630) and his wife.

From floor to ceiling the design of choir and transepts is a perfect unity. The tall clerestory windows; the rectilinear tracery made necessary by the size of the end-wall windows; the one-storey design of the tracery, carried up on unbroken vaulting-shafts, that covers the Norman triforium and pier arcades; the lierne *Vaulting, whether in the complicated pattern of the choir roof, with its galaxy of angel-bosses, or in the simpler but more subtly skilled vaulting of the S transept: all these are the quintessence of Perp architecture. (Note the desperate but effective expedient of carrying the W division of the vault on slender flying arches across the transepts.) The great *East or Crécy Window, 80ft high by 38ft wide and the largest in the country, is often said to have been erected by Lord Bradeston c 1352 to commemorate the battle of Crécy (1346), in which he had fought. The light tone of the glass, which depicts the coronation of the Virgin, is as much an innovation as the architecture, and the walls have been made slightly wider than the chancel by tilting them outwards. The Reredos, brightly painted and gilded, is Victorian (1873, by Sir Gilbert Scott, figures by Frank Redfern), as are the sub-stalls. The 14C

*Stalls, with their vigorous and often grotesque misericords, have been restored. The W window of the choir—an unusual feature, due to the difference in height between nave and choir—contains some old glass from other windows.

Of various noteworthy tombs in the choir, the most interesting and beautiful is the canopied *Tomb of Edward II, erected by Edward III; the effigy is alabaster. The tomb stands under the N arcade of the presbytery, between the monument of Osric of Mercia, who founded the first abbey in 681, and the tomb prepared for Abbot Parker (1539) but occupied by two bishops. The bracket tomb on the S has been assigned to Serlo (see above), but the figure with the church in its hand is probably Abbot Foliot (d 1243). Prominent in the centre of the presbytery is the painted wooden effigy of Robert Curthose (d 1134), eldest son of William the Conqueror, who died a prisoner in Cardiff Castle; the carved effigy of bog-oak (c 1290) rests on a 15C mortuary chest. In front of the altar are well-preserved encaustic tiles of 1455. The NE chapel (Chapel of St Edmund the Martyr), which has good tiles and fragments of a reredos of c 1450, is the war memorial chapel of the Gloucestershire Regiment; opposite, in the N ambulatory, stands the small cross carved in 1951 by Col. Carne, VC, commander of the Gloucestershires, while he was a prisoner of war in Korea. The SE chapel is dedicated to St Stephen; in the ambulatory near it is a fibreglass group of the Holy Family, by Josephina de Vasconcellos.

The *Lady Chapel was the last great work at Gloucester (1457–98). It is detached from the E end of the choir to avoid obscuring the E window, and the W end diminishes in height and breadth to form a gracefully vaulted vestibule. Open tracery fills the upper part of the W arch; and the exquisite lierne vaulting (with leaf-bosses), the crisply carved tracery of the windows and of the narrow wall-spaces between, the vaulting shafts, the ruined reredos, the sedilia, and the remaining 15C tiles all contribute to the architectural harmony. Side chapels (Bp Goldsborough's on the N and the Mothers' Union chapel on the S), with oratories or music galleries in the upper stories, are delicately vaulted. The nine-light E window (late 15C) contains old glass, some of it not designed for this window, which represented the Tree of Jesse. There are several charming monuments, including one to Elizabeth Williams (d 1622). At the W end of the Lady Chapel a bridge links the N and S sides of the triforium (tribune gallery).

The Choir Triforium, with a half-barrel vault, is reached from the N transept. In 1981, as part of the 1,300th anniversary celebrations, the triforium was laid out as a permanent exhibition illustrating the two halves of the cathedral's history: on the N, the abbey period, and on the S, the cathedral period from 1540 to the present. The two halves are linked by the Whispering Gallery which runs outside the great E window and across the W end of the Lady Chapel.

The Norman Crypt, entered from the S transept, consists of an apse and five chapels. The Norman columns of Abbot Serlo's crypt had to be reinforced c 1130, and again when the new choir was built above them in the 14C.

The Central Tower, 225ft high, commands extensive views towards the Severn Estuary and across the surrounding countryside. In the lower part hangs 'Great Peter', which weighs more than 3 tons; cast c 1420, it is the only medieval 'great bell' remaining in England. There are 12 bells altogether, forming a carillon that plays tunes at 08.00, 13.00 and 17.00.

The *Cloisters (c 1370–1410), entered from the N aisle of the nave, are remarkable both for their state of preservation and their beauty. The fan-tracery vaulting is claimed to be an invention of the Gloucester masons, and the fan vaults are certainly the first of any extent in Britain. The S side has 'carrel' recesses for desks; and on the N side is the lavatorium with a long stone trough at which the monks washed their hands, with a recess for towels in the wall opposite. The spacious Chapter House (on the E), restored Norman, with a Perp E bay, is now used for receptions and other functions, as well as for meetings of the Dean and Chapter. On the W side of the cloisters a medieval undercroft has been turned into a shop and refectory. From here a door leads out into College Green, on the other side of which is the medieval St Mary's Gateway, formerly the main gate for provisioning the abbey.

Gloucester Cathedral is one of the homes of the week-long Three Choirs Festival, held each August in rotation at Worcester, Hereford and Gloucester. The Festival developed in the 1720s to raise funds for the benefit of widows and orphans of clergy in the three dioceses. Elgar and Vaughan Williams had many of their works performed at the Three Choirs, which is now the chief bastion of the English tradition of choral singing, visited by musicians from all over the world.

Gloucester: Greyfriars

E of Southgate Street, S of Cathedral.

The 13C Franciscan friary has disappeared, apart from the nave of the church, which was rebuilt in Perp style early in the 16C. At the W end the nave and N aisle are attached to a Georgian town house.

Gloucester: St Oswald's Priory

N of Archdeacon Street, NW of Cathedral.

In Saxon times this was an important monastery, and may have been the burial place of Oswald, King of Northumbria, killed in battle in 641 and later canonized. Four 11–12C arches of a Norman church survive, but there are also traces of 10C Saxon work above ground, while excavations have revealed a 10C apse at the W end.

Grace Dieu Priory, Leicestershire

On S side of A512, 3 miles W of Shepshed.

Fragments of this 13C Augustinian foundation, heavily overgrown, can be seen in a field beside the road.

Great Malvern Priory, Hereford and Worcester

Ded: St Mary and St Michael.

Sited on the slopes of the Malvern hills, Great Malvern's priory church is, from the outside, a noble Perp building, its walls particoloured in stone of every shade from yellow to brown and purple. However, the interior is largely that of the original Norman church, with massive round piers in the nave dating from the Benedictine foundation in c 1085. In the 15C the church was largely rebuilt, with a tower recalling that of Gloucester Cathedral and superb windows, of which the great E window is one of the largest in any English parish church. Much of the 15C glass survives, including the 'Joys of Mary' (c 1500) in the N transept, with a portrait of Prince Arthur, the eldest son of Henry VII; the choir clerestory windows; and a certain amount in both the E and W windows. The priory was dissolved in 1539, and the church was bought by the parishioners; after centuries of decay and neglect, it was restored in the 1860s by Sir Gilbert Scott. Apart from its fine glass, the church has a unique chancel screen panelled with more than 1,200 15C wall tiles; a tile of 1456, on one of the N nave piers, is known as the 'Friends' Tile because it encouraged donors to give to the church.

Hailes Abbey, Gloucestershire

Ded: St Mary.

E side of A46, 2 miles NE of Winchcombe.

Hailes was founded in 1246 by Richard, Earl of Cornwall, later King of the Romans, and younger brother of Henry III, in thanksgiving for escape from shipwreck. A Cistercian monastery and a daughter house of Beaulieu in Hampshire, it was dedicated with great pomp in 1251 in front of the king and queen, and no fewer than 13 bishops. It is beautifully sited on the lower slopes of the Cotswolds, and the ruins are surrounded by neat rows of trees. In 1270, Earl Richard's son Edmund gave the abbey a phial of the blood of Christ (guaranteed by the Patriarch of Jerusalem), which soon made Hailes a centre of pilgrimage. To house the relic, the E end of the abbey church was built in the form of a *chevet*, with the shrine of the Holy Blood at the centre. The relic is mentioned in Chaucer's Pardoner's Tale; as examples of oaths that break the commandments, the Pardoner lists

"By Goddès precious herte" and "By his nayles"
And "By the blood of Crist that is in Hayles".

The abbey was dissolved in 1539. The blood of Christ was promptly declared by the Bishop of Rochester to be honey, coloured with saffron, while another analyst claimed that it was the blood of a drake renewed each week by the monks. The W range of the cloister buildings was turned into a private house; but this was demolished in the 18C, and now only some arches of the cloister survive, dating from the 15C and thus considerably later than the original foundation

There is an excellent small museum on the site, with displays of roof bosses, medieval tiles, and documents relating to the abbey.

Across the lane is a marvellous little 12C church, with extensive wall paintings of c 1300, including greyhounds hunting a hare, a double-headed eagle (the arms of Richard as King of the Romans), and two saints in the deep splays of the Norman windows (St Catherine of Alexandria, patron saint of learning, on the N; and St Margaret of Antioch, patroness of childbirth, on the S).

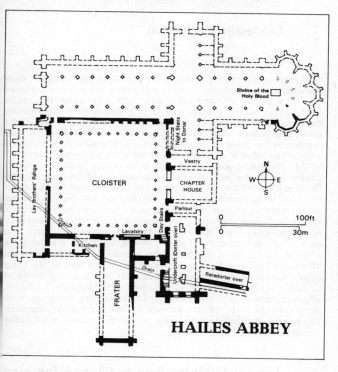

Hurley Priory, Berkshire

Ded: St Mary the Virgin.

N of A423, 4 miles E of Henley-on-Thames.

The aisleless church, long and narrow, was the nave of a Benedictine priory church, founded c 1085. The remains of the cloisters and domestic buildings (on N side), including the refectory, are now incorporated in a private house adjacent to the church.

Leicester Abbey

On N side of city, off Abbey Park Road.

Little is left of Leicester's once rich Augustinian abbey, where Cardinal Wolsey died in 1530. The conjectural foundations and boundary wall are still to be seen, across the river from Abbey Park.

Leicester Cathedral

Ded: St Martin of Tours.

On a cramped site in the centre of the city, St Martin's was the civic parish church of Leicester, until it was raised to cathedral status in 1927. It is mainly 13C and EE in style, with a Perp chancel; but in 1844–67 the whole church was largely refashioned by Raphael Brandon, who rebuilt the chancel and nave clerestory, added the lofty tower and broach spire (220ft high), and renewed the whole roof copying in the chancel the late medieval tie beams with their carved angels. The S porch, used as the main entrance, was designed in 1897 by J.L. Pearson. Inside, the church is unusually wide, as it has a double S aisle, the outer aisle being used in the Middle Ages by the Guild of Corpus Christi, and forming the Lady Chapel. The E end of this aisle, with piscina and sedilia, contains the 18C furniture of the old Archdeacon's Court, now the bishop's consistory court; and the W end is St George's Chapel, the chapel of the Royal Leicestershire Regiment, nicknamed 'the Tigers'. At the E end of the church, the high altar, designed by Temple Moore, and the stained-glass window, by Christopher Whall, form a memorial to Leicester men killed in World War I. An inscribed stone on the floor of the choir commemorates King Richard III (1483–85), killed at the Battle of Bosworth, near Leicester. N of the choir is St Katherine's Chapel which contains a number of memorials to the Herrick family; the poet Robert Herrick (1591–1674) is portrayed in the window over the altar. The large four-manual organ in the W gallery contains much of the Snetzler organ of 1774.

Leonard Stanley Priory, Gloucestershire

Ded: St Swithin.

3 miles SW of Stroud.

This small church, still largely Norman, was part of a priory founded in the 1120s for Augustinian canons. The nave is without aisles, and the square tower is unusually massive for a church of this size. Inside there is some fine Norman carving, notably the capitals in the chancel. During the 15C a rood-stair was cut in the S wall of the nave showing that at the time the W end of the church was used by the parish, while everything E of the rood-screen was monastic. The priory's domestic buildings, S of the church, were turned after the Dissolution to farming and other uses.

Lichfield Cathedral, Staffordshire

Ded: St Mary and St Chad.

The only ancient church in England with three spires (the 'Ladies of the Vale'), Lichfield is one of the most beautiful of English cathedrals. It owes much of its charm to the local red sandstone of which it is built. In style it is mainly an EE and Dec building of the 13C and 14C. The central spire is a restoration (ascribed on very uncertain evidence to Sir Christopher Wren) in the style of the older W spires. The *W Front, a richly decorated screen of carving with a single large window, is almost entirely a 19C reproduction of the original, which was begun c 1275 but not finished until c 1320; of its 113 statues all but five (in the top row of the NW tower) are 19C. The W doors are ornamented with fine metalwork.

History. St Chad (d 672), Bp of Mercia, transferred his bishopric from Repton to Lichfield (though he built his church at Stowe, 1 mile NW). The first church on the site of the present cathedral was founded in 700 by Bp Hedda, as a shrine for St Chad's body; but there are no visible remains of this church, and only two doubtful remnants of the 12C Norman church that succeeded it. The earliest parts of the cathedral are the three W bays of the choir and the sacristy (1195–1208). These, like the transepts and chapter house (1240–50), are EE, while the nave (1280) is early Dec, and the Lady Chapel (1320–36) and presbytery (1337) are in the full Dec style. The cathedral suffered great damage during the Civil War. It was twice besieged (in 1643 and again in 1646) by Cromwell's Parliamentarians; during the second attack the central spire was destroyed and the interior was damaged. After the Restoration Bp John Hacket (1662–69) repaired the fabric and introduced many Perp features in the process. Towards the end of the 18C the nave walls were saved from imminent collapse by James Wyatt, who removed 500 tons of stone vaulting; and in the 19C a thorough restoration, begun in 1842 by Sidney Smirke, was continued after 1856 by Sir George Gilbert Scott and his son John Oldrid Scott. In 1950 the central spire and tower were renovated and a new summit cross placed on top.

Interior. Long in proportion to its width, but the interior is graceful and unified, and the eye is carried along the unbroken vista of arches up to the famous stained glass in the Lady Chapel. The *Nave*, built in the transitional period between EE and Dec, is richly ornamented. The finely carved capitals and all the stone bosses in the roof are unrestored work, though Wyatt substituted wood-and-plaster groining for most of the original roof. The beautiful triforium, with dog-tooth moulding, is unusually large, and the clerestory windows are of elaborate and uncommon design. Just inside the NW entrance are wall tablets to the poetess Anna Seward (1747–1809), known as the 'Swan of Lichfield', and the writer and traveller Lady Mary Wortley Montagu (d 1762). At the W end of the S aisle is a monument to Dean Addison (d 1703), father of the 18C essayist Joseph Addison. The *Transepts* are earlier than the nave (c 1220–40), but the stone-vaulted roofs date from the late 15C and are lower than the original roofs (thus the fine rose window in the S gable is invisible from the interior). The windows are either Perp (Restoration period) or EE (19C). In the N transept is the skeleton monument of Dean

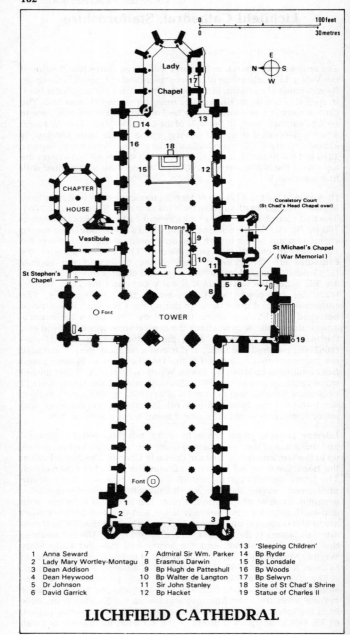

1 Anna Seward
2 Lady Mary Wortley-Montagu
3 Dean Addison
4 Dean Heywood
5 Dr Johnson
6 David Garrick
7 Admiral Sir Wm. Parker
8 Erasmus Darwin
9 Bp Hugh de Patteshull
10 Bp Walter de Langton
11 Sir John Stanley
12 Bp Hacket
13 'Sleeping Children'
14 Bp Ryder
15 Bp Lonsdale
16 Bp Woods
17 Bp Selwyn
18 Site of St Chad's Shrine
19 Statue of Charles II

LICHFIELD CATHEDRAL

Heywood (d 1492). In the S transept are busts by Westmacott of Dr Samuel Johnson (d 1784) and David Garrick (d 1779), both of whom spent their youth in Lichfield and are buried in Westminster Abbey; Dr Johnson once said that the townspeople of Lichfield were 'the most sober, decent people in England—the genteelest in proportion to their wealth, and spoke the purest English'. The S transept also contains a war memorial chapel (St Michael's) and the monument of Admiral Sir Wm Parker (d 1866), the last survivor of Nelson's captains. The window above contains some glass from Herkenrode, in Flanders (see below).

The first three bays of the *Choir* (which is deflected 10° to the N from the line of the nave) are EE and the oldest part of the cathedral. The place of the triforium is taken here by high arcaded windowsills, with a passage through the piers. The tracery is of the Restoration period, except for the fine Dec window on the S side. The canopied statues and angels on the piers date from c 1860, as do the stalls by William Evans (a cousin of the novelist George Eliot, the pen name of Marian Evans). In the S Choir Aisle is a small two-storey extension to the S (c 1225), the lower stage being the sacristy (now the consistory court), and the upper, with its charming minstrel's gallery, known as 'St Chad's Head Chapel' and probably used for exhibiting the saint's head to pilgrims. This aisle has a medallion to the naturalist Erasmus Darwin (1731–1802), the grandfather of Charles Darwin of evolutionary fame; the effigies of Bp Hugh de Patteshull (d 1242) and Bp Walter de Langton (d 1321); the strange effigy, naked to the waist, of Sir John Stanley (d 1515), who was publicly scourged as a penance; the tomb of Bp Hacket, who restored the cathedral after Cromwell's destruction; and (at the E end) the *Sleeping Children (Ellen Jane and Marianne Robinson, both d 1812), the finest of Sir Francis Chantrey's earlier works. The window above contains old Flemish glass representing the Trinity; and in the adjoining piscina is a 14C fresco of the Crucifixion. At the E end of the N Choir Aisle is the monument of Bp Ryder (d 1836), one of Chantrey's last works, beneath a window with old Flemish glass (St Christopher). Further W is the effigy of Bp Lonsdale (d 1867) by G.F. Watts, and a bronze bust of Bp Woods (d 1953) by Epstein.

The lofty and elegant *Lady Chapel, a beautiful example of the Dec style, is in plan a polygonal apse, with nine tall windows resting on an arcade. In the seven easternmost windows is the famous *Herkenrode glass (c 1530–40), from the Cistercian abbey of Herkenrode, near Liège in Belgium. After the French Revolution the abbey was dismantled; and in 1802 Sir Brooke Boothby, who had bought the glass for £200, sold it to the Dean and Chapter for the same price. The other two windows have glass of the same period, acquired in 1895. On the S are three mortuary chapels, in one of which is the effigy of Bp Selwyn (d 1878) of New Zealand and afterwards of Lichfield.

The exquisite *Chapter House, reached through a vestibule from the N choir aisle, with beautiful arcading and wonderfully undercut capitals, corbels and bosses, was completed in 1249. In plan it has been described as an 'irregular decagon', and the central shaft is carried through into the chamber above, formerly the treasury and now the cathedral library. The 13 canopied stalls in the vestibule may have been for visitors attending the Chapter on business, or used in the Maundy Thursday feet-washing ceremony. The chapter house now contains a permanent exhibition relating to the library's chief treasure, the Lichfield Gospels (adm. weekdays 10.30–12.30,

Lichfield Cathedral, the ornate W front with its twin spires, and the central spire behind.

14.00–16.00, Sun. 16.30–18.30; fee). Often called 'St Chad's Gospels', this is a vellum MS probably written in Ireland c 730, beautifully lettered and intricately decorated with Celtic motifs.

The cathedral stands in a quiet *Close, surrounded by old houses, some of them half-timbered. Outside, on the E corner of the S transept, is a crumbling statue of Charles II, the monarch in whose reign the cathedral had its first restoration.

Lilleshall Abbey, Shropshire

Off A518, 3 miles SW of Newport.

Founded c 1148 by Philip and Richard de Belmeis, Lilleshall was originally a monastery of the small Order of Arrouaisians, who later became merged with the Augustinians. The first monks came here from Dorchester Abbey, Oxfordshire (see above). Dissolved in 1538, the abbey suffered great damage during the Civil War, when it was made into a Royalist strong point and besieged by the Parliamentarians; at present it is propped and shored up due to mining subsidence. A good deal of the church remains, notably the round-arched W doorway and part of the NW tower, from the 13C W front. Of the first 12C church, a considerable amount of the transepts and E end survives; a later addition is the huge 14C Geometric E window. The 13C nave is aisleless, and has the footings of three screen walls across it. The 12C E processional door from the nave into the cloister is richly carved with chevron ornament. On the W side of the cloister, the chapter house has a number of abbots' tombstones; and in the wall between the sacristy and the E processional door is an unusual double book-locker, which would originally have had wooden doors. The monastic buildings S of the cloister are on private ground and cannot be visited, while the W range is fragmentary.

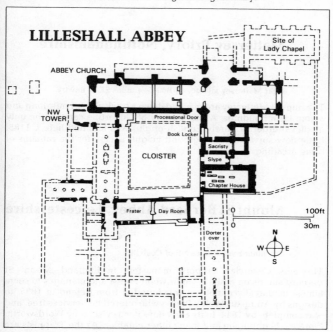

LILLESHALL ABBEY

Site of Lady Chapel

ABBEY CHURCH

NW TOWER

Processional Door

Book Locker

CLOISTER

Sacristy

Slype

Chapter House

Frater | Day Room

Dorter over

0   100ft
0   30m

N
W—E
S

Little Malvern Priory, Hereford and Worcester

Ded: St Giles.

By A4104, 3 miles S of Great Malvern.

A Benedictine monastery was founded here in 1171, on a magnificent site on the Malvern escarpment. Discipline became progressively lax, until in 1480 Bp Alcock of Worcester discharged the prior and monks 'by reason of their demerits', sent them to Gloucester Abbey for two years to mend their ways, rebuilt their church, and in 1482 reinstated them, no doubt suitably chastened. The priory was dissolved in 1535, and the monastic buildings were pulled down, apart from the refectory which was incorporated into Little Malvern Court. The present church consists of the 14C monks' chancel, crossing and central tower, together with Bp Alcock's E end; everything W of the tower has gone, and the transepts and side chapels are in ruins. The 15C tiles on the sanctuary floor are similar to those at Great Malvern (see above), and include a 'Friends' Tile' recommending generosity to the church.

Mattersey Priory, Nottinghamshire

Near Mattersey village, off B6045, 4 miles SE of Bawtry.

The ruins of Mattersey are reached down a track about 1 mile long and adjoin farm buildings. A small priory of Gilbertine canons (the only medieval order of purely English origin) was founded here c 1185. Little now survives above ground height, except for the remains of some arcading.

Mount St Bernard Abbey, Leicestershire

On minor road 3 miles NE of Coalville.

The only Cistercian Trappist monastery in England, Mount St Bernard stands on a hill in Charnwood Forest and manages to seem almost medievally remote. It was founded from Ireland in 1835, to designs by Augustus Welby Pugin, who offered his services free, and was complete by 1844. In its early days it was visited by Wordsworth, Florence Nightingale and many other notables. As the Trappists are an enclosed order, the public can only visit the church, which is a simple, austere building in EE style, with a square tower that dominates the surrounding landscape.

Newstead Abbey, Nottinghamshire

Ded: St Mary.

Off A60, 12 miles N of Nottingham.

House open p.m. Good Fri.–end Sept., grounds all year; fee.

Famous as the ancestral home of the poet Lord Byron (1788–1824), Newstead was founded in 1170 by Henry II for Augustinian canons. It was dissolved in 1539 and the following year was bought by Sir John Byron, who turned it into a family mansion; it remained in the Byron family until Lord Byron's day. During the poet's minority the house was let, and in 1817 he sold it, to pay his debts, to Col. Wildman, who largely restored it. In 1931 it was presented to the City of Nottingham. Chief of the medieval survivals is the magnificent W front of the church (13C), which is still largely intact to gable height; however, the rest of the church has largely disappeared. The cloister square, containing the chapter house which the Byrons turned into their family chapel (though Lord Byron used it for his menagerie), remains practically perfect. Other medieval rooms, more or less altered, include the refectory and the canons' dormitory.

Northampton Cathedral (RC)

Ded: St Mary and St Thomas.

In Barrack Road.

In 1844 a church by Augustus Welby Pugin was begun on the site of the present E end, incorporating a chapel of 1825, now the sacristy (N side). Made a cathedral in 1850, Pugin's church was enlarged by his son Edward, who added the nave and aisles; and the final building phase took place in 1954–60, when the squat crossing tower and lancet-windowed chancel were built by Albert Herbert in succession to A.W. Pugin's church. Inside, the cathedral is gracefully arcaded, with a heavy-looking wooden roof; the bishop's throne is of Italian workmanship, and there is a brass to Bp Amherst (d 1883) in the floor of the nave.

Northampton: Delapré Abbey

Ded: St Mary.

Off A508, 1 mile S of town centre.

Now the Northamptonshire Record Office, Delapré was founded c 1145 as a house of Cluniac nuns, one of only two nunneries of this order ever established in England (the other was at Arthington in W Yorkshire). The name means 'of the meadow', and Delapré still stands in a parkland setting near the busy centre of Northampton. In 1290 the body of Queen Eleanor of Castile, wife of King Edward I, lay for a night in the church at Delapré; one of the three surviving 'Queen

Eleanor's Crosses' (on Delapré Hill nearby) commemorates the event. The nunnery was dissolved in 1538 and a Tudor house was built on the site, considerably added to over the next three centuries. Of medieval Delapré, little that is identifiable stands above ground, though the original cloister plan survives in the inner courtyard. The range on the N side was probably the nave of the nuns' small church (c 65ft by 20ft).

Oxford Cathedral

Ded: St Frideswide (now Christ).

In Christ Church.

The smallest cathedral in England, it is the college chapel of Christ Church as well as the cathedral church of a diocese.

History. Originally it was the church of a monastic community, founded by St Frideswide c 720, probably a joint establishment for both monks and nuns; apart from the name of the founder, its early history is obscure. The church was rebuilt for secular priests in 1004 by King Ethelred II, and became a church of Austin canons in 1122; the present late Norman appearance dates from a late 12C restoration or rebuilding, probably after a fire in 1190 which burnt much of the city. The 13C spire (144ft high) is one of the earliest in England. In 1525 Cardinal Wolsey got possession of the priory and began to tear it down, beginning in its place a magnificent college to be known as Cardinal's College. By the time of his disgrace in 1529 he had pulled down four bays of the nave and the rest of the priory buildings apart from the chapter house, the refectory and part of the cloister. Henry VIII refounded Cardinal College as King Henry VIII's College (an ecclesiastical establishment only) in 1532; this survived until 1545, and the following year was succeeded by Christ Church. What Wolsey had left of the old priory church became the cathedral of the new Oxford diocese as well as the college chapel (a unique situation), and the Dean became head of both the cathedral chapter and the college. Additions and alterations have been made to the building at various times since, notably the 19C W front and E end by Sir George Gilbert Scott (1870).

Interior. Due to Wolsey's destruction of its W bays, the cathedral seems very wide in proportion to its length. This impression is increased by the side chapels (the Latin Chapel and Lady Chapel on the N, and St Lucy's Chapel on the S). In the *Nave*, the massive Norman pillars of the arcades are alternately round and octagonal, and an illusion of height is given by the unusual placing of the triforium inside the main arches, with a secondary arch below (as at Romsey Abbey, in Hampshire). The roof was renewed in 1816, the pulpit and organ screen are 17C, and the stalls 19C. There are monuments to the philosopher Bp Berkeley (1685–1753) and to the Tractarian scholar Dr Edward Pusey (1800–82). The *Choir* has a gloriously vaulted late 15C *Roof, described by John Ruskin (a member of Christ Church) as 'true Tudor grotesque'. The E end, by Scott, is in Norman style.

   The *Transepts*, like the lantern, have early 16C roofs. At the S end of the S transept is a conjectural restoration by Scott, consisting of a slype surmounted by a gallery. St Lucy's Chapel, in the former E aisle of this transept, has a flamboyant *E Window, with fine old glass (c 1330). The central light shows the martyrdom of Becket, with his head replaced by a piece of plain glass, presumably in deference to Henry VIII's dislike of that saint. In this chapel and in the S transept are monuments to Royalists who died in the Civil War (when Christ Church was Charles I's headquarters); in the transept hangs the Garter banner of Prince Paul of Yugoslavia, a member of the college. The S choir aisle is the regimental chapel of the Oxfordshire and Buckinghamshire Light Infantry. Opening from the N transept are three parallel aisles: the N Choir Aisle, the Lady Chapel and the Latin Chapel. Between the first two is the fragmentary base of the late 13C shrine of St Frideswide, once a goal of pilgrimage; and opposite, between the Lady Chapel and the Latin Chapel, is the finely carved oak watching chamber (15C) from which guard was kept on the treasures of the shrine. The saint is commemorated on 19 October each year by a special service attended by dignitaries of the cathedral, university, county and city, in fully robed splendour. The Latin Chapel is so called because the daily service was said here in Latin until 1861 (except for a break during the Commonwealth); it was also used for divinity lectures until the late 19C. It has massive oak stalls, some probably 14C, others 16C; interesting monuments including a bust of Robert Burton (1577–1640), author of *The Anatomy of Melancholy*; and some 14C stained glass in the N windows. Of the three N aisles, two have E windows by William Morris, while the Latin Chapel has an early window (1858) by Burne-Jones. At the W end of the N aisle is a spectacular window by Abraham van Linge (c 1630) depicting the prophet Jonah and the city of Nineveh. The late 17C organ was rebuilt in Austria in 1979.

The visitors' entrance into the cathedral is into the S aisle via the Perp Cloister (1499, W side pulled down in 1525). It was here that in 1556 Abp Thomas Cranmer was formally degraded, before being burnt at the stake in Broad Street. On the E side of the cloister a Norman doorway leads into the EE Chapter House (c 1225, restored 1968), used for exhibitions of church plate; the showcases were donated by the Goldsmiths' Company. On the S side of the cloister is the priory refectory (later the 'Old Library', now undergraduate rooms).

Pershore Abbey, Hereford and Worcester

Ded: Holy Cross.

Towards the end of the 7C Oswald, King of Mercia, founded a church and religious house at Pershore. Destroyed by the Danes c 960, it was refounded as a Benedictine monastery by King Edgar in 972. Some time before 1100 a great Norman church was built on the site, largely rebuilt in EE style during the 13C. At the Dissolution the nave of the church and the monastic buildings were pulled down; but the townspeople paid £400 for the choir and transepts and kept them as their parish church. The magnificent 14C lantern tower, which originally stood over the crossing, is now at the W end of the building; the full extent of the nave is marked out by wooden posts in the churchyard. Of the Norman church, the lofty crossing arches survive, as does the austere S transept. The apsidal E end, with its narrow lancet windows, is 13C EE; the stone vaulting was built after a disastrous fire in 1288. Additions made in the 19C include a wooden 'cat's cradle' platform built high under the tower ceiling for the bellringers; and (in the S aisle) two 'historical windows' (1870) giving the story of the abbey from Oswald's foundation until Victorian times. The W side of the tower is supported externally by two vast flying buttresses dated 1913.

Prinknash Abbey, Gloucestershire

Off A46, 6 miles NE of Stroud.

Prinknash (pronounced 'Prinnersh') stands on a magnificent escarpment site, with wide-ranging views northwards to Gloucester and westwards across the Severn valley. In the Middle Ages it was a hunting lodge and country retreat for the Benedictine abbots of Gloucester, and was enlarged and rebuilt c 1520 by William Parker, the last abbot. His H-shaped Tudor house was added to in Victorian times; and in the 1930s the Benedictines returned to Prinknash, and began a major new monastery incorporating the old building. Designs for a modern church and monastic buildings were prepared by H. Goodhart-Rendel, and work began in 1939; but such was the scale of the scheme that it took 20 years before even the lower crypt of the planned church was completed. So a new, less ambitious scheme (1973) was prepared by F.G. Broadbent, who turned the crypt into the abbey church (open to visitors), with the library and monks' bedrooms above. Prinknash is well known today for the quality of the pottery it produces and sells.

Reading Abbey, Berkshire

On W side of town, by Forbury Gardens.

Apart from the heavily restored gatehouse, little is left of Reading's great Benedictine foundation, which once ranked as third abbey in all England. Founded in 1121 by Henry I, who was buried before the high altar, Reading was dedicated by Becket in 1164, and during the Middle Ages was constantly visited by monarchs and lesser dignitaries. At the Dissolution in 1539 the last abbot was hanged; and the abbey fabric was finally destroyed in the Civil War. The fragments are in a fairly ruinous condition. Among them are the remains of the enormous chapter house, which has on its walls a tablet inscribed with 'Sumer is Icumen In', the earliest known round for several voices, composed by a monk of Reading c 1240. In the 18C the gatehouse was a school, and had Jane Austen as one of its pupils.

St Albans Cathedral, Hertfordshire

Long and narrow, and with a massive central tower, St Albans is built on higher ground (320ft) than any other cathedral in England. In origin it is an early Norman building, and the nave, at 275ft, is the longest medieval nave in existence. The tower, with its striking arcade, is largely constructed of Roman bricks and tiles, as are the other Norman portions. The harsh W façade and the transeptal façades are mainly 19C, while the brickwork theme is taken up again in the new chapter house (1982).

History. The town of Verulamium was founded soon after the Roman conquest of Britain in A.D. 43; sacked by Boadicea in 61, it was rebuilt on a larger scale and flourished until c 410, when the Romans left Britain. It owes its present name to St Alban, a Roman soldier and the first Christian martyr in England, beheaded for giving shelter to a priest called Amphibalus who had converted him. (The traditional date for his martyrdom is given as 303, but recent research puts it in 209). Offa, King of Mercia, founded a Benedictine abbey here c 793 in honour of the saint. The first Norman abbot, Paul of Caen, built a church on the site of Offa's church in 1077–88, and this is still substantially the central part of the cathedral we see today. Dedicated in 1116, this seems to have ended in seven apses, just E of the present transepts. Since the area round St Albans is short of building stone, Paul of Caen collected bricks from Roman Verulamium to build his church, no doubt as his Saxon predecessors had done before him; inside the church the bricks were plastered over and painted. Later builders could afford to import stone, which was used for the present E end, and for the W bays of the nave which was rebuilt c 1200–35. During the Middle Ages St Albans Abbey rose to great wealth and power, so that from 1154 to 1396 its mitred abbot was the premier abbot in England. Nicholas Breakspeare, the only Englishman ever to become Pope (in 1154, as Adrian IV), was born in St Albans (though as a youth the abbey refused to take him as a novice); Matthew Paris (d 1259), the chronicler, was a monk at St Albans; and Robert Fayrfax, one of the greatest of early Tudor composers, was organist from c 1498 until his death in 1521. At the Dissolution in 1539 the monastic buildings were demolished and the church was sold to the parishioners for £400. In 1856 a major restoration was begun by Sir Gilbert Scott, succeeded by Sir Edmund Beckett (later Lord Grimthorpe), an eccentric millionaire who designed and paid for a new W front and transept windows. In 1877 the church became the cathedral of a new diocese. In 1982 a new chapter house, built in brick like the Norman church, was opened by HM the Queen.

Interior. The plain but graceful W end of the enormously long *Nave* is EE, abruptly joining the severe early Norman work on the N side and continued on the S side by five Dec bays constructed in 1323. On the W and S sides of the Norman piers are considerable remains of 13C and 14C *Wall-paintings, cleaned since 1955. The Crucifixion (the westernmost painting) is probably by Walter of Colchester (c 1220), whom Matthew Paris called 'an incomparable painter'. On the wall of the S aisle are four colourful embroidery panels symbolizing the religious significance of Earth, Air, Fire and Water. A stone Rood screen (c 1350) separates the nave from the Norman ritual *Choir*,

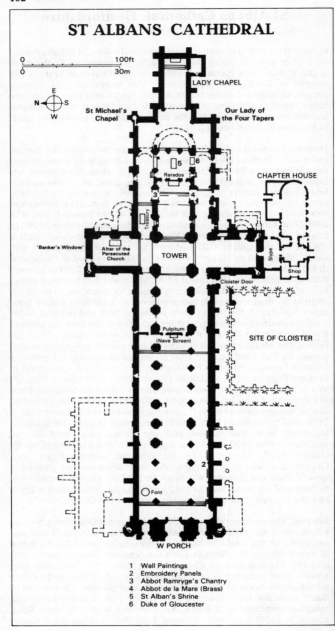

ST ALBANS CATHEDRAL

0   100ft
0   30m

N W E S

LADY CHAPEL

St Michael's Chapel

Our Lady of the Four Tapers

5   6

Reredos

CHAPTER HOUSE

3   4

Treasury

'Banker's Window'

Altar of the Persecuted Church

TOWER

Slype

Shop

Cloister Door

SITE OF CLOISTER

Pulpitum (Nave Screen)

1

2

Font

W PORCH

1   Wall Paintings
2   Embroidery Panels
3   Abbot Ramryge's Chantry
4   Abbot de la Mare (Brass)
5   St Alban's Shrine
6   Duke of Gloucester

which is continued E by the Presbytery. The fine ceiling over the choir, divided into square painted panels, dates from the late 15C; the tower ceiling was renewed in 1952, when one original panel was removed to the N aisle. A larger panel of c 1530 from the N transept, representing the Martyrdom of St Alban, is preserved in the S choir aisle; and in the same aisle is the magnificent *Brass of Abbot Thomas de la Mare (d 1396). Most of the presbytery and the retrochoir was rebuilt by Abbot de Hertford (1235–60); the unique wooden vault was painted with foliage and symbolic motifs c 1450. Behind the high altar is an elaborate stone Reredos completed by Abbot William of Wallingford in 1484, with statues of c 1900 in the niches; the altarpiece of the Resurrection is by Sir Alfred Gilbert. On the N side of the presbytery is the ornate little chantry of Abbot Thomas Ramryge (d 1520); and on the S side the chantry of Abbot Wallingford (long thought to be that of Abbot John Wheathampstead), now a chapel for private prayer.

The *Transepts* are the best preserved portions of Paul of Caen's Norman church. The arches on their E sides led originally into apsidal chapels. In the N transept is a 15C fresco ('Doubting Thomas') and a plan of the abbey as it was before the Dissolution. The large rose window, filled with plain glass, in the N wall is Lord Grimthorpe's 'Banker's Window', so-called because the circular shapes of which it is composed correspond to the various sizes of the coins of the realm. (Lord Grimthorpe himself is carved in the role of St Matthew in the W porch.) In the S transept the blind *Triforium on the E wall has arches separated by small circular shafts assumed to be from Offa's Saxon church, though they have Norman capitals and bases. The S wall, with its five-lancet window, was rebuilt by Lord Grimthorpe, who incorporated into it some late Norman arcading.

Immediately. E of the presbytery is *St Alban's Chapel*, in the middle of which is the elaborately carved marble base of the saint's shrine, pieced together in 1872 from more than 2,000 fragments. The oak *Watching Loft (c 1400), on the N side, has carvings of rural scenes on the back; it consists of a relic cupboard below, and a watching loft above. On the S side is the *Monument to Humphrey, Duke of Gloucester (d 1447), brother of Henry V; it has a tall canopy with statuettes of English kings, and a grille of Sussex ironwork. E of the retrochoir is the *Lady Chapel*, built by Abbot Hugh de Eversden (1308–26); and on either side of the retrochoir are chapels, St Michael's (N side), restored as a World War I memorial, and Our Lady of the Four Tapers (S side).

A door from the S transept leads into the Slype, across which is the new *Chapter House* (1982), on the site of the chapter house demolished in 1539. Designed by William Whitfield, it is built of locally made red bricks to harmonize with the old Norman work. As well as the traditional functions of a chapter house, it provides a refectory, a shop, a youth centre and a variety of other facilities. Before it was built the bones of medieval abbots buried in the old chapter house were disinterred and buried in the cathedral presbytery.

W of the cathedral is the magnificent 14C gatehouse, which survived the destruction of the rest of the abbey buildings.

St Albans Cathedral, the magnificent brass of Thomas de la Mare, c 1360.

Southwell Minster, Nottinghamshire

Ded: St Mary the Virgin.

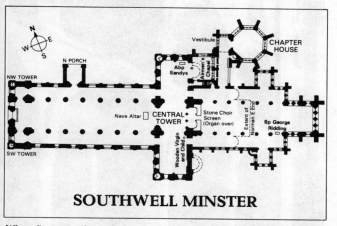

SOUTHWELL MINSTER

When first seen through the entrance gateway, the minster's twin W towers, capped by pyramidal spires, look far more French than English, and give a curiously foreign look to this attractive little town. The church is a textbook illustration of three successive styles of architecture. The severe W towers, flanking the large Perp window above the fine W door, the low central tower, and the nave and transepts with porthole-like clerestory windows, are all Norman (early 12C), and on the N side is a rare late Norman porch. The choir is a beautiful example of EE (c 1234–50), while the Dec chapter house (1295–1300) is the chief glory of the minster.

History. A church is said to have been founded here c 630 by Paulinus, first Bp of York; but the first authentic mention is in a charter of c 956, when King Eadwig granted Southwell to Oskytel, Abp of York. Oskytel established a collegiate foundation of canons, more or less under the wing of successive Abps of York, which survived until 1840, though temporarily suspended under Henry VIII and again under Edward VI. Throughout all this long period Southwell was unique in retaining the loose, democratic Saxon form of organization, with no recognized head of the chapter: unlike Norman foundations, which were always under the authority of a dean. Almost the only remaining fragment of the Saxon church is the tympanum, showing St Michael and the dragon, which now forms a lintel over the doorway in the W wall of the N transept. The present church was begun by Abp Thomas of York c 1108, and the crossing, transepts, nave and W towers are largely of this period. The original E end was considerably shorter, and terminated in a squared end, with an apsidal choir aisle on each side. The transepts had apsidal chapels on the E. The next major building phase was the enlargement and rebuilding of the choir in the EE style (c 1234–50), followed by the chapel (now the Airmen's Chapel) which took the place of the E transept apse. Last of all came the small octagonal chapter house

Southwell Minster, the triple Norman arcading at the W end of the nave. (K. Spence)

(1295–1300) and its vestibule, sumptuously carved with foliage. Unlike monastic foundations, the minster did not suffer at the Reformation, though it was neglected during the 17 and 18C. In 1880 Ewan Christian restored the two W spires, which had been removed at the beginning of the 19C, bringing them back to their Norman design. In 1884 the new diocese of Southwell was created, taking in the counties of Nottinghamshire and Derbyshire; Derby (see above) became a diocese in its own right in 1927.

Interior. The magnificent *Nave*, with its massive Norman piers and lofty triforium, is flooded with light from the Perp W window and the Perp windows inserted in the aisles. The tower arches are decorated with well-cut cable moulding. In the N Transept is the fine alabaster tomb of Abp Sandys (d 1588), with angels at his head and feet, and his family carved below him. Steps lead down to the Airmen's Chapel, which contains an altar made of fragments of aircraft destroyed in World War I. The outline of the Norman apse is marked in the chapel paving. In the S transept is a wooden sculpture of the Virgin and Child (1952), by Alan Coleman; and part of a Roman tessellated pavement (probably from the Saxon church) has been exposed.

The graceful EE *Choir* is separated from the nave and transepts by a Dec stone rood-screen (c 1335), with organ over; the screen's elaborate carving is said to include 220 human heads (many restored c 1820 by Bernasconi). The capitals of the arch above it are carved in

Saxon-looking rather than Norman style, and under the stalls behind the screen are fanciful misericords. The clerestory and triforium of the choir are ingeniously combined so as to add to the impression of height. Two heads on corbels on the N side of the choir are supposed to represent Walter de Gray and Henry III, the archbishop and the king under whom the choir was built. The E window has two rows of four lancets instead of the more usual three or five; the Flemish glass in the lower lights was formerly in the old Temple Church in Paris. The patchwork window in the S choir aisle is of old glass, perhaps from the chapter house. The praying figure under the SE arch is Bp George Ridding (d 1904), first bishop of the diocese. The splendid brass lectern (c 1500) was recovered from the lake at Newstead Abbey, into which it had been thrown by the monks of Newstead at the Dissolution, and was presented to the minster in 1805. The sedilia on the S side are in the same style as the screen and were likewise restored by Bernasconi.

A short passage leads from the choir to the exquisite octagonal *Chapter House* (c 1295–1300). The marvellous carving on the entrance doorway and on the chapter house arcading is of every variety of foliage: oak, maple, hawthorn, vine and ivy riot over the capitals and the canopies of the arcading. It is the earliest sculpture of its kind in England. The roof is not supported by the usual central pillar, and is the only example of a stone-vaulted chapter house of this type (the vault at York Minster is made of wood).

A short way S of the minster are the remains of the Palace of the Archbishops of York, with the 20C Bishop's Manor built inside them. The palace was built c 1380, but fell into disuse and was largely demolished in the 17C.

Stoneleigh Abbey, Warwickshire

Ded: St Mary.

Off A444, 3 miles N of Leamington.

A Cistercian abbey was founded at Stoneleigh c 1150. The main gateway (14C) still stands; and the Italianate mansion, built on the site by 'Smith of Warwick' in 1714–26, incorporates fragments of the abbey. The park is now the permanent site of the Royal Agricultural Show, held every July.

Tewkesbury Abbey, Gloucestershire

Ded: Blessed Virgin Mary.

Almost as large as Westminster Abbey, Tewkesbury's magnificent abbey church is remarkable for its blending of Norman and Dec architectural styles, and for the quality of its medieval tombs.

History. The successor of a Benedictine monastery founded in 715, it was begun in 1092 by Robert Fitzhamon, a cousin of William Rufus; after his death in 1107 the work was carried on by Fitzhamon's

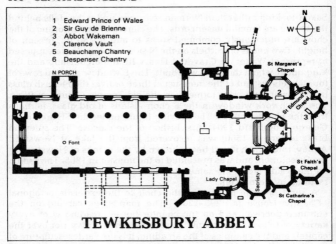

1 Edward Prince of Wales
2 Sir Guy de Brienne
3 Abbot Wakeman
4 Clarence Vault
5 Beauchamp Chantry
6 Despenser Chantry

N PORCH

O Font

St Margaret's Chapel

St Edmund's Chapel

St Faith's Chapel

Lady Chapel

Sacristy

St Catharine's Chapel

TEWKESBURY ABBEY

son-in-law Fitzroy, the 1st Earl of Gloucester, and the church was consecrated in 1121. The upper stages of the noble Norman tower were added c 1160. Though neglect and frequent restoration have affected both the exterior and interior, it is substantially as it was when it was reconsecrated after the Battle of Tewkesbury in 1471. In this battle the Yorkists, led by Edward IV, defeated the Lancastrians, some of whom fled into the abbey for sanctuary; they were killed in the church, which had to be reconsecrated after this pollution. The abbey was dissolved in 1539; the monastic buildings were pulled down, but the church was saved by the townspeople, who bought it for £453. Extensive restorations were carried out in the 1870s and again in the 1950s.

Exterior. The splendid *Central Tower is the largest Norman tower in existence, 46ft square and 148ft high (the pinnacles were added in 1660). The later North Porch is impressively plain; and the W front is almost entirely taken up by a grand recessed arch, rising almost to roof height (the large Perp-style window was inserted in 1686). The original far steeper roof line is shown by the Norman gable-ends clearly marked on the outer walls of the tower. In contrast to the austerity of the Norman work is the fanciful cluster of Choir Chapels, added in 1330–50.

Interior. Here is an even more varied range of architectural beauty. Although the great pillars of the *Nave dwarf the triforium and the later (Dec) clerestory and vaulting, built c 1340, they justify their predominance by the grandeur of their scale. Along the centre of the nave are vigorously carved roof bosses depicting scenes from the life of Christ. The tower vaulting has shields and a circle of suns representing the 'sun of York' mentioned by Richard III at the start of Shakespeare's play ('Now is the winter of our discontent/Made glorious summer by this sun of York'), triumphant over the Lancastrians at Tewkesbury. A brass in the pavement below marks the traditional site of the grave of Edward, the young Lancastrian Prince of Wales (son of Henry VI), who was killed in the battle or murdered shortly after it. The *Transepts* are Norman, with 14C windows. In the beautiful S arm is the apsidal Lady Chapel, with a mosaic reredos, and on the side wall Raphael's painting 'The Madonna del Passeggio', which once belonged to Mme de Pompadour.

The choir is surrounded by an *Ambulatory*, with radiating chapels in the form of a *chevet*. On the N side is the elegant EE St Margaret's Chapel, with the tomb of Sir Guy de Brienne, who fought at the Battle of Crécy in 1346 and d in 1390, aged 90; and St Edmund's Chapel, with bosses showing his martyrdom at the hands of the Danes. Beside this chapel is the cenotaph of Abbot Wakeman (made Bp of Gloucester by Henry VIII), with the effigy of a decaying corpse with creatures crawling over it (worm, snake, frog, mouse and spider or snail). On the S side are the chapels of St Faith and St Catherine. Behind the high altar is the Clarence Vault, where the Duke of Clarence (by tradition drowned in a butt of Malmsey) and his wife were buried in 1478. The truncated Norman pillars of the *Choir* support pointed arches and a tall superstructure with a richly groined and bossed roof (14C); the vaulting is stellar, contrasting with the lierne vaulting of the nave. Brasses, monuments and 14C *Windows of the choir commemorate the Fitzhamons, De Clares, Despensers, Beauchamps and other lords of Tewkesbury in its great days. Finest of all is the exquisite late Gothic *Beauchamp Chantry, which still has traces of its original coloured decoration. Next to it is the Fitzhamon Chantry (1397); and to the E the canopied tomb with alabaster effigies of Hugh Despenser and his wife (c 1349), who together largely financed the rebuilding of the choir and E end of the church. On the S side of the high altar is the Despenser Chantry (also called the Trinity Chapel), restored in 1983, which is Perp of c 1390 and is roofed with some of the earliest fan vaulting in the country. On the roof of the chantry the unique kneeling figure of Edward Despenser, painted and gilded, faces the altar. To the E is the tomb of Hugh Despenser's father, also Hugh, who supported Edward II and was executed as a traitor in 1326. The old organ S of the choir stalls is known as the 'Milton Organ'; during the Commonwealth it was at Hampton Court Palace, and was almost certainly played on by the poet John Milton, who was Cromwell's secretary. A larger 19C organ, used only for recitals, occupies the N transept.

Of the monastic buildings, the only survival is Abbey House (W of the abbey), the 15C abbot's lodging, much altered in the 18C. The nearby gatehouse is a 19C restoration.

Tutbury Priory, Staffordshire

Ded: St Mary the Virgin.

On A50, 3 miles NW of Burton-upon-Trent.

Soon after the Conquest (c 1080) Henri de Ferrières, one of William I's Domesday commissioners, founded a small Benedictine priory at Tutbury, on the site of a Saxon church. The present parish church consists of the nave of the Norman building, with later additions (S aisle c 1305, N aisle c 1830, apsidal E end 1867). The church's chief

Tutbury Priory, the elaborate Norman W doorway. (K. Spence)

feature is its magnificent W door (c 1160), carved with naturalistic and stylized ornament. The monastic buildings, now vanished, stood on the N side of the church.

Ulverscroft Priory, Leicestershire

On minor road off B5330, 7 miles NW of Leicester.

Hidden away in Charnwood Forest, this priory of Augustinian canons was founded in the 1130s and dissolved in 1534. A good deal of the church survives, including the tower; the domestic buildings are incorporated in a farm. (Ulverscroft discourages visitors with 'Keep Out' notices, and can only be seen from the lane that runs beside it.)

Wenlock Priory, Shropshire

Ded: St Milburga and St Michael.
In Much Wenlock, off B4378.

The substantial and beautiful medieval remains are on the site of a foundation that goes back to the 7C. In c 680, Merewald, King of Mercia, founded a nunnery here for his daughter, the saintly Milburga. It was refounded c 1050 by Leofric, Earl of Mercia, and his wife Lady Godiva (see also Coventry above), and after the Conquest, c 1086, was made into a priory of Cluniac monks by the powerful Norman earl, Roger de Montgomery. It owed allegiance to the abbey

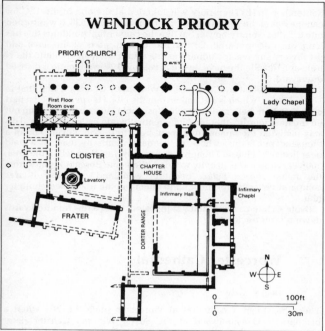

of La Charité, in France, and was thus an alien priory, heavily taxed
and penalized throughout the Hundred Years' War in the 14C. It was
dissolved in 1540, when the monastic buildings were mostly
destroyed, apart from the 15C prior's lodging, which was turned into
a private house. The church was rebuilt on a grand scale in the 13C to
house the shrine of St Milburga, whose body had been discovered by
the monks c 1100. A good deal of it survives, including the S transept
to gable height and much of the N transept. A unique feature is the
small first-floor room above the S nave aisle, at the W end; it seems
likely that it was a chapel dedicated to St Michael. The cloister is
unusually and attractively laid out with clipped topiary; on the E side
is the 12C chapter house, with well-preserved Norman blind
arcading, and in the SW corner the 12C lavatorium, decorated with
fine Romanesque sculptured panels.

White Ladies Priory, Shropshire

Ded: St Leonard.

Off minor road, 3 miles S of Weston-under-Lizard (A5), and ¾ mile W
of Boscobel House.

White Ladies is closely connected with a crucial event in English
history: the flight of Charles II after the Battle of Worcester in

September 1651. The priory was founded at the end of the 12C for canonesses of the Augustinian Order. Dissolved in 1538, it was turned into a Tudor country house; but like the conventual buildings this has long since disappeared. Of the 12C church, parts of the nave and presbytery survive, including the fine round Norman arch into the N transept; outside the nave, to the S, is a low 19C wall round a disused graveyard.

After his defeat by Cromwell at Worcester, Charles II fled first to White Ladies, which is c 40 miles from the city. He spent the best part of a week both here and at nearby Boscobel House, before setting out on the long journey that led him eventually into exile in France. This stay included the famous day spent up a tree—the 'Royal Oak' of a thousand pub signs, whose descendant stands by itself in a field near Boscobel House. Though there are now few trees left in the area, 300 years ago it was heavily wooded (the name Boscobel comes from the Italian *bosco bello*, 'beautiful woodland'), and so it was comparatively easy for the king to hide from the troops searching for him.

(Note: White Ladies is badly signposted; it lies a few hundred yards down a farm track.)

Worcester Cathedral

Ded: St Mary.

There has been a cathedral at Worcester since the 7C, when a bishopric was established at the Saxon Wigorna Ceaster (later abbreviated to the present name) c 680. Standing near the River Severn and slightly above it, Worcester Cathedral's commanding tower is a landmark in the surrounding countryside; the building is cruciform, mainly EE and Perp, with aisleless transepts and secondary choir transepts. In the 19C it was extensively restored by A.E. Perkins and Sir George Gilbert Scott, with the result that the exterior is now almost exclusively Victorian in structure and appearance, and the interior contains a number of Victorian features. In recent years the approach to the E end has been largely ruined in the interests of traffic flow. Worcester is one of the homes of the Three Choirs Festival (see also Gloucester, above; and Hereford, below).

History. The original church was dedicated to St Peter and served by secular canons. Bp Oswald (961–92), canonized in the 11C, rebuilt the cathedral and converted the secular foundation into a Benedictine monastery. St Wulstan (bp 1062–95), the only Saxon bishop to retain his see under the Normans, pulled down St Oswald's church, which had suffered greatly at the hands of the Danes, and in 1084–89 built a cathedral in the new Norman style, of which the crypt—rededicated in 1984 to celebrate its 900th anniversaray—is the chief remaining part. In 1202 the cathedral was devastated by fire, but in 1218 it was dedicated after restoration, in a splendid ceremonial attended by the young Henry III, ten bishops, and many other ecclesiastics and nobles. Wulstan was canonized in 1203, after miracles had begun to happen at his tomb; and the consequent influx of pilgrims necessitated—and paid for—the building of the noble EE Lady Chapel and the rebuilding of the choir (begun 1224 by Bp William de

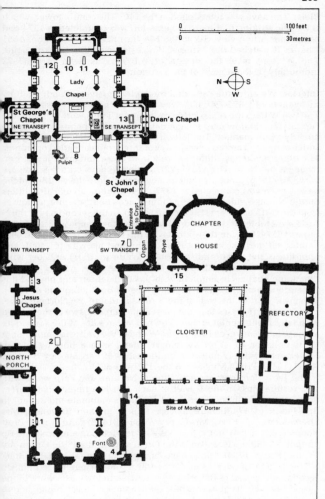

100 feet
30 metres

N E S W

12 10 11
Lady
Chapel

St George's
Chapel
NE TRANSEPT

Dean's Chapel
13
SE TRANSEPT

Pulpit

8

St John's
Chapel

Entrance to Crypt

Slype

NW TRANSEPT

SW TRANSEPT

Organ

7

CHAPTER
HOUSE

15

6

3

Jesus
Chapel

2

CLOISTER

REFECTORY

NORTH
PORCH

14

Site of Monks' Dorter

1

5

Font

4

1	Elgar Meml. Window	9	Prince Arthur's Chantry
2	Sir John Beauchamp	10	Bp Cantelupe
3	Bp Bullingham	11	Bp Blois
4	Bp Johnson	12	Charlotte Digby
5	Stanley Baldwin	13	Sir Griffith Rice
6	Bp Hough	14	'Miserrimus' Stone
7	Bp Philpott	15	Medieval Bells
8	King John		

WORCESTER CATHEDRAL

Blois). The nave was remodelled in the 14C. The central tower, which is the one striking feature of the exterior, was completed in 1374 and commands a fine view SW to the Malvern hills; in September 1651 Charles II watched the Battle of Worcester from this vantage-point. The W front is to the design of A.E. Perkins, who in 1857–73 thoroughly restored most of the exterior.

Interior. We enter the cathedral by the impressive N Porch, built by Bp Wakefield (1375–94), half-way along the nine piers of the *Nave*. The two W bays are remarkable examples of Trans work (c 1160); the capitals foreshadow later foliage designs, and the pointed arches are already EE in manner. The lofty triforium is unusual, consisting of a series of pointed arches over groups of three round-headed openings. The other seven bays differ entirely from these and are not uniform: those on the N are Dec (1317–27); while the bays on the S side are very early Perp, probably built immediately before the vaulting of the nave, which was completed in 1377. The triforium arcade also differs on the N and S side. The tympanum spaces bear sculptured figures from the Old Testament (19C on the S side). In the second bay of the N Aisle is a tablet and a memorial window to the composer Sir Edward Elgar (1857–1934). In the sixth bay of the N arcade is the tomb, with painted effigies, of Sir John Beauchamp and his wife (c 1400), and opposite is the altar-tomb of Robert Wilde (d 1607) and his wife. Further E the Jesus Chapel opens off the aisle, one of the few remaining chapels in England with this dedication; and beyond it is the curious tomb (not in its original place) of Bp Bullingham (d 1576). The lower part of the wall of the S Aisle is that of the Norman nave. Five Norman recesses face the present pier arches, two of them filled with later monumental arches. The two W bays are of the same date as those of the nave (c 1160). At the W end of the S aisle is a monument to Bp Johnson (d 1774) by Robert Adam, with a bust by Joseph Nollekens. At the W entrance lie the ashes of Earl Stanley Baldwin (1867–1947), Prime Minister in the 1920s and '30s.

The *West Transepts* are a mixture of Norman and Perp work, with 19C restorations. In the E wall of each arm is a fine Norman arch. Below this arch, in the N arm, is Roubiliac's elaborate monument to Bp Hough (d 1743); here too are tablets to three novelists, Mrs Sherwood (1775–1851), Mrs Henry Wood (1814–87) and Francis Brett Young (1884–1954). In the S arm is a large Victorian monument to Bp Philpott (d 1892). Here also is the Great Organ; the Little Organ (by 'Father' Smith, 1704), said to have belonged to Handel, is in the choir.

The *Choir of Worcester Cathedral is one of our most English, second only to that of Beverley Minster (see below), as a work of the period 1220–60. Its quality is best seen in the EE Lady Chapel, begun in 1224, with its tall lancet windows and sculptured arcade below, and in the E transepts. The sculptures in the spandrels are worth studying; one of them (E end of S aisle) is the Worcester Crucifix, with expressive figures of the Virgin and St John (restored 1862). The piers and arches are loftier at the E end of the cathedral than they are in the Presbytery; this is built over the Norman crypt, which raises the floor considerably above that of the transepts and Lady Chapel. The detached shafts of Purbeck marble were added by Bp Giffard (1268–1302). The late Victorian stalls incorporate the medieval *Misericords (14C), which are lively and varied, mixing scenes from medieval life with themes from classical mythology. The pulpit is 16C and the other furniture 19C. In the middle of the presbytery is the tomb of King John (d 1216), of which the Purbeck marble effigy alone is contemporary. The lion at the king's feet bites the end of his sword, allegedly referring to the curbing of royal power by the barons by means of Magna Carta. The king's skeleton is still in the tomb. The tomb-chest on which the effigy rests is probably of the same date as the adjacent *Chantry of Prince Arthur, erected in 1504; the prince, who was the elder brother of Henry VIII and the first husband of Catherine of Aragon, died at Ludlow Castle in 1502, aged only 15. Within the screenwork below are two fine effigy tombs, probably of Bp Giffard (d 1302) and a kinswoman. In the Lady Chapel are the tombs of Bp Cantelupe (d 1266) and Bp Blois (d 1236), and on the N wall is a tablet to Izaak Walton's second wife (d 1662), with an epitaph by him. To the left is a monument to Mrs Digby (d 1820) by Sir Francis Chantrey. The NE Transept is now St George's Chapel, dedicated to the Worcestershire Regiment; opposite is the tomb of Bp de Cobham (d 1327), who built the Jesus Chapel and began the 'new' nave (c 1317). In the SE Transept (now the Dean's Chapel) is the effigy tomb (14C) of Sir William de Harcourt, the massive tomb of Sir Griffith Rice (d 1523), and an alabaster statuette of the Virgin and Child, carved c 1470 by Nottingham craftsmen. Looking into the N choir aisle is the projecting Sacrist's Window, from which the sacrist could watch over the high altar and the shrines of St Oswald and St Wulstan.

The many pillared *Crypt, entered from the SW transept, was begun by St Wulstan in 1084. The largest Norman crypt in England, its complexity and beauty must have been even greater in its original form, extending to the E. It is the second in date of the four apsidal crypts in English cathedrals (Canterbury is earlier; Winchester and Gloucester later).

The Library, in a room over the S nave aisle, contains some 4,000 volumes, both MSS and printed books of the 15–18C. (Visits by prior arrangement with the Librarian.)

The remains of the monastic buildings lie to the S, connected with the church by the late 14C *Cloisters*, which are entered from the S nave aisle. A second entrance on the S side (from College Green) is by a richly moulded late Norman door. Of the fine roof bosses, those in the S walk represent the ancestors of Christ (Jesse Tree), while in the N walk adoring angels turn towards the central boss, carved with the Virgin and Child. At the W end of this walk is a tombstone inscribed *Miserrimus* ('most wretched man'), said to be that of a Jacobite canon unable to adjust himself to the rule of William III. This one-word epitaph inspired Wordsworth's lines:

> Nought but that word assigned to the unknown,
> That solitary word—to separate
> From all, and cast a cloud around the fate
> Of him who lies beneath. Most wretched one.

On the E side of the cloisters is the Chapter House, a circular building of c 1150, with Perp vaulting and windows, which set the pattern for later chapter houses (e.g. Lincoln and Wells). The walls with their Norman blind arcading are constructed of alternate bands of green and brown stone. Left of the doorway are five bells of the original peal, the oldest cast c 1374. Along the S side of the cloisters lies the monks' Refectory, 120ft long, on a vaulted Norman undercroft. Now called College Hall, it has been used by the boys of King's School, Worcester, since the Reformation. (To visit Chapter House or Refectory, apply to verger.)

SE of the cathedral is the Edgar Tower (c 1350), once the fortified great gate of the monastery.

Worksop Priory, Nottinghamshire

Ded: St Mary and St Cuthbert.

Worksop's noble priory church is a remarkable combination of the old and the new: the long and splendid Norman nave with its twin W towers, and the 20C E end, consecrated in 1974, with a low tower topped by a slender needle spire. In 1103 an Augustinian priory was established here, and the Norman church was substantially complete by c 1170. Of this church the grand nave, 140ft long and built c 1150–60, survives in its original form; unusually, the pillars are alternately round and octagonal. Early in the 13C the Norman choir was replaced by a larger EE choir; the EE Lady Chapel, E of the S transept, was added c 1240. The S door has elaborate ironwork of c 1260. The priory was dissolved in 1539 and the nave was made over to the parishioners. After 1845 a major restoration was carried out, with further restoration in 1935. In 1965–74 the works were brought to completion by a new E end, which includes a vestry and meeting-rooms.

Of the rest of the priory buildings, the fine 14C gatehouse survives (S of church), and part of the cloister wall (N of church).

6. NORTHERN ENGLAND

Alnwick Abbey, Northumberland

Off B6346, just N of Alnwick.

Only the 14C gatehouse survives of the abbey, founded in 1147 for Premonstratensian canons on a pastoral site beside the River Aln. In the Middle Ages it had a reputation for hospitality; and the earliest literary record of Robin Hood occurs in a Latin poem by a 14C abbot of Alnwick.

Ampleforth Abbey, N Yorkshire

Ded: St Laurence.

On minor road off B1257, 4 miles S of Helmsley.

Impressively sited on a south-facing hillside, Ampleforth has been the home of a community of Benedictine monks since 1802. In 1793 they were driven out of France by the Revolution and took refuge in England, finally settling at Ampleforth. The Georgian house (Ampleforth Lodge) where they lived still exists, now surrounded by the later buildings of the monastery and boys' public school (main study block built 1861). The abbey church can be visited; designed by Sir Giles Gilbert Scott in the 1920s, it was inspired by French 12C churches, notably Périgueux. The choir and W crypt were completed in 1924, and the tower (120ft high), transepts and main crypt were built in 1957–61. The church contains a number of treasures, notably a 14C French Madonna and Child in painted wood, and a 14C alabaster of the Trinity from Byland Abbey. There is some fine stained glass (by Herbert Hendrie, W window, and Patrick Reyntiens, Lady Chapel). The monks' stalls were carved by Robert Thompson, of Kilburn, N Yorkshire, who signed his work with the carving of a mouse.

Beverley Minster, Humberside

Ded: St John the Evangelist.

One of the few great English churches with a double set of transepts, Beverley Minster is in size and splendour more than the equal of some cathedrals. It is noteworthy for the purity and beauty of the EE work (13C), and the nobility of the Perp W front.

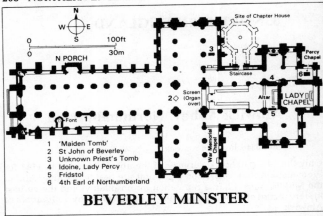

1 'Maiden Tomb'
2 St John of Beverley
3 Unknown Priest's Tomb
4 Idoine, Lady Percy
5 Fridstol
6 4th Earl of Northumberland

BEVERLEY MINSTER

History. John of Beverley (d 721), Bp of Hexham and of York, founded a monastery at Beverley on the site of a chapel of St John the Evangelist, and died and was buried there. Miracles that took place at his tomb led to his canonization in 1037, and kings, from Athelstan in the 10C to Henry V in the 15C, conferred benefits on the church in gratitude for victories they won after making pilgrimages to St John's shrine. The minster was rebuilt in the 11C after destruction by the Danes in 866; but this Saxon and Norman church was badly damaged in 1188 by a fire which destroyed much of Beverley; and in 1213 the central tower fell down. Restoration during the next two centuries was mainly on Gothic lines; and the blending of styles that makes the church seem to be of a single design soon becomes apparent. The choir and transepts are EE (c 1220–60), the nave mainly Dec and Perp. The Perp ·W Front, with its slender twin towers, built c 1390–1420 and 163ft high, is the finest of its kind in England. In 1548 the college of secular canons who ran the minster was dissolved, their chapter house was pulled down, and the minster reverted to the status of a parish church. In the 18C the church was saved from ruin by restoration carried out by Nicholas Hawksmoor (d 1736), and a further restoration was undertaken by Sir Gilbert Scott in 1866–68. In 1977 another major restoration was begun.

Interior. In the *Nave*, the two E bays are EE and the W bay is Perp while the rest is fine Dec work c 1300–50. Exquisite carvings of angel musicians form the label-stops along the nave arcades; the label-stops in the N aisle show bagpipers, drummers etc. In the S aisle are the massive late Norman font of Frosterley marble, with an elaborate cover of 1726, and the canopied Dec 'Maiden' or 'Two Sisters' tomb. St John of Beverley is buried at the E end of the nave. The medieval W doors are decorated with later carvings of the Evangelists, which probably date from Hawksmoor's 18C restoration.

The *Great Transept* (EE) is notable (like the York Minster transepts) for having both E and W aisles. In the S arm is a painting (James I period) of Athelstan making a grant of sanctuary to the minster in 938; and in the E aisle of the N arm is a remarkable 14C tomb with the effigy of a priest, possibly Gilbert de Grimsby (d 1306).

In the N Choir Aisle is the beautiful 13C double ·Staircase, a ver rare feature, which formerly led to the chapter house (destroyed c 1550). The *Choir*, a perfect example of EE, has a wealth of woodcarving in the stalls (c 1520–40); the collection of often humorous misericords (68 altogether) is the largest in England. The elaborate choir screen (c 1880) is by Sir Gilbert Scott; the organ above it, restored by Scott, contains parts of an organ built by the famous maker John Snetzler in 1769. The front of the Dec altar screen was renewed in 1826 and adorned in 1897 with statues and mosaics. On the N side of the altar is the magnificent canopied *Percy Tomb, to the memory of Idoine (d 1365), wife of the 2nd Lord Percy. One of the masterworks of European medieval art, the canopy is carved with knights, angels, fruit, leaves and symbolic animals. Also on the N side of the altar is the pre-Conquest 'Fridstol' or sanctuary chair, traditionally dating from the time of Athelstan (924–39); the minster gave sanctuary to criminals throughout the Middle Ages, until Henry VIII abolished the right in 1540, and it seems likely that the stone Fridstol was used by the magistrate who examined the criminal's plea for asylum.

Beverley Minster, the great W doorway. The medieval door is decorated with early 18C panels of the four Evangelists.

The beautiful *Retrochoir* (sometimes called the Lady Chapel), behind the high altar, has an E window inserted in 1416 which contains fine 13–15C glass, some collected from other windows. The vaulting and blind arcading (c 1340) at the back of the reredos, with Flamboyant tracery, are especially fine. In the small 15C Percy Chapel (to the N) is the mutilated tomb of the 4th Earl of Northumberland (d 1489).

An unusual medieval survival (though constantly repaired as its parts wear out) is the treadwheel crane in the central tower, formerly used to raise building materials through a removable central boss in the crossing ceiling. Last used in 1977, it is still in working order.

Birkenhead Priory, Merseyside

A small Benedictine priory was established near the Mersey c 1150; after c 1300 the monks had the right to control the ferry crossing over the river. The small vaulted chapter house still survives, and is now used as a local church.

Blackburn Cathedral, Lancashire

Ded: St Mary the Virgin.

Blackburn's modern (1961) needle spire, rising above an octagonal lantern, provides a focal point for the town's centre. A church has stood on the site since the 6C; the present building, designed by John Palmer, was consecrated in 1826, and has been greatly enlarged since World War II. Palmer was a pioneer of the Gothic Revival, and St Mary's was an early example of the 'new' style. By the early 20C the population of Greater Manchester had grown so large that there was need for a new diocese; and so the Diocese of Blackburn, 'carved' from the Manchester diocese, was created in 1926. In the 1930s preparations for the enlargement of the church to suit its new cathedral status was set in hand, to designs by W.A. Forsythe. The foundation stone of the extensions was laid in 1938 by the Princess Royal; but work was interrupted by World War II and only begun again in 1950. Work on new transepts, crossing and E end went on slowly. In 1961 Laurence King took over as cathedral architect. A soaring lantern, in the style of a corona and topped by a flèche, was completed in 1967 in place of the larger central tower planned by Forsythe.

The cathedral, spacious and full of light, centres on the high altar placed directly below the lantern. At the W end of the wide Nave, above the ogee-arched doorway from the W tower, is John Hayward's enormous aluminium and fibreglass statue of 'Christ the Worker' (1965), set against a wrought-iron background whose shape suggests a loom. Below the lantern is a large metal corona (crown of thorns), weighing four tons, from which the eye is led upwards to John Hayward's golden abstract glass in the lantern, and a device symbolising the Holy Trinity on the central boss. In the N Transept is a window of Flemish glass, brought to Blackburn in 1826. A modern sculpture of the Virgin and Child, by Josephina de Vasconcellos, stands in the NE corner. The S Transept contains the font, egg-shaped and with a small bronze statuette on the lid, by John Hayward, of the Baptism of Christ. In the same transept is a fibreglass Madonna and Child, an enlarged copy of figures on a 15C 'Pax' (icon-like tablet kissed by the congregation at Mass), which had been hidden in a grave at the Reformation and discovered in 1820. The S window consists mainly of 15C glass taken from the nave and reassembled by John Hayward. At the NE corner of this transept is St Martin's Chapel (1970), the chapel of the E Lancashire Regiment, dedicated to the Roman soldier who in 370 became Bp of Tours.

E of the high altar is the bishop's throne, behind which is an ambulatory bounded by a pierced and painted screen. At the extreme E end is the Jesus Chapel (1977); in the tympanum above is the splendid crucifix carved by Advent Hunston. The fine organ, by J.W. Walker and Sons, was dedicated in 1969. The cathedral is built on a sloping site, creating a large Crypt with space for vestries, a sacristy, a muniments room and choir rehearsal room.

Bolton Priory, N Yorkshire

Ded: St Mary and St Cuthbert.

By B6160, 6 miles E of Skipton.

John Ruskin said that Bolton was 'more beautifully situated than any other ruin in this country', though Rievaulx Abbey might dispute this claim. Situated in parkland beside the River Wharfe, with craggy hills on the opposite side, Bolton is very much part of the landscape and has inspired artists since the time of Turner. (As a matter of terminology, Bolton Abbey is the village and Bolton Priory is the ruin.)

In 1120 Cecily de Rumilly founded a priory of Augustinian canons at Embsay, outside Skipton, which was moved to its present site by Lady Alice, her daughter. The EE nave of the church has been used as a parish church since c 1170, and so was not destroyed when the priory was dissolved in 1539. Of the noble priory church (c 1220) the E window (minus its tracery), choir and transepts remain, almost to roof level, but the monastic buildings to the S have almost entirely disappeared. The parish church is approached through a magnificent Perp W front, begun by Prior Moone c 1520 but still without its tower when the priory was dissolved. Prior Moone's front conceals the original 13C W front, through which we enter the church. This consists of nave and N aisle; the roof and E end were restored in 1875–80 by G.E. Street. The E wall, which consists of the crossing arch filled in, is painted with madonna lilies and other plants in an almost art nouveau style (by A. Bottomley, 1880).

The 19C Bolton Hall, W of the priory ruins, incorporates the medieval gatehouse.

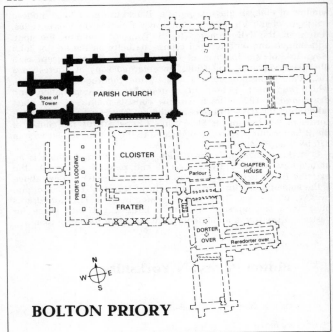

BOLTON PRIORY

Bradford Cathedral, W Yorkshire

Ded: St Peter.

Built on a hillside above the city centre, Bradford Cathedral consists of a mainly Perp parish church embedded in additions of the 1950s and '60s. Until recently the old work could be easily distinguished from the new by its coating of industrial grime, but after cleaning the whole now appears far more homogeneous. An earlier church on the site is said to have been burnt down by the Scots in 1327, and the present church is largely a 14–15C rebuilding; the nave and chancel were completed c 1460, and the tower was finished in 1508. The S porch was restored in 1833 and the transepts were added in 1898. Bradford became a diocese in 1919, when St Peter's was raised to cathedral status. At the W end, a song-room for the choir and rooms for the bishop and church staff were added in the 1950s on either side of the tower; and in the 1960s a new E end was built to designs by Sir Edward Maufe, the architect of Guildford Cathedral.

Entrance is normally through the S porch. From the wide Nave there is an uninterrupted view through to the Lady Chapel at the E end, with its three narrow William Morris windows formed from the original seven-light window of 1863. A unique feature of the nave is the free-standing organ near the W end, used when the choir walks in procession from the song-room, and providing a link in colour and sound between the old and new parts of the cathedral. At the W end of the N aisle is a World War I memorial window to the men of the 6th Battalion of the Prince of Wales Own W Yorkshire Regiment. There are a number of good monuments, notably the Flaxman memorial to Abraham Balme (d 1796) in the N transept. The elaborate wooden font cover (restored) is 15C. Maufe's new E end consists of the Sanctuary (consecrated in 1963), with St Aidan's Chapel (completed in 1965) to the N and the Chapel of the Holy Spirit and Lady Chapel to the E, all opening off an ambulatory. The consecration cross traced by Abp Donald Coggan, inscribed and painted red, is on a pillar S of the sanctuary.

Bridlington Priory, Humberside

Ded: St Mary.

An Augustinian priory was founded at Bridlington in 1113. Of its impressive church (EE and Perp) only the nave survives; because it was being used by the parishioners at the time of the Dissolution, it was not destroyed along with the E end of the church and the monastic buildings. It is still used as the parish church. The oldest work is EE, on the N side; the W end is largely Perp.

Brinkburn Priory, Northumberland

Ded: St Peter and St Paul.

Off B6344, 5 miles SE of Rothbury.

A small gem of a priory church, approached down a steep track through rhododendrons, Brinkburn lies tucked away beside the little River Coquet. A house of Augustinian canons was founded here c 1130; the church, built all of a piece c 1190–1220, is in a Trans style combining Norman and EE elements. The approach is from the N, and so the N side is the first to be seen, giving a good impression of the church's height in proportion to its short length, and its squat central tower. Though the windows are all lancets, and small, there are so many of them that the church is full of light: for example, the E end is pierced with three rows of three lancets. Little survives of the monastic buildings, though traces remain of the S cloister range in the Georgian house S of the church.

Byland Abbey, N Yorkshire

Ded: St Mary.

On minor road off A170, 7 miles E of Thirsk.

Together with Fountains and Rievaulx, Byland makes up the trio of great Cistercian abbeys of N Yorkshire. Less beautiful than Rievaulx

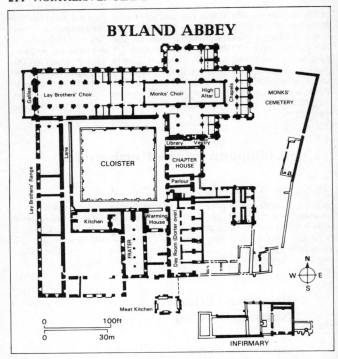

BYLAND ABBEY

and smaller than Fountains, it nevertheless displays the Cistercian layout more clearly than either. The original foundation (on another site) can be dated back to 1134; after various wanderings the present site was occupied in 1177, during the long rule of Abbot Roger, who held office for 54 years (1142–96). The site is flat and open, and so there were no problems (apart from drainage, as the land was originally marsh) in laying out the monastery. The chief survival of the church is the once-magnificent W front (c 1200), with a large door into the nave and a smaller one into each aisle, three lancets above, and the remains of a huge wheel-shaped window over the lancets. The square E end terminated in five chapels, and the transepts had two chapels each. As in all Cistercian churches, there were dividing walls separating the lay brothers in the nave from the monks in the choir and presbytery. The chapels in the S Transept are still floored with medieval tiles, originally glazed green and yellow.

The monastic buildings, whose lower courses still stand, are fairly easy to follow. The E cloister range, beyond the S transept, consists of an almost square chapter house, flanked by a narrow library-vestry on the N and a parlour to the S; the abbot's lodging was SE of this range, linked to it by a passage. On the S side were the warming-house, cellar with frater above, and kitchen. The lay brothers' range, on the W side, is the oldest part of the monastery and enormously long (275ft). Between it and the monks' cloister is a narrow 'lane', flanked by a wall with recesses used as seats.

There is a small museum on the site with a display of carved stones and tiles from the abbey, and a rare four-legged stone base for a lectern.

Calder Abbey, Cumbria

Ded: St Mary.

On minor road E of Calder Bridge, 4 miles SE of Egremont.

The first monastery was founded here in 1135, but after raids by the Scots the attempt was abandoned. A second more successful foundation took place in 1142 (Savignac Order, becoming Cistercian in 1147), which lasted until the Dissolution in 1536. Of the late 12C church a good deal of the W end and the N aisle arcade survives; a redbrick Georgian house now stands on the S side of the monastic buildings.

The abbey is privately owned and cannot at present be visited. The best way to see it is to park in Calder Bridge village and walk along the riverside footpath from the church for about a mile; the ruins can be seen from the path.

Carlisle Cathedral, Cumbria

Ded: Holy Trinity.

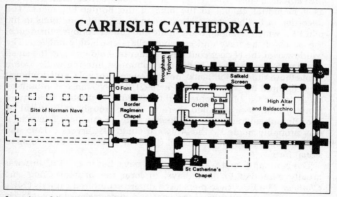

In spite of its small size, Carlisle's cathedral, built of reddish-brown stone and dominating the centre of the city, is full of interest, as is to be expected of a building that has stood for so long at the heart of the turbulent Border region. Originally the church of an Augustinian priory, it became a cathedral in 1133, and was the only Augustinian church that was also the seat of a bishop.

History. In Roman times Carlisle was an important frontier town, called Luguvallium, and it is possible that Christianity had already reached it when the Romans left Britain in 410. The first evidence of

Christian worship appears in 685, when St Cuthbert visited the city. Destroyed by the Danes in 875, and constantly attacked by the Scots, Carlisle attained a measure of security in 1092 when William Rufus captured it from the Scots and began its castle. In 1122 Henry I brought a community of Augustinian canons to Carlisle, to take over a priory that already existed there; and in 1133 he created the See of Carlisle. The original Norman church survives in the crossing, the two W bays and the S transept. (The remaining six bays of the nave were pulled down by the Parliamentarians during the Civil War to provide stone for guardhouses; this accounts for the back-to-front appearance of the cathedral, which extends far more to the E than it does to the W.) The short original Norman presbytery began to be replaced by the beautiful EE chancel c 1225. The choir was destroyed by fire in 1292, and the triforium and clerestory were subsequently restored in the Dec style by Bp Halton in 1292–1324. The final major building works were carried out by Bp Strickland (1400–19), who rebuilt the N transept and constructed the central tower. In 1542 the priory was dissolved, and Prior Lancelot Salkeld became the first dean. In the 17C most of the nave was destroyed; and in the Jacobite rebellion of 1745 the cathedral was used as a prison for captured supporters of the Young Pretender. Sir Walter Scott was married there in 1797. Major restoration began on the initiative of Dean Tait (later Abp of Canterbury) in 1850, under Ewan Christian, who restored the choir ceiling and made good the W end in 1870, and after him under G.E. Street. Since then the cathedral has been constantly restored and redecorated in lesser but equally important ways.

Interior. The entrance, on the S side, leads into the Norman W end of the cathedral. Here what remains of the *Nave* was refurnished in 1948 as a memorial chapel to the men of the Border Regiment. The distortion of the Norman arches is due to drought conditions in the mid 13C, which dried the water-table and caused serious subsidence; the bases of the nave and crossing pillars are highly uneven. The window over the N door contains fragments of old glass. In the small Norman *S Transept* is a Runic inscription set into the wall: 'Dolfin wrote these runes' (Dolfin may have been governor of Carlisle when it was captured by William Rufus in 1092). The *N Transept*, rebuilt by Bp Strickland c 1400, contains the cathedral's greatest treasure, a Flemish altarpiece installed there in 1979. Brought to England by Lord Brougham in the 19C and known as the 'Brougham Triptych', it was probably made by the Antwerp Guild of Carvers c 1505 and shows scenes from the Passion of Christ in naturalistic three-dimensional form.

The Norman E end was of only two bays, but in the 13C this was greatly extended to eight bays, to form the present *Choir* and *Chancel*. The EE arcade piers have superb sculptured capitals (14C), representing the months of the year and their various tasks (March, sowing; November, ploughing; etc). The glory of the choir is the magnificent Dec ˙E Window (tracery c 1340–45). The tracery lights have glass of c 1360 showing the Last Judgement; the main lights have 19C glass. Below the window is a monument to Archdeacon William Paley (d 1805), a distinguished theologian and author of *Evidences of Christianity*, who is buried in the N choir aisle. The splendid wooden barrel-vaulted ceiling, which dates from c 1360, was restored by Ewan Christian and Owen Jones in 1856 and repainted in 1970. The choir stalls, with fine misericords, date from c

1420; their backs were painted in the time of Prior Gondibour (1484–1507) with the Apostles, and scenes from the lives of St Anthony and St Cuthbert (N side) and St Augustine (S side). The paintings were restored in 1936 by Prof. E.W. Tristram, and further cleaned and refurbished by Pauline Plummer (1977–79). There is more fine woodwork: Prior Gondibour's beautiful Flamboyant screen enclosing St Catherine's Chapel (W end of S choir aisle); and the elaborately carved Renaissance *Salkeld Screen (between presby-tery and N aisle). The carved 16C Flemish pulpit was brought to the cathedral in 1964 from a church in Bedfordshire (Cockayne Hatley). In the centre of the choir is a large brass to Bp Bell (d 1496).

Some remains of the monastic buildings survive SW of the church. Chief of these is the *Deanery*, a range of buildings consisting in part of a fortified 13C peel-tower, in which the monks could take refuge from Scottish attacks. The second floor has been turned (1982) into the Prior's Tower Museum, devoted to the history of the cathedral and housed in the prior's bedroom. The floor below was the prior's solar, with a magnificent painted ceiling (cleaned by Pauline Plummer in 1976) from the time of Prior Simon Senhouse (c 1510), whose motto was 'Simon lothe to offend'. The imposing hall known as the Fratry (13C, rebuilt late 15C) is now the cathedral library. The Gatehouse was rebuilt by Prior Slee in 1527.

Cartmel Priory, Cumbria

Ded: St Mary and St Michael.

On minor road 2 miles W of Grange-over-Sands.

Now the parish church of a picture-postcard village, Cartmel church belonged to a priory of Augustinian canons founded c 1190, and is a rare example of a monastic church to have survived the Reformation in its original form. Still basically a Norman church, the S choir aisle is 13C Dec, while the nave and glorious E window are 15C Perp. An external curiosity is the upper stage of the central tower, added in the 15C to the squat Norman tower at an angle of 45 degrees. The priory was dissolved in 1537, not without protest, as some of the canons took part in the 'Pilgrimage of Grace' against the Dissolution and were subsequently executed.

  At an unknown date the church was bought by the parish. Its restoration was due to a local landowner, George Preston, from c 1620 on; he was responsible for inserting the unusual Flemish wooden choir screen which is one of the main features of the church. Inside the predominant feeling is of spaciousness and height, emphasized by the immensely tall crossing arches. The short Nave, of only three bays, contains the large memorial to Lord Frederick Cavendish, assassinated in Phoenix Park, Dublin, in 1882; and an expressive bronze of the Holy Family ('They Fled by Night'), by Josephina de Vasconcellos. On the NW crossing pier is a wooden bread cupboard. The arches of the Choir have well-carved Trans Norman carving; and the choir stalls retain their fanciful misericords of c 1440.

  The *Priory Gatehouse* (owned by the National Trust), in the village square, became a courthouse, then a school, and is now a shop.

Durham Cathedral

Ded: Christ and the Blessed Virgin.

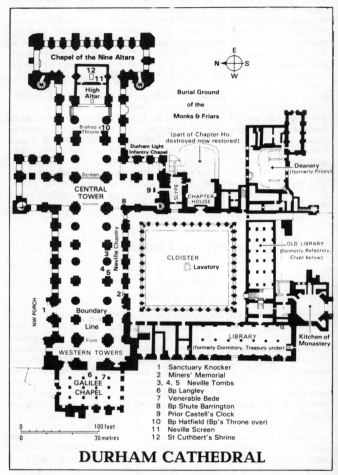

1 Sanctuary Knocker
2 Miners' Memorial
3, 4, 5 Neville Tombs
6 Bp Langley
7 Venerable Bede
8 Bp Shute Barrington
9 Prior Castell's Clock
10 Bp Hatfield (Bp's Throne over)
11 Neville Screen
12 St Cuthbert's Shrine

DURHAM CATHEDRAL

Durham stands on a bold peninsula almost surrounded by the River Wear, and has the most dramatic city site in England. On the summit of a wooded bank that rises abruptly from the river, the great Norman cathedral and the castle of the prince-bishops tower side by side. There are magnificent views of the cathedral from Prebends' Bridge to the S, and from the paths along the river. The usual approach, best made on foot, is up the old shopping streets of the town to Palace Green, where the vista is closed by the impressively austere N side of the cathedral.

History. St Cuthbert, Bp of Lindisfarne, died on Farne Island in 687 and was buried at Lindisfarne, after leaving instructions that if the monks had to leave Holy Island they would take his bones with them. This happened some 200 years later, when Danish raids drove them from Lindisfarne; after a further century of wandering, they found a final refuge on a peninsula in the River Wear. Here in 995, under Bp Aldhun, they founded a monastery and shrine for the saint, but little or nothing remains of the Saxon cathedral (known as the White Church and dedicated in 998). The present great Norman church was begun by Bp William de St Carileph in 1093, starting with the choir and crossing; the nave was completed by Bp Ranulph Flambard (1099–1128). In 1104 St Cuthbert's body was enshrined behind the High Altar. The whole church was designed to be vaulted, and the ribbed vault of the N choir aisle (before 1096) is perhaps the oldest in England; the main choir vault was renewed early in the 13C. The graceful Galilee chapel, at the W end, was added by Bp Hugh de Puiset (or Pudsey) c 1175; and the two W towers (145ft) were probably built between 1150 and 1226. The original church terminated in three apses to the E; but the present Chapel of the Nine Altars, in the shape of an E transept and paralleled only at Fountains Abbey, was substituted in the mid 13C, with Master Richard of Farnham as architect. The great central tower (218ft), built originally c 1260, was struck by lightning in 1429 and rebuilt by Bp Lawrence Booth in 1470.

At the Reformation in 1542 the last prior, Hugh Whitehead, became the first dean, and so continuity of administration was maintained. In the 17C repairs and renovations were carried out by Bp Cosin; but the woodwork was greatly damaged in 1650 by 4,000 Scottish prisoners confined in the church by Cromwell after the Battle of Dunbar. Towards the end of the 18C major repairs to the structure were put in hand, by James Wyatt and others, who pared down the walls (N side, E end, W towers) by a depth of four inches, removing much detail in the process. (Wyatt's proposal to demolish the Galilee aroused so much protest that it was not carried out.) Further work was undertaken by Salvin in the 1840s and Sir Gilbert Scott in the 1870s (choir screen and pulpit).

Exterior. This remains remarkably bold and imposing, in spite of the 18C alterations. The NW porch, with its bronze sanctuary knocker, was spoilt in the 1770s by removal of the upper watchmen's chamber. The famous mid 12C *Sanctuary Knocker (replica) is a reminder that Durham was a place of sanctuary throughout the Middle Ages. The figure of a cow (outside at NE end) perpetuates the legend that a woman looking for her dun cow acted as guide to Bp Aldhun when he was choosing the site for his church.

Interior. Entrance is through the NW porch. As the visitor stands at the W end, the uninterrupted view produces an impression described by Dr Johnson as 'rocky solidity and indeterminate duration'. No other great English church retains its original Romanesque bulk so untouched; and nowhere else is Norman work so strongly individualized (an effect due largely to the mighty circular columns with their remarkable incised ornament, and to the profusion of zigzag moulding).

The *Nave* is built on the system of alternate single columns and clustered piers. The quadripartite ribbed vaulting is designed for single bays; the pointed transverse arches, finished in 1133, are

Durham Cathedral, spectacularly sited above the river Wear.
(Aerofilms)

probably the earliest pointed arches in a high vault anywhere in Europe. In the pavement E of the font is a line of black Frosterley marble beyond which no woman was allowed to go, in accordance with the Benedictine rule. The small Renaissance font is surrounded by a towering 'tabernacle', part of the magnificent woodwork given by Bp Cosin (1660–72). The W window is an insertion of c 1346. Part of the S Aisle was formerly screened off as the Neville chantry, and two Neville effigies, smashed by the Scots after the Battle of Dunbar, remain in the S arcade. Further W, against the S wall, is the Miners' Memorial, placed there in 1948 in tribute to 'the Durham miners who have given their lives in the pits of this county and those who work in darkness and danger in those pits today'. In the same S aisle is the case of the organ built by 'Father' Smith (1683) to stand on the choir screen.

The many-pillared * Galilee, entered from the W end of the nave, is a remarkable example of Trans work begun by Bp Puiset c 1175, and restored and altered by Cardinal Langley (d 1437), who built his altar-tomb in front of the central W door. It contains the simple 16C tomb of the Venerable Bede, who d 735 at Jarrow, and whose remains were brought to Durham c 1020 and moved to the Galilee in 1370. The 12C wall-paintings in the second bay on the N side may be of St Cuthbert and St Oswald. The modern crucifix in the centre space is by George Pace, who also designed the lettering of the panel containing a quotation from Bede (1971).

The original Norman ends of the *Great Transepts* were altered in the 14C (N) and 15C (S) by the insertion of the present windows, but the vaulting of the N transept is original (c 1105). Above the crossing is an open lantern of unusual height and dignity. In the S transept is a fine monument by Sir Francis Chantrey to Bp Shute Barrington (d 1826); and at the end of the transept is Prior Castell's Clock (c 1500, dial and works renewed 1632, case restored 1938). The memorial Chapel of the Durham Light Infantry is on the E side of this transept.

The *Choir* is separated from the crossing by a light, open screen of marble of different colours, replacing the former wooden screen of Bp Cosin removed by Salvin in 1845. Cosin's dignified stalls, however, survive. On the S is the *Bishop's Throne, said to be the highest in Christendom; reached by stairs, it stands above the altar tomb of Bp Hatfield (d 1381), who also erected the throne. The magnificent stone altar screen (c 1375), with its tall open pinnacles, was the gift of John, Lord Neville, and was made of Caen stone in the London workshops of Henry Yevele, the architect of Canterbury Cathedral.

The *Chapel of the Nine Altars* (c 1250) harmonizes admirably with the massively Romanesque choir, though it is wholly different in style. (The tracery of the great E rose-window is to a neo-Gothic design by Wyatt, c 1795). The slender polished shafts are of Frosterley marble. The rich Bede Altar, in the central chapel, was designed by S.E. Dykes Bower (1935). The fine 13C stone cross, to the S, came from the vanished abbey of Neasham, near Darlington. St Cuthbert's Tomb is up a flight of steps behind the high altar; the elaborate shrine that

Durham Cathedral, the Norman Galilee Chapel, which contains the tomb of the Venerable Bede. (A.F. Kersting)

stood there, and was a major goal of pilgrimage, was destroyed in 1540, and the body now lies buried under a plain marble slab inscribed simply 'CVTHBERTVS'. At various times since the saint's death in 687 his body had been found to be without corruption, and so it was in 1540: it was 'whole, incorrupt, with his face bare and his beard as it had been a fortnight's growth'. The four large candlesticks at the corners of the tomb were designed by Sir Ninian Comper. The plan of the original apse is outlined on the floor.

Though Durham, as established in 995, was a secular church, Bp de St Carileph made it monastic in 1083 by bringing monks from Jarrow and Monkwearmouth. The monastic buildings are clustered round the *Cloister* (c 1400), S of the nave; both doors from the church are noteworthy, especially the Monks' Door (W), with splendid ironwork of c 1130. The W range consists of the Monks' Dormitory (1398–1404), which still has its original timber roof. Below it, in the undercroft, is the Treasury; on display are relics of St Cuthbert, including wooden fragments from his coffin and an exquisite little gold and enamel pectoral cross of c 640–70, together with seals and documents, church vestments, and the original sanctuary knocker. The Refectory, on the S side, was rebuilt as a library c 1684 (no adm.). The large vaulted Chapter House (E side, normally closed) was completed c 1140, partly destroyed in 1796 and restored in 1895.

Easby Abbey, N Yorkshire

Ded: St Agatha.

Off B6271, 1 mile E of Richmond.

Easby, which stands on a beautiful site by the Swale, was founded for Premonstratensian canons c 1155 and has a rare dedication to St Agatha of Sicily, martyred at Catania in 251. Its history was uneventful, though it was subject to raids by the Scots, and in 1346 it was damaged by English troops billeted there. It was dissolved in 1536.

It has an unusual layout, since the church stands between two groups of monastic buildings, with the infirmary and abbot's lodging to the N, and the cloister to the S. The church has largely disappeared; of the monastic buildings, the chief survival is the magnificent 13C frater (which occupies the S range of the cloister and still stands to almost its full height, though without its roof. On the W side is a large block, originally three storeys high, which consisted of the monks' dorter linked to an impressive guesthouse; the adjoining reredorter was flushed by a covered millrace to the W. The 14C gatehouse is still substantially intact.

The little parish church, older than the abbey (early 12C), has extensive wall-paintings in the chancel, a font of c 1100, and a copy of what is left of the Easby Cross (7 or 8C); the original stones are now in the Victoria and Albert Museum.

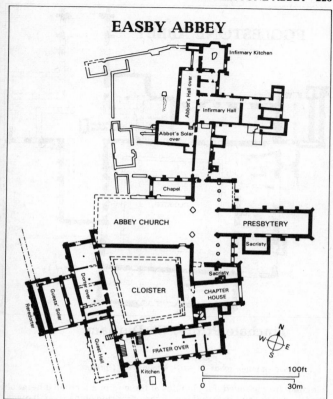

EASBY ABBEY

Infirmary Kitchen

Abbot's Hall over

Infirmary Hall

Abbot's Solar over

Chapel

ABBEY CHURCH

PRESBYTERY

Sacristy

Reredorter

Guests Solar

Dorter over

CLOISTER

Sacristy

CHAPTER HOUSE

Guest Hall

FRATER OVER

Kitchen

N
W · E
S

100ft

30m

Egglestone Abbey, N Yorkshire

Ded: St Mary and St John the Baptist.

On minor road 1 mile SE of Barnard Castle.

Egglestone stands on top of a mound, on a remote site above the River Tees. It was founded in 1195–98 for Premonstratensian canons and was a daughter house of Easby; like Easby, it suffered both from Scottish raids and the depredations of English troops. Always poor and small, it was dissolved in 1536; c 1550 the domestic buildings were turned into a private house, which later became labourers' cottages. A good deal survives of the church, mainly the W and E ends (W end the first church of c 1200, E end an enlargement of c 1250). The imposing tomb in the crossing is that of Sir Ralph Bowes of Streatlam (d 1482). Little remains of the cloister buildings (N of the church) apart from the E range (the Tudor house).

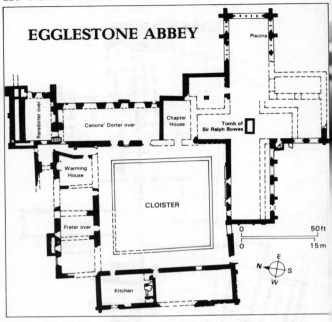

EGGLESTONE ABBEY

Piscina

Reredorter over

Canons' Dorter over

Chapter House

Tomb of Sir Ralph Bowes

Warming House

CLOISTER

Frater over

Kitchen

50 ft

15 m

Finchale Priory, Co Durham

Down minor roads off A167, 4 miles N of Durham.

Finchale (pronounced 'Finkle') lies at the end of a lane on a bend of the Wear, with superb woodland on the other side of the river. It owes its origins to St Godric, who seems an unlikely candidate for sainthood. Born in Norfolk c 1065, he became a travelling pedlar and later took to the sea, as merchant-cum-pirate, venturing to the Mediterranean and making the pilgrimage to Compostela. In 1104 he settled with a hermit at Walsingham, then two years later went on a pilgrimage to Jerusalem. While at Walsingham he had a vision of St Cuthbert, who told him he would have a hermitage at Finchale, which at the time he had never heard of. On his return from Jerusalem he eventually came to Durham, where he at last heard of Finchale and settled there c 1115, building a cell and a small chapel. Here he lived until 1170, wearing a hair shirt and a coat of mail, and dying at the enormous age of 105. After Godric's death two monks were sent to Finchale; and c 1195 it became a proper monastery, colonized by Benedictine monks from Durham. The first buildings were temporary, and permanent building did not begin until 1237. During the 13C Finchale took on an unusual role: that of a 'holiday home' for monks from Durham, who were allowed to go there in rotation in groups of four for three weeks at a time. It was dissolved in 1538.

The ruins are quite substantial. As first built in the 13C the church was larger than its present extent; the aisles were taken down in the

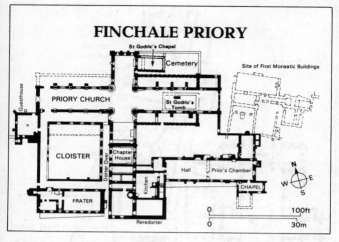

FINCHALE PRIORY

St Godric's Chapel

Cemetery

Site of First Monastic Buildings

Guesthouse

PRIORY CHURCH

St Godric's Tomb

CLOISTER

Chapter House

Dorter Over

Hall

Prior's Chamber

CHAPEL

Kitchen

FRATER

N
W E
S

0   100ft
0   30m

Reredorter

14C for reasons of economy. St Godric's stone chapel, dedicated to St John the Baptist, occupied the chancel E of the choir; a small tomb on the N side is reputedly that of the saint, who was described as an exceptionally short man. The cloister buildings still stand to a good height, especially the 14C frater on the S side, with undercroft below. E of the cloisters is the two-storey Prior's House, which was also used by the Durham monks on holiday.

Fountains Abbey, N Yorkshire

Ded: St Mary.

Off B6265, 4 miles SW of Ripon.

Second in fame only to Tintern among the great abbey ruins of England and Wales, Fountains was founded in 1132 by a breakaway group of monks from St Mary's, York (see below), who wished to return to the original austerity of their order. It stands by the little River Skell, which formed a natural drainage course for the infirmary and other monastic buildings; and adjoins the Studley Royal estate, of which since the 18C it has formed an integral and picturesque part. The name derives from the springs of fresh water (*fontes*) on the hillsides close by. In 1135 the new foundation was adopted by the Cistercians, and building on the largest scale soon began. The buildings are of four principal periods. To the first (1135–47) belong the nave and transepts of the church; to the second (1147–79), the gradual reconstruction of the domestic buildings; to the third (1220–47), the rebuilding of the E end; and to the fourth (1498–1526), the construction of the lofty Perp tower. By the middle of the 13C Fountains was the wealthiest Cistercian abbey in England, with enormous wool-producing estates (granges) throughout Yorkshire. This prosperity, well demonstrated by the vast *cellarium* (undercroft) below the lay brothers' dormitory, continued (with occasional breaks)

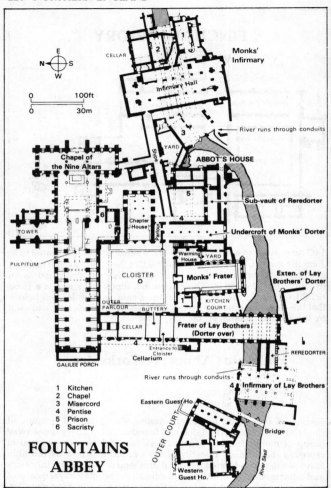

N
E
W
S

0 ——— 100ft
0 ——— 30m

CELLAR

Monks'
Infirmary

2

Infirmary Hall

3 ←--- River runs through conduits

YARD

Chapel of
the Nine Altars

ABBOT'S HOUSE

5

6

TOWER

Chapter
House

Parlour

4

Sub-vault of Reredorter

Undercroft of Monks' Dorter

PULPITUM

Warming
House

YARD

CLOISTER

Monks' Frater

Exten. of Lay
Brothers' Dorter

OUTER
PARLOUR

BUTTERY

1

KITCHEN
COURT

CELLAR

Frater of Lay Brothers
(Dorter over)

REREDORTER

GALILEE PORCH

4

Entrance to
Cloister
Cellarium

River runs through conduits

4 Infirmary of Lay Brothers

1 Kitchen
2 Chapel
3 Misercord
4 Pentise
5 Prison
6 Sacristy

Eastern Guest Ho.

OUTER COURT

Bridge

River Skell

FOUNTAINS
ABBEY

Western
Guest Ho.

until the 16C, when Abbot Marmaduke Huby (1495–1526) built the great tower. The abbey was dissolved in 1539 and was bought by Sir Richard Gresham; in the 18C it passed to the Aislabie family, who incorporated it into the landscaped park of Studley Royal. In 1983 it was acquired by the National Trust.

Substantial remains of the Church survive, notably the Nave, a grand example of austere Cistercian building, 11 bays long and complete to ceiling height. The *Chapel of the Nine Altars (13C), at the extreme E end, is a miracle of delicate design and inspired the similar chapel at Durham Cathedral. Abbot Huby's Tower, placed unusually at the end of the N transept, at 170ft is thought to be the tallest tower ever built by the Cistercians. In the vestry, off the S

Fountains Abbey, a model showing the abbey as it was shortly before the Dissolution, in the museum on the site. (K. Spence)

transept, is the tomb of a knight (c 1300) of the Percy or Mowbray family.

The extensive remains of the monastic buildings stretch between the church and the river. Of the buildings round the cloister, the most remarkable is the *Undercroft of the Lay Brothers' Dormitory on the W side, 300ft long and supported on a central row of 19 pillars; though now unbroken, it was originally divided by partitions into the lay brothers' refectory, storerooms and other apartments. On the E side is the Chapter House, with three fine arches opening into the cloister, book cupboards by the entrance, and the graves of a number of abbots in the floor. Next to it are the parlour and the undercroft of the monks' dorter. On the S side (from the E) are the Warming-house (the only room in a Cistercian monastery to have a fire during the winter), with a huge fireplace and still retaining its vault; the noble Refectory, over 100ft long, with splendid lancet windows and lavers outside the door; and the Kitchen, small for so large an abbey, with a hatch to the refectory. Above the warming-house is the Muniment Room, reached by the monks' day-stairs. To the E of the cloister buildings, and built partly across the Skell, are the foundations of the huge Infirmary.

Fountains Hall, outside the W entrance, was built in the 16C largely of stone from the abbey.

Furness Abbey, Cumbria

Ded: St Mary.

Off A590, 1 mile NE of Barrow-in-Furness.

The remains of Furness, a Cistercian abbey on the grandest scale, lie hidden in a valley on the outskirts of Barrow. Built of the attractive local red sandstone, the abbey was founded in 1123 by Stephen, Count of Boulogne (later King Stephen of England), for monks from Savigny in Normandy. During the Middle Ages it was second in importance only to Fountains among the abbeys of northern England; but owing to its remote position on the wild Furness peninsula, it suffered from frequent Scottish raids, which limited its prosperity. Peel Castle near by, built by the abbot of Furness, played a brief part in English history when Lambert Simnel, pretender to the throne, landed there in 1487. The abbey was dissolved in 1537.

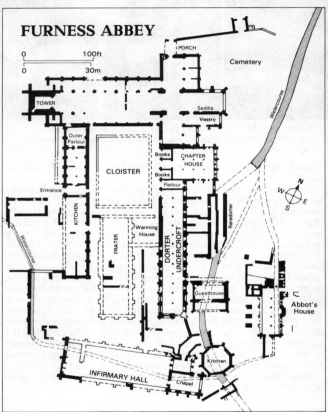

Entrance to the ruins is through a small exhibition hall, with displays of stonework and other abbey relics. Of the church, little remains of the 12C Norman nave. The transepts, with a fine N doorway, are late Norman and EE work with 15C windows; the beautiful sedilia and piscina (in the presbytery) are Perp, as is the W belfry tower, which was added c 1500. The E cloister wall is pierced by superb round-headed arches (c 1230), and the elegant chapter house, of four bays, is EE. Little survives of the S and W ranges. S of the chapter house is the long dorter undercroft; and S of this again the large 14C infirmary, with the remains of an octagonal kitchen, and a vaulted chapel which contains effigies of knights in armour (assigned to the 13C), perhaps the oldest of their kind in England.

Furness Abbey, the sturdy Norman arches of the cloister with the remains of the transepts behind. (K. Spence)

Guisborough Priory, Cleveland

Ded: Blessed Virgin Mary.

In town, off A171.

Standing at the foot of the Cleveland Hills, Guisborough was founded c 1119 for Augustinian canons by Robert de Brus (or de Bruce), ancestor of King Robert the Bruce of Scotland. The first church was destroyed by fire in 1289; the present scanty but beautiful remains are of the second (Dec) church, built early in the 14C. Chief among them is the lofty gabled E end, nearly 100ft high; the central window is almost 60ft tall, and now extends down to the ground, as the wall below it was knocked down in the 19C. The abbey was dissolved in 1540.

Hexham Abbey, Northumberland

Ded: St Andrew.

Hexham's magnificent church, larger than some cathedrals, stands at the town's highest point and dominates the Tyne valley. Though popularly called an abbey, because it was originally founded as a Benedictine monastery, it is in fact the church of a priory, founded for Augustinian canons in 1113. Built mainly in the late 12C and early 13C, it has been called 'the textbook of EE architecture'.

The first church was built here in 674, on land given by Queen Etheldreda of Northumberland to St Wilfrid, and was constructed of stone from the Roman Wall camp of Corstopitum (Corbridge). Of this first church, there survive the foundations of the apse, some

HEXHAM ABBEY (PRIORY CHURCH)

Map labels:
- N DOOR
- W DOOR
- Font
- Stairs to Crypt
- CRYPT UNDER
- Leschman Chantry
- Pulpitum
- Choir
- Ogle Chantry
- Sedilia
- Procession Path and Chapel of Five Altars
- MARKET PLACE
- Chapel or Sacristy
- Night Stair
- CLOISTER
- Vestibule
- CHAPTER HOUSE
- BEAUMONT STREET
- Buildings
- Cellarer's
- Lavatory
- W RANGE
- Refectory
- CANONS' DORMITORY OVER

1 St Wilfrid's Chair
2 Painted Panels
3 Monument of Flavinus
4 Acca Cross

fragments of the nave, and the Crypt, among the finest Saxon crypts in England, in whose walls are some Roman inscribed stones from Corstopitum. Between 681 and 821 this church was the cathedral of a Saxon bishopric. Sacked by the Danes in 876, it was succeeded by an Augustinian priory (founded 1114, dissolved 1536); the canons built the existing beautiful choir and transepts (c 1175–1225), the latter of disproportionate length (c 150ft). The S transept retains the canons' *Night-stair from the dormitory, much worn but still used occasionally by the abbey choir before services. The Nave, destroyed by the Scots in 1296, was rebuilt in 1908.

There are rich furnishings of all periods. The Rood-screen, set up by Prior Smithson (1491–1524), includes 16 painted panels of saints and bishops. In the Choir, immediately above its former presumed position in the apse of the Saxon church, is a stone Saxon Bishop's Chair (known as St Wilfrid's Chair), possibly used as a coronation chair for the Kings of Northumbria and later serving as a sanctuary stool or 'Fridstol', as at Beverley Minster. The choir has some grotesque 15C misericords; on the N side of the chancel is the 15C Leschman Chantry and on the S the Ogle Chantry with a triptych altarpiece; and a screen in the sanctuary contains painted panels of seven bishops of Hexham and four panels from a 'Dance of Death' (Cardinal, King, Emperor and Pope). In the S transept is a large Roman funeral slab commemorating Flavinus (a Roman standard-bearer), and the famous Saxon *Acca Cross of c 740 (St Acca was Bp of Hexham in the early 8C).

Some of the priory buildings (partly restored) can be seen S of the church, and in Cowgarth, off Market Street (NW), are the ruins of the late 12C priory gateway.

Holm Cultram Abbey, Cumbria

Ded: St Mary.

In Abbey Town, off B5302, 6 miles W of Wigton.

The small red sandstone church at Holm Cultram is an oddity, reflecting an unusual history. An abbey was founded here in 1150 by Henry, son of King David I of Scotland, for Cistercian monks from the Scottish abbey of Melrose. Prosperous in its early days, it was raided several times by the Scots in the 12 and 13C and gradually declined; at the Dissolution the inhabitants petitioned Chancellor Cromwell successfully for the preservation of the church, and in 1557 Queen Mary handed over the living to the University of Oxford, who retain it to this day. The present church is only two-thirds the length of the original nave; in the 18C the side aisles were demolished and the arcades blocked in. It is entered through a small 16C porch, leading to the original 12C Norman W doorway, and contains the imposing tomb of Abbot Rydekar (d 1434). The monastic buildings have almost entirely disappeared, apart from foundations E of the present church, and two cottages (formed from part of the cloisters) which were renovated in the 1960s and turned into offices and a reading-room.

Hulne Priory, Northumberland

In Hulne Park, 1½ miles NW of Alnwick.

Founded c 1240 and standing on a hill above the Aln valley, Hulne is the earliest example of a Carmelite friary in England, and the ruins are the most perfect of their kind. Walled and remote, it looks like a castle rather than a monastic building, and was a defensible position in the turbulent Border region. The 13C guesthouse is still lived in; the ruins include the W and S walls of the small aisleless church. Hulne was dissolved in 1539 and the buildings were put to other uses, being 'gothicized' in the 18C, when the fortified gatehouse became a hunting-lodge.

The priory is now privately occupied, but can be seen with the tenant's permission. It is reached on foot (no cars or dogs allowed) through the beautiful grounds of Hulne Park, either from Alnwick or from a gate on B6346 (admission pass obtained from the Estate Office, Alnwick Castle).

Jarrow Monastery, Tyne and Wear

Ded: St Paul.

Jarrow is famous as the monastery where the Venerable Bede, author of the *History of the English Church and People*, lived and worked from its foundation in 682, until his death in 735. It was founded from nearby Monkwearmouth by St Benedict Biscop, and consisted originally of a stone church, and wooden huts for the monks to live in. Part of this church survives as the chancel of the present parish church, which has an 11C Norman tower, and a nave built by Sir Gilbert Scott in the 1860s. The dedication stone, placed above the chancel arch, gives the names of King Ecgfrith and Abbot Ceolfrith, and the date 685. One of the small Saxon windows contains fragments of 7C stained glass, probably the oldest such glass in the country; also in the chancel is an ancient wooden chair, traditionally known as 'Bede's Chair'. A fine wooden sculpture of Bede, by Fenwick Lawson, stands at the chancel entrance. The N porch contains a display of Saxon carved stones and other objects.

Part of the cloister of a later Norman monastery (a refoundation of 1074) stands S of the church. The bones of the Venerable Bede, kept as relics at Jarrow, were moved to Durham in 1020.

Jarrow Hall, just up the hill from the church, is now the Bede Monastery Museum (closed Mon. exc. Bank Hols.), which illustrates the lives of the Jarrow monks with models and archaeological finds.

Jervaulx Abbey, N Yorkshire

Ded: St Mary.

By A6108, 5 miles SE of Leyburn.

The ruins of this great Cistercian abbey (pronounced 'Jervo'), still in private hands, have the ivy-mantled, romantic appearance beloved by 18C engravers of monastic remains. It stands by the River Ure (or Yore), from which it takes its name (Yorevale, or Jervaulx in Norman French). The original foundation of 1145 was up the valley near Aysgarth, but 11 years later the monks moved downstream to the present, more suitable site. The church, 270ft long and on the grandest scale, can still be traced along its foundations; the SW door is well preserved, as is the altar in the N transept. Around the cloister, S of the church, are the remains of (E side) chapter house and monks' dorter (the latter with one wall almost to full height); (S side) warming-house, refectory and kitchen with two vast chimneys; (W side) lay brothers' quarters. To the SW are the infirmary and abbot's lodging. Jervaulx made its appearance in literature in Scott's *Ivanhoe*, as the monastery from which Prior Aylmer came. It was dissolved in 1537, after the last of its abbots had been unjustly implicated in the Pilgrimage of Grace (the northern rebellion of 1536 against Henry VIII's religious reforms), and subsequently hung, drawn and quartered at Tyburn.

Kirkham Priory, N Yorkshire

Ded: Holy Trinity.

Off A64, 5 miles SW of Malton.

The scanty remains of Kirkham stand in an attractive setting beside the Derwent. It was founded in 1122 for Augustinian canons by Walter l'Espec (who later founded Rievaulx, see below), in memory of his son killed by falling from a horse. Though the remains are few, they are very fine. Chief among them is the late 13C gatehouse, with a

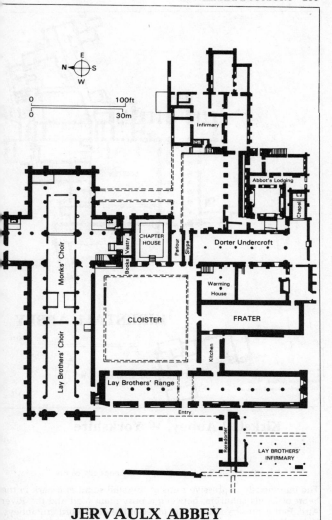

N ←→ E
  ↓
  W   S

0 _____ 100ft
0 _____ 30m

Infirmary

Abbot's Lodging

Chapel

Monks' Choir

CHAPTER HOUSE

Vestry

Books

Parlour

Slype

Dorter Undercroft

Lay Brothers' Choir

Warming House

CLOISTER

FRATER

Kitchen

Lay Brothers' Range

Entry

Reredorter

LAY BROTHERS' INFIRMARY

JERVAULX ABBEY

wide entrance arch and superb Dec windows on the first floor; the
facade is richly adorned with stone-carved figures and coats of arms.
In the cloister is an exquisite lavatorium of the same date, in two bays,
with fine arcading; and a moulded Romanesque doorway into the
refectory.

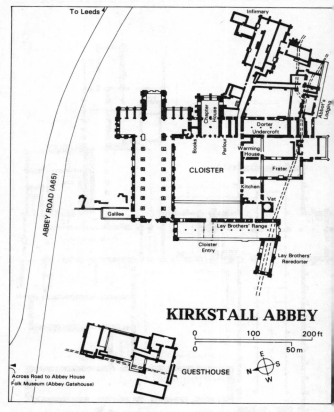

KIRKSTALL ABBEY

Kirkstall Abbey, W Yorkshire

Ded: St Mary.

By A65 (Abbey Road), 3 miles NW of Leeds city centre.

The enormously impressive ruins of Kirkstall stand in a park in the heart of Leeds suburbia, between a busy main road and the River Aire. Better preserved than any other of the great northern abbeys, Kirkstall gives an excellent idea of medieval monastic life in its most vigorous and creative years. It was founded in 1152 by Cistercians from Fountains, who five years previously had made an unsuccessful start on another site. Most of the remains date from this early period, notably the superb W front and nave of the church, with its near perfect Trans arcading. Kirkstall was dissolved in 1539 and gradually fell into picturesque decay, inspiring Turner, Cotman and Girtin among the artists, and Gray and Horace Walpole among the writers of the Romantic movement. Preservation work was carried out throughout the 19C, and a major programme of restoration was begun in 1980, including excavation of the guesthouse area to the W. The work can be followed in regular news-sheets provided at the site.

The most striking feature of Kirkstall is the tall crossing tower, of which the S wall still stands to its full height; the upper (belfry) stage, in Perp style, was added to the squat 12C tower in the early 16C. The church (kept locked at present) is long and narrow, with two nave aisles, three chapels in each transept, and a presbytery that is only as wide as the nave. The windows are round-arched, except for the great E window, inserted in the 15C. Until 1827, when a new road was built to the N, the valley road ran down the church from end to end, surely a unique thoroughfare. The cloister buildings are unusually well preserved, especially on the E side. Immediately S of the S transept is a small Library, still tiled; next come the vaulted Chapter House, entered through a fine pair of round-headed doorways, the Parlour, the Stairs to the monks' dorter, a narrow Passage, and the Dorter Undercroft. On the S side (from the E) are the Warming-house, the Frater, the Kitchen (all basically 12C), and the 15C Malthouse with a huge beer-vat behind. On the W side, one wall of the Lay Brothers' Quarters survives almost to roof level. At the SW corner of the site are the impressive remains of the Infirmary and Abbot's Lodging.

Across the main road is the 12C abbey gatehouse, which now forms part of the excellent Abbey House Folk Museum.

Lancaster Cathedral (RC)

Ded: St Peter.

In East Road.

The cathedral's tall spire, 240ft high, dominates the E side of Lancashire's county town. Raised to the status of a cathedral in 1924, the church was completed in 1859 to the designs of E.G. Paley, a Lancashire architect. The entrance, at the SW corner, leads into the big nave, which is mainly plain and white-painted. The E end is apsidal, with fine Victorian glass. A large statue of St Peter stands at the W end.

Lancaster Priory

Ded: St Mary.

Few churches can have a finer situation than St Mary's, which stands within a stone's throw of the castle, high above the River Lune. The Romans had a fortress on the site, and in Saxon times a church was built here, of which a small door survives in the W wall of the present church. In 1094 the church and attached priory became a cell of the Benedictine abbey of Séez, in Normandy; traces of the 12C church, in Trans style, remain in the SW entrance doorway. After suffering from Scottish raids in the 14C, in 1414 Lancaster was handed over to the Bridgettines (followers of St Bridget, of Sweden) of Syon in Middlesex, as part of Henry V's suppression of alien priories (priories owing allegiance to a French mother house). The present church, in Perp style, dates almost entirely from this period. At the Dissolution it was handed over to the parishioners, and has been little altered since. The tower was largely rebuilt in the 1750s to designs by Henry Sephton, and the large NW memorial chapel was built after the Boer War to commemorate men of the Royal Lancaster Regiment, and now honours in addition the dead of both World Wars.

Internally, the body of the church is a simple rectangle, with no transepts, and with aisles that run the whole length. There is no W window, as the base of the tower abuts on the W end of the nave. There are plenty of monuments (mainly 18C), and colour is added to the plain stonework by the stained glass, by the painted organ pipes, and notably by the cheerful embroidery panels on the choir stalls, worked by lady parishioners in 1962–77. The superb carved oak stall canopies are of c 1340, and the wooden pulpit and font cover are Jacobean.

Lanercost Priory, Cumbria

Ded: St Mary Magdalene.
Off A69, 2 miles NE of Brampton.

Lanercost's splendid priory church stands in remote countryside immediately below Hadrian's Wall. Founded c 1166 by Robert de Vaux for Augustinian canons, Lanercost was complete by 1220; its existence was far from peaceful, as between 1280 and 1350 it was constantly attacked by raiders from across the Border. It was dissolved in 1536, and was implicated in the Pilgrimage of Grace (the rising in the North against Henry VIII's religious reforms), as a result of which the king ordered all its monks to be hanged. Of the noble church, the nave survived to become the parish church.

The EE W front (c 1200–20) is particularly fine, with three tall lancets set in elegant arcading, and a statue of St Mary Magdalene (c 1270) in the gable end. Inside, the church consists of the EE nave (blocked W of the crossing by an 18C wall) and N aisle, which has window glass by William Morris and Burne-Jones. To the E, the squat central tower, transepts and chancel are still remarkably well preserved, though without roof or windows. In the transepts are several medieval tombs, among them those of Sir Rowland de Vaux (nephew of Sir Robert, the priory's founder), Sir Humphry Dacre, Lord Warden of the Marches (d 1485), and other members of the Dacre family.

The monastic buildings, S of the church, are quite easy to follow. The cloister was a small one; the best-preserved remains are on the S side, and consist of the beautiful vaulted undercroft of the refectory, with the square block of the prior's house at its SW corner.

Leeds Cathedral, W Yorkshire (RC)

Ded: St Anne.
In Cookridge Street.

Designed by J.H. Eastwood and built in 1902–04, this big church, grey with industrial grime, took the place of an earlier church which had

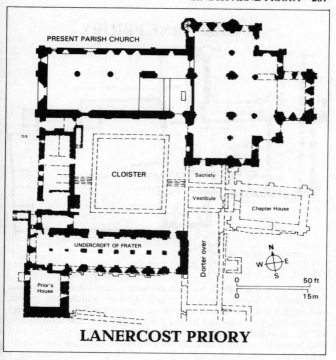

PRESENT PARISH CHURCH

CLOISTER

Sacristy

Vestibule

Chapter House

UNDERCROFT OF FRATER

Dorter over

Prior's House

N
W E
S

0   50 ft
0   15m

LANERCOST PRIORY

been raised to cathedral status in 1878. The entrance (on the S side) leads into a spacious nave, with narrow aisles and several side chapels. The style is a sturdy late Gothic, with a boldly painted, barrel-vaulted roof, and nave arcading in which the upper tier is far taller than the lower. Behind the altar is a huge wooden reredos; and in the Lady Chapel a smaller, brightly painted reredos of 1842 by Augustus Welby Pugin, brought from the old St Anne's.

Lindisfarne Priory, Northumberland

On Holy Island, reached across causeway from A1 8 miles S of Berwick.

The pink sandstone ruins of Lindisfarne, often shrouded in mist and smelling of the sea, form the remotest outpost of monasticism in England. As the name Holy Island suggests, the place has had a reputation for sanctity for the past 13 centuries, as one of the earliest and most shining centres of English Christianity. In 634 King Oswald of Northumbria gave Holy Island to St Aidan (d 651), a missionary from Iona, who was consecrated first Bp of Lindisfarne in the following year. Aidan's most celebrated successor was St Cuthbert, who was made bishop in 685, died in 687 and was buried on the

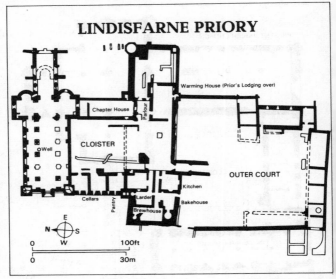

LINDISFARNE PRIORY

Warming House (Prior's Lodging over)

Chapter House

Parlour

CLOISTER

○ Well

OUTER COURT

Cellars

Pantry

Larder

Kitchen

Brewhouse

Bakehouse

N E / S W

0 _____ 100ft

0 _____ 30m

island. A glorious relic of the first monastery survives in the famous Lindisfarne Gospels, now in the British Museum, which were written and exquisitely illuminated by a monk named Eadfrith c 698. In 793 the monastery was sacked by the Danes, and after a second raid in 875 the monks fled, taking with them the body of St Cuthbert and wandering for a further century before finally settling at Durham. In 1083 the Normans resettled the site on Holy Island, founding a Benedictine priory as a cell to Durham. The present ruins, consisting of superb Norman work badly eroded by nine centuries of rain, spray and sea wind, date from this period. Lindisfarne survived the Scottish wars without being attacked, and was dissolved in 1537.

The ruins are splendidly sited almost on the shore, with views S down the coast to Bamburgh Castle, and E to nearby Lindisfarne Castle (16C, restored by Sir Edwin Lutyens in the early 20C). The church (late 11C–early 12C) has aisles, transepts with apsidal chapels, and a later square E end of c 1140, extending beyond the original apsidal E end. It is a fine example of Norman work, very like the mother house at Durham (see above), and remarkable for its fortified character. Best preserved is the W end, with the main front and SW tower still standing to a good height; and the most striking survival is the diagonal vaulting-rib, complete with keystone, linking two of the massive crossing piers. The nave pillars have deeply incised decoration similar to that at Durham. The remains of the monastic buildings (to the S) are a century or more later than the church. On the E side of the cloister are the foundations of the chapter house (c 1300); on the S a large square block was built in the 14C as the prior's lodging, while a large outer court extended southwards almost to the sea wall; and on the W are kitchen, larder, brewhouse and cellars.

Adjacent to the ruins is the little parish church, mainly EE, with a massively buttressed bell-tower; and by the entrance is a small

Lindisfarne Priory, on Holy Island, the most remote outpost of monasticism in England. (K. Spence)

museum with carved stones, pottery and other remains salvaged from the priory.

The causeway from the mainland to Holy Island is covered for 1½ hours on either side of high tide. Safe crossing times are posted at both ends.

Liverpool Cathedral, Merseyside

Ded: Cathedral Church of Christ.

Built high on the ridge of St James's Mount, and looking down on the cranes and shipping of the Mersey, Liverpool's mighty Anglican cathedral was completed in 1978, after almost 75 years of continuous work. Though the concept may seem an anachronism for the 20C, the execution is superbly realized in a highly original Gothic style that does not conform to any of the recognized architectural periods. The brown-red sandstone of which it is built was quarried at Woolton, within the city boundaries. The dominant feature of the church is the huge Vestey Tower (331ft high), which rests unusually on the outer walls of the building. (The church is built N and S, following the line of the rock ridge, but in this description the points of the compass are used in the ecclesiastical sense, with the actual S end referred to as the E, etc.)

History. In 1880 the Diocese of Liverpool was created, and five years later a cathedral committee was set up. In 1902 the design for a new cathedral was opened to public competition; the winner was Giles

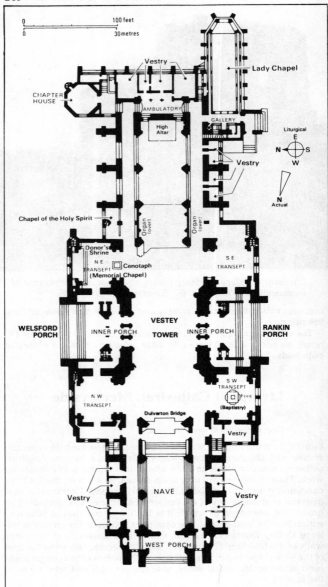

0 100 feet
0 30 metres

Vestry

Lady Chapel

CHAPTER HOUSE

AMBULATORY

High Altar

GALLERY

Liturgical
E
N · S
W

Vestry

N
Actual

Chapel of the Holy Spirit

Organ (over)   Organ (over)

Donor's Shrine

NE TRANSEPT   Cenotaph (Memorial Chapel)

SE TRANSEPT

WELSFORD PORCH   INNER PORCH   VESTEY TOWER   INNER PORCH   RANKIN PORCH

NW TRANSEPT

SW TRANSEPT
Font (Baptistry)

Dulverton Bridge

Vestry

Vestry   NAVE   Vestry

WEST PORCH

LIVERPOOL CATHEDRAL (C of E)

(later Sir Giles) Gilbert Scott, then aged only 22, who was still working on the cathedral at his death in 1960—a span of time that even exceeded the 42 years spent by Wren on St Paul's. The building bears little resemblance to Scott's original design, owing to changes introduced at his suggestion as the work progressed. His concept was 'a vast hall quarried out of a solid mass of stone', and the cathedral is on the grandest scale: it is the largest church in Britain, and is exceeded in Europe only by St Peter's in Rome, and by Milan and Seville cathedrals. The first part to be finished was the Lady Chapel at the E end, consecrated in 1910 (reopened in 1955 after war damage); the choir, E transepts and chapter house were consecrated in 1924; the central space under the tower and the W transepts in 1941. The central Vestey Tower and the N and S porches were completed in 1949. The W front has been completed more simply than was originally planned; the completion of the last bay of the nave was marked by a rededication in the presence of HM the Queen in 1978. The tower (ascent in summer by lift) contains 13 bells, of which the largest ('Great George') weighs 14½ tons.

Interior. The principal entrances open into the under-tower through triple doorways leading from the Welsford Porch (N) and the Rankin Porch (S; the usual way in), decorated with sculptured figures by E. Carter Preston. The plan is unique, the outstanding feature being the rectangular *Central Space* (203 by 73ft), comprising the Under-tower and the two Transept Crossings. This area, unobstructed by pillars, has space for 4,000 people. Most striking of all is the tremendous height (107ft) of the arches of the Under-tower, with its superb vaulting, the apex of which is 175ft above the floor. The *Windows, by James Hogan, form two groups of triple lancets 70ft high, surmounted by a rose. The SW Transept is the baptistry; the font of Languedoc marble, carved by Carter Preston, has a tabernacled oak cover, and stands beneath an elaborately carved oak baldacchino 39ft high.

The *Nave* occupies a subordinate position in comparison with the central space. Its E bay, lit by windows depicting Bishops and Scholars, is spanned by the huge stone Dulverton Bridge (1961), an arch supporting a musicians' gallery. The two W bays of the nave form a well that is reached down eight steps from the side aisles and is popularly known as the 'swimming-pool'. The NE pier of the nave is carved with a lovers' knot and the initials E and P, commemorating a visit by the Queen when Princess Elizabeth and Prince Philip.

To the E of the central tower are the E transepts, and the lofty *Choir* (116ft high) of three bays, which has a triforium but no clerestory; the oak stalls are noteworthy. The stone reredos, with carved and gilded panels by W. Gilbert and L. Weingartner, is unusual in forming an integral part of the E wall. The E window, the largest in England (76 by 44ft), has the 'Te Deum' as the theme of its stained glass. The NE Transept is a war memorial chapel, with a cenotaph and colours of the King's (Liverpool) Regiment. Next is the Chapel of the Holy Spirit, with an alabaster reredos and a 15C polychrome Madonna. The SE Transept contains a bronze effigy (designed by Giles Gilbert Scott) of the 16th Earl of Derby (d 1908), first President of the Cathedral Committee. The Choir Aisles, above the W ends of which are the two parts of the great organ, are connected by an ambulatory, with the octagonal chapter house opening off it at the NE corner of the cathedral. In the S choir aisle is a memorial to the orthopaedic surgeon Sir Robert Jones (d 1933); and memorials (designed by Scott) to the first two Bps of Liverpool, Bp Ryle (d 1900) and Bp Chavasse (d 1928), and (by Carter Preston) to the first Dean, Dr F.W. Dwelly (d 1957). In the N choir aisle is a splendid *Cope-chest, wholly medieval in concept and of superb 20C craftsmanship.

The *Lady Chapel* (see above), SE of the choir and on a lower level, is completely different in style from the rest of the building. Entered from the S choir aisle, it is in elaborate Dec Gothic, rising to a stone traceried vault. The ornate reredos has carved panels representing Christ's Nativity and Baptism; and the theme of the tall windows is womanhood as portrayed in the Bible and Church history.

Liverpool Metropolitan Cathedral (RC)

Ded: Christ the King.

At the other end of Hope Street from the Anglican cathedral, Liverpool's Roman Catholic cathedral is at the opposite extreme architecturally, as it was built in record time (five years) in uncompromisingly 1960s style. Their only similarity is that both are products of architectural competitions. Designed by Sir Frederick Gibberd, begun in 1962 and completed in 1967, the cathedral is a circular skeleton of 16 concrete trusses, faced with Portland stone and white mosaic, with sloping buttresses, and surmounted by a glass-panelled lantern tower with a crown of slender pinnacles. The Roman Catholic archdiocese of Liverpool was created in 1850, and a cathedral in high Gothic style was designed by Edward Pugin; but the scheme was abandoned, and only revived in the 1930s, when Sir Edwin Lutyens designed a huge Baroque church that would have had

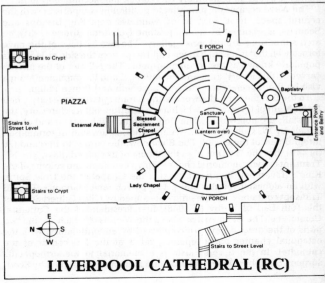

LIVERPOOL CATHEDRAL (RC)

Liverpool Metropolitan Cathedral, Pope John Paul II
celebrating High Mass in 1982. (Catholic Pictorial, Liverpool)

a dome bigger than that of St Peter's. Only the crypt of Lutyens's cathedral was completed, and this now forms the podium on which the modern cathedral stands.

The cathedral is designed completely 'in the round', and so has no conventional E or W end. The main entrance porch is on the S side, below a sharply-angled open belfry deeply incised with a design of crosses and crowns by William Mitchell, who also designed the barbaric bronze fibreglass emblems of the Evangelists on the doors at the entrance. The interior takes the form of a vast open pavilion, lit from the sides by narrow panels of blue glass, and from above by the lantern, designed by John Piper and Patrick Reyntiens, which represents the Trinity and is filled with glass of all the colours of the spectrum. In the centre is the Sanctuary; the high altar is made of a 19-ton slab of white marble from Skopje, in Yugoslavia, and the bronze figure of Christ poised over it is by Elizabeth Frink. A baldacchino made of linked tubes hangs from the ceiling over the sanctuary. The spaces between the buttresses form a ring of chapels round the cathedral's perimeter. Immediately to the right of the main entrance is the beautifully simple, circular Baptistry, entered by bronze gates. Diagonally opposite is the Lady Chapel, lit by golden glass by Margaret Traherne; a ceramic statue by Robert Brumby, depicting Mary with the child Jesus, stands high above the altar. Largest of the chapels is the Blessed Sacrament Chapel, on the far side from the entrance, which has windows, tabernacle and a painting above the altar, all by Ceri Richards.

The Lutyens Crypt is reached down stairs on the far side of the large piazza N of the cathedral. Built of brick in Renaissance style, it has massive pillars, cavernous vaults, and maze-like aisles, with a series of chapels, one of which shelters a notable Madonna by David John.

Another, the Relics Chapel, with the tombs of Abps Whiteside, Downey and Beck, is closed by a 'rolling gate' formed from a 6-ton disc of stone. The roof of the crypt forms both the piazza and the podium of the cathedral.

Manchester Cathedral

Ded: St Mary, St Denys and St George.

Looking across the grimy waters of the Irwell, and dwarfed by modern tower blocks, Manchester's cathedral keeps its medieval splendour among the dinginess of more recent times. The old parish church ('t'owd church') of Manchester was made collegiate in 1421 by a charter of Henry V; the same charter authorised Thomas de la Warr, who was both lord of the manor and rector, to build a new church—hence the addition of the patron saints of France and England to the dedication, since Henry had conquered France and married the French Princess Katherine. The present building is entirely in the Perp style, with a few later additions, and dates from 1422–1520. It was raised to cathedral status in 1847. The square W tower (130ft high) was resurfaced and heightened in 1867, when the building was much restored; and further major restoration was carried out after World War II, in which a landmine did extensive

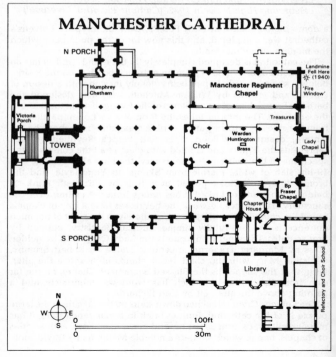

damage to the E end. Though only 220ft in length, the church has a disproportionate width of 114ft, which makes it the widest in England, exceeding even York Minster (104ft).

Interior. The *Nave* has double aisles, the outer aisles having originally accommodated six chantries. The tall and graceful tower arch is a relic of the earlier St Mary's; the tower fan vaulting is a fine example of Victorian craftsmanship. The W window under the tower is filled with glowing blue glass by Antony Hollaway (1980); known as the St Mary Window, it forms a trio with the St George and St Denys Windows (by the same artist) on either side of the tower. In the NW corner is the seated figure of Humphrey Chetham (1580–1653), founder of Chetham's School near the cathedral, by William Theed (1853). Angels with musical instruments (bagpipe, recorder, trumpet, dulcimer etc) support the main beams of the 15C roof and are typical of the superb woodwork throughout the building. The magnificent Perp choir screen is also 15C.

The *Choir* contains elaborately carved stalls (late.15 and early 16C), which have been described as the finest in Europe, with fanciful misericords (men playing backgammon, a scolding wife, fox and goose etc). These, and the splendid 15C panelled roof, suffered from blast in 1940 and have been well restored. Noteworthy also in the choir are the fine brass of Warden Huntington (d 1458), builder of the choir, the 18C ironwork, and a chandelier of 1620.

In the retrochoir is the Lady Chapel, destroyed by the 1940 landmine and rebuilt by Sir Hubert Worthington. On either side of the entrance arch are rebus carvings on Warden Huntington's name: a man hunting, and a vintner with his tuns. The chapel is entered through a screen of c 1440 (restored) and is decorated with modern tapestries by Theo Moorman; on the exterior wall is a gilded bronze figure of the Virgin and Child by Sir Charles Wheeler. On the wall immediately to the N is a silver cabinet containing a display of treasures from the cathedral and other Manchester churches. At the NE corner of the church is the large Chapel of the Manchester Regiment, founded as the chapel of the Stanley family in 1513, shattered in 1940, and carefully restored (1951). The roof has carvings by Alan Durst; the bright red E window, by Margaret Traherne, known as the 'Fire Window' from the fact that the landmine fell outside this corner of the church, is in memory of Sir Hubert Worthington (d 1963). S of the choir are (from the E) the Bishop Fraser Chapel (1887), in memory of the 2nd Bp of Manchester (d 1885); the small Chapter House, rebuilt as an octagon in 1485, with paintings above the entrance of the Sermon on the Mount and the Beatitudes in modern dress (by Carel Weight, 1962); and the Jesus Chapel, founded 1506, with a 16C screen, beside which hangs a copy of the royal charter of 1421, the earliest of three on display.

Middlesbrough Cathedral, Cleveland (RC)

Ded: St Mary.

In town centre.

Like Leeds, Middlesbrough became a separate diocese in 1878, and St Mary's was raised to cathedral status. Built in the 1870s to designs by George Goldie, it is a somewhat barn-like church of mixed stone and brickwork, without a tower. Inside it has a hammerbeam roof, and an E wall with a rose-window above a mixture of stone and mosaic. Among the side chapels is one dedicated to the Yorkshire Martyrs (Middlesbrough was in the North Riding until the creation of the new county of Cleveland in the 1970s).

Monk Bretton Priory, S Yorkshire

Ded: St Mary Magdalene.

Off A268, 2 miles NE of Barnsley.

The ruins of the priory lie on a gently sloping site on the outskirts of the village of Monk Bretton. It was founded c 1154 by Adam Fitzswane for Cluniac monks, but in 1279 it broke with the mother house at Cluny and became Benedictine. It was dissolved in 1538. To the N of the church and monastic buildings, the outer gatehouse survives to first-floor height. Little of the church (mainly 12C) survives above ground level; it consisted of an aisled nave, transepts with chapels, and a narrow presbytery. The cloister buildings date from the 13 and 14C, and are later than the church. On the E side is a small chapter house, parlour and warming-house; a large refectory occupies the S side; and the W range consists of the lower stages of cellars and storerooms. Best preserved is one wall of the separate Prior's Lodging, which retains its first-floor fireplace and chimney. The priory was drained by a system of channels and sluice-gates, which can still be traced.

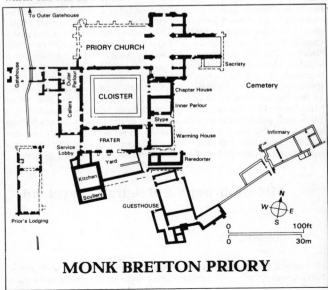

MONK BRETTON PRIORY

Mount Grace Priory, N Yorkshire

Ded: The Assumption and St Nicholas.

Off A19, 6 miles NE of Northallerton.

Standing at the western edge of the Cleveland Hills, Mount Grace is the most perfect Carthusian monastery in England. It was founded in 1398 by Thomas Holland, nephew of Richard II, led a quiet existence for 140 years, and was dissolved in 1539. The Carthusians led a solitary rather than a communal life, and the layout of their monasteries reflects this. In place of the large refectory and dormitories of the other orders, they lived in small cells or cottages built round a huge central cloister-garth. Each cell was of two storeys, with its own small garden and lavatory, and the monks had their food pushed to them through a hatch in the wall of their cell.

Mount Grace consisted of two courtyards, separated by a central cluster consisting of the church (which still survives to tower height), a small frater where the monks ate communally on Sundays and feast days, the chapter house, the prior's accommodation, and other rooms. The cells were built round the N cloister (longest side 272ft); while S of the church are traces of a few more cells, and a large outer court with guesthouse, granaries and storehouses on its W and S sides. The guesthouse was converted into a private house in the 17C and is still privately occupied.

Newcastle, Tyne and Wear: Blackfriars

In Monk Street.

The Dominicans are known to have been active in Newcastle by c 1250, and it seems probable that the present Blackfriars was built some ten years later. In the 14C the friary became very prosperous, and was visited from time to time by monarchs on their travels. It was dissolved in 1539, and in 1543 was sold for just over £50 to the Newcastle Corporation, who leased it to nine craft guilds, including the smiths, the cordwainers and the tanners. Down the centuries the buildings continued to be used by the guilds and private individuals, until in 1951 they were handed back to the Corporation. They have since been restored to form a multi-purpose complex, including crafts workshops and studios, historical exhibition centres, a tourist information centre and a restaurant (in the old refectory). The church, which lay N of the domestic buildings, is at present being excavated.

Newcastle Cathedral

Ded: St Nicholas.

In St Nicholas Street.

The cathedral's pinnacled lantern tower is a landmark of central Newcastle, half-way between the Tyne Road Bridge and the Central Station. Formerly one of the largest parish churches in England, it was raised to cathedral status in 1882, and is England's most northerly cathedral. The *W Tower, crowned by a spire (194ft) supported in the air by diagonal flying buttresses, is the earliest (c 1448) and best example of a 'crown spire' in Britain, and set the pattern for other such spires, notably St Giles's, Edinburgh.

Unusually, the columns of the Nave (1330–60) are without capitals. Below the striking lierne vault of the tower stands the font, with a superbly carved *Canopy (c 1500), inside which is an exquisite miniature vault with a boss showing the Coronation of the Virgin. Near it (in the NW transept) is a bust of Admiral Collingwood (d 1810), second-in-command to Nelson at Trafalgar, who was baptized and married in the church. In St Margaret's Chapel (off the S aisle) is a roundel of 15C stained glass showing Mary suckling the infant Jesus. The chapel off the S Transept, known as St Mary's Porch, contains several monuments, notably a fine painted 17C memorial to Henry Maddison (d 1634) and his family. The lectern dates from c 1500; and the upper part of the organ case (N Transept) survives from the original Renatus Harris organ of 1676. The alabaster reredos, with figures of saints in the niches, dates from 1882. In the N Choir Aisle is an elaborate canopied tomb to Bp Arthur LLoyd (d 1908); and on the wall of the S Choir Aisle a magnificent Flemish *Brass, one of the largest in the country, commemorates Roger Thornton (d 1429) and his wife Agnes. The Crypt Chapel (off N transept), formerly used as a charnel-house for bones from the churchyard, has 14C ribbed vaulting and a small internal 'wheel' window. Among the cathedral's treasures is the so-called Hexham Bible (c 1220), which can be seen on request.

Newcastle Cathedral (RC)

Ded: St Mary.

In Clayton Street.

Standing on an island site facing the Central Station, the cathedral's Gothic architecture is in striking contrast to the classical of the station. It was built in 1844 by Augustus Welby Pugin as a parish church, but was soon raised to cathedral rank. The lofty spire (220ft) was added by Joseph A. Hansom in the 1860s. The entrance (SW corner) leads past the baptistry into the large, plain interior. The most unusual feature of the church consists of encaustic tiles inscribed with the names of Roman Catholic martyrs and running as a frieze round both side walls.

Nun Monkton Priory, N Yorkshire

Ded: St Mary.

Off A59, 9 miles NW of York.

The beautiful little church (Trans and EE) of a Benedictine nunnery, founded in the 12C, stands at the end of a by-road, at the junction of the Ouse and the Nidd. As often happened, the nuns used the E end and the parish the W (nave) end, with the result that at the Dissolution the E end and monastic buildings were pulled down, while the parochial W end survived. The W tower is c 1200; the W door has well-carved moulding; and the nave is lit by EE lancet windows.

Old Malton Priory, N Yorkshire

Ded: St Mary.

By A169, on N outskirts of Malton.

A priory of Gilbertine canons (the only monastic order to originate in England) was founded at Malton c 1150. The fine W front, with SW tower, and nave survive, as the W end of the church was parochial at the Dissolution, and so was not demolished. It is late Norman and EE in style, with a large Perp window added in the 15C; the aisles were pulled down in the 18C to make a more compact church. The W front was originally symmetrical, but the NW tower has disappeared, apart from a buttress with blind arcading and part of the base.

Peel Cathedral, Isle of Man

Ded: St Germanus.

On W side of Peel Harbour.

The roofless remains of the cathedral stand inside Peel Castle, on St Patrick's Isle. St Patrick (d c 460) may possibly have come to Man in the 5C and made his disciple, Germanus, the first bishop of a new diocese. By the 8C there was a Celtic monastery on the island: the present cathedral, founded by Bp Simon (1230–48), dates from the 13–14C. (The name of the diocese, Sodor and Man, derives from the Norse Sudr-Eyjar, meaning 'South Islands', as it originally covered both Man and the Hebrides.) During the early Middle Ages the cathedral was constantly open to attack from the sea; but c 1400 the castle was built by Sir William le Scrope, who also rebuilt the cathedral transepts and the upper levels of the fortress-like central tower. The cathedral gradually fell into decay, and by the end of the 18C was in a ruinous condition.

To judge from the present remains, there never was a N nave aisle; and the S arcade may also have been blocked, without an aisle leading off it. The sturdy S transept is battlemented. The crypt was used as a prison until the late 18C. In the N wall of the chancel is the tomb-recess of Bp Simon, founder of the cathedral.

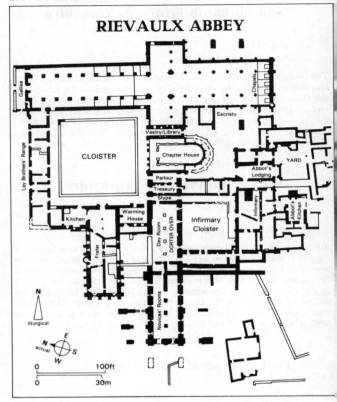

RIEVAULX ABBEY

Rievaulx Abbey, N Yorkshire

Ded: St Mary.

Off B1257, 3 miles W of Helmsley.

In the pastoral tranquillity of its remote setting below the North York Moors, and in the nobility of its substantial remains, Rievaulx (pronounced 'Reevo') is the most beautiful of all the ruined abbeys described in this book. It takes its name from the little River Rye (Rievaulx=Rye Valley), which flows down from the hills to the NW. The earliest Cistercian house in Yorkshire, it was founded in 1132 by Walter l'Espec, who had already founded the Augustinian priory at Kirkham (1122; see above). It was successful and prosperous from the outset: by c 1150 there were 140 monks and 500 lay brothers, and in the words of a contemporary, 'the church swarmed with them like a hive with bees'. The abbot at this period (1147–67) was Ailred, renowned in his lifetime for his learning, the friend and correspondent of kings and bishops, and later canonized. From c 1300 the story of Rievaulx is one of slow decline; when it was dissolved in 1538 the number of monks was down to 22.

*Rievaulx Abbey, the substantial ruins of the transepts and E
end. (K. Spence)*

Since the river valley at this point runs N-S, and the ground on
which the abbey stands slopes to the W, the church is orientated from
N to S, with the ecclesiastical E end pointing to the S; when
describing Rievaulx the ecclesiastical orientation rather than the
actual compass is used. By far the finest of the remains is the E end of
the church, which dates from the 13C. Of the original Nave (c 1140),
long and narrow, with aisle chapels on either side and a galilee porch
at the W end, only the stumps of the columns survive, together with
the bases of the outer walls. E of the nave, the Transepts still keep
their Norman W, S and N walls, with upper stages of the 13C; these
were added c 1230, as part of the rebuilding, on the most imposing
scale, of the Choir and Presbytery, with five chapels at the E end
behind the high altar. Here the arches are pointed in full EE style;
there are twin arches in each opening of the triforium, and the E end is
pierced with two superimposed rows of three lancet windows.

Of the cloister buildings, the most interesting is the Chapter House
(E range, beyond the combined vestry and library). Entered through a
vestibule, it is apsidal in plan, thus differing from the usual Cistercian
simple rectangle. In the W wall is a shrine to William, the first abbot (d
1148), and graves of other abbots are set in the floor. S of the chapter
house are the narrow Parlour and Treasury. On the S side of the
cloister, the large Refectory still stands to a considerable height, with
the remains of a lavatorium on either side of the door; to the E is the
Warming-house, and to the W the Kitchen. As always, the W range
formed the Lay Brothers' Quarters, at Rievaulx far too small for their
number, and insignificant compared with the W range at Fountains or
Byland. To the SE are the remains of the Infirmary, with its cloister;
and the Abbot's Lodging.

Ripon Cathedral, N Yorkshire

Ded: St Peter and St Wilfrid.

Standing on a small hill beside the River Skell, Ripon is one of the least self-assertive of our cathedrals. However, this has not always been the case; since all the predominant lines in the building are vertical, and formerly the Minster (as it then was) had three lead-covered spires. Though fairly small (270ft long), it is fascinating for its mixture of architectural styles, typified by the squat central tower and the choir (see below). It celebrated its 1300th anniversary in 1972.

History. A monastery was founded at Ripon (called 'In-Rhypum' by the Venerable Bede) c 660. About ten years later St Wilfrid (d 709) built a church here, and for a short time (681–86) Ripon was a bishop's see (revived in 1836, when the diocese of Ripon was made separate from York). The crypt of St Wilfrid's Saxon church survives, but in the 9C the Danes destroyed the rest of the building. A second Saxon church on the site was destroyed by the Normans in 1069; but they soon built a third, Norman, church, part of which survives in the apsidal chapel at the E end of the chapter house and the undercroft below it. The present (fourth) church was begun by Abp Roger of York (1154–81) as a church for secular canons. His plan, unique in England, included an aisleless nave, an aisled choir, transepts with E aisles only, and a central tower. The existing W front, with its twin towers and two rows of five lancet windows, is probably due to Abp Walter de Gray (1215–55); it is the sole EE example of a twin-towered facade of its kind in England (at Wells, see above the towers stand clear of the aisles, as was originally the case at Ripon). The E end of the choir is a Dec reconstruction of the last quarter of the 13C. In c 1450 the SE corner of the central tower collapsed, and plans were made to rebuild the whole tower; but in the event only the S and E sides were rebuilt, in Perp style, while the N and W sides remained Norman Trans. Finally, in the first quarter of the 16C, the nave was

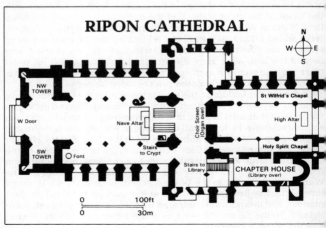

RIPON CATHEDRAL

Ripon Cathedral, medieval ceiling boss showing Adam and Eve expelled from the Garden of Eden.

enlarged by the addition of aisles. Until the mid 17C all three towers had leaded spires, which must have given Ripon from a distance the appearance that Lichfield has today. However, the central spire fell in 1660, and the two W spires were taken down as a safety precaution four years later.

Interior. On entering by the W door, visitors will be struck by the great width (87ft) of the *Nave* and aisles, and the contrast between the Perp clerestory windows and the much older work to the E. Part of Abp Roger's work survives at both the W and E ends, and in the N aisle is a pillar-base from the 10C (second) church. The nave altar and nave choir stalls occupy the two E bays. The pulpit, in beaten metal on marble columns, is a fine work of 1910. The *Transepts* retain Abp Roger's design in fair completeness; but the crossing has an unfinished appearance with the Trans N and W arches of the tower and the recast Perp S and E arches (see above). The Gothic pulpit, in the N transept, was originally above the rich stone Choir Screen (c 1480), which is decorated with carved figures of kings and clerics by Esmond Burton (1848); the organ above the screen has a case designed by Sir Gilbert Scott (1860).

The *Choir* is a remarkable mixture of three building periods (Trans, Dec and Perp), and is unusual for having a glazed triforium (or double clerestory). The Geometric tracery of the great E window (50ft high), and the naturalistic foliage of the capitals in the two E bays, are characteristic of the finest Dec work. The roof has some superb gilded bosses (c 1300). The splendid 15C stalls, which have fanciful and comic *Misericords, were restored by Scott. The ornate reredos (1922), by Sir Ninian Comper, commemorates the men of Ripon who fell in World War I. A curiosity is the wooden hand, jutting out from the organist's seat above the chancel arch, which can be used for beating time. The Choir Aisles terminate at their E end in chapels: St Wilfrid's Chapel (N), where the saint's shrine is once believed to have stood; and the Chapel of the Holy Spirit (S), closed off from the rest of the aisle by a jagged metal screen, representing Pentecostal lightning flashes and tongues of fire, by Leslie Durbin (1970). On the S side of the choir is the apsidal Norman Chapter House, with an undercroft below, which was restored in 1948–60 as a chapel and choir vestry. The altar of this chapel is formed from a circular pillar base from the 10C (second) church. Above the chapter house, and reached by stairs from the S transept, is the Lady Chapel (or Lady Loft), in a very unusual position; it now houses the cathedral Library (seen by request), which contains many books from before 1500, including a beautiful 13C illuminated Bible.

The remarkable *Crypt*, one of the half-dozen Saxon crypts in the country, was built by St Wilfrid (as was the crypt at Hexham), and takes the form of a narrow zigzag passageway. It was designed to display relics brought from Rome, and was lit by oil lamps placed in niches in the stonework. It now houses church treasures (mainly 17 and 18C) from churches in the diocese. A narrow hole on the N side of the crypt is known as 'St Wilfrid's Needle'; in former times the ability to crawl through it was taken as a proof of chastity.

Roche Abbey, S Yorkshire

Ded: St Mary.

By A364, 1½ miles SE of Maltby.

Romantically sited in a rocky glen, Roche gets its name from the cliff on its N side. It was founded for Cistercian monks in 1147, and virtually nothing is known of its history, apart from the fact that it was dissolved in 1538, when the local inhabitants descended on it and 'all things of price were either spoiled, carped away, or defaced to the uttermost'.

The abbey is entered through a gatehouse (14C), which has a narrow passageway for pedestrians and a wider one beside it for horses and wheeled traffic. The church (c 1160–70) was never altered; though little is left of it apart from the E walls of the transepts and the N and S walls of the presbytery, it is easy to follow on the ground, and is of standard Cistercian pattern. The aisled nave is divided half-way along by a screen, which separated the monks on the E from the lay brothers on the W. The transepts have two chapels each, and the presbytery is short and narrow. There are a number of grave-slabs on the nave floor. The monastic buildings (mainly 13C) lie between the church and the stream, and make use of it for drainage purposes. Little of them is left above ground; they consist of (E range) chapter house, parlour and undercroft, with monks' dorter over; (S range) warming-house, frater and kitchen; and (W range) lay brothers' quarters. The abbot's lodging was on the other side of the stream, which is still spanned by the arches that supported the S ends of the frater and the dorter.

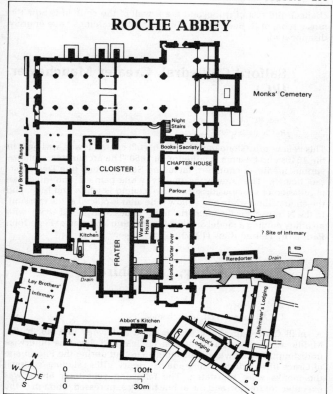

ROCHE ABBEY

Monks' Cemetery

Night Stairs

Books Sacristy

CHAPTER HOUSE

CLOISTER

Lay Brothers' Range

Parlour

Kitchen

Warming House

? Site of Infirmary

FRATER

Monks' Dorter over

Reredorter   Drain

Drain

Lay Brothers' Infirmary

? Infirmer's Lodging

Abbot's Kitchen

Abbot's Lodging

N W S E

0   100ft

0   30m

St Bees Priory, Cumbria

Ded: St Mary and St Bega.

On B5345, 3 miles S of Whitehaven.

The little seaside town of St Bees gets its name from Bega, an Irish girl saint who landed on the coast and settled as a hermit c 900. Some time after 1120 a small Benedictine priory was founded here; the church, built of red sandstone, with a square central tower, was begun c 1150 and enlarged c 1200. After the Dissolution it was saved from ruin by the parishioners, who carried out extensive repairs in the early 17C. The finest medieval survival is the splendid Norman W door, which has three orders of columns and is ornamented with zigzag carving and grotesque birds and animals; opposite it is a 'dragon stone' of 11C Scandinavian type. The nave arcades are EE, and the Perp clerestory windows probably date from the parishioners' restoration of c 1610. The crossing arches and transepts are largely Norman. The E wall dates from a major restoration by William Butterfield (1855–68), which included rebuilding the tower and much of the S transept and nave aisles. The modern chancel takes up only one bay of the monks' chancel; the rest of it (beyond the E wall of the church) is now the music room of St Bees School. The monastic buildings have entirely disappeared.

Salford Cathedral, Greater Manchester (RC)

Ded: St John.

In Chapel Street.

This yellow-grey stone building, with a tall central tower, was built in the 1840s and became a cathedral in 1850. The architecture imitates various medieval churches, including Selby Abbey (the Dec choir; see below). The interior is mainly white-painted and gives an impression of spaciousness; the nave ceiling is white and blue, and the choir ceiling white and yellow. The altar is placed at the crossing. In the N transept is the memorial to Bp James Sharples (d 1850), with an effigy holding a model of the cathedral; and a portrait of Pope John Paul II, by Harold Riley (1982).

Sawley Abbey, Lancashire

Ded: St Mary.

Off A59, 3 miles NE of Clitheroe.

A small Cistercian abbey was founded at Sawley in 1148. In the Middle Ages it won a reputation for learning, but was otherwise undistinguished. It was dissolved in 1536; but during the Pilgrimage of Grace (the northern rising against Henry VIII's religious reforms) the monks were reinstated. The following year their abbot was executed for treason and the abbey finally suppressed. Enough of the church walling survives to make out the plan; it had an aisleless nave, transepts with three chapels each, and an aisled chancel. At some stage during the abbey's history the nave was considerably shortened (possibly for reasons of economy), which left the nave far smaller than the chancel. The best-preserved survival of the monastic buildings is the night-stair that led from the monks' dorter to the S transept. Just inside the gate are shelves with a display of stones excavated from the ruins.

Selby Abbey, N Yorkshire

Ded: Christ, St Mary and St Germanus.

Formerly the church of a Benedictine abbey, Selby is one of the most perfect monastic churches in England. The abbey was founded in 1069 by Benedict, a monk who had absconded from the abbey of Auxerre, SE of Paris, with the finger of St Germanus (Germain), which became Selby's chief relic (Germanus was a 5C French nobleman who was converted to Christianity, became Bp of Auxerre, and was subsequently canonized). Presumably Benedict and his monks worshipped in a temporary wooden church, as nothing remains from his time; harsh as an abbot, even by the standards of his day (he had two monks castrated for stealing silver), he was forced to resign in 1097. His successor was Abbot Hugh, who c 1100 began the present church.

The original building, completed c 1230, consisted of the existing nave, transepts with apsidal chapels, and a short choir, with an apse at the E end; the W front with its superb Norman doorway is of this period (apart from the Perp W window, and the upper stages of the twin towers, which were added in 1935). Between c 1280 and 1340 a new and enlarged choir was built in Dec style, including the magnificent Flamboyant E window, and the nave windows were enlarged. Disaster struck the church in 1690, when the central tower collapsed, demolishing the S transept; and again in 1906, when a fire totally destroyed the roof. A complete restoration was carried out by J. Oldrid Scott; the church was re-roofed by 1909, and the S transept was rebuilt in 1912. In 1935 Scott raised the two W towers by their upper storey; previously they had risen no higher than the nave roof. In 1969 the Queen distributed the Royal Maundy Money at Selby, on the occasion of the 900th anniversary of its foundation.

Interior. The *Nave* displays several distinct periods of building. Norman work from Abbot Hugh's time (c 1100–20) occurs in the four E bays on the N side of the nave and two on the S side, and the four tower arches; the second pillar on the S side, with incised decoration similar to that at Durham, is known as 'Abbot Hugh's Pillar'. Several of the arches on both the N and the S sides are distorted due to the unstable foundations of the church. At the W end of the nave the architecture becomes Trans, with pure EE in the S triforium and both clerestories. The simple font is Norman; its tall ornate wooden cover is 15C. The lofty Perp window (15C) in the N Transept is filled with early 20C glass depicting the life of St Germanus; the Lathom Chapel (E of the transept) has a leper's squint cut through the stone in its SE corner. The open choir screen is by Oldrid Scott.

The *Choir* is Dec throughout, of more than one period, with the remains of rich sculpture and a fanciful triforium balustrade. The coat of arms of the Washington family (stars and stripes) appears in a window of the S clerestory. The choir stalls are by Oldrid Scott, and the large and elaborate reredos was carved by Peter Rendl, of

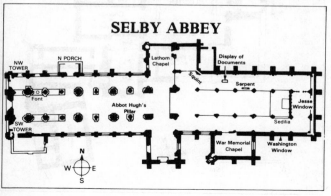

SELBY ABBEY

Oberammergau (1909). The sedilia were almost certainly designed c 1380 by Henry Yevele, the architect of the Canterbury Cathedral nave. The great *E Window (c 1340) is a Jesse Window showing the ancestry of Christ (top centre) back to Jesse (bottom centre); at the top is a 'Doom' showing St Michael weighing souls. About a quarter of the glass is original 14C. In the N Choir Aisle is a glass case displaying old documents, and a serpent from the old church orchestra hangs on the screen near by. The 14C Sacristy (off the S choir aisle) was made into a War Memorial Chapel in 1955 (furnishings by George Pace); it contains a good alabaster *Deposition, made in the 15C by the Nottingham school of carvers. The N porch has a Norman doorway as fine as that in the W front; the upper storey, decorated with blind arcading, is EE.

Shap Abbey, Cumbria

Ded: St Mary Magdalene.

Off A6, 10 miles S of Penrith.

At the end of the 12C an abbey was founded at Shap, on the E edge of the Lake District beside the River Lowther, for Premonstratensian canons (White Canons). Little is known about the abbey or any of its

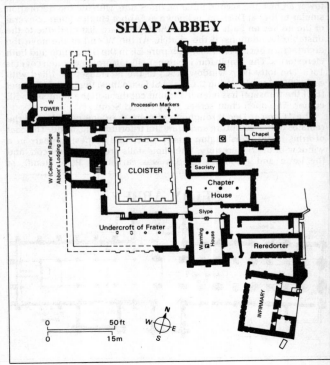

SHAP ABBEY

monks, apart from Abbot Richard Redman (d 1505), who became successively Bp of St Asaph, Exeter and Ely. Shap was dissolved in 1540. The most spectacular feature of the ruins is Redman's great W tower (c 1500), which stands to almost its full height. Little is left of the rest of the church (nave with N aisle only, transepts with chapels, and narrow presbytery), which is almost entirely 13C, lengthened at the E end in the 15C. Some of the nave flagstones have survived, inscribed with stone circles showing where the monks had to stand in two rows at the end of their regular Sunday procession round the abbey. The small cloister survives as foundation walls only. The E range contained the sacristy and chapter house, with the warming-house in the SE corner; the S range was taken up by the refectory, with undercroft below; and the W range was used to store provisions on the ground floor, with rooms for the abbot or guests above. SE of the cloister is the reredorter, draining into the river, and the infirmary set at an angle to the rest of the buildings.

Sheffield Cathedral, S Yorkshire

Ded: St Peter and St Paul.

The Diocese of Sheffield was created in 1914, and the parish church was made a cathedral. Its tall crocketed central spire is a landmark in the centre of the city. In spite of modern additions which give it a confusing appearance when seen close to, it is still basically a 15C Perp church, built on the site of a late 13C church which it superseded, and much altered in the 19C. Before World War II the architect Sir Charles Nicholson (d 1949) planned to swing the whole layout through a right angle, with a new nave on the space now the S

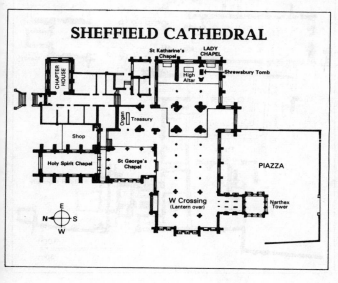

SHEFFIELD CATHEDRAL

forecourt. But the total plan had to be abandoned; though it survives in part in the Chapel of the Holy Spirit to the N, which would have been in the position of a Lady Chapel if the new orientation had come about.

Entrance is under a modern narthex tower, designed by Arthur Bailey, who succeeded Nicholson as cathedral architect. It leads into a tall W Crossing (1966), at the W end of the nave, lit from overhead by a lantern of glowing stained glass, with wooden pendants symbolizing the Crown of Thorns. On the N side of the nave is St George's Chapel (originally intended as the sanctuary of Nicholson's cathedral), the chapel of the York and Lancaster Regiment (Hallamshires), with a curious roof of hollow boxlike structures. N again is the Chapel of the Holy Spirit, with stalls by Sir Ninian Comper, and a window on the theme of the 'Te Deum' by Christopher Webb (1940). In the N Transept the organ by Noel Mander (1966) makes a striking pattern with its combination of vertical and horizontal pipes; in front of it is a display of cathedral treasures. Beyond the short Choir, the E end is divided into three spaces of almost equal width. On the N is St Katherine's Chapel, furnished in memory of the work of women in Church ministry; central is the Sanctuary with the high altar; and on the S is the Lady Chapel (formerly the Shrewsbury Chapel), which has a brightly painted pre-Reformation stone *mensa* (table altar). Set in the arcade between the chapel and the sanctuary is the superb tomb of the 4th Earl of Shrewsbury (d 1538), with alabaster effigies of the Earl and his two wives. Another monument commemorates the 6th Earl, the husband of Bess of Hardwick.

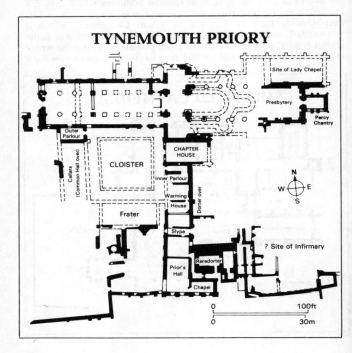

TYNEMOUTH PRIORY

Tynemouth Priory, Tyne and Wear

Ded: St Mary and St Oswin.

Off A193, 8 miles E of Newcastle.

Visitors to Tynemouth might be excused for thinking that they have come to a castle rather than a religious foundation, as the ruins of the priory are reached through a massive gate-tower set in a fortified wall. For centuries Tynemouth, built on a lofty headland guarding the N side of the Tyne estuary, was a fortress as much as a priory, and its history is military as well as ecclesiastical. Today it serves a practical purpose as well, since there is a large coastguard station next door to the church.

There was certainly a monastery here by the mid 7C, as in 651 it received the body of St Oswin, King of Deira (part of Northumbria), who had been murdered by his rival King Oswy of Bernicia. Miracles were recorded at his shrine, and the monastery became a popular pilgrimage centre. During the 9C it was attacked and plundered by the Danes on several occasions, in spite of being fortified against them. Abandoned in 1008, it was refounded c 1090 by Robert de Mowbray, Earl of Northumberland, as a priory of Benedictine monks. In 1127 St Oswin's relics were joined by those of another saint, Henry of Coquet, a hermit who had died of self-inflicted privations in his cell on Coquet (a small island off the coast near Alnwick). The monastic ruins date mainly from 1090 to c 1250. The massive battlemented wall across the headland was built against the Scots c 1296, and the towering gatehouse was added a century later. After the priory was dissolved in 1539, Tynemouth continued to be used as a castle; the fortifications were altered and added to in the 16C and also in the 18C, and it remained in the hands of the War Office until 1960.

Of the Norman Church (c 1090–1140), parts of the nave walls and S transept survive. At the end of the 12C the apsidal Norman E end, with its three radiating chapels, was demolished, and a new EE presbytery was built; the E wall and part of the S wall, pierced with tall lancet windows, still stand almost to full height. The fine W front, of which the moulded W doorway survives, was built c 1220–50. At some stage (probably 14 or 15C) a large room of unknown purpose was built over the ceiling of the presbytery and choir, lit by the topmost windows at the E end. In the middle of the E wall a small door (normally kept locked) leads to the 15C Percy Chantry (Percy was the family name of the Earls of Northumberland). At the E end is a rose-window, and there are 33 carved stone bosses crammed into the vaulting. The Cloister is marked out in the turf S of the church; little more than foundations survives. On the E side, the Chapter House stood directly against the S transept. Beyond the stairs and a narrow parlour is the warming-house, still with some tiles on the floor. The Frater took up most of the S range; and the W side consisted of cellars and storage, with a 'common hall' above. Other buildings include the Priors' Hall (a continuation of the E cloister range), with its own chapel to the SE.

Wakefield Cathedral, W Yorkshire

Ded: All Saints.

Wakefield's soaring spire (247ft) is the tallest in Yorkshire, and still dominates the town, in spite of the challenge of modern tower blocks near by. Formerly the parish church, it was raised to cathedral status when the Diocese of Wakefield was created in 1888. There was almost certainly a Saxon church on the site, succeeded by a Norman cruciform church (much smaller than the present building) which was begun c 1100; aisles were added c 1150 (N) and 1220 (S). The church was virtually rebuilt at the beginning of the 14C; the W tower was added c 1420; and c 1470 the chancel and aisles were rebuilt and the clerestory was added, giving the church its present plan of a rectangle without transepts and overall Perp appearance. Only the pronounced tilt in the line of the chancel in relation to the nave remains as evidence of the former cruciform plan. The only recent alteration to the church took place in 1905, when a new E end (by J.L. Pearson and his son F.L. Pearson) was added, to give the space needed for its cathedral status.

Inside, the slender pillars of the Nave give an impression of lightness and grace; some of them are Norman in their lower sections. In the SW corner is a fine font, placed there at the Restoration of Charles II and dated 1661. The wooden rood-screen (1635) is surmounted by a Crucifix and angels by Sir Ninian Comper (1950). In the N Choir Aisle is an organ screen of 1743, and (at the E end) a display case of church treasures, including a pewter chalice from Monk Bretton Priory (see above). At the E end of the church, behind the altar, is St Mark's Chapel (Pearson's 1905 extension). The S choir aisle forms the Lady Chapel; in a shallow transept opening off it is the effigy of Bp Walsham How (d 1897), the first Bp of Wakefield and author of the famous hymn 'For all the Saints who from their labours rest'. Next to it is a replica of the Saxon Wakefield Cross (c 970; original at present in Wakefield Museum). The chapel also contains several memorials to the Pilkington family. Nearly all the stained glass throughout the church is by Charles Kempe (late 19C).

Whalley Abbey, Lancashire

Ded: St Mary.

Off A59, 6 miles NE of Blackburn.

During the 1280s a community of Cistercian monks moved from a site by the Mersey that was constantly liable to flood, to a new inland site at Whalley, beside the River Calder. The church, completed in 1380, took half a century to build, and the monastic buildings were not finished until the 1440s. The last abbot, John Paslew, was executed for his part in the Pilgrimage of Grace of 1536 against Henry VIII's religious reforms. In the 1550s part of the buildings was converted into a private house, now owned by the Diocese of Blackburn and run as a centre for conferences and retreats.

Entrance is through the NE gateway (c 1480), which originally gave access to the abbot's house. The foundations of the large church (260ft long) can be easily followed; in 1964 a new high altar was reconsecrated in the position of the medieval altar. There are remains of several tombstones in the transepts. More survives of the cloister than of the church. In the E range, the chapter house, entered through a vestibule, is unusual in being octagonal in plan; the range continues S past a parlour and passageway to the monks' day-room, which was also their warming-house. In the S range, the frater is parallel to the cloister instead of at right angles to it, differing in this respect from the traditional Cistercian layout. The W range (lay brothers' quarters) is still in use as a Roman Catholic church hall. The conference centre (not open to visitors) incorporates parts of the abbot's house, of which foundations can be seen SE of the cloister.

Whitby Abbey, N Yorkshire

Off A171, on E side of town.

In 657 a monastery was founded on the windswept clifftop at Whitby by King Oswy of Northumbria after his victory over the heathen King Penda of Mercia. Called 'Streonaeshalch' by the Venerable Bede, it was a joint community of monks and nuns, with St Hilda (d 680) as its first abbess. In 664 it won a permanent place in Church history as the setting for the Synod of Whitby, at which the date of Easter and other matters were decided in favour of the Roman rather than the Celtic interpretation. The first English poet of distinction, the Northumbrian Caedmon (d c 680) was a monk at Whitby. The monastery was destroyed by the Danes in 867, and remained desolate until the late

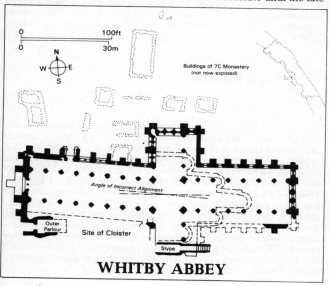

WHITBY ABBEY

11C, when it was refounded as a Benedictine abbey by William de Percy. It was dissolved in 1539. Though the domestic buildings were destroyed, the church was allowed to stand, probably because it was used as a navigational guide. In the 18 and 19C much of it fell down (nave, W front, central tower), and at the beginning of World War I it was shelled by German warships.

Enough survives of the church to show what a magnificent building it once was. The EE N transept and the chancel are still largely intact, except for the S wall; built about 1220, these took the place of a smaller apsidal Norman E end. The E wall is especially fine, having three rows of windows, with three lancets in each. For some unknown reason the nave is considerably out of alignment with the E end and transepts. Not much remains of the nave (mainly 14C) except for part of the N wall and the W end, where the windows change from EE lancets to Dec tracery. The cloister and monastic buildings have disappeared.

Excavations in the 1920s N of the church uncovered the foundations of a number of small buildings from the early monastery, probably the cells of St Hilda's nuns and their successors.

York: Holy Trinity, Micklegate

A small Benedictine priory was founded in Micklegate, across the Ouse from the Minster, in 1089. Until 1426 it was an alien priory owing allegiance to the abbey of Marmoutier, outside Tours; but in that year it became denizen (i.e. no longer subject to foreign control). Part of the W piers of the Norman church's central tower can be seen near the chancel steps; the nave is largely 13C; and the tower at the NW corner is 15C. In the Middle Ages the York Mystery Plays, performed on wagons throughout the city, began their annual progress (on Trinity Thursday in June) outside the gateway of Holy Trinity.

York Minster

Ded: St Peter.

The largest of English medieval cathedrals (almost 500ft long and over 200ft across the transepts), York Minster has a stately grandeur befitting the church that is second only to Canterbury in ecclesiastical importance. The Archbishop of York has the title Primate of England (whereas Canterbury is Primate of *All* England), and his sway extends over 14 dioceses in the N Midlands and the N of England. Though called a minster (derived from the Latin *monasterium*), York was never a monastic foundation, and so (unlike Canterbury) has no cloister or domestic buildings. It lies in the N corner of the old city, and the best view of it is from the city walls. Its architecture gives a comprehensive picture of building developments during three periods: EE (transepts), Dec (nave and chapter house), and early and late Perp (choir and towers). The stained glass is among the most glorious in the country.

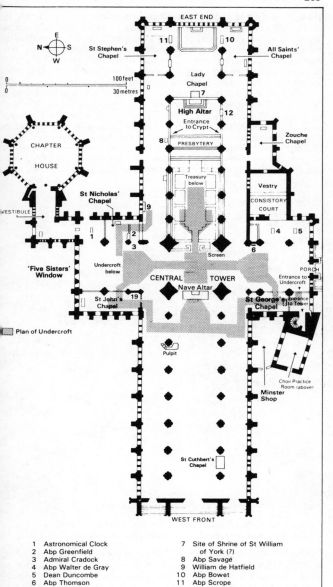

N · E · S · W

0 ——— 100 feet
0 ——— 30 metres

EAST END

St Stephen's Chapel

All Saints' Chapel

11   10

Lady Chapel   7

High Altar   12

Entrance to Crypt

8   PRESBYTERY

Zouche Chapel

CHAPTER HOUSE

St Nicholas' Chapel   9

VESTIBULE

Treasury below

Vestry

CONSISTORY COURT

1

2   6   4   5

3

Screen   6

'Five Sisters' Window

Undercroft below

CENTRAL   TOWER

Nave Altar

PORCH

Entrance to Undercroft

St John's Chapel   19

St George's Chapel   Entrance to Tower

Plan of Undercroft

Pulpit

Choir Practice Room (above)

Minster Shop

St Cuthbert's Chapel

WEST FRONT

1   Astronomical Clock
2   Abp Greenfield
3   Admiral Cradock
4   Abp Walter de Gray
5   Dean Duncombe
6   Abp Thomson

7   Site of Shrine of St William
     of York (?)
8   Abp Savage
9   William de Hatfield
10   Abp Bowet
11   Abp Scrope
12   Abp Dolben

YORK MINSTER

History. In Roman times York (Eboracum, known to the British as 'Caer Ebrauc') was of the greatest importance, as the headquarters of the 6th Legion and capital of the province of 'Lower' (i.e. Northern) Britain. During repairs to the foundations of the central tower (see below) Roman walling was discovered, which made it clear that the minster stands above the legion's main administrative building (the *Principia*). Constantine the Great, the first Roman emperor to support the Church, was proclaimed emperor at York in 306, and York seems to have had a bishop in the early 4C. The first recorded evidence of permanent Christianity in the city dates from 625, when Paulinus, Bp of York, baptized King Edwin of Northumbria in a small wooden chapel, supposedly somewhere on the minster site. This was soon replaced by a stone church, which was burned down c 740. A magnificent successor to it, begun by Abp Albert (767–80), was destroyed in the troubles that followed the Norman Conquest.

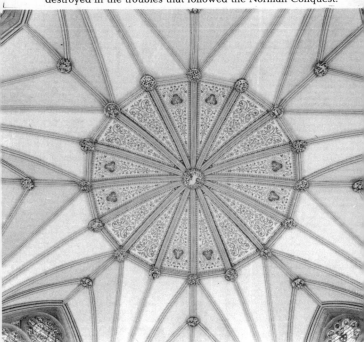

York Minster, the vaulting of the 13C Chapter House, unsupported by a central column. (A.F. Kersting)

The first Norman archbishop, Thomas of Bayeux, began rebuilding c 1080. The choir of his church was rebuilt by Abp Roger of Pont-l'Evêque (1154–81), and the remainder of it was gradually replaced by the present building. The S transept was rebuilt (1220–40) by Abp Walter de Gray, followed by the N transept (1240–60). The present nave was begun in 1291 and completed (1345. Abp Roger's Norman choir was replaced by the present one in

1360–1405. The building of the pinnacled W towers was completed by 1474, and the central tower (replacing a tower that had partly fallen in 1407) by 1480. Thus from the first work of Abp de Gray to final completion the minster had taken over 250 years. Two 19C fires damaged the fabric: in 1829 a maniac burnt out the choir, and in 1840 a fire started by a careless workman destroyed the timber roof of the nave.

In 1967 structural investigations showed that the central tower and the E and W ends were in danger of collapse, due to fatigue and water erosion in the building material, and changes in the water table affecting the foundations. Extensive engineering works were needed to strengthen the fabric; the foundations of the four columns supporting the central tower were encased in reinforced concrete, and the opportunity was taken to create a museum (the Undercroft Museum, see below) in the excavated space. Repairs were also carried out to the W towers. The eroded statues and pinnacles on the exterior were extensively restored in 1965. In the late 1970s the S transept roof was given new bosses and ribs. Repairs to the E end are still in progress.

Exterior. The finest parts are the W facade, particularly the great window and finely sculptured portal; the N Transept, especially the façade and 'Five Sisters' window; the octagonal Chapter House; and above all the great *Central Tower.

Interior. The glory of the minster is the extensive series of Stained-glass Windows, mainly the product of a well-defined local school of artists and craftsmen. It includes some of the earliest glass in England, a masterpiece of EE grisaille glass, a great range of splendid Dec windows, and superb Perp glass. This priceless glass, removed for safety during World War II, was carefully restored under the direction of Dean Milner-White (d 1963).

The normal entrance is by the W end, near which is an 'info-bar' of taped information in English, French and German. The *Nave*, of exceptional height and breadth, has widely spaced piers; the triforium is virtually suppressed, in order to give the largest space possible for the stained glass. The design presupposes a stone vault which was never built, and the present wooden roof (part of the restoration by Sydney Smirke after the fire of 1840), painted to resemble stone, perpetuates the earlier deception. There is superb tracery in the large clerestory windows, and above all in the great *W Window*, given by Abp William Melton in 1338; the upper part of the Flamboyant tracery suggests the shape of a heart. The unusually wide aisles (30ft) are stone-vaulted, unlike the nave. The W windows here have fine glass, and the second window from the W in the N aisle contains a panel of the oldest glass in England (c 1150). Besides the 14C glass elsewhere in the aisles, the remains of 12–13C glass in the clerestories are worth studying. All round the nave and choir, below the triforium, are stone shields painted with the arms of Edward II and the barons who met in parliament at York in 1309–10. The gilded timber jutting from the N triforium may once have been the support for the chain and pulley of a medieval font cover. A recent addition (1982) to the minster is St Cuthbert's Chapel, between two piers at the W end of the S aisle; it commemorates the Yorkshire Volunteers, and its ceiling, painted by Graeme Willson, has as its theme 'St Cuthbert's Vision of Heaven'. An oak pulpit t the memory of Abps Lang and Temple was dedicated in 1948. Th Archbishop's Throne (1959), by Sir Albert Richardson, is a memori to Abp Garbett.

The spacious *Transepts* have aisles on the W side as well as the I The Perp Lantern (by Henry IV's master mason, William Colchester) is the largest example in England, and the impression size in this part of the church is hardly lessened by the obtrusiv triforium and the consequent meanness of the clerestory, or by th rather feeble design of the wooden vault. The huge boss in th centre depicts St Peter and St Paul. In the N Transept the vault, oak ribs with cedar infilling, dates from 1934–51, with many ribs an bosses from the 15C ceiling. In the N wall are the lancet lights (5C high) of the •'Five Sisters', with their wonderful 13C glass interlacing stems on a grisaille background. (The Sisters form th lower row of lancets; the upper row is glazed with modern gla matching the 13C glass below.) The 'Five Sisters' were releaded 1925 (with medieval lead from Rievaulx Abbey) as a memorial to th women who gave their lives in World War I; an oak screen in the aisle bears their names. In this transept is an astronomical cloc designed by Richardson (1955) as a memorial to airmen based in N England who died in World War II; and in the NE corner the fir brass of Abp Greenfield (1306–16), and a memorial to Admir Cradock, killed at the Battle of Coronel in 1914. In the S Transe (which contains the exit door on its S side) is the tomb of Abp de Gr (1215–55), in the E aisle; also monuments to Dean Duncombe 1880) and Abp Thomson (d 1896). Though this transept is slight earlier than the N transept (both are 13C), its rose-window considerably later (c 1500).

In the SW corner of the S transept is the entrance to the *Undercro Museum* (1973), an essential part of any visit to the minste Extensive remains of Roman York lie exposed, and there is extreme of contrast between the ancient exhibits and the concret studded with stainless steel bolt-heads, that encases the foundatio of the four central piers. Adjoining is a treasury with numerous relic including the Horn of Ulf (an oliphant or drinking horn made from tusk), probably 11C from S Italy, the mazer bowl traditional connected with Abp Scrope (d 1405), and magnificent church pla and domestic silver. The treasury is in part of the original Norma crypt.

Back again to the N transept, where a Vestibule leads from the aisle to the •*Chapter House*. Both are among the supreme exampl of Dec work, and both preserve contemporary glass of rare quality tracery of inventive beauty. Built in 1260–85, the chapter house is t largest in England (63ft wide); it was restored in 1844–45 and aga in 1969–70. Its beauty justifies the Latin inscription by the door *rosa flos florum, sic est domus ista domorum* ('As the rose is the flow of flowers, so this is the house of houses'). The vaulting unsupported by any central column; the painted ceiling was restor by John Carr in 1798 and was repainted in 1976. The carvi includes over 250 stone heads, and almost 300 foliage capitals a pendants.

The *Choir* is separated from the nave by an elaborate late Gotl Rood-screen (traditionally c 1475–1500, but perhaps a little earlie with life-size statues of English kings from William I to Henry VI (15C except the last, on the right, which is modern); the central boss

York Minster, carving (c 1390) of a White Hart, the emblem of Richard II, at the entrance to the S choir aisle

the vaulted entrance has a high relief of the Madonna (c 1150), Byzantine in manner. The glass in the great *E Window, by John Thornton of Coventry (1405), is still almost intact and forms the largest expanse of medieval glazing in England, and probably in the world (78ft by 31ft). The soaring windows of the E Transepts (transeptal bays) contain 15C glass depicting the lives of St William of York and St Cuthbert. All the woodwork in the choir was destroyed in the fire of 1829. The present stalls are an approximate reproduction of the originals by Sir Robert Smirke. The miracle-working shrine of St William of York, canonized in 1227, is believed to have stood behind the high altar until the Reformation. The traceried altar screen, the work of John Scott (1831), is a free copy of its predecessor of c 1475. In the N Choir Aisle is the Tudor monument of Abp Savage (1501–07), with a restored chantry above; also the damaged but finely wrought effigy-tomb (c 1370–80) of William of Hatfield (d 1336), the young son of Edward III. In the Lady Chapel is the splendid tomb of Abp Bowet (1407–23); and opposite is the plain, restored monument of Abp Scrope, beheaded in 1405 by Henry IV for allegedly taking part in an unsuccessful rebellion (see Shakespeare's *2 Henry IV*, IV). After his death a cult to him sprang up in the N of England. In the S Choir Aisle are monuments by Grinling Gibbons to Abp Dolben (d 1686) and Abp Lamplugh (d 1691), and in front of the Dolben monument are massive 13C cope-chests. Near by is another 'info-bar'. The Zouche Chapel, reserved for private prayer, is reached down steps from this aisle; it was endowed by Abp Zouche in 1352, and has medieval cupboards and a well.

The late Norman E *Crypt*, entered from the choir aisles, is the oldest part of the building; its structure shows the extent of Abp Roger's choir. The capitals of the pillars have intricate Romanesque carving and probably date from the time of Abp Thomas (c 1080). Beneath a trap-door is the base of a pillar of the Roman Praetorium.

In Dean's Park (N of the minster) is a fragment of a cloister from Abp Roger's Norman Archbishop's Palace. Immediately to the E of the minster is St William's College, founded in 1461 to house the chantry priests attached to the minster. Opposite the S transept is a restored Roman column from the headquarters building of the 6th Legion.

York: St Mary's Abbey

In Museum Gardens, SW of the Minster.

Once the most important Benedictine abbey in the N of England, St Mary's was founded c 1080 by Stephen of Lastingham and enlarged by William Rufus. Only foundations of the apsidal Norman church still exist; the ruins, still graceful, are those of a church begun by Abbot Simon of Warwick in 1259. The N wall of the nave and part of the W front stand to a fair height, Geometric and early Dec in style. The Yorkshire Museum is built over part of the domestic buildings. The abbot's *Hospitium* or guesthouse (now a small museum) survives near the river; and much of the precinct wall still stands.

7. WALES AND THE MARCHES

Abbey Dore, Hereford and Worcester

Ded: Holy Trinity and St Mary.

On B4347, 10 miles NE of Abergavenny.

This magnificently irregular church lies in a remote valley of the
Black Mountains (the Golden Valley, whose name is wrongly derived
from the river's name Dwr, which has nothing to do with gold but
means 'water'). A Cistercian abbey was founded here in 1147 by
Robert of Ewyas, grandson of Ralph, Earl of Hereford. Of Robert's
church nothing survives; the present church, consisting of choir and
transepts only, dates from 1180 to c 1280 and is architecturally mainly
EE. After the abbey was dissolved in 1535 the monastic buildings
were pulled down and the church fell into such decay that it was used
as a cattle shed. In 1632 the owner, Lord Scudamore, restored it and
made it into the parish church; the work was carried out by John Abel
of Hereford, who rebuilt the roof in local oak. Most unusually, the
upper parts of the presbytery columns were continued in oak rather
than stone. There was a second major restoration in 1902.

The most notable feature of the interior is the heavy wooden
•Screen, by Abel, which bears the arms of Charles I in the centre,
flanked by those of Scudamore (N) and Archbishop Laud (S).
Through the screen, the choir, with its clustered columns, represents
EE architecture at its simplest and best. Inside the altar-rail is a large
altar or *mensa*, 12ft long; after the Dissolution it had been used for
making cheese and salting meat on, but it was restored to its rightful
position by Lord Scudamore. On the floor on either side of the altar
are 13C tiles collected at the 1902 restoration, and under an arch (S)
there is a mutilated 12C effigy of Robert of Ewyas, the abbey's
founder. Except for the lectern, all the furniture is by John Abel. The E
end of the church consists of an ambulatory with five chapels, the
foundations of whose dividing walls can be seen. On the floor of the
chapels are 13C bosses, possibly from the former nave. Worth noting
is the 13C upper hinge of the EE N door: it terminates in an animal's
head, said to commemorate an order given by Edward I to
exterminate the wolves in the region.

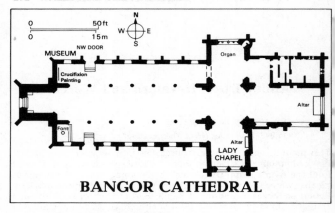

BANGOR CATHEDRAL

Bangor Cathedral, Gwynedd

Ded: St Deiniol.

This small and unpretentious church, built of reddish-brown stone, is probably the oldest cathedral in Britain in continuous use as such, since it was founded c 525, more than 70 years before Canterbury. It lies on the lower slope of a valley, dwarfed by the University College building on the opposite side.

History. Bangor owes its origin to St Deiniol, a Welsh nobleman who founded a monastic community here c 525; the word bangor means 'the binding part of a wattle fence', and no doubt Deiniol's community had a fence of this sort round it. In 546 St Dubricius (Dyfrig), Bishop of all Wales, divided his large see into three parts, consecrating St Deiniol as the bishop responsible for Gwynedd (St Padarn became Bp of Central Wales, and St Teilo Bp of S Wales). For the next five centuries the history of the see is virtually blank. In 1071 the Normans tried to impose their own nominee, a Breton called Hervé, as bishop; but as an unwelcome symbol of Norman power he was at constant odds with his Welsh flock and soon departed. Between 1120 and 1139 Bp David built a Norman cathedral, terminating in an apse at the E end; and it would have been here that Abp Baldwin preached in 1188, on his tour of Wales to win support for the Third Crusade. In 1211, and again during the wars of Edward I in the 1280s, the cathedral was much damaged. Rebuilding was begun before 1291 by Bp Anian I (1267–1305), who was responsible for a central tower (burnt c 1308), the Lady Chapel and an enlarged S transept. Building continued throughout the Dec period until c 1350, Bp Anian II (1309–28) probably being responsible for the N transept and nave. Disaster came in 1402, when the cathedral was badly damaged by followers of Owain Glyndŵr; the ruins lay virtually untouched for nearly a century, and the Lady Chapel was never rebuilt. Bp Deane (1496–1500) largely rebuilt the choir, including the E window; and Bp Skevington (1509–34) added a nave clerestory and W tower. During the Civil War and the two centuries that followed the cathedral again suffered damage and neglect. Major restoration was carried out in

1868–84 by Sir Gilbert Scott and his son Oldrid Scott; the choir and transepts were largely reconstructed, the chancel and S transept were refloored, and the whole interior layout was changed. Scott's plans envisaged a lofty central tower and spire, but subsidence made this impracticable. In 1967–71 the tower was battlemented at its present stumpy height and given a small cap spire.

Exterior. Points worth noting are a blocked window and plain buttress (both S wall of choir), the sole surviving visible remains of the Norman cathedral; the Latin inscription of 1532 over the W doorway recording Bp Skevington's building of the tower; the unusually thin buttresses of the N aisle; and the late Dec (? 1350) windows of the aisles, which survived Owain Glyndŵr's damage of 1402. The transept ends were rebuilt by Scott in what is probably the original design, to judge from fragments discovered in the 16C walls. The fine buttresses on the end of the S transept, including the curious dwarf example in the middle, also escaped destruction in 1402. On the E of the S transept are traces of former chapels, probably demolished in the 15–16C and their stone used in the repair of the transept walls.

Interior. The cathedral is entered through the NW doorway. On the right is a small museum of stonework, tiles and documents; the ancient stones include the 14C sepulchral slab known as the 'Eva Stone', from the name of the lady carved on it ('Here lies Eva, wife of ...anwel' etc). The tiles on the floor are probably early 14C and were discovered under the floor of the choir during the 19C restoration. Here too are 'dog tongs', used to remove unwanted dogs from the church; a 15C miserere; some 16C Flemish wooden figures; and a modern painting of the Crucifixion by Margaret Cross (1968). On a nearby pier in the *Nave* hangs the moving •Mostyn Christ: the carved wooden figure (c 1518), thought to have been hidden by a Roman Catholic branch of the Mostyn family at the Reformation, depicts Christ seated on a rock, bound and wearing a crown of thorns. All the woodwork in the nave is modern. The nave altar frontal (1975), whose main motif is the Celtic cross, was designed by Iris Martin; and the hanging rood above the screen (1950) by Alban Caröe. In the S Transept (now the *Lady Chapel*) the arched tomb in the S wall was once thought to be that of Prince Owain Gwynedd (d 1170), originally buried before the high altar; but since the tomb is 13C, it is now thought that it may have been prepared for Bp Anian I (see above). Also in the S transept are a mural (1950) by Brian Thomas ('Christ on the Road to Emmaus'); a memorial to Edmund Prys (1544–1623), author of Welsh metrical psalms; and a tablet to the poet Goronwy Owen (1723–69). The N Transept is occupied by the organ. In the Choir the stonework of the large Perp windows in the E and S walls dates from 1494–1500, while the glass is 19C. The bishop's throne dates from 1879; the stalls were designed by Sir Gilbert Scott; and the reredos was the work of Oldrid Scott.

The former close, just N of the cathedral, is now the *Bible Garden*. The S side of the path is planted with flowers and shrubs traditionally associated with the medieval church, while on the N side are examples of trees, shrubs and plants mentioned in the Bible that are able to survive the climate of N Wales.

Bardsey, Gwynedd: St Mary's Abbey

On Bardsey Island, off the tip of the Lleyn Peninsula.

Known also as the 'Island of 20,000 Saints', Bardsey was an important goal of pilgrimage from the 5 or 6C onwards, three pilgrimages there being reckoned as the equivalent of one to Rome. St Cadfan, from Brittany, is said to have founded the first monastery here in 429; and in c 545 St Dubricius (Dyfrig) is thought to have died and been buried here. In 607 the surviving monks of Bangor-is-Coed, near Wrexham, are said to have taken refuge on Bardsey. Their monastery was the oldest in Britain, founded c 180; in 607 it was destroyed by King Ethelfrid of Northumbria in the last great battle of Saxon paganism over British Christianity, and more than 1,200 monks were slaughtered. In the N part of the island are the 13C remains (little more than a bell-tower) of the Augustinian St Mary's Abbey, in whose churchyard lie some of the 20,000 saints reputedly buried on Bardsey.

Basingwerk Abbey, Clwyd

Ded: St Mary.

Off minor road joining A248 and A55, 1 mile N of Holywell.

Built on a plateau above the estuary of the Dee, Basingwerk stands on a fortified site that was occupied as far back as Roman times. The abbey was founded in 1131 by Ranulf, Earl of Chester, as a house of the Savignac Order. The abbey was dissolved in 1536 and almost entirely destroyed, though enough is left to give a good idea of the church and monastic buildings. The few remains of the church comprise the S and W walls, some pier bases, and fragments of the transepts. The cloister adjoined the church to the S; along the E side were (N to S) the sacristy, chapter house (with traces of the bench round the walls), parlour, novices' dorter, and warming-house. The large room W of the warming-house is the frater; it has internal arcading on its W wall, and traces of the hatch to the kitchen can be seen. Of the kitchen, on the W side of the refectory, little remains, apart from the base of the fireplace against the S wall.

Brecon Cathedral, Powys

Ded: St John the Evangelist.

The cathedral, built as a priory church and raised to cathedral status in 1923, is a sturdy foursquare building standing on high ground above the Honddu River in the northern part of the town, and largely enclosed by a surrounding wall.

History. The priory was founded, probably on the site of an earlier church, by Bernard of Newmarch at the close of the 11C as a cell of the Benedictine monastery of Battle in Sussex, a connection recalled by

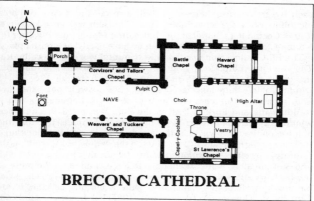

BRECON CATHEDRAL

the village of Battle 3 miles north-west. Giraldus Cambrensis (c 1147–c 1223), the Norman-Welsh historian, was archdeacon of Brecon in c 1172. Of the early church nothing remains except part of the nave walls immediately W of the crossing. The choir and transepts were entirely rebuilt in the first half of the 13C, when the tower was added; and during the 14C the nave, with the N and S aisles, was newly built, and the E chapels of the transepts were reconstructed on a larger scale. The church was restored in 1862–65 by Sir Gilbert Scott. In 1923 the church was made cathedral of the diocese of Swansea and Brecon, and in 1927 such parts of the priory domestic buildings as had survived the Reformation were restored by William Douglas Caröe (1857–1938) and rededicated for cathedral chapter use.

Interior. The *Nave* is entered by the NW porch, above which is an upper chamber. Before the Reformation, the present beautiful vista up the whole length of the church was broken by a rood-screen, reached by the still remaining staircases W of the crossing. The screen divided the church into two, the E part being for the monks and the W serving as parish church. Above the screen was suspended a great rood, the Crog (Cross) Aberhonddu, which gave the church its second title, Church of the Holy Rood, celebrated by the Welsh bards of the 15C. At the W end of the nave are a Norman font, and several sepulchral slabs, notable for their retention as late as the 17C of the medieval floreated cross; similar slabs can be found elsewhere in the cathedral. The N Aisle, formerly the chapel of the Corvisors (shoemakers) and Tailors, has a beautiful 14C tomb-niche and recumbent effigy; a part of the 15C screen; and a dormer window portraying three 6C Welsh saints (Cynog, Brychan and Alud) connected with the area. In the S Aisle, the former chapel of the Weavers and Tuckers, are the tombs of Sir David Williams (d 1613) and his wife Elizabeth Vaughan; the wooden effigy of a lady (c 1555), the only surviving figure from a tomb—made up of three tiers of oak beds—to the memory of the Games or Gams family; and, at the W end, a medieval cope-chest. In the N Transept (known formerly as the Battle Chapel, after Battle Abbey, or the nearby village of Battle) are a remarkable stone cresset (candle-holder) with 30 cups, unique in Wales and the largest found in Britain; a stone thought to have been used by archers for sharpening their arrows; and a case of books including a rare Breeches Bible. The S Transept was once known as 'Capel Cochiaid' ('Chapel of the Red-haired Men'), possibly after the Norman garrison of the castle, who may have used it as a burial place.

The EE *Chancel* contains the most beautiful work in the cathedral. The vaulting, completed by Sir Gilbert Scott, conceals two roofs, one the great roof of the 15C, the other dating from the 17C. The E window, of five large lancets, completely fills the wall space; the glass is in memory of officers and men of the 24th Regiment killed at Isandhlwana and Rorke's Drift in the Zulu War of 1879. The lancet windows at the sides are arranged in graduated triplets; the full effect of those on the N, however, is impaired by the later (14C) blocking of their lower parts. Also worth noting are the exquisite 13C sedilia; the rare triple piscina; the trefoiled niches (concealed by the reredos) N and S of the altar, which seem once to have opened on the outer air but perhaps afterwards served as aumbries; and the sepulchral slab on the N wall of the sanctuary, with a curious carving of the Crucifixion. The reredos (W.D. Caröe, 1937) has figures of saints and others in relief. Rich archways at the W end of the choir open into the transept chapels on either side. In the Havard Chapel (N), with a 14C doorway to the sanctuary combined with a squint, is the tomb of Walter Awbrey (?1312) and his wife, with an inscription in old Saxon and Norman French characters. Here also are four old houselling benches (two now cut down for footstools) that formerly took the place of fixed altar rails at the celebration of Holy Communion (linen cloths were placed on the benches, to catch crumbs of consecrated bread that would otherwise have fallen on to the floor). The Havard Chapel is the regimental chapel of the South Wales Borderers, now amalgamated with other regiments to form the Royal Regiment of Wales. The Chapel of St Lawrence (S), after lying in ruins for 300 years, was rebuilt by Caröe in 1930; it contains a small 13C piscina, and a memorial with effigy to Bp E.L. Bevan (d 1934), the first bishop of the diocese.

The domestic buildings of the priory (entered from the SW door), after serving as stables etc for three centuries, were skilfully adapted by Caröe to form the canonry, deanery and chapter house.

Caldy Island, Dyfed: Priory and Abbey

In Carmarthen Bay, 2 miles S of Tenby.

There have been monks on Caldy for 1,500 years, in a succession of foundations at varying intervals of time. The first monastery, founded in the late 5C, was probably established by monks from St Illtyd's monastery of Llantwit Major in South Glamorgan (though some authorities claim that Caldy was the older foundation). Its most famous abbot was St Samson of Dol, the patron saint of Caldy, who was born c 490 and educated by Illtyd at Llantwit. How long this Celtic Christian monastery lasted is unknown, but it was presumably still in existence when the Caldy Ogham Stone was put up. This is a slab of sandstone, with a cross and a double inscription, one in the ancient British alphabet known as Ogham (5–6C) and the other in Latin, added in the early 9C, which bids passers-by to pray for the soul of Catuoconus (Cadogan). In 1127 the island was given to Benedictine monks from St Dogmaels (see below), who remained there for over 400 years, until the priory was dissolved in 1534. The monastic buildings became a farm, and they and the small 12C church have largely survived. In 1906 the priory was bought by Aelred Carlyle, the founder of a community of Anglo-Catholic monks who in 1913 joined the Roman Catholic Church as Benedictines. In 1928 the Benedictines moved to Prinknash Park, in Gloucestershire (see above), and their place on Caldy was taken by Cistercians from Chimay in Belgium. The monastery was raised to abbey status in 1958.

On the cliffs, facing Tenby, there is a round Norman tower, now converted to a chapel. The main building on the island is the Abbey, built in 1907–11 (conducted tours for male visitors only); the church, seriously damaged by fire in 1940, was restored in 1950–51. The peal of bells is one of the largest in Wales. Near the abbey is St David's Church, which in plan resembles Irish churches of the 8 and 9C and which is probably in origin as old if not older. The W door is Norman. Beyond, the Old Priory dates mainly from the 13–14C, with 15C additions. The restored St Illtyd's Church can be visited; it has a leaning tower, and the Ogham Stone (see above) is at the E end of the nave.

There are regular boats between Tenby Harbour and Caldy, from late May to Sept. (not Sat. and Sun.).

Cardiff Cathedral, S Glamorgan (RC)

Ded: St David.

Built in the 1880s as a Roman Catholic parish church, St David's was raised to full cathedral status in 1920. The architect was Peter Paul Pugin, son of A.W. Pugin, the prophet of the Gothic Revival; he designed a building with a wide nave and no side arcades to obstruct the view of the altar. The unusual E window is circular and has delicate stone tracery. Much of the decoration and furnishings are modern, including the baldacchino at the E end of the church, and the ceramic Stations of the Cross by Adam Kossowski.

Chester Cathedral, Cheshire

Ded: Christ and the Blessed Virgin Mary.

Bounded on the E by the city wall built by the Romans and on the other sides by the buildings and streets of the city, Chester Cathedral is closely integrated with the life around it. It is built of red sandstone in a wide variety of architectural styles, from Norman to late Perp.

History. Chester was founded by the Romans possibly as early as A.D. 48, as Castra Devana ('the Camp on the Dee'); after they left c 380, it was occupied successively by the British, the Saxons and the Danes. In 907 it was rebuilt and refortified by Ethelfleda, the warrior

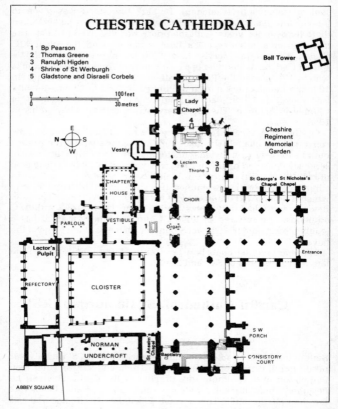

CHESTER CATHEDRAL

1 Bp Pearson
2 Thomas Greene
3 Ranulph Higden
4 Shrine of St Werburgh
5 Gladstone and Disraeli Corbels

Bell Tower

100 feet
30 metres

N—E—S—W

Lady Chapel

Cheshire Regiment Memorial Garden

Vestry

Lectern
Throne

St George's Chapel St Nicholas's Chapel

CHAPTER HOUSE

CHOIR

PARLOUR

VESTIBULE

Organ

Entrance

Lector's Pulpit

REFECTORY

CLOISTER

S W PORCH

NORMAN UNDERCROFT

St Anselm's Chapel

Baptistry

CONSISTORY COURT

ABBEY SQUARE

daughter of King Alfred and wife of Ethelred, Earl of Mercia. Soon after, a church was built on the site of the present cathedral, and the relics of St Werburgh, a Mercian princess and abbess who d c 700, were placed there to give it added sanctity. In 1092 it was refounded as a Benedictine abbey by Hugh Lupus, nephew of William the Conqueror and Earl of Chester, with the assistance of St Anselm, who came over from his own abbey of Bec in Normandy to take part in the work. The chief remains of this Norman abbey church are to be found on the N side. The rest of the cathedral, beginning with the Lady Chapel (1250–75), reflects successive building periods up to the 19C. The choir, largely the work of Edward I's military engineer, Richard of Chester, dates from c 1300; the arcades of the S transept and the S arcade of the nave from the mid 14C; the rest of the nave, the clerestory of the S transept and the top stages of the tower from the end of the 15C. The S front of the S transept is the work (1819–20) of the Chester architect Thomas Harrison. In 1868–76 Sir Gilbert Scott carried out a major restoration affecting much of the exterior and interior; his work includes the turrets on the central tower and W front, the pinnacles at the E end of the Lady Chapel and the flying buttresses on the S side.

Until the Reformation the abbey was in the diocese of Lichfield; but in 1541 Henry VIII converted the abbey church into the cathedral of the new diocese of Chester. The title 'Bishop of Chester' was often used at an earlier date, because for some years in the late 11C the Mercian see of Lichfield was transferred to Chester, with St John's Church (E of the city wall) being used as the cathedral.

Exterior. The W front, in spite of its fine Perp window, is somewhat lacking in dignity. On the S side, the enormous S transept has a war memorial on the W and the memorial garden to the Cheshire Regiment on the E. Worth searching for on the SE corner of the transept are the Victorian caricature corbels depicting Gladstone attacking the Church of Rome, and Disraeli defending the Crown of England. In the SE corner of the precinct is a free-standing bell-tower (1975), designed by George Pace; built of concrete with slate cladding, it is called the Addleshaw Tower, after Dean Addleshaw (1963–77). The best view of the E end, and of as much of the N side as is not concealed by the cloister and other buildings, is from the city wall.

Interior. Entrance is normally either from St Werburgh's Street, into the large S transept, or from Abbey Square and through the cloister on the N. From the W end of the *Nave*, raised a few steps above the rest of the pavement, there is a vista of great simplicity and beauty, enhanced by the warm red of the stone. The S arcade of the nave is Dec, and the N arcade late Perp. The place of a triforium is taken by a plain frieze; the clerestory is late Perp. At the bottom of the second clerestory window from the E on the N side is the 'Chester Imp', said to represent a man tied and bound, and placed there to discourage the Devil from entering the church. The glass in the W window (1961) is by W.T. Carter Shapland. At the W end of the late Perp S aisle, in the base of the unfinished SW tower, is the Consistory Court (1636). The

Chester Cathedral, corbel outside the S transept showing Disraeli as defender of the Church of England.

court of the bishop, presided over by the chancellor of the diocese, it was used for settling ecclesiastical disputes, and still retains its 17C panelled furnishings. The wall of the N aisle is Norman, now covered by mosaics by J.R. Clayton (1886) of scriptural scenes (Abraham, Moses, David and Elijah); and at its W end is the base of an unfinished Norman tower, now the Baptistry, with a 6C Venetian font placed here in 1885. From both ends of this aisle, doors (the E one Norman of c 1100) lead into the cloisters (see below).

The small *N Transept* was part of the original church and is thus the oldest part of the cathedral. Over the entrance is the organ loft, surmounted by Gilbert Scott's magnificent organ case (1876; organ rebuilt 1969). The windows and roof are Perp; the roof (1518–24) offers a fine display of Tudor heraldry (cleaned and redecorated 1969). In the centre of the transept is a monument (by Sir Arthur Blomfield, 1864), to Bp John Pearson (1673–83), a famous 17C theologian; and a mural tablet commemorates the artist Randolph Caldecott (1846–86), a native of Chester. A Norman archway on the E side opens into the Sacristy (Trans style), which replaces a Norman apse; above is a small row of triforium arches of the earliest period. In a niche in the E wall is the so-called 'Cobweb Picture'; about the size of a playing-card, it depicts the Virgin and Child, and was painted in the Tyrol in the early 19C on the 'net' of a species of caterpillar.

The *S Transept* (14C Dec, completed in 15C Perp) is remarkable for its huge size; including two aisles it is as large as the choir and nearly as large as the nave. The reason is that the monks of the 14C wished to extend their church, but could not touch the N transept without destroying their domestic buildings. From the early 16C until 1881 this transept was used as the parish church of St Oswald. The great S window (1887) is by Blomfield. There are four chapels along the E wall: colours of the Cheshire Regiment in the SE chapel (St Nicholas's) are said to have been used to cover General Wolfe's body at the battle for Quebec (1759); and the adjoining chapel (St George's) is that of the Cheshire Regiment. On the W wall of the transept is the RAF memorial, with a wooden propeller; and near it a carved stone (1980) in memory of Czechs who fought in World War II. In a case against the NW pier is the roll-of-honour of HMS *Chester*, which took part in the Battle of Jutland (1916). On the E side of this pier is a fine monument to Thomas Greene (d 1602), Mayor of Chester, and his two wives.

Above the entrance to the *Choir* is a large rood, designed by Giles Scott (1913). The choir was built in the 13 and 14C, principally by Richard of Chester; above is a beautiful triforium. The *Stalls (c 1390), with their spired canopies and lively misericords, are among the chief treasures of the cathedral; particularly noteworthy is the Tree of Jesse which decorates the end of the Dean's stall (formerly the Abbot's stall). The two large bronze candelabra were made in Rome in the 17C. The bishop's throne (1876) was designed by Sir Gilbert Scott. The S choir aisle was lengthened to the E about 1500; but its present apsidal end was the work of Scott. Its curious conical roof—a feature of the exterior as seen from the city wall—was designed by Scott from evidence provided by old masonry. Buried in this aisle is Ranulph Higden (d 1364), a monk at Chester and the author of many books including the *Polychronicon* (1352), a history of the world since the Creation. The gates of both choir aisles are of Spanish wrought-iron (1558). In the N choir aisle can be seen the base of a Norman column, and a capital which has been turned over and used as a foundation for later building. A band of dark marble in the pavement marks the line of the Norman apse. This aisle still keeps its prolongation of c 1500, now St Werburgh's Chapel. In the Lady Chapel (c 1250–75), reached from the N choir aisle, are the reconstructed stone fragments of St Werburgh's Shrine, which until the Reformation formed the base of the reliquary housing her remains. Noteworthy in this chapel are the three original ceiling *Bosses (recoloured 1960), particularly the delightful Madonna and Child which forms the central boss.

The *Cloisters* are reached through either of two doors from the nave N aisle. They were rebuilt c 1526 and restored by Giles Scott in 1911–13; they are thus considerably more recent than the conventual rooms that open off them. The windows on to the garden (1921–27) illustrate the calendar of the Church of England prayer book. Off the E walk, a graceful vestibule leads into the rectangular 13C Chapter House, which contains display cabinets of ancient cathedral books and a notable 13C cupboard. Also off the E walk are a slype (which probably led to the infirmary), and a staircase, lit by a 13C quatrefoil window, which would have led to the dormitory occupying the whole of the E upper floor. The wall of the S walk is partly Norman; the double arcade on the garden side marks the position of small compartments used by the monks for study. Along the W walk runs the 12C undercroft (monks' storeroom); part is now used as the cathedral workshop and part as a bookstall. In the N walk is the large Refectory (13C with 15C windows), now a cafeteria. Here a staircase leads to the *Pulpit from which the lector would read to the monks during meals; it is one of the only three such pulpits surviving in England (see also Beaulieu, above, and Shrewsbury Abbey, below). The fine hammerbeam roof is modern (1939). The large tapestry at the W end was woven at Mortlake c 1637 from one of the cartoons of the Acts of the Apostles designed by Raphael for the Sistine Chapel. It formerly hung behind the high altar. In the centre of the cloister garth was the water tank, supplied by pipe from Christleton 2 miles to the SE.

From the NW corner of the cloister there is an exit into Abbey Square, a charming precinct of mainly 18C houses. The Abbey Gateway is 14C. St Anselm's Chapel (adm. on request), reached from the square, lies between the W end of the nave and the conventual buildings. Dating from the 12C, it was the chapel of the abbot's lodging; its most notable feature is the plaster ceiling and oak screen from the time of Charles I.

Craswall Priory, Hereford and Worcester

Off minor road 12 miles N of Abergavenny.

One of the remotest monastic ruins in the whole of England and Wales, Craswall is hidden away in the Black Mountains, down an unmarked track 1 mile N of the village of Craswall. The priory was founded in 1222 by Roger de Lacy for monks of the austere Grandmontine Order. The ruins, overgrown and largely obliterated, reveal traces of an apsidal E end to the church, and a chapter house running N-S instead of the normal E-W.

Cwmhir Abbey, Powys

Ded: St Mary.

On minor road off A483, 6 miles N of Llandridod Wells.

Invisible from the road, the scanty ruins of Cwmhir lie in a beautiful pastoral setting in the winding valley of the Clywedog (*cwm hir* means 'long valley'). The abbey was founded in 1143 for Cistercian monks from Whitland, near Carmarthen, and a second foundation followed in 1176. It was also twice destroyed: in 1231 by Henry III; and in 1401 by Owain Glyndŵr, who is said to have suspected that the monks were Englishmen in disguise. At the Dissolution there were only three monks. Although after Henry III's destruction an ambitious rebuilding was planned, in fact the choir was never built, the transepts were left unfinished, and the nave (242ft long) was destroyed by Glyndŵr. Today's remains comprise little more than the foundations of the nave and some battered lower courses of its wall. By tradition, the body of Llywelyn ap Gruffyd ('Llewellyn the Last'), killed by the English in 1282 at Cilmeri a few miles to the S, was buried below the high altar, the position today being marked by a blackthorn, and by a stone slab with a Welsh inscription.

Cymer Abbey, Gwynedd

Ded: St Mary.

On E side of A470, 1½ miles N of Dolgellau.

The remains of Cymer (pronounced 'Kummer') lie among farm buildings and through a caravan site, on the E side of the Mawddach River. In 1199 a Cistercian house was founded here by monks from Cwmhir (see above), on a site whose name is in full *kymer deu dyfyr* ('meeting of the waters'). The ruins are mainly those of the abbey's never-completed 13C church, which is in plan a simple rectangle, with a nave and twin aisles, and a small 14C W tower. Surviving remains include the N nave arcade, three tall lancets at the E end, battered sedilia and a piscina in the S wall. The cloister foundations remain; of the domestic buildings, the refectory is S of the cloister, and something of the chapter house can be seen in the farm's yard. The farm is probably on the site of the guest-house, important at a site where travellers were often delayed by floods. The ruins are beautifully tended, and in spring are bright with daffodils.

Denbigh Friary, Clwyd

On NE side of Denbigh, at end of Abbey Road.

A house of Carmelites (White Friars) was founded at Denbigh c 1285, probably by Sir John Salusbury, a Crusader buried here in 1289. A good deal of the small church survives, notably the E end, which has a large window of c 1300, given new tracery in the early 15C. A door in the S wall led into the cloister, but this has long since disappeared; though part of the S range is incorporated into a private house. The friary was dissolved in 1538, and the deep well on the N side of the nave was dug at some subsequent date.

Ewenny Priory, Mid Glamorgan

Ded: St Michael.

Off B4524, 2 miles S of Bridgend.

At first sight, Ewenny looks more like a castle than a monastic foundation, as the lane leading to it skirts a battlemented curtain wall past a massively fortified gatehouse. It was founded by Maurice de Londres, a Norman knight with large estates in S Wales, in 1141 as a cell to the Benedictine abbey of Gloucester; the church, which became the priory church, had already been built c 1120 by Maurice's father, William de Londres (builder of Ogmore Castle nearby). The priory is a good example of early Norman building, part ecclesiastical and part defensive. The military aspect appears in the crenellation (at this period not mere ornament) of the strong precinct wall (12–13C)

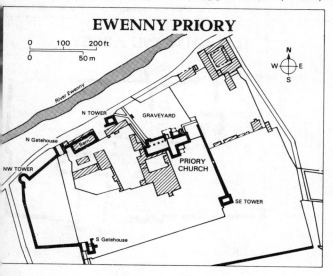

and in the gateways (c 1300), in both of which are loopholes for archers; the N gatehouse also has a portcullis.

The Church is in two parts: the nave, which is the parish church and was probably always parochial; and the chancel, now disused, which was monastic. The two parts are separated by a 13C stone rood-screen. The nave exhibits good Norman work in its arcade, in the sturdy arches of the crossing, and in the open wall arcade (late 12C) on the W of the S transept (only the foundations survive of the N transept). The nave was heightened and the central tower was built in the late 12C, and the N aisle, built at the same time, was rebuilt in the 16C and again (partly) in 1895. The font has a basin of c 1200, and under the E arch of the crossing there is a wooden screen of the 14–16C. In the surviving transept are the tomb of the founder (the inscription in Old French begins 'Ici gist Morice de Lundres le Fundur'), and various monuments and stonework fragments. Traces of the chapel (mid 12C) to the E of the now vanished N transept can be seen outside.

Apart from the church, most of the priory is in private hands and cannot be visited.

Haughmond Abbey, Shropshire

Ded: St John the Evangelist.

By B5062, 4 miles NE of Shrewsbury.

Haughmond stands on a 'shelf' on a steep, rocky escarpment above the Severn; and the awkward site has influenced both the overall layout, and the floor of the church, which is on no fewer than four different levels. The approach is also unusual: through a Tudor or Jacobean garden gate. The abbey was founded by William Fitzalan o

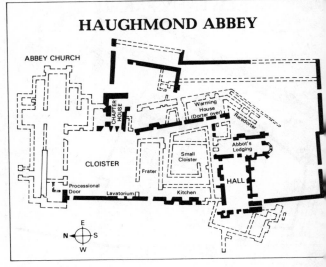

HAUGHMOND ABBEY

1135 for Augustinian canons; it was rebuilt towards the end of the 12C, at which time the church was much enlarged, and there was more rebuilding in the 14 and 15C. It was dissolved in 1539, and part of it was turned into a private mansion, which however burnt down, possibly in the Civil War.

The ruins are mainly of the domestic buildings, which were built round two cloisters instead of one, since the slope of the hill, rising steeply to the E, made it impossible to build E of the cloister in the usual way. Facing the entrance is the Tudor oriel window of the Abbot's Lodging, probably inserted shortly before the Dissolution; the rest of the lodging, and the great hall adjoining it on the W side (probably the infirmary hall), with its grand W window, are 14–15C. The site of the Kitchen, still with its two vast chimneys, extends N from here; and beyond are the sites of the Refectory and Cloister, of which virtually only the W walls survive. The Chapter House (12C), on the E side of the cloister, has a superb triple-arched ˙façade; the timber ceiling and Tudor windows at its E end were put in after the Dissolution, when the abbey became a mansion. The Church (N of the cloister) is entered through a 12C processional doorway, with figures of St Peter and St Paul on either side. There is a small museum on the site, and a reputed 'monks' well' just E of the entrance.

Hereford Cathedral

Ded: St Mary the Virgin and St Ethelbert the King.

Though Hereford is not among the most spectacular of cathedrals, it has its own quiet beauty. Built in many architectural styles, it contains unusual treasures, notably the 13C Mappa Mundi and a medieval chained library (for both, see below). In 1976 Hereford celebrated 1,300 years as a diocese; and the cathedral is one of the homes of the annual Three Choirs Festival, along with Worcester and Gloucester Cathedrals (see above).

History. Towards the end of the 7C the see of Hereford was detached from that of Lichfield, the first bishop, Putta, being appointed in 676. In 794 King Ethelbert of East Anglia, on his way to marry the daughter of King Offa of Mercia, was murdered by Offa near Hereford; and legend has it that his ghost demanded burial in the town. Miracles occurred at his tomb and Ethelbert was canonized; in 825 what was probably the first stone church on the site was built over the tomb, followed by another church built by Athelstan and probably destroyed when the Welsh burnt the town in 1055. The first Norman bishop, Robert de Losinga, began to rebuild in 1079. Losinga's church was largely obliterated by the work of Bp Reynelm (1107–15), who is called on his tomb 'founder of the church'—an excessive claim, in view of the 11C character of parts of the E end. During King Stephen's reign (1139) supporters of Queen Matilda captured the cathedral and used the tower for hurling missiles at the castle, forcing Stephen's followers to surrender. Bp Robert de Béthune (1131–48) completed the nave and restored the choir; and Bp William de Vere (1186–99) radically altered the E end and probably began the Lady Chapel (completed c 1220), beneath which was constructed a spacious crypt. Bp Peter of Aquablanca (also known as Peter of Savoy, d 1268) built

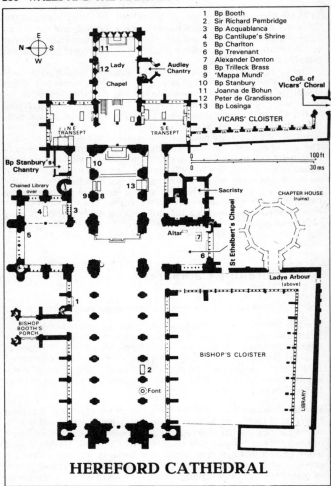

1 Bp Booth
2 Sir Richard Pembridge
3 Bp Acquablanca
4 Bp Cantilupe's Shrine
5 Bp Charlton
6 Bp Trevenant
7 Alexander Denton
8 Bp Trilleck Brass
9 'Mappa Mundi'
10 Bp Stanbury
11 Joanna de Bohun
12 Peter de Grandisson
13 Bp Losinga

Audley Chantry

Lady Chapel

Coll. of Vicars' Choral

VICARS' CLOISTER

N E TRANSEPT

S E TRANSEPT

Bp Stanbury's Chantry

Chained Library over

Sacristy

CHAPTER HOUSE (ruins)

Altar

St Ethelbert's Chapel

Ladye Arbour (above)

BISHOP'S CLOISTER

BISHOP BOOTH'S PORCH

Font

LIBRARY

0   100 ft
0   30 ms

HEREFORD CATHEDRAL

the N transept c 1260. A favourite of Henry III, he was so unpopular in Hereford that the local citizens sided with Simon de Montfort against him, and in 1263 expelled him from his own cathedral. Another 13C bishop, Thomas Cantilupe (1275–82), was canonized in 1320, and his miracle-working shrine at Hereford became a centre of pilgrimage. The inner N porch was added by Bp Swinfield (1283–1316); the central tower (165ft), built on Norman piers and arches, and the chapter house are due to Bp Adam of Orleton (1317–27); and Bp Booth (1516–35) added the outer N porch. During the Civil War the cathedral was ransacked by Cromwell's troops, and when in 1645 Dean Croft preached a sermon against their sacrilege, he was only saved from being shot on the spot by the intervention of an officer.

The fall of the W tower in 1786 gave the architect James Wyatt the chance to pull down two W bays, destroying much Norman work in the nave, and build a new W front after his own idea of Gothic. In 1908 Wyatt's W front was replaced by a new 14C-style façade by J. Oldrid Scott. The E end and crossing were restored in 1841 and the whole building in 1856–63; in 1967 Sir Gilbert Scott's ornate choir screen of 1862 was removed, opening up the whole church.

Exterior. The best view is from the NE, taking in the Lady Chapel, the choir clerestory, Peter of Aquablanca's N transept, and the Dec Gothic N choir aisle and NE transept. On the W front, the N medallion shows Dean Croft menaced by Cromwell's soldiers.

Interior. The usual entrance is through the imposing Bp Booth's Porch (on the N side), decorated with small figures round the arch. The 12C *Nave*, one of the richest Norman designs in England, is notable for its massive piers, its main arches with their rich carvings and mouldings, and the arches that support the tower. The present triforium, clerestory and wooden vaulting are the work of Wyatt (1788). The 12C sculptured font rests on a 14C pedestal. Near the font is the early 16C pulpit from which Dean Croft berated the soldiers. The aisles are late Dec on Norman lower courses. In the N aisle is a monument to Bp Booth (d 1535) complete with its original iron grille; and in the S aisle one to Sir Richard Pembridge (d 1375), who fought at Poitiers in 1356, has a curious addition in the form of a new right leg.

The *N Transept* was built c 1260 by Peter of Aquablanca, probably to house his own exquisitely arched and pinnacled tomb. Here too is the Shrine of St Thomas Cantilupe (d 1282), canonized in 1320, notable for its naturalistic foliage and figures of mourning knights. Under the great window, one of the largest examples of Geometrical tracery in England, is the canopied tomb of Bp Thomas Charlton (d 1344). The *S Transept* retains its Norman character, much of it probably being Robert de Losinga's work (1079) and thus the oldest part of the cathedral. On the wall is a triptych of the S German school (c 1530). Bp Trevenant (d 1404), who made the Perp alterations in this transept, lies under the S window. On the W side there is a fireplace of probably Norman origin but with 18C alterations, and beside it are a few 14C stalls with their original canopies. In the corner of the transept is the Denton tomb, with coloured effigies of Alexander Denton (d 1577) and of his first wife and child. Hung in the Norman arcading on the E side are three tapestries designed by John Piper and woven in Namibia, on the theme of the Tree: Adam and Eve, the Crucifixion, and the Tree of Life. Until 1843, the Tower Lantern, with its shafts and remarkable gratings, was hidden by a 15C roof.

The noble *Choir*, dedicated in 1110, has a rich Norman triforium below a graceful EE clerestory, which, like the vaulting, dates from the 13C. The main arches are supported by massive piers, and the capitals of the semi-detached shafts are elaborately carved. At the E end, the grand Norman arch, surmounted by a blind arcade, originally gave access to the centremost of three apses, which were replaced, by transepts and Lady Chapel, over a long period (c 1190–1370). In the axis of this arch now rises a pier of the processional aisle which was an important part of Bp de Vere's alterations of 1186–99. The stalls (with carved animals) and bishop's throne are

Hereford Cathedral, part of the 13C Mappa Mundi (map of the world), showing the countries of Asia.

14C. A marble slab opposite the throne commemorates St Ethelbert, and there is a 14C statue of the saint on the S side of the sanctuary. The 12C wooden chair to the left of the altar is said to have been used by King Stephen in 1138; and on the floor near by (under carpet) is a good brass to Bp Trilleck (d 1360). The organ (1893), which includes a few pipes from the organ of 1676, was rebuilt in 1977–78 with money donated by the Bulmer's cider firm.

In the N Choir Aisle hangs the famous *Mappa Mundi*, drawn on vellum c 1290 by Richard of Haldingham, a prebendary of the cathedral. This is a typical medieval map, with Jerusalem in the centre, the Day of Judgement at the top, and the continents (Asia top, Europe left, Africa right) liberally decorated with Biblical scenes and mythical men and beasts. It is likely that it was used for teaching purposes. Opening from the aisle is the Perp *Chantry of Bp Stanbury (d 1474), with rich fan vaulting and heraldry; and across the aisle is his alabaster tomb. In the S Choir Aisle are several 14C effigies of early bishops.

The *Chained Library* (open weekdays 10.30–12.30, 14.00–16.00 summer; 11.00–11.30, 15.00–15.30 winter; fee), reached by a stairway opposite the Mappa Mundi, occupies a room built for muniments by

Bp Aquablanca (c 1260), and giving a view down into the N transept. With almost 1,450 chained books, the collection is the largest in the world. Among the MSS the oldest (7C) is two pages of St Matthew's Gospel. There are 227 MS volumes from the 8C onwards, including the Four gospels (8C); the Hereford Breviary (1265–70), with music, probably an original service book of the cathedral, found in a London shop in the 19C; and the 15C Cider Bible, in which the translator wrote 'wyn ne sidir' instead of the usual translation 'strong drink'.

Between c 1190 and 1370 the Norman apsidal chapels were replaced by the E Transepts. The main work dates from 1290, but the SE transept, built on cheaper lines, probably due to a lack of craftsmen after the Black Death, was not carried out until the 1360s. This transept contains a bust by Roubiliac, probably of James Thomas (d 1757); and there are several good brasses on the walls.

The *Lady Chapel* (1220) is a beautiful example of EE work, especially the clustered window shafts and the E end with its five elegant lancets (restored). On the S side is the 15C tomb of Precentor Swinfield, carved with his rebus of swine; and behind a tall screen of painted stone is the *Audley Chantry*. Edmund Audley (d 1524) was Bp of Hereford in 1492–1503; he then became Bp of Salisbury, and is buried in a similar chantry chapel there (see above). On the N side are two fine effigy tombs: Joanna de Bohun, Countess of Hereford (d 1327); and Sir Peter de Grandisson (d 1358), unusual in having a dog looking alertly at its master, instead of lying passive at his feet.

Below the Lady Chapel is the vaulted *Crypt*, which was opened in 1980 as the cathedral Treasury (open 10.30–12.30, 14.00–16.00 summer; 10.45–11.15, 14.45–15.15 winter; fee). This was the last crypt to be built in any English cathedral (c 1220) and is in an elegant EE style, as opposed to the usual ponderous Norman. Until the 19C it was used as a charnel-house for bones dug up in the graveyard near by. At the W end is the large tomb of Andrew Jones (d 1497), a prominent cider maker, and his wife. The altar and reredos (1920) are a World War I memorial.

A covered walk with a carved oak roof (the Vicars' Cloister) leads from the SE transept to the College of Vicars Choral, built round a quadrangle (1475). A second cloister, with two walks (Perp), known as the Bishop's Cloister, is entered from the S side of the nave. Off the E walk are the remains of the *Chapter House* (14C); unusual in being ten-sided, it was stripped of its lead roof in the Civil War (the lead was made into bullets) and used as a quarry in the SE 18C. The W walk was demolished in 1760; part was rebuilt in 1897 with two storeys. (Hereford was not a monastic foundation, and so there were never any domestic buildings opening off the cloister.)

The *Bishop's Palace* (no adm.) stands between the cathedral and the River Wye. A tablet on the wall of the bishop's garden (in Gwynne Street) marks the supposed birthplace of Nell Gwynne (1650–87), Charles II's favourite mistress. Immediately E of the cathedral is the Cathedral School, which dates back to 1381 and still educates the cathedral choristers.

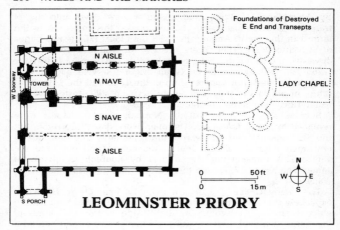

Foundations of Destroyed
E End and Transepts

N AISLE

N NAVE

TOWER

LADY CHAPEL

S NAVE

S AISLE

S PORCH

0   50 ft
0   15 m

LEOMINSTER PRIORY

Leominster Priory, Hereford and Worcester

Ded: St Peter and St Paul.

The present magnificent priory church, which illustrates every architectural style from Norman to Perp, stands on a site that has been Christian for more than 1,300 years. In 660 King Merewald of Mercia founded a priory here, appointing Ealfred, a Northumbrian missionary, its first abbot. According to legend, Ealfred tamed a ferocious lion by offering it bread, and took this as a good omen for his work among the savage pagans. Hence one explanation for the town's name: Leonis Monasterium ('monastery of the lion'). It seems more likely, however, that it takes its name from Leofric, Earl of Mercia, who founded a nunnery here in the 11C, since in Domesday Book it appears as Leofminstre.

In the 12C the original priory was succeeded by a Benedictine priory, a cell of Reading Abbey (see above); of the original Norman church, consecrated in 1130, there remain the North Nave with its massive pillars, and the superb W Doorway (best seen from outside) under the tower, very slightly pointed and with fine carvings on the capitals (one on the N side, of a monk and a lion, may illustrate the story of St Ealfred). The wall at the W end of the main S Nave is the original wall of the S aisle of the Norman church; on the floor, immediately below this wall, are some 14C tiles. The main nave, added in 1239 as the parish church (on the site of the Norman S aisle), has a beautiful Perp window, 45ft high. The S aisle was built c 1340 and has ball-flower ornamentation—a style which also appears on the outside of the church. The tower is of three periods: Norman 12C, Perp 14C, and 19C (battlements and pinnacles added). When the priory was suppressed in 1539, the whole E end and the central tower were demolished; thus the present E end is little more than half-way down the original church, on the W side of the crossing. In 1699 the church was almost totally destroyed by fire; in 1705 it was partly rebuilt, and the work was completed in 1872–79 by Sir Gilbert Scott. There was further restoration in 1921–23 and 1948–50. In the chapel at the E end of the S aisle are a pre-Reformation silver chalice, an old Leominster seal, and a piscina of c 1239 surrounded by three expressive heads. In the N aisle is a ducking stool, last used in 1809 for submerging one of the local scolds in the river.

The cloister and domestic buildings lay on the N side of the church. Part of the Old Priory Hospital on this side may have been the infirmary, or possibly the reredorter.

Llandaff Cathedral, S Glamorgan

Ded: St Peter and St Teilo.

About two miles NW of Cardiff city centre, Llandaff lies just above the River Taff, from which it gets its name. Largely rebuilt after damage in World War II, it is a fascinatingly varied cathedral, dominated inside by Epstein's majestic figure of Christ.

History. That this was once a pagan site is known from the evidence of pre-Christian, probably Romano-British, burials discovered under the W part of the cathedral. Tradition connects the founding of the church with the ministry of St Dyfrig (early 6C) and the mission from W Wales of St Teilo (mid 6C), and it is known that a pre-Norman church stood here, or near here. Another saint associated with Teilo and Dyfrig was Euddogwy, the trio being the reason for the three mitres on the present coat of arms of the see. The existing church was begun c 1120 by Bp Urban, who, though probably a Welshman,

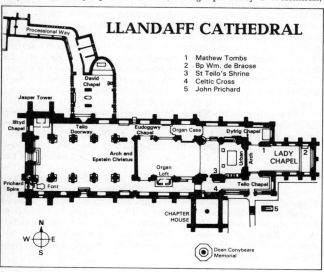

LLANDAFF CATHEDRAL

1 Mathew Tombs
2 Bp Wm. de Braose
3 St Teilo's Shrine
4 Celtic Cross
5 John Prichard

Processional Way

David Chapel

Jasper Tower

Illtyd Chapel

Teilo Doorway

Eudoggwy Chapel

Organ Case

Dyfrig Chapel

Arch and Epstein Christus

Organ Loft

Urban Arch

LADY CHAPEL

Prichard Spire

Font

Teilo Chapel

CHAPTER HOUSE

Dean Conybeare Memorial

N W E S

would have been appointed by the Normans. Of this early church the chief remains are the Norman arch dividing the presbytery from the Lady Chapel and some traces of blocked windows in the S wall of the presbytery. It seems that the completion of the nave was delayed by some 50 years, for the N and S doorways (perhaps no longer *in situ*) date from c 1170. Two events of the 12C may be mentioned: the death of the historian Geoffrey of Monmouth at Llandaff in 1154; and the visit in 1188 by Abp Baldwin of Canterbury, accompanied by Giraldus Cambrensis, preaching the Third Crusade (the next recorded visit by an Archbishop of Canterbury was that of Abp Temple in 1907, followed by Abp Ramsey in 1972).

The present nave and chancel arcades, as well as the W front, which was flanked by EE towers, date from the earlier 13C, and the chapter house was completed in 1250. In 1266 the cathedral was the scene of a great dedication service, coinciding with the enthronement of Bp William de Braose, during whose time the Lady Chapel was added in Geometric style. During the 14C the nave walls and aisles, which on the N had apparently begun to lean outwards, were rebuilt, and large windows with pointed heads were inserted. The presbytery was also remodelled by the cutting of arches through Urban's outer walls and windows, and the medieval history of the fabric closed with the rebuilding of the NW tower by Jasper Tudor (d 1495), uncle of King Henry VII (Henry Tudor).

There followed nearly 300 years of neglect. The building was already in dangerous decay by 1575; Cromwell's soldiers used the nave as a tavern and post-office, and the font as a pig trough, and burnt the cathedral's books at a formal ceremony at Cardiff Castle; after storms in 1703 and 1723 the SW tower collapsed and the nave roof fell in; and in the 18C 'restoration' took the strange form of an Italian temple, built within the walls by John Wood, better known for his work at Bath.

Real restoration began in 1835, when Precentor Douglas devoted two years of his stipend to this purpose. Later years saw the removal of Wood's temple (all that remains are the screens at the N and S entrances to the Lady Chapel, and two urns outside the NW of the cathedral); the restoration of the Lady Chapel, presbytery, choir and part of the nave; and the reopening of all these parts for divine service in 1857. Much of the later restoration was under the care of John Prichard, son of a priest of the cathedral and a pupil of the Gothic Revival architect Augustus Welby Pugin (1812–52). Prichard rebuilt the SW tower, gave the chapter house its distinctive roof, added the row of sovereigns' heads (S wall; modern heads N wall), and carved four Evangelists on the E face of the tower. It was Prichard's partner, J.B. Seddon, who brought in the Pre-Raphaelite work in glass, carving and painting. By refounding the Cathedral School in 1880, Dean Vaughan completed the restoration of the choral services, which had declined in the 16C and were abandoned entirely in the early 18C.

In 1941 a German landmine fell near the S wall of the cathedral, destroying virtually the whole of the previous century's work (Llandaff was, next to Coventry, the worst damaged of Britain's cathedrals). Restoration, completed in 1960, was largely by George Pace, who added the parabolic arch at the entrance to the choir, the Welch Regiment Memorial Chapel (David Chapel), and the Processional Way which passes through this chapel and leads from the vestries to the N aisle.

Exterior. Llandaff is unique among British cathedrals in having no transepts, and the absence of a triforium is also remarkable in so early a building. Externally the most notable feature is the gracefully irregular W front with its 13C centre. The curious pendent tympanum of the doorway (there never was a central shaft) has an original statue (St Dyfrig or St Teilo), and in the apex of the gable there is a Christ in Majesty. The S doorway of the nave (c 1170) is a rich example of Norman Trans work. Jasper Tudor's Perp NW tower has 19C pinnacles and elaborately panelled battlements. The SW tower and spire, rebuilt from Prichard's designs of 1869 and bearing figures of saints and clerics, resemble those found in southern Normandy. Prichard and his father are buried in the churchyard near the SE door.

Interior. This is immediately striking, the dominant feature being Pace's concrete arch, surmounted by a cylindrical organ case (with gilded Pre-Raphaelite figures, formerly in the niches and canopies of the pre-war choir stalls) bearing Jacob Epstein's huge Christus in unpolished aluminium. The effect is to separate nave and choir while not interfering with the lower-level vista. The long arcades of the *Nave* and *Choir*, with foliated capitals, are 13C; and the flat-panelled ceiling is modern, the hardwood being from Central Africa and Malaya. At the NW corner of the nave is the Illtyd Chapel, dedicated to the fallen of the 53rd (Welsh) Infantry Division. The Rossetti Triptych (1846–64) here, which formed the reredos of the high altar until 1939, illustrates the Seed of David; Rossetti's models were the poet Swinburne, the artist Burne-Jones, and the craftsman-philosopher William Morris and his wife. The font, at the SW corner of the nave, is by Alan Durst (1952) and depicts Man's fall, Christ's redemption, and scenes from the lives of St Dyfrig and St Teilo. Most of the windows in the S aisle are Pre-Raphaelite, but the small panels in the second window are English 17C glass. Above the S door hangs a Madonna and Child attributed to the 17C Spanish artist Murillo. In the S Presbytery Aisle a 10C Celtic Cross is the only relic of the pre-Norman church. Hidden at the time of the Commonwealth, it was found in 1870 in the garden of the Bishop's Palace. The Teilo Chapel, at the E end of the S aisle, contains an alabaster figure of Lady Audley (? early 15C).

The *Lady Chapel* (c 1287), finely proportioned and with lovely vaulting, contains in its NE corner the tomb of the builder, Bp William de Braose. The E window tracery is 19C, and the glass is modern. In the niches of the 15C reredos are 12 bronze replicas of wild flowers named in Welsh in honour of Our Lady; they were designed in 1965 by Frank Roper. The richly carved and strangely flattened Urban Arch dividing the Lady Chapel from the Presbytery is a remnant of Bp Urban's church of c 1120. On the S side of the presbytery, on the site of St Teilo's shrine, is a 13C effigy of the saint. The silver-gilt shrine, a centre of pilgrimage, stood here until the Reformation when the canons dismantled it rather than see it destroyed; the various pieces soon disappeared. Note the remains of the old Norman window on the S wall. On either side of the altar are heavy 17C Florentine candlesticks, and the windows above the Urban Arch contain stained glass by John Piper and Patrick Reyntiens (1960; see also Coventry Cathedral, above). In the Choir the bishop's throne and the stalls are 19C work (restored 1960).

The *Dyfrig Chapel*, the E end of the N aisle, is so called because Urban is said to have buried the saint's bones here in an attempt to boost his cathedral's reputation. The chapel contains the badly broken 14C reredos (originally three-tiered), removed from its place behind the high altar during the 19C restoration, and, to its S, the tombs of Sir David Mathew, standard-bearer to King Edward IV at the battle of Towton in 1461, and of Sir Christopher Mathew (d 1500). The Mathew family had the right of burial in this N aisle until the 18C, when they failed to continue to maintain the roof. Six porcelain panels on the W organ case were designed by Burne-Jones and are from the Della Robbia pottery at Birkenhead; the model was Elizabeth Siddal, wife of Rossetti and inspiration to the Pre-Raphaelites. In 1980 the chapel was restored and the memorial screen commemorating Abp Glyn Simon (d 1971) erected. The brightly coloured hanging was designed and worked by Barbara Dawson. W of the organ case is the Euddogwy Chapel, commemorating the third saint traditionally associated with the founding of the cathedral and now the memorial chapel of the 614 RAF Auxiliary Squadron. Here, opposite a painting of the Assumption (15C, on board), is the marble monument of Dean Vaughan (d 1897) by Goscombe John. Further W, on the S side of the N aisle, a modern pulpit commemorates Abp John Morgan (d 1957), 4th Abp of Wales. Below it is another Mathew tomb (Sir William and his wife, 1526).

The Norman Teilo Doorway leads into Pace's *David Chapel* (1956), the memorial chapel of the Welch Regiment, with furnishings that are gifts from Commonwealth regiments (in 1969 the Welch Regiment was amalgamated with the South Wales Borderers to form the Royal Regiment of Wales). In the Processional Way (1956) there hang four medieval gargoyles, rescued from the damage caused by the 1941 landmine.

The early 14C *Chapter House*, entered from the S presbytery aisle, is a solidly vaulted room, only about 20ft square, supported on a central column. Above is another small room, formerly the museum, now used as a storeroom.

On the green immediately S of the cathedral are a restored Cross and the remains of a 13C Bell-tower; traditionally Exeter's bell 'Great Peter' came from here (see above). On the E an attractive garden (1972) is surrounded by fragments of the medieval Bishop's Palace, destroyed by Owain Glyndŵr in the 15C.

Llanthony Priory, Gwent

On B4423, 9 miles N of Abergavenny.

Standing in the beautiful valley of the Afon Honddu, with a backcloth of majestic hills, Llanthony was founded c 1100 by William de Lacy on the site of a chapel dedicated to St David. In 1103 he was joined by a priest called Ersinius, formerly chaplain to Queen Matilda of England; the two men and their followers then built a church, which became the centre of a community of Augustinian canons. During the 12C the priory was harassed by the Welsh, and the monks migrated first to Hereford and then to Gloucester, where they founded a daughter priory known as 'Lantonia Secunda'. In 1175, with the

Llanthony Priory, the remains of the nave arcading. (K. Spence)

coming of more settled times to Wales, the community returned to 'Lantonia Prima', where they built a new church, the ruins of which are those we see today. Of the church, 212ft long, the noble W front, with its twin towers, and parts of the nave, transepts, central tower and choir remain. The style is plain and severe early Trans, combined with EE. There was no triforium; doorways rather than arches lead from the aisles to the transepts; and there is in general a sparing use of capitals and correspondingly frequent use of continuous mouldings. Of the monastic buildings, to the S of the church, the best preserved is the slype to the cemetery, which is still vaulted; the remains of the prior's house on the W side of the cloister are now incorporated in a hotel, as is the SW tower.

The priory was dissolved in 1538 and fell into neglect. In the 18C it was bought by a Brecon landowner, who converted the SW tower into a shooting lodge. In 1807 the estate was bought by the author Walter Savage Landor, who was reduced to near-bankruptcy by his ambitious plans for restoring the priory and improving the neighbourhood.

At Capel-y-Ffyn, 3 miles to the N, are the remains of 'Lantonia Tertia', a Victorian church and monastery built c 1870 by the self-styled 'Father' Ignatius Lyne. In the 1920s the buildings were occupied by Eric Gill, the pioneer of lettering design, and a community of artists, who decorated the roof beams and other areas with painting and lettering.

Margam Abbey, W Glamorgan

Ded: St Mary.

Off A48, near M4 Junction 38.

The abbey was a Cistercian house, founded in 1147 by Robert, Earl of Gloucester, near the site of a long-vanished Celtic monastery. The greater part of the nave (115ft long) of the original abbey church survives, and is today used as the parish church. The lower part of the W front with its deeply recessed doorway, the plain and massive arcades, and perhaps the groining of the aisles, date from the 12C. The twin Italianate campaniles were added in 1808. The windows at the W end contain glass by William Morris, and in the S aisle there is a group of alabaster tombs of the Mansel family, who bought the abbey estate at the Dissolution. Little survives of the monastic buildings, apart from the beautiful polygonal chapter house, which still stands to above-window level, with a central column up to 20ft. Where the S side of the cloister once stood is now an orangery, which provides an audio-visual display on the history of the abbey.

Beside the church is a small museum (Welsh Office), containing an important collection of inscribed and sculptured stones, mostly from the neighbourhood of Margam. These include a Roman milestone from Port Talbot, with a Latin inscription on one face and an early Christian one on the other; and several pre-Norman crosses, including the 9C 'wheel-cross' of Cynfelyn, richly decorated and bearing representations of the Virgin and St John, and among the finest of its kind in existence.

On a spur above the church is a ruined 15C chapel known as Capel Mair ('Mary's Chapel'), which may either have been a private oratory for the Cistercians, or kept for lay worship. Below the chapel is a secluded pool which was the monks' fishpond.

Monkton Priory, Dyfed

On W outskirts of Pembroke, ½ mile W of the castle.

The priory church stands on a hill, with a fine view across a small valley to the castle. The priory was founded in 1098 for Benedictine monks by Arnulf de Montgomery; originally a cell of Sées in Normandy, it was given to St Albans in 1473. The church, which lay in ruins for many years until a restoration in 1878–87, has a long, narrow barrel-vaulted nave; the monastic chancel, though part of the original structure, was recast in the 14C. The detached chapel to the N is apparently contemporary. Under the tower is the altar-tomb of Sir Francis Meyrick (d 1603), the upper part in a style which suggests Italian Renaissance influence. On the exterior, the tower is of the local fortified type. In the gable above the E window there is a decorated niche with a headless figure. From traces of two small half-blocked windows on the N exterior of the nave, it has been suggested that the masonry incorporates the S wall of a pre-Norman church.

Neath Abbey, W Glamorgan

Ded: St Mary.

At end of Monastery Road, in Neath Abbey village.

Hemmed in by houses and industry, with a canal to the S and a railway to the N, the impressive ruins of Neath manage to preserve a sense of grandeur among the surrounding grime. The abbey was founded by Richard de Granville in 1130, on land taken from the Welsh, beside the River Neath or Nedd (the name means 'sparkling stream'). It was colonized by a community of Savigniac monks. The monastery became prosperous, mainly by trading in wool and hides; though it was in continual dispute with Margam Abbey (see above), only 8 miles away, over fisheries, the right to wrecks, and the pasturage of sheep. The wealth it acquired during the 13C was used to build the present church (1280–1330); but it reached its zenith at the beginning of the 16C under its last abbot, Leyshon Thomas, when

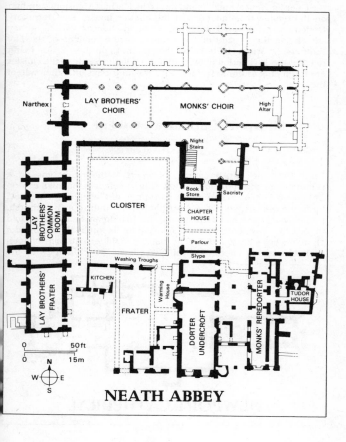

NEATH ABBEY

a Welsh poet called it 'the admiration of England, the lamp of France and Ireland', and the antiquary John Leland described it as 'the fairest abbey in all Wales'. Dissolved in 1539, Neath was bought in the late 16C by Sir John Herbert, who converted the abbot's house into a country mansion. With the rapid industrial development of the 18C the abbey was used as a forge for copper-smelting, while the decayed Herbert mansion housed the workmen.

Of the abbey Church, little remains except the outer walls of the nave and part of the W front. It comprised a nave of seven bays and two aisles, the five W bays forming the lay brothers' church, and a presbytery of three bays; in the centre of the church was the monks' choir and presbytery screened off from the rest of the building. The transepts were each of two bays with two chapels, and an ambulatory with chapels opening off it ran round behind the high altar. In the S Transept is a wall tablet to Mr Glen Taylor, who led the excavations in 1923–35, during which period 4,000 tons of debris were removed; and in this transept can be seen two altars, a piscina and (on the W side) the night-stairs. To the S, beyond the sacristy, is what little remains of the Chapter House, and beyond this is the Herbert Mansion, standing on the medieval foundations of the abbot's house. The Dormitory Undercroft, with good medieval vaulting, houses various abbey stones. On the W side of the cloister are the remains of the Lay Brothers' Quarters (1170–1220), the chimneys on their E side being relics of the 18C period of industrial use. On the S side of the cloister are fragments of the Refectory, with washing-bays on either side of the entrance doorway.

Newport Cathedral, Gwent

Ded: St Woolos.

Until 1921 the parish church, Newport Cathedral stands on a commanding site at the top of Stow Hill, ¾ mile S of the town centre. The name Woolos is an English corruption of Gwynllyw, a local 6C lord who was converted to Christianity and built the first church, probably of wattle and daub, on the site. In a dream he had been told to look for a white ox with a black spot on its forehead and build a church where he found it. The narrow Galilee (entrance chapel) probably stands on the site of Gwynllyw's 6C church, with the

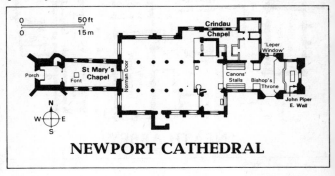

NEWPORT CATHEDRAL

Norman church to the E; in the 15C, after destruction by Owain Glyndŵr, the N and S aisles were rebuilt and the tower was added. Thorough restorations were carried out in 1853 and 1913. With the creation of the Diocese of Monmouth in 1921 the church became a pro-cathedral, and in 1949 it was raised to full cathedral status. In the 1960s a new and enlarged E end was built to designs by Alban Caröe.

The cathedral is entered through a door in the 15C W tower; the headless statue above the door is supposed to be that of Jasper Tudor (d 1495), uncle of King Henry VII and reputed builder of part of the tower. E of the tower is the long and narrow St Mary's Chapel (see above), from which a superb *Norman Door leads into the main body of the church. The chapel's E wall is 12C and the other walls are 13C; the columns supporting the Norman arch, with their Corinthian capitals recarved by the Normans, are thought to have come from the Roman town of Caerleon near by. The Nave (12C, with 15C aisles) is typically Norman, with a clerestory of narrow round-headed windows, formerly external but now internal. The new Chancel terminates in a striking E wall designed by John Piper, consisting of marbling painted on canvas, surrounding a circular window of Norman inspiration. The mural painting was carried out by the scenery painters of the Royal Opera House, Covent Garden. The N wall of the chancel incorporates a 15C traceried window known as the 'leper window'. The bishop's throne and canons' stalls came from the workshop of Robert Thompson, the Yorkshire woodcarver who signed his creations with the carving of a wooden mouse. The cathedral has the only peal of 12 bells in Wales.

Norton Priory, Cheshire

In Warrington Road, Runcorn.

In 1134 a priory of Augustinian canons was founded at Norton. Their original small aisleless church and cloister were greatly expanded at the end of the 12C; the priory prospered, due largely to its possession of the 'Holy Cross of Norton', and in 1391 it was raised to abbey status. It was dissolved in 1536; a Tudor mansion was built on the site of the W range (the abbot's lodging), succeeded by a Georgian country house in the 18C. In 1928 this was demolished and the site became derelict. Excavation began in 1970 under the auspices of the Runcorn Development Corporation, and during the 1970s the foundations were revealed, showing the outlines of the phases of church building, and the cloister with chapter house, dorter and reredorter in the E range, frater in the S range, and undercroft (surviving from the Tudor and Georgian houses) along the W side. The surviving masonry includes an exceptionally fine Norman doorway of c 1180, and an arcaded passageway; and quantities of patterned tiles from both the 14 and 15C have been uncovered.

Penmon Priory, Anglesey

Ded: St Seiriol.

3 miles NE of Beaumaris.

A priory was founded here, at the easternmost corner of Anglesey, by St Seiriol in the 6C. The church was rebuilt 1120–70, and in 1237 Llywelyn the Great granted the monastery and its property to the prior and canons of Priestholm (Puffin Island), off the Penmon peninsula, who then apparently moved to Penmon, reorganizing the community as Augustinian canons. The church and domestic buildings are now separate, the former serving as the parish church, and the latter being in the care of the DoE. The nave of the Church is the oldest part (c 1140); the crossing and S transept (the latter with fine chevron-moulded arcading) are of 1160–70; and the choir is a rebuilding of c 1220–40, coinciding with the arrival of the canons from Priestholm. There is a fine Norman pillar piscina in the nave. The base of a pre-Norman cross (c 1000) has been converted into a font, and another cross of the same period stands in the S transept.

Immediately S of the choir is the site of a small Cloister, the W side of which was the prior's house, now much altered and privately occupied. S of the cloister are the domestic buildings, a three-storey 13C wing containing the refectory, with a cellar below and dormitory above. Adjoining on the E is an early 16C addition, which contained the warming-room on the ground floor and the kitchen above.

By the E entrance to the priory is a large square Dovecote of c 1600, with a domed roof and open cupola, containing nearly 1,000 nests. A path E of the church leads N to St Seiriol's Well, possibly at the site of the 6C priory. The upper part of the small building covering the well seems to be 18C, but the much older lower part may incorporate something of the original chapel. The adjacent foundations of an oval hut may be those of the saint's cell.

St Asaph Cathedral, Clwyd

This little town of approximately 4,000 inhabitants, on a ridge between two rivers, is the second smallest city in Britain after St Davids, and its cathedral is the smallest of the ancient cathedrals (182ft by 65ft, and 108ft across the transepts). Yet for all its parish-church dimensions, the plain exterior and solid central tower give it a quiet dignity.

History. The town grew round a cathedral and monastery founded in 560 by St Cyndeyrn or Kentigern (also known as 'St Mungo' and the founder of the first church on the site of Glasgow Cathedral). His successor as bishop c 570 was Asaph, who held an administrative post at the monastery. In its early days the place was known as Llanelwy (the religious enclosure beside the Elwy river), the English name St Asaph not being recorded before 1100; it is still called Llanelwy in Welsh. There are few records of any bishop between St Asaph in the 6C and Bp Gilbert in 1143. The most distinguished of the later bishops was William Morgan (1601–04), who in 1588 completed the first translation of the Bible into Welsh; on the N side of the cathedral is a monument to him and his fellow translators. In 1282 the cathedral was burnt down by English troops; Edward I wished to rebuild it at Rhuddlan, a fortified town 2 miles N, but Bp Anian II (1268–93) insisted that the new cathedral be at St Asaph and got his way, such was the power of the Church even against a conqueror like Edward I. Today's building was therefore started by Bp Anian and completed by his two successors. The woodwork was burnt in 1402, but the church was reroofed and restored by Bp Redman (1471–96). The tower was rebuilt in 1715, after being destroyed in a storm, and the choir was remodelled c 1780. There was major restoration by Gilbert Scott in 1869–75, and further restoration in 1929–32. In 1920 Dr A.G. Edwards, bishop since 1889, was enthroned as the first archbishop of the disestablished Church in Wales.

Interior. The roof painting and gilding (1968) celebrate the investiture of Prince Charles as Prince of Wales in 1969. The Dec Nave, begun by Bp Anian II, has 14C arcades with continuous moulding, and a good 15C clerestory. Looking down the nave, it will be seen that the aisle columns lean outwards, making the nave wider at the top than at the bottom. The S Aisle contains the recumbent effigy of a bishop, almost certainly Anian II; also the unusual 'Greyhound Stone', carved with unexplained heraldic decoration. In this aisle, too, are tablets to Mrs Hemans (d 1835), poetess of 'The Boy Stood on the Burning Deck', who lived near St Asaph; and to the explorer H.M. Stanley (d 1904), who, born John Rowlands, was as a youth an inmate of the St Asaph workhouse. The transepts are contemporary with the nave, and something of Bp Redman's 15C roof has survived. In the N Transept is the Translators' Chapel (see above); and the S Transept now serves as the Lady Chapel and Chantry Chapel. The exquisite little 16C Spanish ivory Madonna is said to have come from a wrecked Armada galleon. The alcove in the S wall was made a Treasury in 1978. It contains rare books and documents, including the William Morgan Bible of 1588 (see above), a prayer book annotated by Roger Ascham, tutor to Queen Elizabeth I, and an early 17C hornbook, unique in Wales. The aisleless Choir, mostly rebuilt by Scott in the style of the 13C, incorporates some genuine work of that period which escaped destruction in 1282. The stalls, with their carved elbows, date from the 15C restoration by Bp Redman; the sedilia and E window, with glass of 1968, are 14C (restored). The Victorian bishop's throne stands over Bp Morgan's tomb.

St Davids Cathedral, Dyfed

St Davids is a straggling village on an almost treeless windswept plateau above the River Alun, less than a mile from the sea. The smallest cathedral city in Britain, since the 6C it has been the seat of a bishop, whose see now embraces all the county of Dyfed. The partly ruined Tower Gate is the main entrance to the cathedral close, about ¾ mile in circumference and still mostly surrounded by a wall (c 1300, though often restored). The gatehouse (the last survivor of four) and

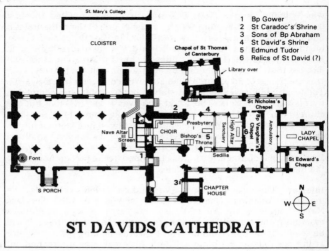

St. Mary's College

CLOISTER

Chapel of St Thomas of Canterbury

Library over

1 Bp Gower
2 St Caradoc's Shrine
3 Sons of Bp Abraham
4 St David's Shrine
5 Edmund Tudor
6 Relics of St David (?)

St Nicholas's Chapel

Presbytery

Nave Altar
Screen

CHOIR

Bishop's
Throne

Sanctuary

High Altar

Bp Vaughan's Chapel

Ambulatory

LADY CHAPEL

Font

Sedilia

St Edward's Chapel

S PORCH

CHAPTER HOUSE

N
W — E
S

ST DAVIDS CATHEDRAL

the precinct wall are in the main attributed to Bp Gower (1328–47); but it has been suggested that the octagonal flanking tower on the N, which is 50 years older than the rest, was originally a detached bell-tower. The cathedral and ruined Bishop's Palace are both in the deep Alun valley, known also as Glyn Rhosyn ('Valley of the Small Bog'). The pedestrian approaches the cathedral up a flight of 39 steps, nicknamed the 'Thirty-nine Articles'. The cathedral is the largest and finest church in Wales. Its core is a late 12C building, but alterations have given its exterior a style largely of the 14C.

History. The see was traditionally founded by St David (Dewi Sant), the patron saint of Wales, c 550, when he transferred his monastery from Whitesand Bay (on the coast NW) to Glyn Rhosyn, but both the church and the monastery he is supposed to have built here have long disappeared. In 1081 William the Conqueror paid homage at the shrine of St David, but in 1088 the town was sacked by the Norsemen and the church burnt. Despite this, St Davids flourished, and kings continued to make it a place of pilgrimage, two pilgrimages here being equated with one to Rome. The present building was begun in 1180 by a Norman bishop, Peter de Leia (1176–98). In 1220 the central tower fell, demolishing the choir and transepts; but these, with the lower stage of the tower, were rebuilt practically in the original style by 1250. The successive addition of the Chapel of St Thomas, the ambulatory and the Lady Chapel (by Bp Martyn, 1296–1328) completed in broad outline the ground-plan of the church.

Later bishops included: Bp Gower (1328–47), largely responsible for the Bishop's Palace (see below); Bp Houghton (1361–88), Lord Chancellor to Edward III, famous for being excommunicated, and then himself excommunicating the Pope from the cathedral steps; Bp Vaughan (1508–22), who completed the top stage of the tower, and also vaulted the Lady Chapel; Bp Ferrar (1548–55), the Marian martyr burnt at Carmarthen; and Bp Davies (1561–68), who commissioned the first Welsh translation of the Bible (see also St Asaph, above). Abp Laud (1621–26) was appointed bishop on relinquishing the presidentship of St John's College, Oxford, but he never came to St Davids. During the Civil War much of the lead was stripped from the roofs, and the E parts of the cathedral became dilapidated.

The W front was rebuilt by Nash at the end of the 18C. The work of restoration, begun in 1846, was afterwards carried on (1862–78) by Sir Gilbert Scott, who rebuilt the W front to what is thought to be its original design.

Exterior. This is plain but dignified. Note the lack of high-pitched roofs to the nave and choir, the 125ft high tower, and the huge buttresses on the N side of the nave. The 13–14C building (Chapel of St Thomas, and library) in the angle between the N transept and the presbytery was originally of three storeys. The S porch is the work of Bp Gower (1328–47), except that the parvise was added c 1515.

Interior. The general impression is of softly tinted purple slate and lavish late Norman ornament. The *Nave* is of six bays, clerestory and triforium, with a varied wealth of chevron and other ornament. The flat *Roof of Irish oak, probably constructed during the treasurership of Owen Pole (1472–1509), is unique in having a number of arches of fret-like delicacy that apparently carry the ceiling but are in fact pendants of it. The slope of the floor, due to its original construction on ill-drained and ill-prepared ground, is very noticeable; there is a rise of 14ft between the W door and the high altar. Against the S wall is the monument of Bp John Morgan (1496–1504), with his recumbent effigy and sculptures round the base, including, at the foot, a vigorous panel representing the Resurrection. On the adjacent (W) pier there are traces of murals. At the E end of the S aisle there is a beautiful 13C tomb-niche of a vested priest with a curiously shaped canopy. The elaborate and beautiful *Rood-screen, one of the glories of the cathedral, is the work of Bp Gower (1328–47), whose tomb, with

St Davids Cathedral, 15C misericord showing wild boars devouring a hound. (K. Spence)

304 WALES AND THE MARCHES

effigy, occupies the S compartment. To the N of the central opening, notable for its unusual skeleton vaulting, is a striking stone reredos. On either side of this opening are tombs of unknown priests, probably chaplains to Bp Gower. Above the N tomb is a wall-painting of c 1350.

The transepts, entered from the nave aisles by Norman doorways instead of by the usual arches, were largely rebuilt after the fall of the tower in 1220; but here, and in the presbytery, the builders assimilated their new work to the Norman character of the nave, though they adopted the pointed arch. In the *N Transept*, at the back of the choir stalls, is the reputed Shrine of St Caradoc (d 1124), buried in the cathedral. The two pierced quatrefoils in the base (like those in the shrine of St David, see below) may have been intended for the insertion of a diseased limb in hope of cure, or for the reception of alms. The great window on the N of the transept was put in by Butterfield in 1846. The Chapel of St Thomas of Canterbury (off the E of the N transept), a vestry until 1952, has been restored as a memorial to Bishop Prosser (Archbishop of Wales, d 1949); it contains a beautiful 13C double piscina. The room above, reached by a stair from the N aisle of the presbytery and formerly the chapter house, is now the Library. Originally this was divided into two floors, of which the upper—once the Treasury—has now been converted into a gallery in memory of Bp Havard (1956). The library cases were restored in 1955 by the Pilgrim Trust. The oldest book is Bp Lyndewode's *Provinciales Constitutiones Angli* (1505), still quoted today as an authority on Church law. Also in the library are some beautiful fragments of the former organ case (? by Grinling Gibbons), broken up during restoration work. In the *S Transept*, beyond the vestry door, there are fragments of two Celtic slabs, one of which commemorates the two sons of Bp Abraham (1076–78), who was bishop before the present building had been started. In the W wall a doorway gives access to the tower.

The *Choir* takes the place of the crossing below the tower, which rests on four fine arches. The circular-headed arch on the W is part of the original wall of Peter de Leia (c 1180), while the other three are pointed and date from the rebuilding after 1220. The lantern exhibits the beautiful Dec work of Bp Gower. The 28 choir stalls date from c 1470, and their design, without the usual canopies, is unusual if not unique. Most of the misericords are highly original; they include four men in a boat, one being seasick (Archdeacon of Brecon's seat), and two men doing a country dance, or rubbing their sciatica (Succentor's seat). On the S side is a stall for the sovereign, with the royal coat of arms above. The *Bishop's Throne, nearly 30ft high and one of the few medieval examples left in Britain, is perhaps from the time of Bp Morgan (c 1500), though incorporating earlier work by Bp Gower. On either side there is a seat for a chaplain. Another rarity (though found in some parish churches) is the parclose screen (late Dec) between the choir and presbytery. The painting on the ceiling of the lantern and presbytery is by Gilbert Scott.

The choir aisles are on either side of the presbytery and sanctuary. In the *N Choir Aisle* is the tomb of Rhys Gryg (d 1233), fourth son of Rhys ap Tewdwr, who in 1176 held the first Eisteddfod at Cardigan; the effigy is, however, 14C. The *S Choir Aisle* contains the tombs of Bps Gervase or Iorwerth (1215–29) and Anselm de la Grace (1231–47), and the recumbent effigy of a knight, possibly Rhys ap Gruffydd (d 1197). Another effigy may be that of the chronicler Giraldus Cambrensis (d c 1223). One slab bears an interesting Latin inscription (?13C): 'Here lies Silvester the Physician; his present state of dissolution shows that medicine cannot resist death'.

To the E of the choir is the *Presbytery*, consisting of three and a half bays, with chevron and other ornament, and originally lighted on the E by two tiers of lancets. The lower row, which formerly looked into the open space now occupied by Bp Vaughan's Chapel, is blocked, and enriched with richly gilt glass mosaics by Salviati (1871). The door jambs and arches are decorated with imitation ornament that is richer than any other in the cathedral. The upper tier was reconstructed by Gilbert Scott, from surviving fragments, in place of a poor but genuine window of the 15C. The roof, of 1461, was likewise restored by Scott. On the N of the presbytery is the late 13C Shrine of St David, once a magnet for crowds of pilgrims. The stone base has holes for receiving pilgrims' offerings; the relics were kept in a feretory on top of this base. In the middle of the presbytery is the large altar-tomb (with a handsome modern brass) of Edmund Tudor (d 1456), father of Henry VII, brought here at the Dissolution of the Monasteries by his grandson, Henry VIII, from the church of the Grey Friars at Carmarthen.

On the S side of the Sanctuary is a rare series of wooden sedilia (1460–81), and here the floor is paved with encaustic tiles, many of which are late 15C and form one of the finest sets of medieval tiles still in position.

Bp Vaughan's Chapel, entered from the aisles, is a fine example of late Perp work, with a fan-tracery *Roof (1508–22). Originally this was an open space, bounded by the presbytery and by the three walks of the ambulatory. It was also apparently neglected and dirty, being described in 1492 as 'the nastiest and most sordid place in the whole church', when the sum of fourpence was paid for its cleaning. The arrangement, unique among British cathedrals, may have been due to the 13C builders' reluctance to block up the three lower lancet windows on the E of the presbytery. An unexplained feature is the recess on the W side, with an opening at the back that looks into the presbytery. This is 12C work of Peter de Leia's time; but of the four crosses (brought from elsewhere) built into the wall around the opening, the one below it, hidden by a coffer, may possibly be a relic of a pre-Norman church. This recess, found walled up by Gilbert Scott, concealed a quantity of bones—possibly those of St David, or St Justinian (who lived on the island of Ramsey and was David's friend and confessor), or both—embedded in mortar and probably hidden here at the Reformation; they are now in the coffer just referred to. On the E side of the chapel stands the Altar of the Holy Trinity, made up of old fragments, with a niche and window on either side, an unusual and curious arrangement.

The Ambulatory contains several 13–14C recumbent effigies. Its E walk is vaulted, while the side walks show evidence of a similar but unfulfilled intention, with the truncated bases of vaulting arches.

The Lady Chapel was the last part of the cathedral to be restored, with a replacement for Bp Vaughan's vault, which fell in 1775. In addition to fine sedilia, the chapel contains two tomb-niches, probably the work of Gower. The one on the S (restored, no effigy) is thought to be that of Bp Martyn (1296–1328), the original builder of the chapel. The other (N)—perhaps the tomb of Bp Bek (1280–96), who built the Bishop's Palace—has been restored as a tomb for Bp Owen (1897–1926).

On the N side of the nave, and once connected with it by a cloister, are the ruins of St Mary's College (restored since 1933), founded for secular priests in 1377 by Bp Houghton and John of Gaunt. The chief feature is the chapel, above a barrel vault, with a plain tower attached to its SW corner. The original formed the S range of the quadrangle. During work on the conversion of the buildings into a cathedral hall (1965), a tomb, believed to be that of Bp Houghton, was discovered.

The remains of the *Bishop's Palace* are across the Alun. Started about 1200, and continued by Bps Bek (1280–96) and Gower, the palace was mostly built between 1280–1350 and may have had the additional purpose of serving as a reception centre for pilgrims to the shrine of St David. The decay of the palace dates from the time of Bp Barlow (1536–48), who stripped the lead from the great hall—though perhaps not, as local tradition asserts, to provide dowries for his five daughters, all of whom he married off to bishops.

The palace consists of a single large quadrangle. The open arcade and parapet that run round the top of the whole building on the outer side are typical of Gower's work. The entrance to the quadrangle is by a disproportionately plain gateway at the E end of the N face. Immediately to the left of this is what is supposed to have been the Private Chapel (c 1350), raised, like the rest of the palace, on a series of vaults, which provided basement rooms and storage. The Bishop's Hall (late 13C, c 60ft by 24ft), on the E side of the quadrangle, has a later entrance porch with a curious doorway, exhibiting the semi-octagonal head characteristic of Gower's work. To the S of this hall is the Kitchen; to the N is the Solar. The Great Hall (1327–47, c 120ft by 31ft), on the S side, is noticeably larger than the Bishop's Hall and was doubtless used for public purposes. It is approached by a fine porch at its NE corner, with a striking ogee doorway enriched by canopied niches with now mutilated figures, and has a beautiful rose-window at the E end. At its NW corner is the Chapel, with a piscina and a W bell-turret. The W side of the quadrangle seems to have been occupied by domestic buildings, stables etc.

St Dogmaels Abbey, Dyfed

Off B4546, 1 mile W of Cardigan.

Now in a public park on the S side of the Teifi estuary, the ruins of St Dogmaels stand on a hill above the river. The abbey was founded c 1115 by Robert FitzMartin, Lord of Cemais, on the site of an old Welsh *clas* ('monastic community'), destroyed c 1000 by the Vikings. The monks were Benedictines of a reformed Order (Tironensian). Situated in a remote part of Wales, the abbey suffered from the lawlessness of the times and was never prosperous; it was dissolved in 1536. The small ruins comprise part of the church (originally apsidal, enlarged and altered in the 14–15C), fragments of the refectory and other domestic buildings round the cloister S of the church, and a small detached infirmary (SE corner of site). Of the Church, the N and W walls of the nave survive, the most notable feature being the ball-flower ornament on the moulding of the N door. The 13C Infirmary stands almost to roof level on three of the

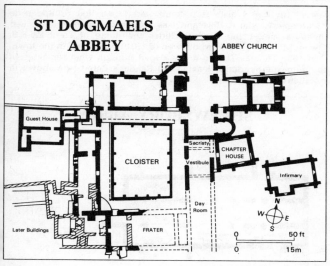

sides, and is used to house inscribed stones and effigies. After the
Dissolution, the W cloister range was turned into a private house and
probably used as the rectory.

Shrewsbury Abbey, Shropshire

Ded: St Peter and St Paul.

In Abbey Foregate, on E side of River Severn.

Founded by Roger de Montgomery in 1083, Shrewsbury abbey was
once one of the foremost abbeys in the Welsh Marches. What survives
is the magnificent abbey church, and the elegant little reader's pulpit
of the 14C refectory, now half-hidden among nondescript buildings
on the S side of the main road. The church, built of purple-brown
stone, has an imposing Dec W tower, the base of which, together with
the doorway, is Norman. The statue above the W window is said to be
of Edward III, in whose reign Abbot Stevens (1361–99) built the
tower. Inside the church, the two W bays of the nave were rebuilt at
the same time as the tower; the other bays are powerful Norman
work. The transepts and chancel are Victorian, built by J.L. Pearson
in 1886–88; the original choir and Lady Chapel extended
considerably to the E, into what is now an open space. Pearson also
built an imitation Norman clerestory over the triforium arches, which,
unlike much restoration of this sort, blends in well with the original
work. During the Middle Ages Shrewsbury was famous for the Shrine
of St Winifred, martyred in Wales in the 7C; opposite the N door are
fragments from the shrine, with figures of St John the Baptist, St
Winifred and St Beuno, recovered in 1933 from a garden in the town.
In the N aisle are a monument to Richard Onslow (d 1571), Speaker to
the House of Commons under Elizabeth I, and a 13C effigy of a

lawyer. In the S aisle is a tomb said to be that of Roger de Montgomery, who d 1094 and was buried in the abbey. The war memorial under the tower includes the name of Lieut. W.E.S. Owen, MC: the poet Wilfred Owen (d 1918), who lived in the town.

In 1836 Thomas Telford drove a road through what remained of the monastic buildings, leaving the Reader's Pulpit (see above) in isolation across the road.

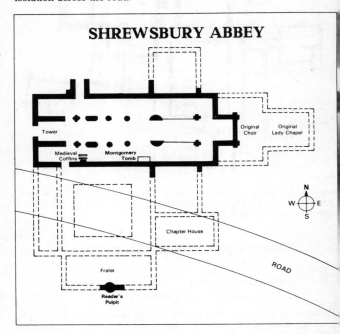

Shrewsbury Cathedral, Shropshire (RC)

Ded: Our Lady Help of Christians and St Peter of Alcantara.

Standing on the S side of the town adjoining the 13C town walls, the cathedral was built in the 1850s to designs by Augustus Pugin (d 1852) and his son Edward, for a diocese established in 1850. Small for a cathedral and without a tower, inside it is of EE design, with a timber roof divided into painted panels. In the NW chapel (Sacred Heart) is an elaborate reredos by Augustus Pugin.

Strata Florida Abbey, the Norman W doorway. (K. Spence)

Strata Florida Abbey, Dyfed

Ded: St Mary.

Off B4343, 6 miles NE of Tregaron.

Set in gently hilly countryside on the upper reaches of the Teifi, Strata Florida is as beautiful a spot as its name suggests. One of the most celebrated abbeys in Wales, during the Middle Ages it was important politically, and a centre for Welsh learning and literature. The name is a Latinized form of the Welsh Ystrad Fflur, meaning 'Plain of Flowers'. It was founded by a Norman baron, Robert FitzStephen, in 1164, on a site 2 miles SW of the present one; but two years later his estates were overrun by a Welsh prince, Rhys ap Gruffydd, who in 1184 began a new Cistercian monastery on the present site. The church was consecrated in 1201, though it and the monastic buildings were not completed for a further 70 years. The greater part of the ruins date from the late 12 and early 13C, the chapter house and the monks' choir are 14C, while the cloister is 15 or early 16C. In 1238 Llywelyn the Great summoned an assembly of Welsh princes to Strata Florida to swear allegiance to his son Dafydd. In the late 13C the church was struck by lightning, and the monastery suffered during the wars of Edward I. Economically, the abbey flourished largely from wool, provided by sheep grazing on its lands which stretched as far as Rhayader, 15 miles to the E. The national annals of Wales were written at Strata Florida, and the greatest medieval Welsh poet, Dafydd ap Gwilym (c 1320–80), was buried there. During the Owain Glyndŵr rebellion at the beginning of the 15C the abbey was abandoned for a time, and when it was dissolved in 1539 there were only seven monks left.

The Church, in Trans Norman style, is on the usual Cistercian plan, with an aisled nave of seven bays, transepts each with three chapels, and an aisleless chancel. Finest of the remains is the superb *W Doorway into the nave, richly ornamented, with a framing cluster of five rolls, tied together at intervals by bands ending in crozier-like ornaments. Inside, the aisles were completely cut off from the body of the nave by screen walls 5ft high, an arrangement not known elsewhere in England or Wales, though occasionally found in Ireland. In the transept chapels, remains of altars can be seen, and many of the medieval tiles have been relaid, and are now protected by hangar-like roofs. On the wall of the N transept is a slate memorial (1951) to Dafydd ap Gwilym (see above), who is said to be buried under the giant yew in the churchyard just to the N. Immediately S of the S transept is the narrow sacristy, and beyond this the remains of the chapter house; behind them are rows of graves thought to be of abbots and Welsh princes of the House of Dynevor (Dinefwr). On the N side of the cloister is an alcove for a lectern.

At the entrance is a small exhibition telling the story of the Cistercians and their abbey. Some of the fragments of sculptured work are of a delicacy and richness strangely at variance with the reputed severity of the Cistercians at this period.

Talley Abbey, Dyfed

Beside B4302, 6 miles N of Llandeilo.

The E wall of the tower, pierced with a tall arch, is the main survival of Talley, which stands on a fine site, commanding wide views, above the picturesque Dulais valley. It was founded in the late 12C by Rhys ap Gruffydd, Prince of South Wales, for Premonstratensian canons, and was the only monastery of this order in Wales. The canons were ejected c 1200 by the powerful Cistercians of Whitland Abbey (see below), but by 1208 they had been reinstated as the result of an appeal to the Archbishop of Canterbury. In 1215 the Abbot of Talley, Iorwerth, left his abbey to become Bp of St Davids (see above). The remains of the church, of very plain architecture, consist (apart from the tower) of the transepts with their chapels, part of the choir, and fragments of the nave. To the S of the nave are the lower courses of the cloisters; but most of the monastic buildings now lie under a farmhouse and barns. Talley disputes with Strata Florida the honour of being the burial place of the poet Dafydd ap Gwilym. Just to the N is a lake once used by the monks as a fishpond (the name Talley is a shortened form of Tal-y-Llychau, 'Head of the Lakes').

Tintern Abbey, Gwent

Ded: St Mary.

By A466, 5 miles N of Chepstow.

The subject of a famous poem by Wordsworth and painted by Turner, Tintern is the best known of all our ruined abbeys. The substantial

Talley Abbey, the remains of the crossing arch and central tower. (K. Spence)

remains lie beside the Wye, against a backcloth of steep tree-covered hills across the river. It was founded in 1131 by Walter FitzRichard, Lord of Chepstow, for a community of Cistercians from the monastery of L'Aumône in Normandy. Little remains of this first abbey, and most of today's ruins date from rebuilding in the 13 and 14C. Concerned mainly with agriculture, the abbey was at its most prosperous during the early 14C, before the Black Death of 1349 took its toll of the monks and of the lay brothers who carried out the farm work. In 1326 Edward II spent two nights there as a refugee; but that was Tintern's only brush with history. The abbey was dissolved in 1536 and mouldered quietly away, until the Romantic vogue for ruins at the end of the 18C made it a popular goal of pilgrimage.

The entrance, on the N side of the precinct, leads first of all to an excellent exhibition centre, telling the story of Tintern and its abbey. Among the themes illustrated are the geology of the district, early man, and the various stages of the abbey (including information on the Cistercians and monastic life in general) from its foundation to today's rescue and conservation.

The *Church* is on the far (S) side of the precinct from the entrance, beyond the two cloisters and their attached monastic buildings. Its chief feature is the great W Window of seven lights, whose fine tracery is best appreciated from outside the precinct, above the W doorway with its twin trefoil-headed openings. The Nave, mostly late 13C, retains its clerestory on the S side. The four large and beautiful arches of the crossing formerly supported a tower, and beyond is the huge and beautifully proportioned *E

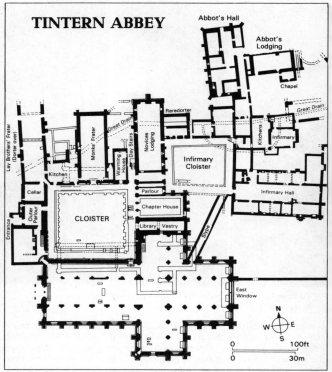

TINTERN ABBEY

Window, covering almost the whole of the wall. From the nave, a processional doorway beside the N transept leads into the *Cloister*, built unusually on the N side of the church, possibly to allow easier drainage into the Wye. Off the E walk of the cloister are the Library and Vestry, which now form one room because of the disappearance of the wall between them. From the vestry there is a door into the N Transept, which incorporates remains of the original 12C church, and retains the night-stairs to the monks' dormitory and a six-light window with much of its tracery. The E walk of the cloister continues past the Chapter House and Parlour. A walk along the N side of the parlour leads to the small Infirmary Cloister, across which (E) is the Infirmary, with its Kitchens to the N, their wastes (like those of the whole abbey) being carried by the great drain that runs across the site.

N of the infirmary kitchens is the *Abbot's Lodging*, with his hall, camera, and chapel. From the lodging, a walk leads back (S) into the infirmary cloister, passing (right) the Reredorter and its drain. Beyond is the long room, running N–S, which formed the Novices' Lodging. From here a passage leads past the day-stairs into the N walk of the main cloister, along which are in turn the Warming-house, the Monks' Frater (early 13C, a fine room 84ft by 29ft), the Kitchen with its serving-hatch, and the Lay Brothers' Refectory. This is even larger

Tintern Abbey, water-colour drawing by J.M.W. Turner.

than that of the monks since, with the Cistercian emphasis on agriculture, the lay brothers normally outnumbered the monks.

The abbey made great use of the river as a waterway, and the adjacent hotel is on the site of the watergate, where a 13C arch gives access to a slipway.

Valle Crucis Abbey, Clwyd

Ded: St Mary.

By A452, 1½ miles N of Llangollen.

In a steep-sided valley, with a caravan site as its neighbour, Valle Crucis is one of the prettiest of all the Welsh abbeys. A Cistercian monastery, it was founded in 1201 by the ruler of Powys, Madoc ap Gruffydd Maelor (d 1236), who was buried in the abbey. The 'Valley of the Cross' takes its name from the 9C Pillar of Eliseg, formerly surmounted by a cross, which still stands on a mound ¼ mile N of the abbey. The original abbey was seriously damaged by fire during the 13C, leading to major alterations, and the tower collapsed in 1400. Though only a small abbey, it was a prosperous one, where by the 15C the monks were living a life of un-Cistercian luxury: a Welsh poet, Guttyn Owain, praised the generosity of the abbot, who kept a good table with fine claret, and described the fretted ceiling of his lodging. The abbey was dissolved in 1538.

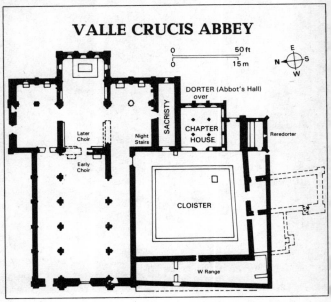

VALLE CRUCIS ABBEY

The EE Church keeps to the usual Cistercian plan of aisled nave, transepts with E chapels, and short aisleless choir. In the walls of the N aisle can be seen the original masonry, heightened by small flat stones added after the fire. The W front (c 1250–75) is a beautiful composition, with three fine plate-tracery windows enclosed in a common frame, and with a delicate rose-window in the gable. The E end (c 1240) is notable for the way in which its external pilaster buttresses split above the lower row of three lancets so as to embrace the upper pair. Worth looking for are the remains of the pulpit including the stairway (under the vanished W arch of the crossing); the recess, with remains of a shafted screen, on the N side of the choir; the bases of altars in the two chapels on the E side of the S transept; and the arch at the end of the S transept which led to the now-vanished night-stairs up to the monks' dormitory. The crossing piers were heavily buttressed after the tower fell in 1400. In front of the choir are six mutilated tombs, said to include those of Myfanwy Fechan, a beauty who inspired the Welsh bards and lived at Castell Dinas Bran above Llangollen, and Iolo Goch, the bard of Owain Glyndŵr.

The E range of the Cloister is entered by a door from the S aisle. Adjoining the S transept is the narrow Sacristy; then comes the square Chapter House, with its vaulting and four supporting columns still in good condition. The screen of decorated tracery in the N bay probably enclosed a book-cupboard. S of the chapter house entrance a narrow staircase leads to the Dormitory, which occupied the whole upper floor of the E range. In the 15C the N end of the dormitory was turned into the abbot's hall, and the chimney was added. S of the chapter house a passage leads to a large fishpond, fed from the valley stream; and S of this passage is the Reredorter. Only foundations survive of the S and W cloister ranges.

Whitland Abbey, Dyfed

Ded: St Mary.

On minor road, 1½ miles NE of Whitland.

Little remains of Whitland, once one of the greatest Cistercian houses in Wales. Founded by Bernard, the first Norman bishop of St Davids, in 1143, it set up daughter houses at Cwmhir (see above) in the same year, and at Strata Florida (see above) in 1164.

Wrexham Cathedral, Clwyd (RC)

Ded: St Mary.

On SE (Llangollen) side of town.

Built as a parish church in 1857 and raised to cathedral status in 1898, this unpretentious building of yellow-grey stone was designed by Edward Pugin, son of the more famous Augustus. Inside it has capitals decorated with foliage and simple lean-to wooden roofs on the aisles; the nave roof is painted in sober colours, while the choir roof is red picked out with white. The bishop's throne is immediately below the E window.

INDEX

Cathedral and abbey entries in the gazetteer section are printed in bold type, other entries in Roman type. The names of famous people buried or commemorated in St Paul's Cathedral and Westminster Abbey have not been included for reasons of space.

The following abbreviations are used (Devon, Clwyd etc are not abbreviated):

Typeset by Media Conversion Limited.
Printed in Great Britain by Fletcher & Son Limited, Norwich.

SOUTH EAST ENGLAND

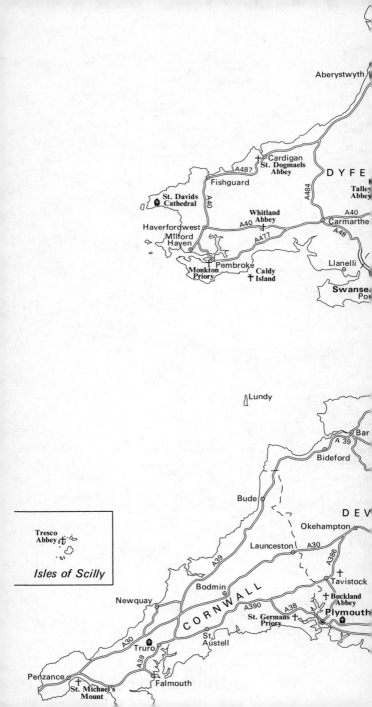

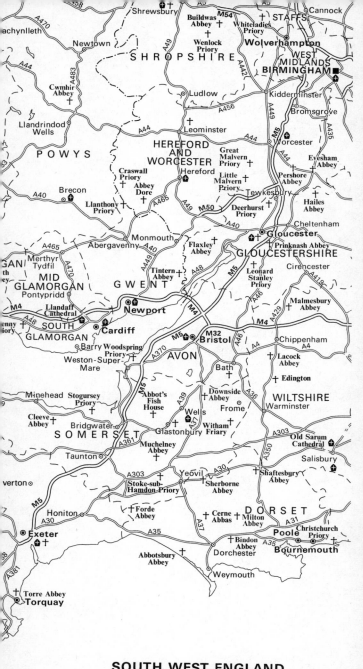

**SOUTH WEST ENGLAND
& SOUTH WALES**